The Man
Time Forgot

The Man Time Forgot

A Tale of Genius, Betrayal, and the Creation of *Time* Magazine

ISAIAH WILNER

HarperCollins*Publishers*

THE MAN TIME FORGOT. Copyright © 2006 by Isaiah Wilner. All rights reserved. Printed in the United States of America. No part of this book may be used or reproduced in any manner whatsoever without written permission except in the case of brief quotations embodied in critical articles and reviews. For information, address HarperCollins Publishers, 10 East 53rd Street, New York, NY 10022.

HarperCollins books may be purchased for educational, business, or sales promotional use. For information, please write: Special Markets Department, HarperCollins Publishers, 10 East 53rd Street, New York, NY 10022.

Photo credits: Hadden and Luce at Hotchkiss, *Yale Daily News* board of 1920, Hadden and Luce with Cleveland's city manager, cartoon of Hadden, painting of Hadden: courtesy Time Inc. Hadden photograph, Luce photograph: Underwood and Underwood, courtesy Time Inc. Early staff of *Time*: courtesy Mary-Kelly Busch. "The Man of the Year" cover: S. J. Woolf/ © Time Inc., all rights reserved. John Stuart Martin: portrait by Orren Jack Turner, courtesy Time Inc. Roy Edward Larsen: courtesy Christopher Larsen. Lila Hotz: courtesy Peter Paul Luce. Deborah Douglas: courtesy Rebecca C. Morey. Mimi Martin: courtesy Barry M. Osborn.

FIRST EDITION

Designed by Nancy Singer Olaguera

Library of Congress Cataloging-in-Publication Data
  Wilner, Isaiah, 1978–
    The man time forgot : a tale of genius, betrayal, and the creation of
  Time magazine / Isaiah Wilner.—1st ed.
      p. cm.
    Includes bibliographical references and index.
    ISBN-10: 0-06-050549-4
    ISBN-13: 978-0-06-050549-3
    1. Hadden, Briton, 1898–1929. 2. Periodical editors—United States—
  Biography. 3. Time. I. Title.
  PN4874.H19W56   2006
  070.5'1—dc22
  [B]   2006043532

06 07 08 09 10 ID/RRD 10 9 8 7 6 5 4 3 2 1

FOR JEFF AND LUCY

CONTENTS

The Man
Time Forgot

Death Wish

In January of 1929, the creator of *Time* magazine lay dying in a Brooklyn hospital bed. He was thirty years old. Briton Hadden did not look like a man with only a few weeks to live. His family had decided not to tell him of his dire condition. But the doctors believed he stood almost no chance. Hadden, who had only just begun the creative revolution that would transform journalism in the subsequent century, had drunk and partied his way to his deathbed.

In the giddy and rebellious decade just ending, a time when youth shattered old rules of behavior, a time that saw the emergence of jazz, modern literature, and transcontinental flight, Hadden had influenced popular culture in ways that would permeate the American mindset, changing the way people thought and acted in the twentieth century. By the age of twenty-five, he had created the first magazine to make sense of the news for a broad national audience. By the age of twenty-seven, he had invented a writing style that brought great events to life, informing a wide group of Americans. By the age of thirty, he had made his first million dollars.

"Anyone over thirty is ready for the grave," Hadden had proclaimed during the heady years of his quick rise to influence. A muscular man with a barrel chest and a square jaw, he looked more like an athlete than an editor. But there were signs of eccentric genius in his intense face: the gray-green eyes that twinkled when he laughed, the pencil-thin mustache that drew attention to a mischievous smile. He had lived fast all the way, dancing to "Hindustan" at the Plaza, hosting outrageous cocktail hours that mixed ministers with call girls, shocking friends by showing up for parties in an asbestos suit and stamping out cigarettes on the arm of his jacket.

In a hurry to achieve all he had dreamed, Hadden had rushed about with his coat collar up, chewing gum, chain-smoking, and swinging his cane. When he talked, he often barked. When he liked a joke, his raucous laugh shot through the room as if fired from a machine gun. Writers called him "The Terrible-Tempered Mr. Bang" because he growled and stamped his feet when they used a word he didn't like, but it was all part of his act—a beautiful insane act that swept people up within his orbit and filled them with the magic of his grand persona. People loved Hadden; they admired him. The dramatist Thornton Wilder called him "a prince."

Now almost thirty-one, Hadden was wasting away of an unknown ailment. Doctors had diagnosed him with an infection of streptococcus, and they guessed that the bacteria had spread through his bloodstream to reach his heart. Hadden, a lover of animals, believed he had contracted the illness by scooping up a wandering tomcat and taking it home to feed it a bowl of milk, only to be attacked and scratched. Now Hadden was losing strength. Without penicillin, his doctors were all but helpless, and they were beginning to consider desperate measures—a direct infusion of the antiseptic Mercurochrome, perhaps, or a massive series of blood transfusions.

In this dark hour, the most frequent visitor to Hadden's bedside, aside from his devoted mother, was a tall, thin man with slightly hooded eyes framed by a pair of thick, bushy eyebrows, a receding line of straw-colored hair, and an open, angelic face. Equally as attractive as Hadden, he also looked his diametric opposite. Hadden's business partner, Henry R. Luce, was penetrating where Hadden was witty, analytical where Hadden was creative, organized and careful where Hadden was spontaneous and reckless. They had been drawn together as only opposites can be almost since the moment they had met. Their rivalry was legend, and so was their friendship.

Conjoined by mutual brilliance, a passion for the news, and the love for a good fight, they had competed ardently and at times bitterly for fifteen years. They had drawn intellectual sustenance from each other. At Yale, in the secret society of Skull and Bones, their fellow club mates had drawn a picture of them on horseback, dueling with lances, because each was the greater warrior for facing the other. During the Great War, at a dusty training camp in South Carolina, they had brainstormed the idea that would shape their lives and those of millions more. Believing people nationwide were outrageously ignorant, they resolved to create a magazine that would make sense of the news for the average American. A few years later, they quit their jobs to launch *Time,* the first newsmagazine. Publishers predicted failure, but within a few years the awkward upstart was growing faster than all of its competitors.

Hadden and Luce launched their magazine in a time when a young nation stood open to the influence of adventurers and iconoclasts, people with new ideas of how the world should be run and the courage, ambition, and drive to make their dreams reality. It was Hadden, *Time*'s creative genius and editor, who would shape the style in which Americans think about and tell the news. In doing so, he set the foundation for the newspaper and magazine chains, radio and television networks, cable stations and Internet sites that have come to occupy a prominent place in the national culture.

Hadden told the news just as he viewed it—as a grand and comic epic spectacle. He hooked readers on the news and sold them on its importance by flavoring the facts with color and detail, and by painting vivid portraits of the people who made headlines. Hadden's entertaining writing style proved so popular that it quickly spawned imitators. As the rest of the media took up Hadden's style of narrative reporting, journalists transformed themselves from mere recorders into storytellers. The burgeoning national news media acquired a grip on the American imagination and a power unprecedented in public life.

That achievement alone would qualify Hadden as one of the few seminal publishers in American history. But that was not all Hadden did. Within a year of printing the first issue of *Time,* he created the first radio quiz show. Three years after that, he began publishing a trade magazine about advertising that took business reporting in a new direction. In the last year of his life, he dreamed up the idea for a magazine devoted exclusively to sports, which later became *Sports Illustrated.* Sniffling with the first hints of illness, he talked excitedly of his idea for a new picture magazine, which he hoped to call *Life*. Hadden's ideas were so influential that a single page from one notebook found among his things after his death would serve as a virtual road map for the next half-century of the company he founded.

Luce called Hadden an "original" and was deeply influenced by his ideas. Throughout their many battles, whether for the editorship of the school paper or for creative control of *Time*, it was Hadden who won. Luce, who couldn't stand to lose, had been forced to content himself with second place for more than a decade. He had worked as Hadden's deputy in both prep school and college. During the founding of Time Incorporated, Hadden had acted more "on the originality side," as one friend put it, while Luce had served as the creative "brake." Luce had continued to live in Hadden's shadow ever since. For years, when Luce walked in the door of the New York Yale Club, the waiters would greet him as "Mr. Hadden," because Luce ate there on Hadden's account.

But Luce was a dogged competitor, capable of acquiring new talents, and each time they raced Luce finished a hair closer. In recent years, Luce had pressed Hadden for control of the company. Offended by Luce's desire for power, Hadden had been further depressed by a string of romantic failures. In his final few years, he had turned to the bottle, driven drunk through town, picked fights in speakeasies, and spent nights in jail. Finally it seemed that the brighter of two brilliant candles was about to flicker out. "It's like a race," Hadden had once said of their strange friendship. "No matter how hard I run, Luce is always there." Now Luce was at Hadden's deathbed, ready to slog out the final grueling lap of their rivalry.

For several months Luce had been developing a plan to publish the company's second major product—a business magazine to be called *Fortune*. Hadden was opposed. Believing the business world to be vapid and morally bankrupt, he had devoted the last few years to lampooning businessmen in print, even when they happened to be *Time*'s own advertisers. Luce was adamant. He kept coming to Hadden's bedside, discussing draft articles and mock-ups. Hadden, true to form, had been drawn into a series of lengthy arguments. Day after day, Hadden and Luce had yelled at each other—so loudly that Hadden's nurse could hear them from behind the closed door.

From the perspective of Luce and others at the company, Hadden was out of his head. "He's a sick man," Hadden's cousin told Luce. An executive later reflected, "He was too sick to know and comprehend." Luce was going ahead without Hadden; it wasn't necessary to fill him in on every detail. But there Luce was at Hadden's bedside, insistently pressing his case. Luce would stay for an entire hour, and when he finally got up to leave Hadden would be visibly exhausted. The doctors, believing Hadden was wasting his precious energies, came to fear the moment of Luce's arrival. But Luce continued to visit, and Hadden's condition continued to deteriorate.

As Hadden lay near death, too weak to speak above a whisper, he and Luce had their decisive conversation. No one else would ever know what transpired that January day in that Brooklyn hospital room. It was only known that Luce came by and sat behind a closed door. But the story that later circulated among *Time*'s employees was that Luce brought up the major financial matter that lay between *Time*'s young founders. Together, Hadden and Luce held slightly more than half of the voting stock in Time Incorporated—just enough, together, to maintain control. Singly, however, each of them owned less than 30 percent of the voting stock. If Hadden died, Luce could lose control of the company—unless somehow he got his hands on Hadden's stock.

In that moment it was nearly certain that Hadden would die, and that he would die holding the shares his successor desperately needed to keep control of *Time*. Given his ambitions, Luce would have been foolish not to ask for those shares. One rumor passed along by Luce's detractors was that he broached the question as Hadden lay dying—an awkward matter that would have abruptly shocked Hadden with the full gravity of his rapidly deteriorating condition. Luce, of course, told a different story. He claimed he did not ask Hadden for his shares; in fact, there was never any "open recognition" between them that Hadden was dying. But if this were the case, it would be difficult to explain what happened next.

A few days later, Hadden took a decisive step. He asked his roommate, a young lawyer named William J. Carr, to draw up a will. Carr, who didn't have much experience with estates, took out a piece of paper and simply wrote, "I, Briton Hadden, declare this to be my last will and testament." He must have strained to hear his friend, who was speaking so quietly by then that he could hardly express his desires at all. Clinging to life but fast approaching death, Hadden forbade his family from selling his stock in Time Inc. for forty-nine years. When Carr handed Hadden the will, he felt too weak to sign his name, but he managed to guide his hand to the line. There Hadden scrawled an "X." In settling his estate, Hadden prevented Luce from gaining immediate control of the company they had founded together.

Hadden's heart gave out one month later—six years, almost to the hour, since he had sent the first copy of *Time* to press. It was four A.M. in New York, three A.M. in Chicago, where the latest issue rolled off the press, too soon to mention Hadden's passing. The next week, a short notice led off *Time*'s National Affairs section: "Creation of his genius and heir to his qualities, *Time* attempts neither biography nor eulogy of Briton Hadden. But there will be privately printed, within the year, a book about him which will be sent to all who ask."

That book was not printed for more than twenty years. Within a week, Luce removed Hadden's name from the masthead of the magazine. Hadden's name would not return until after Luce's death nearly forty years later. Within a year, Luce violated Hadden's death wish by negotiating a deal with his bereaved family to purchase Hadden's shares in Time Inc. at a bargain-basement price. Freed from Hadden's shadow, Luce quickly grew into his talents, becoming the most influential magazine publisher in history and for decades the most powerful media mogul in America. Employing his editor's post as a lectern, Luce became the missionary of the media, an imperialist who consistently urged Americans to spread democracy and capitalism throughout the globe.

As he traveled the world, delivering hundreds of speeches about everything from his childhood in China to his years at Yale, Luce repeatedly claimed credit for Hadden's ideas. In all of his talks before a public audience, Luce mentioned Hadden's name only a handful of times. If asked to discuss Hadden, Luce would downplay his partner's role, saying Hadden died just as *Time* was "beginning to see the light." When a friend who deeply missed Hadden gently brought him up in conversation, Luce sniffed, "*Time* was his monument, and he done it." By the time Luce died in 1967, Hadden was nothing but a faint memory.

Now, nearly eighty years after his untimely death, Hadden is all but erased from history. One recent book described him as a "footnote" in the faded past of the company he brought to life. Luce's face has been printed on a postage stamp and his achievements have been chronicled in multiple biographies, while Hadden has been the subject of a single book, commissioned by Luce. Long out of print, it was derided by the writer's own brother as an "affront to the memory of Briton." Considering the magnitude of Hadden's achievements, it seems natural to ask why he has all but vanished from the historical record.

For more than half a century, the answer to this question has been kept under lock and key in the archives of the company Hadden and Luce founded together. Recently I was permitted to view these records. Suddenly a world long hidden from view lay bare, revealing the extraordinary story of a tortured friendship that ignited a media revolution. The following narrative describes how two young men transformed the way we make sense of the world around us. It is the story of perfect opposites who formed an epic partnership, of a rivalry so ferocious as to create the best of friends. It begins with their birth, on opposite sides of the world, at the dawn of the twentieth century.

1

Birth

ON FEBRUARY 15, 1898, the last masked participants in Havana's Carnival were drifting toward their brightly painted homes, the plazas were falling silent, and the American reporters gathered outdoors at the Inglaterra Hotel were enjoying a starry Cuban night. Suddenly they felt the force of a fantastic explosion. Down in the harbor, a giant plume of fire was shooting into the sky, carrying with it wood, steel, and body parts. Racing to the harbor, the reporters saw an American battleship in flames and quickly sinking.

No one knew why the USS *Maine* exploded. But the cause hardly mattered to the newspaper publishers who soon whipped the United States into a flag-waving frenzy. The jingoists cried for war against Spain—a chance, they said, to spread liberty abroad. Within five months, the American military had traveled across the Caribbean and the Pacific, triumphed in Cuba and occupied the Philippines, creating the foundations of a global empire. Rising alongside the American empire were the editors and publishers who had fought for the war in print—the powerful Fourth Estate.

At the dawn of this great change, as newspapers blared their loud headlines, newsboys waved their latest editions, and crowds gathered around newsstands to discuss the explosion in Havana Harbor, two young boys who would together transform the world of journalism were born—one in a wealthy neighborhood in Brooklyn, and the other in a dusty, impoverished village in rural China. It would be their fate to race against each other almost from the moment that they met. And it was the winner in all but the last of these races who was born first.

Two days after the explosion of the *Maine*, Crowell Hadden Jr., an attractive and well-dressed sportsman frequently seen at the evening balls in the affluent community of Brooklyn Heights, was walking home from the circus to his pregnant wife, Bess. Crowell was in high spirits that night. Finding Bess at rest, he jumped onto the railing of their bed and began a series of ferocious imitations of the animals he had seen at the show—an act so startling that it shocked his wife into her first contractions. Briton Hadden was born in the early morning hours of February 18, 1898.

Several weeks premature, Hadden was a frail baby, and it was said that he spent his first days in an incubator. Even after leaving the hospital, he suffered from poor circulation and could easily have fallen ill. But he fought for life with the help of his mother, who swaddled and rocked him, and surrounded him with hot water bags in the cold morning hours. Nervous and high-strung, Hadden would wake up and go through crying jags when his circulation sank particularly low. But he quickly gained strength and grew into a healthy and active boy.

Hadden was born into a family of wealth and local prominence. His grandfather, Crowell Hadden, was the head of the Brooklyn Savings Bank. A stern but kindly man with a gentle sense of humor, he was easily recognizable in the chandeliered drawing rooms of the Hamilton Club by his erect posture and big broom mustache. He was wealthy but not ostentatious, keeping a stately brownstone and a summer home in the seaside town of Quogue. The Haddens, of English stock, were modest, private, and reserved. They had a long American pedigree and even a family crest, which bore the grim motto "Suffer."

Crowell Hadden's eldest son, Crowell Hadden Jr., was of a lighter disposition than his father. When he reached marrying age, he fell in love with the five raven-haired daughters of Peter Busch, together known as the "Belles of Brooklyn." The Busch girls lived in a great house in south Brooklyn, laughing, debating, and making cracks at their father's expense. Not knowing which girl he liked best, Crowell finally selected the eldest, Maud. Sadly, she died while delivering their first child, Crowell Hadden III, but the baby survived and was carried to the Busch home. The youngest daughter, Bess, began taking care of the child, and soon she and Crowell fell in love. They married and had two children—first Briton Hadden and then, two years later, a daughter named for the departed Maud.

Shortly after Hadden's birth, his young parents moved to picturesque Joralemon Street, a narrow, tree-lined hill that climbs from Brooklyn's docks to the civic center. The Haddens' brownstone wasn't showy, but its dimensions were luxurious for a family of five. The top floor, crowned by a mansard roof, was given over to the children as a nursery. Years later, in a nostalgic book about Brooklyn, the woman who grew up in the brownstone next door would proudly recall its social location, its vast dimensions, and its deep extension overhanging "a garden whose flowering fruit trees and magnolias were a delight through all the happy Springs of what now seems a long and sun-lit childhood."

Hadden, his elder brother, Crowell III, his younger sister, Maud, and their numerous cousins were free-spirited souls. They loved to work, to play, and, in the case of the men in later days, to drink. Fiercely competitive, they were somewhat eccentric and delighted in skirting the rules. Several were hunters and sportsmen, and most shared a love for and ability to commune deeply with animals. They were all sharp dressers, much like Hadden's uncle Briton Busch, the baby brother of the Busch sisters, known as one of the best-dressed men on Wall Street. Though an instinct for finance ran strong in the elder generation, three of Hadden's cousins would become successful writers. But it was Hadden who would be the most influential.

From early childhood, Hadden showed a love for language and a photographic memory that would later serve him as an editor. At the age of two, he began to shock his mother's friends by reciting nursery rhymes. By two and a half, he had memorized a deck of ornithological playing cards his mother had taken to showing him. Each card in a suit featured the picture of a different bird. Hadden enjoyed looking at the cards and calling the birds by their names. Recognizing Hadden's interest in words, his mother read to him such vivid and patriotic verse as John Greenleaf Whittier's "Barbara Frietchie," the Civil War legend of a brave old crone who defied Confederate Soldiers by protecting the Union flag with her body. Hadden devoured the poems and by the age of four he was quickly memorizing them, too.

Before the age of five, Hadden began to do his own writing. He gripped his pencil with two hands and labored over his work letter by letter. At his desk in the upstairs nursery, which he kept fastidiously clean, Hadden would turn out poem after poem, many of which came to him at night. Hadden's mother put a little bell by his bed stand. Often, just before dropping off to sleep, he would give the bell a tinkle. "I have a little verse, Mother," he would say. "Do you want to put it down?" Bess would rush to her son's bedside and take the poem down immediately.

At the age of five, Hadden caught a cold that lingered and grew severe. He was forced to stay home for a year while his friends went to kindergarten. At first Hadden felt sad and lonely, but he soon found a way to draw the other children to him. When Bess read her son "The Rime of the Ancient Mariner," Hadden, thinking Coleridge's poem must be the longest in the world, set out to beat the Romantic poet's effort. Every morning for the next year, Hadden would rush upstairs to the nursery to write a few lines, almost as if reporting to work. His poem, "The Mouse's Party," based on observations of his mother's card parties, eventually edged out Coleridge's poem at 155 verses. Hadden added pictures and tied the effort together as a "book."

Word of Hadden's writing spread through the neighborhood, and each afternoon a little gang of boys would troop over from Mrs. Jonathan Buckley's kindergarten to knock on the Haddens' door. "What have you written today?" the boys would ask when Hadden appeared behind his mother. Bess would serve the boys milk and graham crackers, and the boys would munch away as Bess read them her son's latest "epic poems." Hadden's mother proudly displayed the pictures as she turned each page. She would always remain her son's devoted reader.

Hadden was from the outset a bright-eyed enthusiast. Ideas for games came easily to him. He presented his notions sharply, often in the harsh tones of a tough boy from the Brooklyn streets, before breaking into gales of laughter. Early in his childhood Hadden developed an obsession with baseball. He would stand for hours outside the office of the *Brooklyn Daily Eagle* in order to survey a giant scoreboard posted on the building's wall. As the numbers changed, Hadden memorized each inning's occurrences. Later, in his friend Stuart Heminway's backyard, Hadden would recount the entire game from memory. "This is the way

Ty Cobb did it," he would say, setting up at the plate and spewing an imaginary stream of tobacco juice. "Now watch."

Hadden's twin obsessions, statistics and personalities, and his ability to recount true stories before a crowd would remain chief characteristics of his work throughout his life. He thought quickly and expressed himself with a unique punch and agility—a style of thought that sparkled in his childhood poetry and drawings. Asked once by his friend Rice Brewster how he had managed to depict a horse, Hadden replied that he simply saw the animal in his mind's eye and "drew around it." All his life he would continue to amuse his friends with invented games, drawings, and doggerel poetry, which held in common a raucous sense of humor and a pungent bite.

Far from questioning his eccentricities, Hadden's family indulged them. In the attic, Hadden was allowed to keep more than a dozen pets, including rabbits, turtles, cats, and guinea pigs. Hadden doted over his pets. If he had to leave home for even a few days, he would leave the nurse a quarter and a long list of minute instructions for his animals' care. Once, when headed to Quogue for the summer, Hadden adamantly refused to leave a single one of his eight Belgian hares behind. His grandfather bought a ventilated valise and packed the pets inside. Another summer, Hadden had twenty-two turtles on Long Island, each turtle named for a friend or relative. Hadden kept his family amused by holding turtle races on his grandparents' lawn.

The inspiration for Hadden's first recognizably journalistic efforts would come from his father. In the living room of the Haddens' brownstone, Crowell Hadden Jr., an amateur genealogist, studied the history of the English Haddens. It was he who had discovered the family crest. Generation by generation, Crowell Hadden recorded the lives of his progenitors in short, journalistic descriptions, and the charts he created impressed his young son. Captivated by his father's method, six-year-old Hadden began to write a genealogy of his Belgian hares.

Much like the Haddens, the rabbits were unfortunately destined to suffer, as is clear from Hadden's dramatic account of the life and death of the athletic Peter II:

> Bought with Benjamin I at the Long Island Bird Store. When young had a foot which turned in when he hoped but this cured.

Almost half the hairs on him black. King and champion jumper of his day. One day ate some meat got very sich for two days at first not blieved to live, but was given parsly, at lengh pulled through. Deid by jumping out 6th story window landing half on curb of yard and half on ground came with great force because some leaves were found where he jumpt flatend out like paper.

Although Hadden had left out some crucial information, such as how the rabbit managed to get so near the window ledge, he was already beginning to observe and deduce.

In 1905, when Hadden was seven, his father caught typhoid fever. Crowell Hadden Jr. died five weeks later. He was not yet forty. "In the death of Mr. Hadden, society loses one of its great individualities," the *Brooklyn Daily Eagle* remarked. A great crowd came to the funeral, and at least one society columnist considered the showing "quite out of the ordinary." Hadden's mother, having lived through the deaths of both her sister and her husband, sank into a period of fatigue, anxiety, and depression, and was often directed by her doctors to take rest cures in the country. Bess Hadden was a buoyant soul, however, and her condition improved. Eventually, she would marry Dr. William Pool, an obstetrician who lived a few blocks away. But even after Bess returned to her old self, a faint aura of tragedy and sadness hung over the otherwise gay Hadden house.

For six years, the significant part of Hadden's childhood, Bess Hadden raised her children alone. In the absence of a father, Hadden developed an unusually close relationship with his mother. Bess took pride in her son's storytelling and writing exploits, chuckled over his jokes, and encouraged his wit. Unusually sensitive to the feelings of others, Hadden was quite solicitous of his mother. He never disobeyed her, and at times he even courted her attention. Later, when he went off to boarding school, Hadden would keep his mother entertained with letters that began "Dearest Mother" and closed "More love than I can write, Mother Dear." The total connection between mother and son would never wane on either side.

The loss of his father did not seem to permanently trouble Hadden. Writing may have helped him come to terms with the experience: Hadden wrote a story about some young bunnies in the burrow who had forgotten their father and had to be reminded of him by their mother. Nevertheless, a feeling of pain and loneliness seeped into Hadden's soul at a tender age, and a remnant of that feeling would persist throughout his life. Friends would later remark that as much as they loved Hadden they often felt that they couldn't reach him. Despite his energy and enthusiasm, Hadden was intensely shy and guarded, and always quite secretive about his personal feelings. Loyal to the extreme, he could not bear to be injured by those close to him.

By 1908, when he enrolled at Brooklyn Poly Prep, the private boys' school his father and grandfather had both attended, Hadden's interest in journalism was quickening. He had been lucky to grow up in New York, where the rival titans of the "yellow" press, Joseph Pulitzer and William Randolph Hearst, battled each other for circulation, and newsboys hawked the papers on street corners. Hadden's grandfather probably read the *New York Times* and the *Brooklyn Daily Eagle,* along with the *Wall Street Journal* for business news and any number of Republican papers, from Charles Dana's *Sun* to the *New York Tribune.* The Haddens' friends and neighbors were often featured in a large society weekly called *Brooklyn Life.* Hadden also would have seen the large illustrated magazines like the *Saturday Evening Post,* which blanketed many a coffee table. Less frequently, he would have come across the progressive magazines, which, as Hadden entered his preteen years, began to feature the "muckraking" reports that inspired the urban reforms of the progressive movement.

Sitting ringside as the great age of American journalism began, Hadden developed the notion that there was too much news in the newspapers—so much news that it would be impossible for one person to learn all of it. From the outset, Hadden sought to simplify things. In the fifth grade, when he joined Poly Prep's school paper, he surprised his bosses with a markedly terse style. As the reporter for his class, Hadden was assigned to write a story that he considered relatively unimportant. When Hadden handed in a mere four inches of type, his editor, an older boy, upbraided the young newshound for failing to make use of the full column and a half to which he was entitled. "That is all the space the story warrants," Hadden shot back. "I don't believe in 'padding.' I'm a journalist, not a press agent."

In 1913, Hadden launched a publication of his own, an underground sheet that he wrote during class and distributed to his classmates, perhaps at Poly's rosewood lunch tables, where the boys were served by "chocolate-colored gentlemen." Though Hadden produced the entire paper, he called himself the reporter and general manager and appointed his friend Robert Honeyman as editor. He named the paper the *Daily Glonk,* in honor of the Hearst comic strip "Krazy Kat," in which a mouse found ingenious ways to wound an amorous cat.

Hadden's paper printed school gossip and joked about teachers. In one copy of the *Glonk* preserved by his mother, Hadden ribbed a friend who must have struggled with a lisp for his choice of attire: "At half past theven thith morning Theo. Oswald Clarke thallied forth to thcool arrayed in a thplendid new thuit. Unhappily for Theo., however, he forgot to remove the Moe Levy price mark which bore the inscription $4.98. Take it off Theo. We know you!" Something about that middle name of Oswald cried for ridicule. Hadden had searched out the funny bone and given it a playful whack. Later, in the pages of *Time,* Hadden's tendency to poke fun at public figures previously accustomed to respectful treatment would become a key aspect of his writing style.

Writing remained a competitive performance for Hadden. He did not merely report in the *Glonk*; he took center stage in a grand comedy of his own invention. When some of his schoolmates started a rival sheet, Hadden quickly added them to the *Glonk's* regular entertainment. He sketched their faces in the style of a newspaper mug shot and penciled in the headline "Ruffneck Fakirs Go to Jail." Chiding his friends for daring to compete with him for attention, Hadden found a moral in their demise: "Don't imitate a good news sheet with cheap and inferior material. The *Glonk* is the First and the Best."

The origins of *Time* can be traced to Hadden's years at Poly Prep, when he first became involved in a conversation about politics. Hadden, who lived almost entirely among Republicans, was surprised to learn that—horror of horrors—one of his friends was a Democrat. To a young member of the banking class, the party of Jackson and Tammany Hall conjured up uncouth images of spit-soaked saloons and rigged elections. Hadden and his friends began to get into political discussions, which came as a revelation to Hadden. Perhaps, he thought, facts of all kinds were open to dispute. "I'm going to put out a magazine . . . when I grow up which will tell the truth," Hadden proclaimed to his family. "Then there won't be all this confusion about who's right."

Hadden talked of founding a magazine throughout the rest of his childhood. He told his family that he wanted his magazine to be on the small side, just large enough to hold the essential facts. Having folded the periodical twice, a reader would be able to carry it about in his pocket. This was quite a specific plan for a boy to dream of at such a young age. More remarkable would be the way Hadden held to his dream as he grew and changed. The idea was so much a part of his personality that it almost seemed to be holding him captive rather than the reverse. In time, Hadden would refine his concept, but his life's work would only take form with the help of a boy growing up on the other side of the world.

Six weeks younger than Hadden, Henry R. Luce was born in rural China. His father, Henry Winters Luce, was a grocer's son from Scranton, Pennsylvania, who had gone off to Yale, joined the student religious movement, and decided to become a missionary. Home in Scranton for the weekend, the young preacher had walked into a church and seen a sad-eyed, voluptuous woman praying in a pew. Abandoned by her parents, fallen members of an illustrious family, Elizabeth Root had found refuge in the church, only to catch scarlet fever at eighteen and lose most of her hearing in both ears. Luce's optimism seemed heaven-sent. Elizabeth shocked her friends by marrying Luce quickly and embarking with him for China. She made the sea voyage while pregnant, traveled the mainland on a rickety pole conveyance strung between two donkeys, and finally covered the last miles on the backs of Chinese coolies.

The Luces were full of vigor and eager to begin the work of converting China's many millions of lost souls. But when they reached the Presbyterian mission compound in Dengzhou, a small town in impoverished Shandong province, the Luces saw only a fortress topped by a spiked gate—designed, they learned, to protect the missionaries from the peasants who lived nearby. Elizabeth, her courage flagging, recalled the lines from Dante: "Abandon all hope, ye who enter here." Two months later, she went into labor. Her first son was born after a harrowing delivery on April 3, 1898. She named him Henry Robinson, after his father and the pastor who had married them, or Harry for short.

The Luces arrived at Dengzhou just as news began to spread of the Righteous and Harmonious Fists, a secret society that whipped up anti-foreign sentiment, along with the belief that its members could not be killed. In 1898, the Chinese "Boxers," as Westerners called them, began to attack Christian missionaries and Chinese converts. By the summer of 1900, a rebellion had spread throughout Peking and nearby Shandong province. One night the Boxers came for the Dengzhou compound and the missionaries were forced to flee. Luce's mother held his one-month-old sister and his father grabbed him by the hand. They ran down into the sorghum fields and through the dark crop to the shore, where a friendly boat captain helped the missionaries escape to Korea. Spending a tense summer in Seoul, the Luces learned their closest friend had been beheaded in Peking. "What days these are for China!" the Reverend Luce wrote friends in Scranton. "Days of blood and death! . . . God's kingdom will still be set up."

After an alliance of foreign powers including the United States brutally ended the rebellion, reasserted control of key trading regions, and compelled the Chinese government to pay hundreds of millions in reparations, the Luces returned to Dengzhou. Reverend Luce taught his students to play basketball and angered his fellow missionaries by campaigning to move the mission to the capital of the province. In 1904, partly acceding to Luce's appeal, the missionaries moved to the larger town of Weifang. They surrounded their new compound with a ten-foot wall topped by jagged shards of glass.

Harry Luce inherited the brilliance and idealism of his father. The boy was dictating notes to his mother, often concerning the Psalms, before he could write by hand. But Luce also revealed a cold confidence of his own. At the age of six, he began to gather the other mission children and sit them down as if in church so that he might stand up on a barrel and preach to them. Patient and resolute, Luce had a calculating, analytical mind. On the top floor of his family's house, he laid out hundreds of soldiers and moved them about in complicated war games. He required his younger sisters to tiptoe around these strategic constructions lest a single piece be moved and the delicate dance to an endgame be nudged off track.

When the reverend donned the robes of a Chinese scholar, hitched the mules to a wagon, and set off to preach in the villages nearby, he would bring along his son. Walking through the dust, they would come across Chinese villagers bearing gongs and drums and carrying elaborate bamboo replicas of houses and temples—a funeral procession meant to ease the path of the deceased toward the afterlife. Looking at these filthy peasants, some covered in sores, others weighed down by goiters, Reverend Luce felt pained that they had never heard of Jesus Christ. With the sureness of one who had undergone a spiritual revelation, he told his son that the United States held a divine mission to spread Christian civilization to the heathen lands.

In 1905, the Presbyterian mission asked Reverend Luce to raise funds in America. The Luces set off for San Francisco aboard the SS *Manchuria*. The family always traveled second class. Reverend Luce barnstormed the nation and solicited funds from wealthy Presbyterians with an interest in foreign lands. In Chicago, the Reverend arranged to meet the widow Nettie Fowler McCormick, whose husband had invented the reaper and built the company that grew into International Harvester. Profits long since reaped by the industrial goliath still funded the widow's many progressive causes. Mrs. McCormick appeared to Reverend Luce almost as a saint. Ushering the traveler into her great house, she took one look at his tired face and insisted that before doing anything he must get some rest. When Reverend Luce awoke, she asked him to send for his family.

The Luces followed their father to the Midwest. Seven-year-old Harry was still a bit fragile; he had only just recuperated from a bout with malaria. He was astounded by the commotion of Chicago's vital Loop: the winter sleighs sliding through the snow, the telegraph wires jutting overhead, the power and energy of America. Seeing this grave little boy with the angelic blue eyes, Mrs. McCormick instantly fell in love. The widow astonished the young couple by asking for permission to take their child and raise him in America. The Luces, in turn, mortified their son by stopping to pray over the offer. Though the couple decided to take their son back to China, Mrs. McCormick would pay for much of Luce's education in any case. Her love for the boy only deepened, and she became to him a kind of godmother.

That fall Luce fell ill again, and the doctors, believing his tonsils were infected, decided to take them out. An uncomfortable procedure worsened considerably when the anesthetic wore off too soon. Luce awoke to the the rending pain of operation—an experience that may also have seared his mind. Around that time, Luce's parents noticed he was having difficulty getting his words out. His stammer worsened until it became painful to the ears of others. Luce spoke in violent bursts punctuated by long, awkward silences. Often it seemed as if he was fighting to control his tongue or to keep up with his racing thoughts. At times the stammer completely defaced Luce's speech. "Oh! It was terrible, just terrible!" recalled his younger sister Elisabeth. Embarrassed by his problem, Luce began to turn inward. He developed a prickly stridency, an urge to win at all costs, and at times a rough male hostility.

The Luces returned to China in 1907. They moved into a simple brick house paid for by Mrs. McCormick. She called it their "Renaissance villa," and by missionary standards it was indeed luxurious. The Luces had a laundry boy, a housekeeper, a nurse, a gardener, a table boy, and even a talented chef. He soon learned to cook with cream since the Luces did not eat Chinese food, apart from an occasional dumpling. Mrs. Luce served afternoon tea on her white damask tablecloth, and Reverend Luce played the violin during parties. Young missionaries traveling through Weifang requested to be boarded with the worldly family.

The Luces rose early and studied most of the day. They read by candlelight, bathed in cold water, and looked forward to Christmas, when a crate arrived from Montgomery Ward full of books and games from friends in Scranton. At dinner, the conversation always managed to circle back to the eldest child, and Reverend Luce couldn't help drawing his son into the study for further philosophical argument. The Luces loved their daughters, Emmavail and Elisabeth, but they admired young Henry the most. Both the Reverend and Mrs. Luce believed their son would travel into the world to represent the family's ideals. Luce's journey began in the fall of 1908 when he boarded a steamship and headed north to boarding school. He was ten years old.

The China Inland Mission School was based in Yantai, a fishing port in northeast Shandong province that Westerners called "Chefoo." Most of the boys at the school were the children of British missionaries who could not afford to give their children a proper English education. The schoolmasters boasted of their tennis courts and swimming beach, but they closed the school down for six weeks each winter just to save on heating costs. With few fireplaces, the school was drafty, and as many as eight boys were forced to share a single load of bathwater. Luce felt desperately lonely. "It sort of seems to hang on not in spells of homesickness but a hanging torture," he once wrote his parents. "I well sympathize with prisoners wishing to commit suicide now."

Though Chefoo lacked the resources of a British boarding school, the boys retained the abusive habits for which those schools later became infamous. Younger boys, who were known as "fags," were forced to "toady" to the older boys and run errands for them. The small group of American boys, who included the budding writer Thornton Wilder, did not take well to the British system. Luce rebelled by refusing to share his sweets and newspapers and by looking askance at boys who failed to keep the Sabbath. When a master, testing Luce, commanded him to agree that the moon was made of green cheese, Luce refused to go along. The next day the rest of the school watched Luce take a caning across the backside.

Wounded by the cries of "skunk" and "mark" that followed him through the halls, Luce acquired a tough exterior and hid his emotions deep within. When his mother bore another son, Sheldon, Luce badly wished to share his joy with his schoolmates, but he decided not to mention his brother's birth for fear of being teased for sentimental thoughts. When his sisters' pet mice had babies, Luce advised his parents to give the girls two weeks to enjoy the newcomers, then "kill them unless you feel that you can afford the grub." Luce found comfort in studying the Bible and took inspiration from the Psalms. By the age of eleven, he began to feel that God had opened a door to him. "I seem more on the same pedestal with him, more at home, more as one of his chosen," he wrote his parents, "and I feel certain that he is at my side."

As Luce entered adolescence, he formed a close friendship with his roommate, an older British boy named Sydney Cecil-Smith. The boys studied together, tried their hands at poetry, and scuffled in their room. Luce thought the competition was "great fun," and when he bought a new camera the first picture he took was of his friend and rival. A mood of rigor and excitement emanated from Smith. A school prefect, he was charismatic and popular. He freed Luce from his Calvinist burdens and inspired him with the feeling of possibility. Not for the last time, Luce felt himself powerfully drawn into the aura of a glamorous friend.

Emboldened by their high academic records, Smith and Luce formed a debating society. "I hope you do not mind my developing those qualities which you say are already too marked in me," Luce wrote his father. During their debates, Luce and Smith faced off in suspenseful showdowns. They lobbed quips, cracked jokes, and competed to rally the crowd. Luce cocked his head to the side and worked his hand in circles as he struggled to control his words. Smith seemed "impregnable" to Luce, but gradually he began to win more of their contests. When the masters broke the society into competing squads, Luce and Smith were picked to head one each. Luce happily wrote his parents that he and his roommate would constitute "a permanent rivalry-ship."

Smith was elected the society's president, but Vice President Luce felt the urge to challenge his roommate. By the spring of 1912, Smith held the edge in their string of debates by just one victory. When Luce received his chance to even the score, the rivals competed in a thrilling debate that ended in a tie. The winner would be determined by the debate chairman, a much younger boy. He twitched a few times before finally awarding victory to Luce. "Long after the sound of the clapping had died away, those words that spoke of my victory echoed and reechoed in my mind," Luce wrote his parents. He assured them that he and Smith were "better friends now than ever," but Smith began to snub Luce, and the two no longer talked as much. The boys' intense rivalry had destroyed their special closeness, and ultimately they did not stay in touch.

Soon a new activity excited Luce's interest. "Now—a surprise," he wrote home. "A school paper has been urged and so—as Smith refused to be editor of any kind—I am the 'Editor in Chief.'" Luce dug into the job with characteristic spirit. He compiled ten pages of campus news, fiction, and poetry. In addition to the lead story, Luce wrote the editorial and a satire about British football. For printing purposes, the boys had nothing but glue and a gelatin reproducer known as a hectograph. Luce managed to print thirty papers on a tight budget. "This is the first thing that makes me realize what really financing is!" he wrote home. During school vacation, Luce produced his own newspaper, which he wrote in longhand on spools of blotting paper. He had found his lifelong love.

In October of 1911, the last Chinese dynasty began to appear dangerously unstable as armed revolutionaries in the large city of Wuchang revolted against the monarchy. The insurrection widened into a revolution for a more democratic form of government, and within a few months soldiers were marching by Luce's school. Chefoo's servants promptly demanded higher wages. When the principal refused their demands, the servants walked out to join a revolutionary army. The Chefoo boys would have to serve their own tea. "Noble pursuit!" Luce cracked to his parents.

Reverend Luce remained committed to spreading the word to China, but he took steps to protect his children from the threat of violence. The Luce girls were studying with a German governess who recommended them to a school in Switzerland. Luce's mother would head to Europe with the girls and little Sheldon. Harry would apply to Hotchkiss, the Connecticut boarding school where an old mentor of the Reverend's had taken up teaching duties. Because the Luces could not afford their son's tuition, he would try to win an academic scholarship. While waiting for the result, Luce would live in St. Alban's, England, at the home of a prep school principal who had devised a method to help boys afflicted with stammering.

Luce rode the train to Nanjing, stood for a moment above the giant Yangtze River, and a week later waved at his father from a ship that floated down the river and into the great sea. Luce traveled through the Suez Canal and the Strait of Gibraltar, then across the English Channel to England. In St. Alban's, reading aloud from Dickens and *Julius Caesar,* Luce wrote his parents that he would soon be rid of his stammer, but it proved to be more stubborn than he hoped. After traveling to Paris, Luce finally arrived in Switzerland, where he hired his own tutor and studied French. Luce hadn't stayed long before he decided to tour Italy. Saving money by sleeping on the train, he traveled the whole country in three weeks.

When he returned to Switzerland in the spring of 1913, Luce had worn out the soles of his walking shoes. He was finally reunited with his family, but only briefly: Hotchkiss had granted him a scholarship. With a friend from Chefoo, Luce traveled down the Rhine into Germany, visited Belgium, and went on to Hamburg. Reverend Luce was there, getting set to begin another grueling fund-raising effort for the Presbyterian mission. In August, father and son boarded a boat for the motherland. "I wonder what you will think of him!" Luce's mother wrote her cousin. "I *hope* he is not going to be eccentric. I hope he will develop into a sane, well-poised person. I know his faults *so well,* but he is very dear, and I will say this—he has only noble instincts."

Standing on the deck with a book by Winston Churchill in hand, Luce, tall and willowy, pointed his steel-blue gaze toward America. At the age of fifteen, he had seen more of the world in a few months than most people see in a lifetime. He had survived a rebellion, witnessed part of a revolution, and made it through a strict boarding school. Now he was headed for his homeland to struggle on a larger scale. Brilliant, dedicated, hardworking, he was ready to race against a new rival. He would find one in Briton Hadden, who had recently passed the Hotchkiss entrance exams, and would soon travel up, golf bag in tow.

2

The Hill

WHEN HADDEN AND LUCE arrived at Hotchkiss, they saw a cluster of yellow brick buildings crowning a gentle hill that sloped down to a lake. Behind the lake was a low mountain, and on the other side more hills rolled away in pillows of yellow and green. The setting conveyed elegance and splendor, as did Hotchkiss boys themselves, who stepped up the hill in cordovan loafers, the pockets of their tweed suits stuffed with money for chocolate sundaes.

Hotchkiss, "the school on the hill," was one of the wealthiest boarding schools in America. So many trust-fund boys arrived from the Midwest that an investment house took out advertisements in the school paper to encourage the boys to buy real-estate bonds. The campus had a Calvinist atmosphere, and its main hall featured a foreboding Latin inscription: "Having been admonished, let us follow better ways." The headmaster, Huber Gray Buehler, was a pompous old sermonizer known to the boys as "the King." With his double chin flapping away behind a stiff collar, he told the boys that what they were at twenty so they would be at forty, "only more so."

The most popular boys at Hotchkiss were the wealthiest and the best at sports. The football greats led the hazing rituals by making younger boys get down on all fours and push matchsticks with their noses, or forcing them to graze the walls with their elbows as they walked the corridors. Anyone who didn't fit the mold was studiously ignored. Hadden and Luce, both fifteen, would be skipping the freshman year and joining the sophomore class, scheduled to graduate in 1916. As new boys, they had a precise position in the Hotchkiss hierarchy, later spelled out in a school newspaper editorial: "Forget not your diminutive stature, your lowliness of rank, the complete nonentity of your existence, for you still are fresh and green, childish and inconsequential."

Hadden walked the halls with his chest puffed out and a baseball cap slung low over his brow. He grinned widely and spewed forth wise-cracks. His harsh Brooklyn accent was often heard above the din, and he smiled a lot, at which times his face would crinkle up in such a way that the boys took to calling him "Cat." Hadden was fascinated by people's quirks and found an element of humor in almost anyone's character. In his high, squeaky voice, he bestowed nicknames on many of his classmates, including Luce. Hadden named his fellow new sophomore, in honor of the catch in his speech and his place of origin, "Chink."

Luce had come to campus in an imitation of a Western suit cut by a Chinese tailor. As a scholarship boy, Luce slept off campus in the town of Lakeville. His roommate, a poor boy from Kansas, had arrived without blankets, so at first Luce shared his bed. Early in the morning, Luce hitched a ride to school on a farmer's buggy. He just had time to sweep out the chapel and wolf down a shredded-wheat biscuit before serving breakfast to his classmates. In the afternoons, he sponged the blackboards. The scholarship work was so burdensome that in later years Luce's speech would fail him when he attempted to describe its horrors.

Hotchkiss boys tended to squirm about in chapel, a habit the King dissuaded with his icy glare and a sermon entitled "Satan in Church." When Luce exhorted his schoolmates to be better Christians, the elo-cution master complimented him for being able to "sling the religious bull"—a sign that perhaps even the masters didn't take religion all that seriously. Within a few months, Luce began to lose interest in follow-ing his father down the missionary path, and gradually he lost that old sense of closeness with God. "I knew it then, there on the hill, that I was really only a back-row Christian," Luce recalled. "And something went outside of me." But Luce admired the glamour and vigor of the wealthy boys who surrounded him. He wanted to befriend them, to achieve success on their terms, and eventually to join their number.

As social opposites, one gregarious and the other quite shy, one active and eccentric, the other reserved and intellectual, Hadden and Luce took little notice of each other. But each in his way impressed the other boys of their class, so that by the winter of their first year they almost seemed to stand out together. Hadden befriended much of the class and he even helped to bring some unpopular boys within the fold. Luce earned honors. When he discovered a miscalculation in his grade-point average, he rose to the rank of First Scholar, edging out another boy and forcing the school newspaper to run a front-page correction. One master told Luce, "You can do one thing that most boys can't—think!" New boys were barred from attending the school dance, but a vote by the sophomore class allowed Hadden and Luce to go. Luce, mentioning Hadden to his parents for the first time, described him as a "general pet."

Classmates took note of Hadden's manic personality, his need to do things to extremes. He seemed to be looking for something that would require his whole heart and soul. In the dining hall, he took on the school cherry-eating record by cramming twelve cherries onto a single spoon and trying to get them all into his mouth. In the dormitory, he excitedly competed in handstand contests. "Time me! Time me!" he would yell, flipping upside down. If he was about to break a new record, nothing could interrupt him, not even the need to go to class. An augury of Hadden's future, hardly remarked upon but intensely felt, was his mania for newspapers and magazines, dozens of which he read daily. Luce, by contrast, was ambitious and self-conscious. He did not easily bond with the scholarship boys, whom he considered uncultured. He especially disliked being forced to sit with them at dinner, since their table manners disgusted him. Luce hoped that if he went out for some extracurricular activities some of the other boys might begin to notice him.

In a school controlled in the classroom by stern masters and in the dormitory by giant football players, one way for an intellectual boy to assume a place of leadership was to edit the weekly newspaper, the *Hotchkiss Record*. To make the staff, boys first had to endure an arcane form of hazing known as "heeling." The word "heeler" had been inherited from New York City, where it described the lackeys who pledged allegiance to Tammany Hall. The heelers, a dozen or so, raced for months to accumulate the most points by writing articles and selling ads. Every few weeks the editor would run a heeling update in the paper, with point totals for the school to see and occasionally an article chiding the heelers for their laziness. At the end of the competition, a few boys would be "taken in."

In May, the *Record* editors announced a new competition for sopho-mores only. It would last only a month. At its end, the sophomore who showed the most "natural ability" would be taken onto the board—a year before his classmates. Luce's father would have preferred that he skip the competition and try to make the high honor roll instead, but Luce wrote his parents that he planned to make the *Record* his "whole-hearted hobby." It seemed to him that he had a good shot at making the board. As it turned out, Hadden, who had yet to distinguish him-self in extracurricular activities, decided to enter the competition, too. It would be a life-changing experience.

Hadden had a habit, when he took an interest in something, of doing it with abandon. Working for the *Record* stoked the love for reporting that had been within him since the earliest days of his child-hood. He began working with a passion he had never felt before, stay-ing at the office during his free hours, proposing story ideas, taking assignments, and selling ads. For a while he stopped writing home. "Maybe you are wondering whether I'm sick or dead or something," Hadden finally wrote his mother. "I'm not. I'm only 'heeling' the *Record*. Gee, it's *some* job, too. I am working hard."

Luce sunk far below Hadden, who clinched the victory when the track team went to a meet in New Haven, and the team's manager gave Hadden the results. "I believe I am still second though quite far behind the first fellow," Luce wrote home. "Added to good hard work he has had very great luck and while I am not satisfied with second place, yet I think it was worthwhile." At the end of the year Hadden became the only sophomore to make the *Record*, a distinction that practically guaranteed him the editorship in his senior year. Having discovered his talent, Hadden held to it tightly. Journalism became his lifelong fixation, and at an extremely young age he began to think of himself as a working reporter.

Luce had a wider range of interests and, perhaps consequently, he lacked Hadden's singular focus. Still considering himself a scholar, Luce wrote poetry, fiction, and essays that quickly found their way into the *Hotchkiss Literary Monthly,* a new publication that most of the boys ignored. The *Record* editors reviewed the *Lit*'s contents each month, often unfavorably. They called Luce's writing "affected and over-ornate." When he wrote a story about China, they jeered, "We can only ask why it was not written in Chinese. The meaning would have been just as clear." But Luce did not let the teasing stop him. He eventually won the *Lit* heeling competition, made the *Record* staff, and joined the yearbook. He was incensed when the faculty forced him to quit the yearbook, because the masters believed that three publications were too many for a scholarship boy.

In the spring of 1914, shouts echoed across the Litchfield Hills when Hotchkiss bested its rival, The Hill School, in both baseball and football, and the boys marched into town to raid the general store of horns, bells, tin pans, and rattles. By the next afternoon, they had constructed a tower of scrap wood as high as a house, which was set ablaze in a spectacular bonfire. The boys paid little attention to the rumblings of war from the other side of the Atlantic. Luce planned to sail for Europe that summer on Germany's pride, the *Vaterland*. But the ship's passage was canceled, and soon Luce learned that his sisters were on their way from Hamburg to America. They had made the last boat out. "It is as if we were placed in the 15th century," Mrs. McCormick wrote Luce, "and the intervening centuries of struggle toward civilization were blotted out."

When Hadden and Luce returned to Hotchkiss as juniors in the fall of 1914, the nation was immersed in a growing controversy over the war. Most Americans viewed the violence in Europe as the product of a corrupt continent; they did not want to get involved. But an increasingly influential wing of the Republican Party, led by former President Theodore Roosevelt, believed the nation should rush to the aid of England and France. Instead of proposing a war that few would support, Roosevelt preached the mantra of military "preparedness." Moved by the Rough Rider's exhortations, some wealthy Ivy League graduates traveled to Plattsburgh, New York, to participate in a military training camp.

The boys at Hotchkiss took in the currents, and generally they sided with Roosevelt. In the Hotchkiss debating society, a relatively lax club in which some snoozed and others threw books, the quality of work improved as the boys began to discuss the war. Luce exhorted his fellow students to spread Christian democracy through the world in a thousand-word speech entitled "By the Light of the Battle Flames." Hadden took up the comparatively modest question of whether, in fact, the nation was prepared for war. He found his answer in the low ratio of horses to men in the national cavalry. "Nine militia officers riding to war on one horse!" Hadden cracked. "A pretty sight."

It was typical of Hadden to hit upon a single fact that could settle a case by standing metaphorically for the matter at hand. Hadden's habit of cutting straight to the point with a joke rather than launching upon a grand thesis and his preference for a fact over an opinion would remain chief characteristics of his work. The style struck his friends as original even then, but it did not particularly impress Luce, so highly trained in the florid British style of declamation. And yet the two were sidling up to each other. Hadden had assembled a large group of friends including a few boys who might not otherwise have been accepted. Luce, gradually rising above the status of a typical scholarship boy, found himself conversing and playing with Hadden and his circle.

By the beginning of 1915, Hadden had shot up three inches and gained more than twenty pounds, with another two inches and fifteen pounds to gain in the year to come. His voice had changed from a squeak to a squawk, which his friends would recall for its ability to pierce the air. At dinner he chatted easily with the masters' wives, never seeming to fear what the other boys would think. After dinner he was an active participant in late-night dormitory raids. During one skirmish, he dressed in a burglar's dark getup and led a sortie against a rival dorm, only to be ambushed, bound, and kidnapped. Hadden remained an enthusiastic adventurer and collector of small delights. Influenced by the novel *Silas Marner,* he and a friend built a hut in the woods by trimming saplings with an ax and weaving other saplings through to create the walls and roof. Hadden revealed his inventiveness with language when he called their activity "marnering."

Beneath the noise, the bombast, the good cheer and exuberant outlook, occasional feelings of anxiety would arise. Back in the Heights, Hadden held his girlfriend Jean Whiting at arm's length during a dance. Jean excoriated Hadden. Dejected, he later confessed to her that he knew he was rough and crude, and he secretly felt more at home with "bummers" than with respectable people. On another occasion, he managed to come a bit closer to admitting his affections by writing his girlfriend a poem of twenty-six lines, each representing a letter in the alphabet: "H is for Hadden, most conventional friend, who may wind up with Jean in the end."

Such sweet testaments of feeling, though expressed only occasionally, showed Hadden's friends the real love behind his teasing, a love he often felt too embarrassed to express. There was something about that wry crooked smile, appealing though it was, that suggested an underlying uneasiness. If he visited a girl in Brooklyn, Hadden would always insist on bringing along a friend; he couldn't screw up the courage to go alone. On the holidays, Hadden received invitations to dancing parties and teas of all kinds. But he didn't always feel comfortable at these sorts of occasions, and he developed a policy of accepting all invitations, so as not to hurt anyone's feelings, but canceling half in the end.

Luce would have gladly made an appearance at some of the dancing parties and teas that secretly vexed Hadden, but the upper crust ignored Luce. His closest friends were two literary fellows, the shy and romantic Culbreth "Cully" Sudler and a younger boy on the *Lit*, the religious Erdman Harris. On long walks through the hills surrounding Lakeville, Sudler would listen as Luce brainstormed, stammering rapid-fire from the classics down to the founding fathers. With his face flushed by the cool winds and his clothes flapping about carelessly, there was something beautiful about Luce, a youth at intellectual war with the world, madly in love with grand ideas.

Sudler could tell Luce felt frustrated. His ambition was great. He was furious at himself for failing to gain notice, and furious with a wealthy, complacent world that had yet to recognize his intelligence. "Harry had a kind of terrifying egotism," Sudler recalled. "Everything was up there in his head. His personality, his manner, didn't matter. Nothing mattered except the idea." One night, peeking around in Luce's room, Sudler opened a drawer and discovered a yellowing packet of pseudoscientific instructions for the cure of stammering. The dog-eared pages seemed much studied, and they gave Sudler an image of Luce alone late at night, struggling determinedly to defeat his inadequacies. Sudler quickly cast the packet aside as if he had discovered an awful secret.

If Luce felt down at times, if he suffered doubts, he never showed it. His letters home were ebullient, loaded with exclamation marks.

Each new essay, each new speech in the debating society, each new article for the *Record* or story for the *Lit* provided him a chance to test his wits. Furthermore, though no one knew it, Luce secretly planned to surprise a few people before he left campus. He hoped to transform the *Lit* from a haphazard collection of poetry and fiction into an essential ingredient of the boys' daily life—a kind of illustrated monthly not unlike the great national magazines. Luce wrote his parents that his plans would "make 'em sit up and take notice!"

In May of 1915, Luce and Erdman Harris were lying on the grass and gazing across the lake. It was a beautiful clear day, a time for reflection. Casually, Harris asked Luce what he might like to do with the *Lit* when he became its editor as a senior in the following fall. Excitedly, breathlessly, Luce began unwinding his audacious plan. First of all, he was going to get Teddy Roosevelt to write an article for the first issue. Not only that, he was going to print pictures for the first time—and not just any pictures, but a glossy photo insert depicting all the scenes of Hotchkiss life. Stunned, Harris asked Luce how he could possibly get a former president to write for a little-known school magazine. When Luce vaguely replied that he had already put in a line to the old Rough Rider, it suddenly dawned on Harris that he was "listening to no ordinary schoolboy."

Luce dashed about New York that summer, touring the Scribner's press and meeting with Lyman Abbott, a friend of Mrs. McCormick who encouraged him to use the *Lit* as a means of "exalting Christ." Hadden, summering at Westhampton beach, concocted a plan to print the *Record* twice a week instead of once, a schedule that would bring in twice the advertising revenue and give the paper a better chance of breaking news. Hadden also moved the editorials page from the middle of the paper to the second page and eradicated the practice of reprinting editorials from college papers. Neither Hadden nor Luce knew it, but they were about to enter into a rivalry that would transform their lives.

At the start of his senior year in the fall of 1915, Hadden released a dramatically changed issue of the *Record*. The newspaper was curt, factual, and fun to read, and in his first editorial Hadden did not mince words. He proclaimed that he intended to provoke controversy, and he planned to print "the facts as we see them in an absolutely unbiased and impartial manner." If boys disagreed with the *Record*'s version of the facts, they could always write a letter to the editor. In fact, Hadden encouraged the boys to do so. "Controversy is unrest," he wrote, "and unrest breathes the spirit of progress."

Little more than a week after Hadden put out his first *Record,* a controversy erupted within the senior class. At its center was Luce, who had stolen the photographs that his former partners on the yearbook staff had taken since the first day of school and saved for publication that spring. Luce planned to print the pictures in the *Lit.* His stunt provoked an ugly feud, and some of his classmates went so far as to call upon the faculty to ban Luce's publication. But the King refused to intervene, and Luce published his first issue over the vocal denunciations of some whom he had once hoped to befriend.

When the boys opened the *Lit,* they were shocked to discover that Luce had transformed the offbeat little monthly into a mainstream magazine of campus life. Luce had not managed to procure a guest essay from Roosevelt, but the boy editor's other plan had succeeded. In the middle of the magazine stood the Pictorial Supplement. Richly plastered with auto advertisements, the glossy insert featured photographs of a recent football game. On the front cover, a brash slogan trumpeted: "First in the Prep School World." The front cover of the *Lit* also featured a new motto: "The 'Better' Magazine." Luce couldn't help cracking a smile when he walked into the senior room and saw the boys reading the *Lit* and chattering. He was less amused when the boys branded him with the new nickname of "Crooked."

Along with the notoriety, Luce attracted the scrutiny of Hadden, who couldn't resist mulling over the controversy. "When such expressions as 'The "Better" Magazine' and 'First in the Prep School World' bring forth unfavorable comment from our own student body, will they not also create adverse criticism from outsiders?" Hadden asked in a review of the *Lit.* "The phrase 'First in the Prep School World' over the Pictorial section, although true enough, seems to us especially uncalled for." The following month Luce eliminated the slogan, and Hadden savored the victory by claiming credit for the change. He wrote, "We notice with pleasure that, upon the advice of last month's criticism . . . 'First in the Prep School World' has been dropped."

Luce had captured Hadden's attention not only by causing controversy but also, no doubt, by improving the *Lit* so dramatically. From that point on, Luce could hardly write a sentence without eliciting an editorial chuckle from Hadden. When Luce wrote an essay suggesting that the boys ought to navigate by the same light the three wise men had used to find the newborn baby Jesus, Hadden called his classmate's writing "noble but vague." Playing on Luce's title, "The Star," Hadden quipped, "If the author had explained more definitely just what star to follow, the piece would have been greatly improved." The rivalry between the two boys grew fierce enough that Hadden's family heard and talked about it. "Competition was the breath of life to Hadden and that's why he and Luce got along so well," a cousin of Hadden's later said. "Neither one could get ahead of the other."

Of the two, it was Hadden who seemed naturally suited toward journalism. He wrote as he spoke, in confident, colorful bursts. Instead of awarding more points for longer stories, Hadden graded his heelers on "terseness." He employed detail cannily, often printing lists of statistics. One story he printed, "What We Eat," informed the boys that they gobbled 350 pounds of steak in a single meal. Hadden's love for chasing a story infused the paper with energy. When the football team traveled to Pottstown to play Hill, Hadden and his reporters made the trip as "war correspondents," phoning back reports of the game's progress to a crier posted outside the office of the *Lakeville Journal.* Immediately following the game, Hadden's staff printed a special edition that brought home the news of defeat even before the weary players returned.

In the main hallway at Hotchkiss, the masters kept a map of Europe dotted with hundreds of pins. Every few days they might adjust a pin, and its movement would symbolize that one army or another had taken perhaps a mile of scorched earth along the Western Front. There were no pins to account for the thousands of lost lives. Hadden was riveted by the news from Europe. He had a vast appetite for newspapers and magazines, encompassing but not limited to the *New York World,* the *Tribune, Cosmopolitan,* the humor magazine *Life,* the *Sporting News,* and the *Wall Street Journal.* Each night, after taking his shower, he would skim through the *New York Times.*

Hadden noticed that most other boys took the news lightly. Many of them read only *Current Events,* a news summary distributed to the boarding schools. Believing that his classmates ought to be better informed, in November of 1915 Hadden began to print his own weekly world news summary. It was a single column running down the left side of the front page. At the top of the first column, Hadden announced what would become his lifelong goal: to tell "the important happenings of the week to those of us who do not find time to read the detailed accounts in the daily papers."

The object of helping busy people to stay current by summarizing the news would guide Hadden throughout his life. But he also proved to be an entertaining storyteller. In the middle of January, when the tiny kingdom of Montenegro surrendered to the army of the Austro-Hungarian Empire, Hadden cracked, "Contrary to last week's reports, Montenegro has not surrendered. Her army is retreating to Albania to join the Swedish forces." In addition to injecting the news with bits of humor, Hadden enlivened his writing by focusing on broad themes. In March of 1916, the news reached Hotchkiss that in February the Germans had attacked the fortress of Verdun, the French had fiercely defended that strategic point, and the trenches were beginning to resemble a mass grave. "That they renew massed attacks undeterred by carnage, speaks well for discipline," Hadden wrote of the German effort, "but it is the work of automatons, not men."

Since he had made the *Record* staff after Hadden, Luce worked as Hadden's assistant managing editor. They came to respect each other as they compressed the news from around the world into the space of a column. Occasionally Hadden would talk about his dream of creating a magazine that contained all the week's news. He later told friends that he first interested Luce in the idea at Hotchkiss. Years later, Luce would not be able to recall those conversations. Watching the classmates spar in print, the friends and teachers of Hadden and Luce came to think of them as great rivals with natures so opposite as to form an epic contrast. Hadden was "brilliant, smiling, face like a round sun at mid-day," the Hotchkiss master H. Brooks Hering recalled. Luce was "heavy-browed, solemn, serious, thinking."

Despite their frequent and fierce arguments, the rivals always ended up near each other. Both had enrolled in the hardest class at Hotchkiss. Though Yale no longer tested its entrants for knowledge of ancient Greek, Hotchkiss required its students to take at least one year. Hadden and Luce were among a small group of boys who elected to take two years. On the first day of class, "Doc" Lester Brown curtly informed his boys that he planned to work them twice as hard as any other master. The boys feared Brown at first, but they admired his integrity, and gradually they began to share his intense love for the classics. They called themselves the Crazy Greek division.

Luce, the scholar of the group, would later place first in Greek when he took Yale's entrance examinations. But it was Hadden who found in Doc Brown's class the inspiration for a writing style that would transform the American media. Homer's *Iliad,* that timeless tale of love and war, grabbed Hadden with its forceful prose and its vivid portrayal of character. Hadden fell in love with the *Iliad*'s backward syntax, in which the noun followed the verb, making a sentence appear to run in reverse. The warriors who marched through the story, speaking eloquently and dying violently, captivated Hadden's young mind with the possibility of portraying people on an epic scale.

Having spent his childhood nicknaming and branding his friends with references to characteristics or traits that seemed to sum up their different characters, Hadden was instantly drawn to the Homeric writing style. The *Iliad* signified the personalities of its main actors by labeling them with epithets such as "helm-quivering Hector," "laughter-loving Venus," and "far-darting Apollo." Though he had never been much of a student, Hadden studied the *Iliad* intensely. He underlined favorite expressions and passages, especially the epithets that connoted character with such brisk enthusiasm. "Brit responded primarily to the freshness and originality of the Homeric point of view," his classmate Cully Sudler recalled. "To Brit everyone was a personality."

Soon Hadden began to coin his own epithets. In nearby Lakeville, he noticed a sort of epithet on a sign posted by a tonsorial shop. The sign simply said "Judd the barber." Hadden laughed over the sign and worked the epithet into conversation whenever he could. Soon his jokes about ancient Greek helped to turn the Crazy Greek division into an informal kind of club. In class, Doc Brown made frequent use of the Greek phrases *Oi men* and *Oi dé*—"on the one hand" and "on the other hand." When Hadden passed other boys from the class, he'd hail them: "Hoy, men!" The boys would respond, "Hoy, dee!"

Hailing and hailing back, Luce and Hadden began to socialize more, partly because of their common interest in journalism, and partly because each found in the other a perfect intellectual partner. Hadden was attracted to Luce's work ethic, raw talent, and inquiring intellect, while Luce appreciated Hadden's wit, his humor, his good fellowship, and his independent judgment. "Brit was just one hell of a guy," recalled Luce's close friend Cully Sudler. "He magnetized Harry, he magnetized anybody. Harry was a bigger person, more intellectual, infinitely better informed, a bigger character—but, as I say, Brit was a tiger and a magnet."

During their senior year, Hadden and Luce found themselves teaming up more often. In the Hotchkiss debating society, Hadden always remained loyal to the team he had joined in his sophomore year, despite its long record of losses. Luce, a key member of the winning team, was shifted over to even up the sides. They must have made funny partners, Luce with his grandiloquent sentences and winding arguments, Hadden with his almost shockingly straightforward exclamations. In the annual debate, the perfect opposites were assigned the question of whether the United States should arm its merchant ships. They argued an emphatically patriotic yes, with Luce crafting the attack, and together they won the competition.

Rivalry remained a crucial aspect of their bond and conflict was embedded in their working relationship. As the assistant managing editor of the *Record*, Luce edited one of the *Record*'s two weekly issues before Hadden did the final proofread. In February of their senior year, an argument broke out in the office when the managing editor suggested that he and Luce ought to control front-page coverage. Luce told his parents that Hadden was forced to surrender "complete control over news columns," adding, "This was not my doings!" Despite their arguments, Hadden was gaining respect for Luce. When Luce published "Stanzas," an ode to the roving life filled with his memories of China, Hadden praised the poem as the *Lit*'s best all year.

Hadden and the rest of the Crazy Greek division were having an influence on Luce. By the spring of his senior year he was playing center for the class football team, campaigning for a friend to be elected class president, and presenting a case to the student court on behalf of a boy who had been caught with whiskey in his room. When the King nastily accused Luce of disregarding his scholarship duties, the headmaster's attack only confirmed Luce's arrival as one of the boys. Luce had shown as much already by saving up funds for a trendy straw hat and Boston garters, and by joining the fellows for an after-dinner Pall Mall. Luce wrote his parents that he and Hadden were "frating it up more." Luce even considered asking Hadden to room with him at Yale, but Hadden had already hooked up with another Crazy Greek division member, the swimming champion "Long" John Hincks.

At the end of the year, Luce was selected as the class poet, a mark of his classmates' respect. He was teased again, however, in the last days of school when the yearbook staff released the Hotchkiss annual. To Luce's dismay, the class history made light of his decision to steal the yearbook pictures. A fictional day in the life of Hotchkiss called Luce "Hindmost Harry" and described him sneaking around campus "with a furtive glance," hiding the yearbook pictures in his coat. In a joke list entitled "Latest Additions to the Hotchkiss Library," the year-book staff included the title *Life in the Underworld* by H. R. Luce, "who for 17 years was an inmate."

It was all in good fun, but the realization that other boys perceived him to be self-interested to the point of occasional dishonesty deeply injured Luce. He had scrapped so hard to be noticed at all, and he knew that wealthier boys could not appreciate his personal hardship as a scholarship boy. Luce struck back in his final piece for the *Lit*, an essay that criticized the Hotchkiss tendency to honor sports captains over editors. "To publish a monthly magazine with 300 pages of, at least, fairly good attempts at stories, articles and verse, to make these pages have any semblance of an appeal to the fellows in school, and to pay for nearly 200 electrotypes—this we submit is no tea-parlor, silk-sock, poetically temperamental game," he wrote. Tipping his hat to Hadden, Luce added that no football game would ever demand more "guts" than editing the school paper.

Despite his evident passion for journalism, Luce still considered himself more of a scholar and a poet than a reporter. His intellectual bent came through clearly when he selected a line by the novelist George Meredith to run alongside his photograph in the yearbook: "All wisdom's armory this man could wield." Hadden, by contrast, selected a quotation attributed to the Supreme Court Justice Joseph Story: "Here shall the Press the People's right maintain, Unaw'd by influence, and unbrib'd by gain."

When the seniors elected Hadden to give the class oration at grad-uation, he gave a strenuously progressive talk—a ringing summons to educated people to return to public life. A call resounded, Hadden proclaimed, not merely for "better men in politics" but for "citizens and voters who are willing to take more than a passive interest in seeing that the right man is elected to the right job." Hadden planned to become this type of citizen. He planned to use reporting to wake people up and encourage them to raise their voice.

It was Luce who received an early look at professional reporting. That summer he clerked for the *Springfield Republican*. Though he did not get a chance to cover news stories, Luce helped write business notices, and a few of his items made the paper. Tailing the police reporter on his nightly trip to the jail, Luce was deeply moved. "I never saw a cell before. I never spoke to a prisoner. I never saw a brave tear-stained mother come to bail out her son, held on sure charge of forgery," he wrote his parents. "These things reveal the Christ who said 'I came not to the righteous.' And they reveal Him because of His apparent absence, and the crying need for Him."

Luce wrote of his trip to the jail as if he had undergone a spiritual awakening, and in a way he had. He had found God in the godless carnival of daily journalism. Such a spiritual view of reporting conflicted with Hadden's approach. Hadden tried to be open-minded; Luce meant to be an advocate and activist. In a letter to Mrs. McCormick, Luce admitted that "real human sympathy and the power of wide friendship is not inherent in me." Journalism would force him into contact with people, and along the way he would learn about everything "from Beethoven to labor strikes." At the end of the summer, Luce wrote his father, "I believe that I can be of greatest service in journalistic work, and can by that way come nearest to the heart of the world."

Journalism was not a common profession for a prep-school boy to choose. In fact, reporting was more of a craft. Most educated men stuck to banking or the law, perhaps the ministry. Newspapermen were considered crass; they took part in a world of corruption. But as Hadden and Luce separately readied for Yale in the summer of 1916, both thought they would lead a life in the press. It was a rare thing for two such driven and kindred spirits to find each other at such an early age. They had yet to grow close, but in the next year events that would change people's lives worldwide would transform theirs as well, speeding them on the path that would lead to a revolution in journalism.

3

Most Likely to Succeed

Rows of elms shadowed Yale's "Old Campus," their great branches forming arches over the flagstone walkways. Towers resembling medieval castles enclosed the quadrangle, presented an ominous face to working-class New Haven, and ensconced the students behind a wall of ivy. Hatless men in letterman sweaters smoked pipes and slapped backs as they ambled among the elms' roots. At the quad's southern end, seniors in the private courtyard of Vanderbilt Hall reverted to childhood pleasures: rolling hoops, shooting marbles, and spinning tops. And on the northwestern corner sat Wright Hall, where a choice few freshmen lived in modern suites swept daily by Irish maids who even took care to clean their boys' tea sets.

Hadden and his Hotchkiss friends lived in Wright, along with students from the East Coast prep schools, athletic stars, and anyone else with money or connections. Luce moved into the more affordable Pierson Hall, an off-campus dormitory on a busy street criss-crossed by trolleys and telephone wires. "There are fellows here of doubtful lineage," he wrote home, "and even more doubtful morality." Hadden spent his days playing touch football on Old Campus, his nights dining with star athletes at a nearby grill, and his weekends watching vaudeville at Poli's Theatre, where he often took a lead role in heckling the performers. Luce spent his evenings studying. Already he felt that he was lagging in the great race for campus prominence.

When Yale alumni gathered at reunions and sang the college song, they waved their white handkerchiefs in the air as they thundered out the final line: "for God, for country, and for Yale." The typical Yale man identified strongly with all three causes. Harvard was more sophisticated, Princeton more debonair, but Yale had the most school spirit. Yale men prided themselves on being good teammates and knowing how to win. Believing success was virtuous, they celebrated a thing called "grit," the mystical blend of desire and determination that could will a team to victory. Valuing tact and consideration, Yale men subordinated their individuality to the culture of the group. A visitor from Harvard once wrote, "'Together' is the great word at Yale."

Social life at Yale was highly regimented. As soon as the freshmen unpacked their trunks, they began to claw their way up a Byzantine hierarchy of sports teams, clubs, and publications together known as the "Yale democracy." If a student was a poet, he didn't wait for the muse to pick up his pen. He manufactured verse on a monthly basis, and with each work he published earned points that brought him one step closer to the editorship of the *Lit*. If he was a strong Christian, he didn't just pray. He preached for Dwight Hall, the campus chapter of the YMCA. A singer never sang alone. He joined the Glee Club, whose star soloists were tapped for an a cappella club called the Whiffenpoofs.

The goal of all this work was to be recognized by the secret clubs run by upperclassmen. Those who earned position or prominence were tapped for the fraternities, which ran college politics. The most successful of all were then tapped for the senior societies, private clubs with vast endowments that met in windowless buildings known as "tombs." Looming over the school was the solemn, brown tomb of Skull and Bones, the oldest society of all, sequestered behind a giant black door, sealed by a heavy lock. The fifteen campus heroes who made Bones each year graduated with connections so far in excess of what the others had acquired that it seemed as if they had attended a school within the school.

Among the most powerful students in the Yale democracy was the chairman of the newspaper. The *Yale Daily News* had been founded in 1878 and promptly listed on the nation's first telephone exchange. It was the oldest college daily and a lucrative one. Each year the top editors split the paper's profits—enough to fund a year of leisure. The chairman, who took the largest share, also held significant authority. He appointed students to the committees that ran undergraduate life, often helped organize the prom, and represented campus opinion at alumni functions. His daily editorials set the tone of the college and could occasionally influence school policy. Near the end of his tenure, he was generally tapped for Skull and Bones. As one former chairman later put it, no doubt reflecting the pomposity of early prominence, "Greatness strode the campus with the chairman of the *News*."

To make the *News*, freshmen had to undergo a complex heeling ritual much like that at Hotchkiss. From October through March, the heelers raced to write stories, sell ads, and even perform chores. The editors awarded a certain number of points for each task—more, for instance, if a reporter broke a big story than if he fetched a cup of coffee. At the competition's end, only the top three or four scorers made the staff. Heelers were easily recognizable on campus by their haggard appearance, the ruthless look in their eyes, and their bicycles, which they pedaled through sleet and snow in pursuit of stories and ads as they cursed the "infernal *News*." The day's work ended when they pedaled the hot copy to the printer. Former heelers described the experience as "murder."

Early in October, when Hadden and Luce were preparing to start this torturous competition, they returned to Hotchkiss for the weekend. Late one night, while the rest of the school slept, the classmates went out for a walk. As they circled the Hotchkiss track, Hadden broached the matter of their rapidly developing rivalry. Perhaps it would be better, he said, if one of them skipped the first heeling competition and entered the second one. That way they could help each other and both would make the board. Luce gave the offer serious thought, but he couldn't get past the problem of who would heel first. "I had one of the longest walks I've ever had in my life," he recalled. "It must have been way after midnight when we both went back to the school with the question unresolved. And so we both went in the first competition. And it *was* a hell of a competition."

The competition to make the editorial board of 1920 survives in *Yale Daily News* lore as one of the hardest ever held. The work was so difficult that fifteen of the forty freshmen quit in the first week. The rest worked blindly, desperately, up to twenty hours a day. Once Luce became so exhausted that he simply sat in a chair and gaped. Hadden drove the pace by sleeping little, skipping meals, and surviving on coffee and cigarettes. "I get up at 5:45 each morning & give the papers . . . the once-over," he wrote his mother. "If there's no news I go back to bed again, but if there is I put on an overcoat & a pair of shoes over my pajamas & beat it across Elm St. to the *News* office." Soon all of the heelers were rising early. The editors, worried for the health of their freshmen, assembled them in the office and issued a stern commandment: "Be in bed at twelve and stay there until seven." But the editors never said to turn off the light, so the heelers worked in bed.

When a group of Yale professors wrote President Wilson to protest Germany's forced deportation of Belgian workers, Luce broke the news on the front page. But the daily work of ferreting out stories—running around campus, trading tidbits, chatting with professors—came more naturally to Hadden, whose winning ways amused his elders. "I went to lunch with Professor Clay today," Hadden once wrote his mother. "Save for a few minor accidents, such as calling him 'doctor' when he isn't a doctor and dropping my cigarette ashes on his wife's parlor rug, I got along nobly."

Hadden took the lead in the competition. Luce, racing to catch up, worried that he wouldn't make the cut. Hadden padded his score with errand credit—cleaning out the *News*' files, then sneaking back into the office late at night to scramble them up again, and earning more points the following day by putting the files back in order. Often he performed such work when he ought to have been in chemistry class. "He would put any old mixture in a test tube, light the Bunsen Burner under it to a low flame, and depart for an hour or so's work on the *News*," Hadden's roommate John Hincks recalled. "My job was to keep something in the test tube so that the inspectors who passed around would not notice his absence."

In the final week, the assignment editor, a Brooklyn neighbor of Hadden's named John Eliot "Doc" Woolley, discovered that he had run out of the stylebooks he would need to give to the new heelers at the start of the next competition. Woolley ordered the heelers to scour the campus for stylebooks and bring them to the *News* by the competition's final night. For each stylebook a heeler brought in, he would receive as many points as he could earn by writing a story. The exhausted heelers ransacked the rooms of former heelers in search of the last few points to put them over the top.

Sunday night they gathered in the chairman's office. Luce had scrounged through several hundred rooms and found about three books. Hadden, who had sneaked into the room of the chairman himself, came forward with twenty-one books. It seemed like no one could top that number when a tall, somber figure stepped forward and sprung open a suitcase. The other heelers cried in dismay, for Alger Shelden, the son of a Michigan millionaire, had gone to New York and paid a printer to run off dozens of books, more than a hundred in all, enough to buy his way onto the board. Hadden won, with more points than any heeler in history. Luce finished fourth, the last man to make the board. Exhausted, he wired his parents one word: "Successful."

In China, it was early in the morning when Reverend Luce, having only just shaved, burst into his wife's dressing room grasping a piece of paper and shouting "Hurray! Hurray!" His cheeks were flooded with tears, and his wife knew it could mean only one thing. Despite it all—his stutter and diffidence, his lack of friends and funds, his position firmly lodged in the shadow of his prep school rival—her son had earned a reputation for grit. After a long sleep, Luce followed up the telegram with a letter. "I have come to Rome," he proclaimed, "and succeeded in the Roman Circus." Certainly Hadden would have a strong claim on the chairmanship, but Luce wrote his parents that the board would function best under a different arrangement: "Chairman, Luce . . . Managing Editor, Hadden."

Shelden invited Hadden, Luce, and the other successful heeler, Thayer Hobson, to spend Easter at his family's estate at Grosse Pointe Shores near Detroit. Hadden wrote his mother that Easter in Brooklyn sounded like better fun, but the Sheldens "may make me a present of a Ford or something—you never can tell." He added, "I want to get better acquainted with Hoy Shelden, Ted Hobson & Chink Luce whom I will have to work with more or less during the next few years." Luce, considerably more excited, wrote his parents that Shelden's father was a Bonesman and a hunting friend of Teddy Roosevelt.

The Sheldens' rambling mansion was full of servants, and the boys partied in high style, often staying up well past three in the morning. One night they took some girls to the theater. The play was quite

sad, and the girls spent much of the night crying into their handkerchiefs. Such delicate creatures befuddled Luce, but he also felt drawn
to console them, and he ended up missing most of the play. Afterward,
there was a party in the grand ballroom, where Luce was love-struck by
Shelden's clever sister. Keep it up, the house and the girls seemed to
say, and we will be yours.

The boys shot billiards, went riding (Luce told his parents that Hadden fell off his horse), watched some female equestrians in action at the
country club, and took a private tour of the Ford factory. Once, shooting
crow in the woods surrounding the estate, Hadden and Luce lost their
way, and together they trekked back through the muddy fields. Ever so
gingerly, they were drawing closer. Early one morning, the boys returned
from a night out to see a large headline stretching across the front page
of the newspaper. President Wilson had asked Congress to declare war
on Germany. "The world must be made safe for democracy," he said.

Hadden and Luce returned to Yale to find students marching through
the streets and performing calisthenics on the Old Campus. This
was the work of Yale's president, Arthur Twining Hadley. Hadley had
encouraged his students to enlist in the National Guard. Well before
America joined the war, Yale had constructed the largest armory in
Connecticut, complete with the latest weaponry from France. But
when the Army nearly sent the Yale regiment in pursuit of the Mexican
revolutionary Pancho Villa, Hadley was unnerved. He took his boys
out of the militia and placed them in the student reserves. Now Hadley
told his boys to stay on campus and train to become officers. This, he
said, was the "highest patriotic service."

The war promised, nevertheless, to be the defining moment of a
generation, and many students felt they had to fight. Most of the campus heroes were disobeying Yale's president and enlisting—even Hadley's own son, the chairman of the *Yale Daily News*. A group of wealthy
boys had founded and paid for the Navy's first air reserve squadron,
known as the "Millionaires' Unit." They had left campus to train in
Palm Beach even before Wilson declared war, and soon they would go
to the front. Even some freshmen were leaving school, among them
Thayer Hobson, who became one of the first Yale students to see action
in France. Students glorified their friends at the front, who sent home

letters about driving ammunition trucks through artillery blasts, sleeping on straw bedding, and drinking red wine to kill the itch of lice.

With flags waving all around, it was natural to dream of shipping off to make the world safe for democracy. As mere nineteen-year-olds, however, Hadden and Luce would not be allowed to serve as officers. If they chose to enlist as privates, they could expect to see battle in the trenches, where no amount of Rooseveltian heroics could halt the fire of the machine guns. Most of the freshmen were electing to stay at Yale, though not without wistful embarrassment. One day Luce was kidnapped by a group of friends who drove to New York to enlist, whooping and hollering all the way. Two enlisted, and ten drove back.

Hadden, badly wanting to join in the excitement, begged his mother for permission to drive an ambulance in France. But Hadden's brother would be enlisting after his graduation from Princeton, and Mrs. Pool felt that one Hadden in France would be enough. Luce's parents, back in China, had less control over his actions, but Luce himself wasn't sure of the right course. "The war of democracy & righteousness needs men at the front and needs them now," Luce wrote home. Still, "if one continues his education, he should become a better & more able citizen, & hence should serve the 'highest cause' best by remaining."

In the spring of 1917, Hadden and Luce launched a campaign to support the war effort by encouraging their wealthy classmates to purchase war bonds. Together they wrote campaign letters, met with prominent Yale graduates, talked with most of their classmates, and succeeded in raising thousands of dollars. Hadden spent most of the summer at Harvard's military camp. He then went to the beach at Westhampton, where he played sports with the military officers on leave. "When they all go away from here there'll be no one left but a bunch of cripples, parlor snakes, old men, & girls," Hadden wrote Luce from the Westhampton Hotel. "Must close now & go in for daily swim. . . . Let me know if we can fix up any dates for parties before college opens."

Luce received Hadden's letter while cleaning out chicken coops on the farm of the Linen family, longtime supporters of the Luces' missionary endeavors. The government had recommended farming as a form of patriotic service. Luce's sisters were sorry to learn he had taken up smoking, but they were impressed by how manly he seemed. Still it seemed hard to feel that way while reading a letter from Thayer Hobson at the front. "Now Harry, a word of advice," he wrote. "You just stay on farming and going to college and when the rest of us are fertilizing France, you will be glad of it. . . . Anybody who can stay out of this little game had better do so."

In the fall of 1917, Hadden and Luce returned to a quieter campus. A third of Yale had left to fight in the war, and many of the rest wished they had left, too. Month by month the juniors drifted off campus to enlist, and soon the sophomores were running the newspaper. As Hadden and Luce began to write editorials together, they gradually succeeded in transforming the *Yale Daily News* from cautious support of the faculty's war efforts toward a blatantly militant stance. "The call of the hour," Hadden cracked to his mother, "is for embryo Teddy Roosevelts." To make extra money, the young editors worked together as table-runners for an "eating joint," one of the places where students took their meals. "We are in partnership," Luce wrote home. "Already our joint has become by far the most popular joint in the class. We now have to have a waiting list!"

They were also lumped together in the same ROTC unit under the command of their assignment editor on the *News*, Hadden's neighbor John Eliot "Doc" Woolley. The contrast between the childhood rivals, always remarkable, had grown more extreme. Hadden had returned from Harvard with a military bearing. With his chest puffed out and his chin tucked in, he looked "determined to be the best soldier that ever was, every inch the man of action," Woolley recalled. Luce, with his long hair blowing into his eyes and his hat on the back of his head, appeared more intellectual. "He was the thinker," Woolley said.

Though outwardly the war did not appear to affect Luce, it had changed him in a far-reaching way. President Wilson depicted the war as a battle between democracy and autocracy. Luce interpreted Wilson's mission with all the charged spiritual and patriotic ardor of his upbringing. He hoped the violence in Europe would awaken the American spirit. "Oh, if only America gets thoroughly into this war, what a wonderful thing it will be," Luce wrote his father, "bringing back to us again the heroism of the idea, and awakening the vision of the ideal."

Hadden didn't think as much about ideals and heroism. He spent his spare time riding the horses and shooting the guns at the armory. Rapidly, he marched up the ranks. Tall and dark, with a voice that ricocheted through the drill ground as if fired from a machine gun,

Hadden stirred up energy and excitement as he charged from place to place. To his classmate Cully Sudler he seemed like "an army of reinforcements, with banners, arriving just in time." Hadden developed a prejudice against people who wasted time reasoning and arguing when the times called for action. He called Luce a "contemplator" and often yapped at him to get a shave or fix his coat. "He used to like to make me the goat of his razzing," Luce recalled. "Well, it got a little tiresome. I didn't really mind it much, except it got a little tiresome."

Competitiveness and resentment added a charge to a friendship growing from cordiality toward mutual admiration and genuine liking. Hadden and the other more popular boys from Hotchkiss took care to include Luce and to support his constant struggle to gain respect from the social elite. When a few of the wealthiest boys in the sophomore class formed a private drinking club, "The White Rats," Luce struck back by forming a rival group, "The Professors," which Hadden joined. Later that fall, Luce wrote his parents that he hoped to join Psi Upsilon, the fraternity that would take "the cream of the class . . . such as Hadden." As it turned out, Hadden and the rest of the Hotchkiss crowd led a charge away from Psi Upsilon, which they considered too cold and snobby, toward the more convivial Delta Kappa Epsilon. The fraternity blackballed Luce, and on pledge night he sat alone in his room while Hadden and his friends tramped through campus, singing, "The Jolly Dekes, they march along!" Luce later joined his literary friends in his father's fraternity, Alpha Delta Phi.

At the *Yale Daily News*, Luce had been politicking for the chairmanship since his freshman year, even going so far as to hold secret talks with classmates. "It is probable that my election as chairman from 1920 will be railroaded through," he had written his parents. Luce's fellow board members held him in awe because of his raw ability and intelligence, but socially most of them did not consider Luce chairman material. Hadden seemed to have the greater love for newpapers. He couldn't walk by a newsstand without buying the latest editions, and his fingers were always stained with ink. People felt inspired by Hadden, partly because he did not express his personal ambitions. He focused on the work, the group, the idea.

Hadden's rise occurred much more quickly than anyone expected, especially Hadden. But the war was an unusual time, a time when the unexpected reigned. At Christmas, Doc Woolley, who was holding down the chairman's job in the absence of President Hadley's son, telephoned Hadden and summoned him down the block to the Woolley house in Brooklyn Heights. "I'm about to enlist in the Army, so now you're chairman of the *News*," Woolley said. Hadden nearly fainted. For several moments he wasn't able to open his mouth. Finally he spoke: "Gosh."

Hadden's emergency appointment would only last until his own board held an election. Luce met privately with the other members of the board and tried to convince them that he would make the best executive. Luce thought he picked up three votes—including those of two fraternity brothers. But one of them voted for Hadden, who won by a single vote. "Briton Hadden is chairman of the *News*, and thus my fondest college ambition is unachieved," Luce wrote home. "Not a soul, I think, has seen what this all means to me, although all are very keenly appreciative of the fact that there were two men for one job, & of course one had to get stung! Happily I have the greatest admiration & affection for Brit, which, in some measure at least, is reciprocated."

As a sophomore chairman, Hadden was placed in an unusual position. He didn't know how long he would be needed, but he would probably serve until the *Yale Daily News* board of 1920 could elect a permanent chairman in the spring. Secretly, Luce met privately with several board members and asked them to switch their allegiances in a couple of months. "One of Brit's supporters told me frankly that he did not feel himself bound by his vote, & in May *would* vote for me," Luce wrote home. "So, if the whole thing is thrashed out again I shall be chairman but if it seems best to unanimously ratify what is now in effect, then I won't. In the latter case, it will be tragic irony indeed!"

In the end, no votes changed sides as Luce hoped. Instead, the board decided to immediately make Hadden's election permanent. On a Sunday night in late January, the entire board convened. Seeing that he had lost the race, Luce made a magnanimous gesture: he gave up his campaign and voted for Hadden. "I could have been chairman of the *News*," Luce wrote his parents. "In the greatest sacrifice of my life I signed away the possibility. Good old Brit Hadden has the high and mighty job."

In China, where Luce's father had recently lost an election to become the president of a college for Chinese Christians, the news from New Haven deeply saddened Mrs. Luce. "It just seems as though a cruel sword were piercing my heart through & through," she wrote her son. "That you, who are supremely worthy, should not attain that which you work & suffer & long for, is the greatest trial for me—not that I covet any of these things in themselves, but simply that *you,* beloved of my heart, desire them, makes me wish to snatch them all & pour them at your feet."

The election left Luce with a pang of envy for Hadden that he would never be able to outgrow. Instead of referring to his defeat, Luce's family called it his "great renunciation." It was not difficult for the sensitive Hadden to sympathize with Luce, especially since Hadden admired Luce's ability and eagerly wished for his help. Hadden quickly patched up their partnership by offering Luce the chance to write half the editorials. Luce busily got to work, contributing to the editorial page, launching a book review section, and writing a series on Yale's preparedness movement. "If Harry was disappointed, there were never any signs," a younger *News* heeler later wrote. "It was always understood among us that Hadden and Luce worked as a team, as they had done at Hotchkiss."

As the youngest chairman ever, Hadden put the paper on a martial footing. President Hadley had outraged Yale's faculty by agreeing to give students academic credit for taking military courses. Hadden not only sided with Yale's president, he did his elder one better by calling for Yale to lessen its academic requirements and offer more classes in subjects like semaphore signaling and drill. Yale ultimately canceled most of its requirements, and for the rest of the war the school became a military academy in all but name. "We give three weeks to Aristotle in Philosophy," Luce wrote his parents. "Aristotle who founded twelve sciences!"

Carried away by Hadden's enthusiasm, Luce came to feel more confident working alongside him. Hadden had the ability to make people feel alive, to inspire them with the notion that *now* was the time that counted, as crucial a moment as any that had ever been. Luce's sense of inspiration burst through his letters home. "Just got a call from my Lord and Master, My Friend, and the man behind whose name I wield what influence I do,—Briton Hadden, chairman of the *News,*" Luce wrote his parents. "What does he want to see me for now? Will we decide to expel Dean Jones? Or is it merely to close the doors of Yale college? At any rate without further ado I must hasten to the councils."

Though he gradually took on some of Hadden's confidence and

even his charm, Luce was not one to suppress his personality to the needs of the group. On the editorial page, Luce's work was clearly visible, not only because he wrote twice as many words as Hadden but also because he took more radical positions. In the space of several months, Luce accused his English professor of being a pacifist, suggested that Yale should ban all student groups that could not be classified as "war industries," and attacked the freshmen for inviting New Haven girls to their rooms. Insensible to temptation, Luce called the prom a waste of war resources. He decided not to go. Hadden had a ball and was eventually found passed out and tangled in a bicycle at the entrance of New Haven's priciest hotel.

One evening in May of 1918, some unruly freshmen ran amok through the city streets, and finally found themselves in a fight with the mayor. Police arrested a dozen students including some ROTC men. "Youth is excitable; old age is irritable," Hadden wrote in that night's editorial. He urged both sides to act with "tact, considerateness," then traveled to Hotchkiss to deliver a talk on college life. The next day Hadden returned to campus to find the *Yale Daily News* at the center of an imbroglio. Luce had published an incendiary editorial that blamed New Haven's "small-town journalists" for blowing the riot out of proportion. "During my absence Chink Luce was indiscreet enough to write a very bombastic editorial," Hadden wrote his mother. "Since then I have been trying to calm things down again between 'Town' and 'Gown.'"

The training at Yale grew intense after the Allies spoiled the German spring offensive and began planning to end the war with a final push of their own. Hadden and Luce spent the summer of 1918 on campus, where the training was arduous, though safer than the active service. Hadden rose to the rank of top sergeant while leading one of Yale's four batteries. A gruff but beloved commander, he organized an ice cream fund, invented silly songs on the march to mess, and called Luce's battery his "inefficient rivals." When Hadden learned that soldiers were supposed to wear their hair short, he shaved his head. Soon a new song spread through the ranks, who celebrated Hadden as "That Bald-Headed Sergeant of Battery B."

President Wilson had all along insisted on an independent American Army. His boys would fight under their own flag, and he would leverage their work to dictate the terms of the peace. More soldiers

were needed, and late in the summer Congress lowered the draft age
to eighteen. Hadden, Luce, and the rest of Yale's junior officer candidates were sent to a dusty expanse in South Carolina dotted by bleak
two-story barracks and, it was said, no more than fourteen blades of
grass. There at Camp Jackson, sixty-five-thousand men were preparing
to deliver the fatal blow to a dispirited German Army.

Most of those sent South to train had grown up among people
like themselves, whether rich or poor, black or white, hailing from the
city or the farm. For the first time they found themselves face-to-face
with people from other places and stations. From this mass meeting
a young country, linked together by effort and exhortation, suddenly
realized a vigorous collective identity. It was an exciting time for Hadden and Luce, children of privilege and conviction who now gained an
appreciation for the raw power and energy of the American people.

Rising to the sound of reveille, they filed into the mess hall for
powdered eggs, cream of wheat, and coffee served in tin cups. They
marched to the bark of sergeants, sweated through their shirts, and
sang, "Over hill, over dale, as we hit the dusty trail, and the caissons
go rolling along." It was hard work, the heat was stifling, and soon
many of the Yale men had broken out in a rash. They were mad at
themselves for not being in France, and mad at the Army for not sending them there. The final insult came when a hundred and sixty fresh
recruits streamed in. These eighteen-year-old boys from the farms of
Ohio would be going directly to France. Instead of fighting alongside
them, Hadden and Luce were ordered to train a platoon each.

Hadden was captivated by the idiosyncratic viewpoints and colorful accents of his "draft rookies." Taking out the pay sheets, Hadden was surprised to discover that some in his platoon could not spell
their own names. Luce, going over some hygiene points, was equally
shocked that he had to teach his boys how to use a toothbrush. But the
recruits were eager to learn, and their dedication filled the Yale men
with pride. One night, Luce asked his platoon to take a knee, and he
told his boys the story of how the Germans had sunk the *Lusitania*.
When Luce was finished, his platoon couldn't wait to get to France
and lick those "goddamn Huns," and Luce experienced a feeling of
confidence he had never known.

At night, after the battalion lined up on the parade ground, the buglers sounded taps, and the flag came down, Hadden would lead the pranks as the Yale officer candidates tramped to town, perhaps looking for a snack or, better yet, a bit of action. Luce, empowered by the risks Hadden took, marched closely in his boot steps. If Hadden made an especially bold move, Luce would wave his arms wildly and titter with glee. Bumping into them one night, Cully Sudler saw in his old friend a new and bursting kind of confidence. Luce was free, released—not a child anymore but a man.

As they studied to take the officers' examination, Hadden and Luce began spending their free evenings at a nearby hotel, where they would drink a pot of tea, smoke a couple cigars, and quiz each other on how to clean out a horse's hoof or blow up a German dugout. One night, walking back to the barracks, they began talking idly about the ignorance that surrounded them. It was then that Hadden first seriously discussed with Luce the idea of launching a publication that would set down the facts. When they passed the barracks, they kept on walking—through a stretch of sand, past the barracks again, through some piney woods, onto and around the drill grounds. They walked for hours, as they talked about the dream of founding some sort of periodical.

It was the first of several conversations that would take place over the next several years. Hadden and Luce did not yet know what form their project would take. They simply agreed that people stood in need of a "paper" that could provide a basic world report. But it was on this night that Hadden's childhood dream finally began to approach a plan. In Luce he had found a partner. "Somehow, despite greatest differences in temperaments and even in interests, somehow we had to work together," Luce recalled. "At that point everything we had belonged to each other."

After six hard weeks, Yale's officers in training marched the recruits to the railroad station, where they would embark for their transport, the *Ticonderoga*. Leaving camp, the group burst into song. "The draft men are lazy, ignorant, but human & interesting," Hadden wrote his mother. "When you hear an entire brigade roaring 'Good Night, Kaiser Bill!' there is something very inspiring in it." A few weeks later, the Yale men learned that a submarine had attacked the transport and nearly all hands were lost. Shocked, Hadden and Luce reported to Camp Taylor near Louisville, having just received their commissions and hoping to make it to France. When they heard bells clanging in Kentucky and the whoops of men setting into their whiskey, they knew they had missed their war.

The disappointment of failing to reach France inspired Hadden and Luce to serve their country in the future. As Hadden put it to his mother, they would serve their country with "word and pen." Coming into contact with people outside their small circle armed the young men with the conviction that ordinary Americans were eager to grow informed. Hadden and Luce believed they could help people learn. Perhaps this was an innocent notion, an instance of noblesse oblige born of a sudden confluence of privilege and poverty. But the very naïveté that allowed Hadden and Luce to be surprised by the ignorance of others also lent them the conviction that what others took for granted they might change.

They sealed their partnership the next year at Yale when Hadden was elected the chairman of the *News* for the second time—a first—and Luce won election as the managing editor. Departing from custom, Hadden gave Luce control of the news pages and confined himself to the editorial page. Hadden spent his nights writing, arose late, and lunched at Mory's, where Yale's student leaders hatched plots over Welsh rarebit, leaving no record but their names carved into the wooden tables. "So far the stuff I have turned out has gotten by the community in fine shape," Hadden wrote his mother, "and Chink Luce has improved the news columns of our journal 100%."

Hadden and Luce gave the *Yale Daily News* an international focus by covering national and world news at the top of the front page. When President Wilson returned from Europe, urging the Senate to accede to a new League of Nations, Hadden held a campus referendum on Wilson's Treaty of Versailles. The idea spread to other colleges, and Hadden set up an "International Treaty Referendum Headquarters" in New York to hold a national student plebiscite. Ninety-two thousand students voted at nearly four hundred campuses. The majority asked President Wilson to compromise with Senator Henry Cabot Lodge in order to salvage some version of the treaty.

Each day Hadden and Luce ran a front-page news summary called "The World at Large," composed directly onto the Linotype by a printer named John O'Donnell. A former American president, William Howard Taft, then teaching at the law school, said he relied on the column. Students read it during morning chapel by sneaking the paper into their prayer books. But Hadden realized that a dry news summary would not appeal to most Americans. In a series of editorials for the *News,* Hadden compared the body politic to a "lazy and laggard lout" who could only be troubled to think of his "immediate personal interests." In order to get people to care about the news, Hadden believed he would have to break with the prevailing journalistic formula.

Hadden began experimenting in his *News* editorials with a writing style that would shock people into paying attention. He honed his skills under John Berdan, an English professor with razor-blue eyes who taught a writing course called Daily Themes. Berdan drew dozens of students to his basement office, where he clouded the air with Latakia pipe smoke and pummeled Victorian literary conventions. The important thing, he said, was to simply observe—to see for oneself. As for style, Berdan advocated brevity, clarity, and wit. "Your job," he would say, with a flourish of his hand toward the crowd, "is to write for them all."

Berdan admired Hadden's fierce bravado and eagerly accepted his proposal to be graded on *News* editorials in lieu of coursework—though they had to keep the deal a secret from the dean. "I can write more respectable & presentable editorials & have the advantage of an expert's criticism on them," Hadden wrote his mother. "Isn't that rich?" With Berdan's encouragement, Hadden trimmed his sentences until they cracked with action. In imitation of Homer's *Iliad,* Hadden began injecting his sentences with the epithets he had come to love at Hotchkiss. He peppered his arguments with classical allusions and quotations. "This gets away big with the college," he wrote his mother. "Folks think I'm literary."

Yale put Hadden's skills to the test in the spring of 1919 when a second and more severe town-gown riot broke out. The argument began when a group of New Haven servicemen returned from overseas and gathered by the campus for a parade. Somehow they gained the impression that students were jeering at them. A row resulted. Hundreds of students jumped in to defend their honor, and several had their heads smashed. Hadden tried to defuse the latest crisis by taking a Homeric viewpoint. "By all the laws of strife and competition, both parties should entertain for each other only the heartiest feelings of respect and approval," he declared. Hadden complimented both "stout clans" for their bravery and urged them to let the matter rest.

As an editor, a writer, and a campus leader, Hadden revealed a natural feeling for nuance that Luce seemed to lack. Like Luce, Hadden held strong viewpoints, but he tried to view an issue from all sides before he arrived at a conclusion. Hadden had his finger on the pulse of the campus. If it seemed too slow, he would administer a shock by printing a fake letter to the editor. Once, when students stopped paying attention to campus affairs, Hadden invented a phony character named "Hatchet Face" who threatened to destroy a Divinity student's piano. The letter sparked three weeks of controversy and nearly caused a fight. But students read the paper.

Every Sunday through Thursday between nine and eleven o'clock at night, friends would walk by the *News* to see Hadden at his desk, writing the next day's editorial. When the heelers brought him the final proof, Hadden would often spend another hour correcting and rearranging the editorials, then send the heelers back to have the proof reset. Sometimes the paper went to bed at midnight, sometimes three in the morning. It didn't matter to Hadden, as long as his editorials came out letter-perfect. "There was a great deal of thought in them somehow, and you actually read them to see what was the temper of the college," Cully Sudler recalled of Hadden's work. "He really was the voice of the college."

At the end of his junior year, Hadden was elected to run the junior prom, the chief social honor of the college and one he did not want. As chairman of the *News*, Hadden tallied such votes, so he undercounted his own ballots and awarded the position of prom chairman to a friend. Hadden was a deacon in chapel and yet a member of the Pundits, the contrarian prankster group that took its name from the British term for an expert or teacher, a term itself derived from the Hindi word for a learned man. The zany pundits paraded through campus in raincoats and rubber boots on the sunniest day of the year.

A rebel yet a compromiser, a sober leader and a writer with a rapier wit, Hadden struck a precarious balance at Yale that elevated him to rare celebrity. Perhaps in doing so he raised outsized expectations of future success. During his long, intense periods of productivity, Hadden could spout off one idea after the next—some fantastic, others original and eminently feasible. His enthusiasm was infectious in those moments. Then suddenly a friend would drop by to find Hadden looking gloomy and sad. He could get surprisingly angry at times and would occasionally growl at the upperclassmen he referred to as "social types." In receiving lines, he was apt to tell the hostess that his mother had just died. After the hostess replied "wonderful, wonderful," Hadden would laugh to his friends that she hadn't been listening at all.

On the weekends Hadden could be found in the Hof Brau Haus, a panatela cigar in one hand and a beer stein in the other. He loved to slap backs and guffaw with friends and acquaintances. Marching across Yale's campus, calling out nicknames and cracking jokes, he was greeted by a chorus of hellos from the dozens of classmates who barely knew him but considered themselves great friends of his. Luce, carried along in Hadden's wake, made an effort to yell out "hi" to everyone he saw, too.

With Hadden as his patron, Luce increasingly found his eccentricities admired and celebrated. He took rides in roadsters and attended fraternity teas. At the prom, the most popular men practically lined up to dance with Luce's beautiful sister, who would later be named Queen of the May Day festival at Wellesley. "Brit Hadden is a mighty interesting fellow," Emmavail Luce reported home. "Rather hard, I should say, but his face shows great strength & I should judge that he might be quite lovable were one to get behind his mask."

Later that spring, Luce ascended to a new height when he viewed the Metropolitan Opera from the private box of Hugh Dudley Auchincloss, who would one day become the stepfather of Jacqueline Bouvier and walk her down the aisle to marry the dashing Senator John F. Kennedy. Alone for a moment in the Auchinclosses' Upper East Side library, Luce hastened to write his parents that he would be dining with members of Manhattan society—"Keys men since the year One." But joining Scroll and Key was not Luce's ambition; he was aiming higher than that.

Each spring, Yale buzzed with anticipation as the secret societies entered into the private negotiations that resulted in the coronation of the new campus kings. The societies selected only fifteen men each. Juniors learned their fate on Tap Day when the society members ran to the Old Campus to choose their new members, and to leave the rejected hopefuls standing before hundreds. As the rumor mill began to spin in the spring of 1919, most people thought Hadden would be left standing until the end, only to be the last man selected by Bones, an elite if nerve-racking honor. Luce's chances of making Bones also seemed fair—until, that is, he stumbled into controversy by running for and winning the chairmanship of the *Lit*. High-ranking *News* editors were expected to steer clear of senior roles on rival publications, and the news that Luce had broken this unwritten rule scandalized the students who ran the Yale democracy. Wary of provoking further protest, Luce decided to step down.

Bones did not appreciate controversy, and for a few weeks it appeared that finally Luce had gone too far in tempting the campus fates. He was deeply distraught. In this darkest of collegiate moments, Hadden took Luce out for a walk. For the first time Hadden let Luce know just how much his old classmate thought of him. Luce was deeply touched. "Now Brit Hadden,—if ever a class had *one* big man,—is the big man of our class,—last man for Bones sure," Luce wrote his father. "Brit took me out for a walk—Brit, my rival since early Hotchkiss days—and said that he was planning to get ten of the sure Bones men together to make it known that none of them would go Bones without me." Luce told Hadden his gesture of support was one of the greatest compliments Luce had ever received. But Bones held up the Yale democracy, and Luce would have to abide by its judgment. His hopes dipped further when the *New York Times*, keen on social news from Yale, predicted who would make Bones. Hadden's name was on the list and Luce's was not.

At five P.M. on May 15, Hadden and Luce walked back to the Old Campus to stand with the rest of their class. The juniors stuck their hands in their pockets and waited nervously under the Tap Tree. Twenty minutes later Luce was still wondering if he would be tapped when the captain of the crew team barreled down the Old Campus, smacked Luce across the back, and yelled, "Go to your room!" Luce wrote his father, "You can easily imagine that said son upon being told to go to his room did so do, and did moreover vouch for his being Henry Robinson Luce, and did accept an election to the so-called society!" A few moments later, Hadden was tapped, though not last as many had predicted. He wrote his mother, "I did not telegraph you or anything that I got Bones because I knew you knew I was going to get it anyway."

The Bones club of 1920 would turn out to be one of the most illustrious. It included Thayer Hobson, who ran the publishing company William & Morrow, and Henry Pomeroy Davison Jr., who rose to the presidency of J. P. Morgan. In later years the club would often meet at Peacock Point, the Davison family's Oyster Bay estate. They forged their bond during senior year, as they met each Thursday and Sunday night for a lobster or steak dinner served by black waiters in white livery. The first part of the ritual was to choose a secret club name. Hadden took Caliban, after the deformed half-human slave in Shakespeare's *The Tempest*, while Luce took Baal, meaning "lord" or "possessor," a term used to describe ancient Semitic gods.

Luce treasured Bones. He planned the weekly menu, accepted the post of class antiquarian, and wrote a poem about the experience in which he called the tomb a "fortress for my peace." He spoke frankly in group discussions, calling government a form of tyranny and openly discussing his sexual experiences, which Thayer Hobson recalled as "naive and ludicrous." Hadden, by contrast, cloaked himself with facetious humor. He tended to give sarcastic responses to pompous discussion topics. Once, while the group discussed communism, Hadden said he couldn't tell what that political theory had to do with baseball and therefore it was "rotten." Hadden's classmates lionized him in their black minute book as the "silver-tongued orator from Brooklyn."

The thirteen other Bonesmen that year ritualized the rivalry of Hadden and Luce. One even drew pictures of the duo in the class scrapbook. It seemed natural somehow to show them dueling with lances on horseback. But it was the other picture, in which the odd couple are shown peeking into a woman's window, that revealed the delight in life Luce picked up from Hadden and their real and strong bond of affection.

The mutual trust of the two Bonesmen had grown so complete that often they traded jobs at the *News*. Luce would spend a week as chairman, and Hadden a week as managing editor. Once, late at night, they fought so vociferously over the positioning of a story that friends worried they were going to wake up the college or, worse, come to blows. But when the argument ended with Luce the victor, both acted like it had never happened at all. "I never could tell how those two got along together," their Bones mate David Ingalls said. "You never knew whether they were ready to fight or agree."

The class of 1920 voted Luce "most brilliant," and Hadden "hardest worker," "done most for Yale," and "most likely to succeed." Their partnership was an attractive one, especially since they seemed so stunningly opposite. It was the writer Dwight Macdonald, a few years younger and yet to arrive at Yale, who would later describe their contrast best: "Luce/ Hadden: moral/amoral, pious/worldly, respectable/raffish, bourgeois/ bohemian, introvert/extrovert, somber/convivial, reliable/unpredictable, slow/quick, dog/cat, tame/wild, efficient/brilliant, decent/charming, Puritanical/hedonistic, naïve/cynical, Victorian/18th Century."

By graduation time, the campus viewed Hadden and Luce as inseparable. They held in common not merely a thirst but a tangible lust for knowledge. With other friends gathered around, they would often talk late into the night—Hadden quizzing his friends on minute points of interest, Luce launching into eloquent tangents. On long walks around Yale's quads, Hadden and Luce would talk for hours on end. Friends, admiring them from afar, thought of what a perfect match they made. The celebrated pair never revealed the details of their private talks with others, but at Mory's they discussed the idea of launching a publication that would bring people all the news.

In the yearbook's section on future plans, both Hadden and Luce wrote "journalism." It was not a Yale man's profession. Toward the end of the school year, Luce spent an afternoon in one of his favorite places, the Elizabethan Club, where Sims, the butler, served the *Lit* men tea. Seeing Luce, the father of Hadden's fellow Pundit Thornton Wilder swept Luce up and sat him down in a corner. "Harry, don't," the former diplomat Amos Wilder said. "Don't go into journalism." He began to speak so feelingly that his eyes filled with tears. "I beg of you. It will corrupt and corrode you. It will turn your wine into vinegar. You will lose your soul."

Wilder went on for nearly an hour, but the frightened Luce was not about to change his mind. Growing up in the progressive movement and coming of age during the war had inspired Luce and Hadden with the dream of contributing to public affairs. Of the two, it was Hadden who had the greater interest in newspaper work. Luce's ambition, though equal to Hadden's, revolved around more personal concerns. "The one thing I want to do is to be an orator," Luce wrote his mother, "but no such profession now exists." He would have time to consider his options. His cut of the *Yale Daily News* profits amounted to $1,500, enough to fund a year of study at Oxford.

Strange as it may seem, Luce did not yet realize how deeply he had influenced Hadden's life, nor how highly he figured in Hadden's plans. In late-night bull sessions, Hadden told his friends three things. He planned to become the greatest editor ever, he planned to make a million dollars before he turned thirty, and he planned to do both by starting a magazine. Hadden's share of the *News* profits was $3,500, which he saved as seed money for the enterprise. He would work for a year at a newspaper, then quit to launch that magazine. And he planned to bring Luce along with him.

4

Destiny

THE DAY HE GRADUATED from Yale, Hadden boarded a train for the Democratic convention in San Francisco. He didn't have a newspaper job, but he thought telling editors that he "went to the convention" would help him to get one. Waylaid by a missed connection in Ogden, Utah, Hadden watched some cowboys shoot craps on the street corner. He arrived in California just in time to see the former presidential candidate William Jennings Bryan lose his temper over Prohibition. In a taut letter home worthy of a newspaper's front page, Hadden compared the Great Commoner to an "angry rooster." He called the convention "the greatest show that I have ever seen—far better than any theatrical comedy."

Luce boarded his friend Morehead Patterson's private railroad car, bound for the Republican convention in Chicago. There Luce stood in the sweat-soaked Chicago Coliseum, watching the "apostle of preparedness," General Leonard Wood, lead a succession of separate ballots without winning a majority. On the ninth ballot, the delegates swung to a little-known senator from Ohio, Warren Gamaliel Harding. On the tenth, he won the nomination. Asked by the press what he stood for, Harding issued a string of bromides, at one point saying that the nation ought to "return to normalcy." The phrase tapped into a widespread feeling of disillusionment with grand moral enterprises. The Republicans were swept into office, and a decade-long business binge began.

While Luce sailed for Europe, Hadden, intent on finding newspaper work, rushed back to New York. Hadden dreamed of working for Herbert Bayard Swope, a celebrated correspondent who had recently been appointed the editor of the deceased Joseph Pulitzer's flagship paper, the *New York World*. Six-foot-one with carrot red hair and a voice like a "dinner gong," Swope was assembling an eccentric group of writers who were transforming the *World* into New York's most beloved newspaper.

Instead of scheduling a meeting, Hadden walked to the gold-domed *World* building on Park Row, slipped past Swope's secretary, and marched into his office. Swope looked up from his reading, expecting to see the managing editor. "Who are you?" he bellowed. "My name is Briton Hadden, and I want a job," Hadden said. Swope promptly ordered Hadden to leave. "Mr. Swope," Hadden replied, "you're interfering with my destiny."

Intrigued, Swope asked Hadden what his destiny entailed. Hadden told Swope that he planned to make the news easy to understand for the first time. The magazine he planned to launch would summarize all the essential facts everybody ought to know. But first, Hadden said, he wished to work for Swope. Other young men had come to Swope and asked for a job on the *World,* but they had usually requested to be columnists. Hadden had no such fancy notions, and it seemed to Swope that his ideas made sense. "All right," Swope said, "You have a job."

Hadden rushed to his desk on his first day of work and barked out introductions. "A gay young sprig," chuckled a nearby obituaries writer before falling back to sleep. Within a couple of days, Hadden was circling his desk and growling, "I'm not getting anywhere here." Walking down the street one day, he noticed a cat stuck under a grate and decided it was worth a feature. When the *World* ran the piece, a star reporter looked up the original copy on the spike, where editors kept their reporters' draft copy. "That's a damn good story," the veteran said. Hadden began supplying the paper with strange accounts of parrots, monkeys, and pigeons.

The editors began assigning Hadden to cover breaking news. Some of his work made the front page. A confident stylist for one so young, he made unconventional choices at times. Sent to report on a Bronx robbery, Hadden began his account in the voice of an old storyteller: "Listen, my children, and you shall hear of the afternoon raid of a boy who thought the Bronx was ripe for a latter day Jesse James." Swope thought the world of Hadden's writing.

Swope invited Hadden to his house in Great Neck, where the parties began at midnight and languidly spilled into the next week. The Swopes knew people in the theater, the underworld, in government and high finance; they came to the house and forgot themselves. Upstairs, with his prosthetic leg removed, Laurence Stallings thumped out the second act of *What Price Glory?* Harpo Marx played croquet on the lawn, encircled by cars with the headlights on, so the game could last all night. F. Scott Fitzgerald, having recently published *This Side of Paradise,* took in the scene and later brought it to life in his master-work, *The Great Gatsby.* Hadden, who showed up at parties munching peanuts, talked volubly of his plan for a magazine. The Swopes considered him a bit of a riddle. "Is he shy?" they asked Hadden's younger cousin. "You're goddamn right," he said.

Hadden moved to Greenwich Village and brought along his air gun. Sitting in a chair and grinding his jaw, he would grab his gun, take aim at the wall, and shoot. When friends asked what he was doing, Hadden would say he was having target practice, only the target was too easy to hit so he had hung it in the room next-door. He never laughed at such practical jokes; instead he shocked his friends by going about ludicrous activities in deadpan earnest. Women found Hadden mysterious and attractive. He would go on dates with debutantes, who would dress for the Plaza, only to be taken to Hoboken for a semi-pro football game. "Don't worry, I won't try to come between you," one disappointed showgirl joked to a male friend of Hadden's. "I've had enough of Brit for a while."

F. Darius "Freddie" Benham, a reporter who had started as Swope's valet, often went to baseball games with Hadden, who ritualized the proceedings. Hadden would hail the cab, promising, "I'll pay it on the way up, if you pay it on the way back." At the stadium, he had to sit in his favorite box, right by third base. When the hotdog man came by, he always bought eight—four for them both, because Hadden was a "four-hotdog man." In accordance with Hadden's style, Benham developed little tricks of his own. He would wave at the players, and occasionally they would wave back. "Gee, do you *know* him?" Hadden would exclaim. "Gee, I'd like to meet *him.*" It was hard to tell who was kidding whom. Benham thought Hadden had an "intelligent brain, with baby thoughts."

Loaded up with bootleg liquor at a party in the Village, Hadden was difficult to take seriously when he announced in his effusive way that he had come up with a "scheme" for a new kind of publication that would solve the problem of human ignorance. At least one friend thought he was joking. Quietly, in free moments, Hadden was doing some heavy thinking, and his idea for the magazine had taken a crucial turn. Instead of gathering his own news—an arduous and expensive chore—he would assemble the most interesting information from the newspapers.

In January of 1921, Hadden took a few days off work to attend a friend's wedding in Texas. Traveling south by train, Hadden bubbled over with excitement as he talked ceaselessly of his plan for a new kind of magazine. Every time the train stopped, he would jump off to buy a copy of the local newspaper. Back on board, he would flip through its pages, chanting, "Wonderful stuff, wonderful stuff!" If he could just skim the best of that stuff and fit it all inside a magazine, he would really have something. The trip south took half a day. Hadden got off the train at least twenty times, even late at night in Rocky Mount, North Carolina. The magazine was all he could talk about the whole way down.

By the following summer, Hadden was singularly obsessed with the idea. He couldn't stop talking about it, even at work. "Ever hear of a fellow named Harry Luce?" Hadden asked Benham one day at the *World.* "Me an' Harry worked on the Yale *News* together. We thought of an idea and I still think it's good."

"What is it?" Benham asked.

"See this?" Hadden said, picking up the *Times.* "Full of wonderful news, tells you everything going on in the world. But you haven't got time to read it all every day. You're a rich millionaire. You live in Glen Cove. You get on the train in the morning. You pick up the *Times.* You skim through it, or maybe you get only halfway through by the time you reach Grand Central. You, a rich millionaire from Glen Cove, haven't got time to read all that wonderful news in the *Times.* I got an idea to start a magazine which comes out on Friday with all the news condensed so you and all the other rich millionaires commuting home for the weekend can catch up on the news they missed. How's that?"

"Not bad," Benham said, "but how you going to put it over?"

"You'd be surprised," Hadden said. "You'd be surprised."

Every time Hadden brought up the magazine, he mentioned Luce. "Me an' Harry," he would say, "me an' Harry."

Luce was staying at Christ Church, one of Oxford's most conservative colleges, in a suite that had once belonged to King Edward VII. The young American had grown a pencil mustache and taken to carrying a cane. His roommate, Morehead Patterson, went foxhunting. Luce, horseless, joined the Tory debating club, squired girls to the Parisian opera, and toured Eastern Europe on the Orient Express. During his journey he dined with diplomats and stayed at the American embassy's palace in Constantinople. "My desire is without doubt to go into public life," Luce wrote his parents. "All I want is a basis so that I can go into politics without being entirely dependent upon the 'boss' for my bread and butter. . . . It's simply a matter of dirty sordid money, until I can get to the point where money will mean nothing to me."

Luce was captivated by the American debutantes he met in Europe, eager to take them to dinner, and even glad to dance—though he tried to steer his partner to the punchbowl as quickly as possible. Despite the stammer, conversation, not dancing, was Luce's forte. Tall and intense, yet somehow angelic with his light hair and steel-blue eyes, he was a hot commodity on the marriage market. The Skull and Bones reputation preceded him.

During his Christmas vacation, Luce and his friend William Whitney traveled to Rome to visit Thornton Wilder, who was studying at the American Academy, a refuge for classical scholarship perched atop the Janiculum, the highest of Rome's hills. The academy's several buildings, including a villa constructed for a Catholic cardinal, were surrounded by acres of gardens. The grounds attracted many varieties of butterflies and afforded views of the city. On New Year's Eve, the academy would host a party attended by American girls touring through Italy. Whitney, who disliked parties, left for Florence. Luce decided to stay.

If one girl stood out that last night of 1920, it was Lila Ross Hotz, a tall Chicago heiress with ivory skin, dark curls, and big brown eyes that made men feel they were staring into something deep. Hotz spun around the floor, first with a composer, then with an archaeologist—"frieks, geniouses," she thought—thrilling the men by feigning interest in their studies and laughing at their jokes. There was something about her, something in the chiseled chin, the arched eyebrow, the pouting lip, that added up to more than beauty. She seemed ethereal, almost pixielike, as if she had danced her way to the highest hill of Rome, not from raucous, rumbling, mad Chicago but from a tea party in the stars.

Luce asked Hotz for a dance. Hotz, no doubt, revealed her sterling résumé: the Presbyterian parents, the brother who had gone to Yale, the fluent French, the taste for poetry. "Are you popular?" Luce asked. After their first dance, he whisked her into a corner, where they chattered for several hours. Hotz was fascinated by Luce's flights from poetry to politics—"superficial as the dickens, but brilliant," she said. They talked through the evening, Luce so excitedly that Hotz never caught his first name. Occasionally they returned to the dance floor, where Hotz would inquire if Luce wished to take a new partner. No, Luce said, he would rather dance with her.

Hotz was everything Luce was not—a dancer and partygoer, wealthy, popular, charming, and poised. She had not been much of a student at Miss Spence's School in New York; the only academic prize she had ever won was for punctuality. But if Hotz appeared to possess more wit than depth, she had a keen social insight that would help Luce to gain acceptance from the social elite he yearned to impress. Her repartee dazzled Luce, who lacked that skill himself. She had an air of spontaneity, and it seemed that she sparkled when she laughed.

At midnight an old man walked into the ballroom dressed as Father Time. "Ring out the old bells, ring in the new!" he sang. Pages holding candles led the way to the moonlit courtyard, where a giant fountain spouted. Luce and Hotz walked out together. Father Time hid behind a curtain, and out popped a little child dressed as an angel. The crowd burst into song, and it seemed a new era had dawned with the year.

The next morning Hotz wrote her mother that she had met "quite *the* king of the evening." After she finished typing her letter, Hotz drew an asterisk and wrote more by hand. "His name is Luce—don't know his first name, or where his home is—or anything. Yet I do know what he thinks about many things! Agreed by us all to be the best looking man ever—which does count! and quite the most heavenly thing to talk to. . . . He left at seven this morning for Florence and then back to Oxford—boo hoo!"

In Florence, Luce's friend Pierrepont Prentice was contemplating the Pitti Palace when all of a sudden he felt a slap across the back. It was Luce, who promptly announced he had just met the most wonderful girl in the world. He said he was going to marry her. "It didn't take Harry any time to make his mind up," Prentice said. Three days later Luce wrote Hotz from Florence. He begged her to mail a letter to Oxford, so it would be there when he returned. Hotz hooked her prize by responding a few days late.

Free for a moment from the lifelong race for power and influence, Luce seemed interested in everything that year. He was friendly and innocent, with a winning outlook, always looking forward and enjoying what life had to offer. Hiking with friends to the Wrexham churchyard to visit the tomb of Elihu Yale, biking from Prague to Potsdam, chatting with the Czechoslovakian foreign minister at a meeting of the League of Nations, Luce seemed at times to be a pilgrim on a quest for truth and beauty. When friends asked him what he planned to do in life, he said he would like to be a statesman. He made no mention of journalism.

Toward the end of his year in England, Luce invited Hotz to Oxford's spring balls. Hotz and her mother hired a small plane from Paris to London and checked into the Berkeley Hotel. Luce dropped in and the couple spent a romantic weekend together, attending the services at St. Paul's Cathedral. "I love you," Luce told Hotz. "I love you, too," she said. At Oxford the courtyards were festooned with decorations and the parties ran for days. Luce and Hotz toured the cloisters, attended a production of *Twelfth Night,* and played grass-court tennis. The score of the first set was 6–0, Luce.

On the last night, Magdalen College set up a pavilion in the courtyard so the students could dance beneath the spires. Luce and Hotz walked out to look at the stars and sat together until dawn's arrival, when they read each other poetry over breakfast. Determined not to lose his head, Luce told Hotz that they must not write for the rest of the summer. But the words he had used a few months before in describing his career plans could also have described his romantic life: "I think the die is about cast."

After a spring spent romancing a wealthy debutante, Luce considered journalism déclassé. When his father managed to introduce him to the editor of *Harper's,* Luce submitted an essay under a pen name

because he did not wish to be known as a "literary hack." Reverend
Luce offered to find his son a job through a family friend at a magazine chain. Luce did not rule out the offer, but long ago Mrs. McCormick had promised him a place at International Harvester in Chicago.
That would be his first choice, so long as the company could make him
wealthy by the age of forty.

Luce returned to the States sporting a mustache, carrying a cane,
and wearing a pair of spats—every bit the upper-class gentleman except
that his Savile Row suit had empty pockets. He briefly stayed with his
parents, who had returned to America and moved to New York while
his father took classes at the Union Theological Seminary. In a quiet
moment, Luce showed his sister a photograph of the girl he had met.
Seeing that enchanting face, Elisabeth realized her brother had fallen
in love. Luce met Hadden at a friend's wedding, where they talked
about the idea. When Luce discussed his plan to move to Chicago,
Hadden told him about a friend with a house on the North Shore.
They could live there together and work on the magazine. Several days
later Luce left town.

Now that his plans were settled, Hadden decided that if he was ever
going to take a vacation this would be the time to do it. He quit his job
at the *World* to join some friends on a boat trip through Latin America. The young men talked their way into free passage to Ecuador by
volunteering to work as deck boys on the SS *Quillota*. Hadden drank
Scotch with the crew and listened to their harangues about women.
Soon he was mimicking their Cockney accents. As the boat headed
south, he grew a pair of bushy sideburns and a ragtag mustache.

At each stop Hadden and his friends would get off to sample the
nightlife. They enjoyed best the port of Colón, where they danced with
a saloon keeper named Black Adalia, all three hundred pounds of her
shaking and shimmering in an emerald dress and bright white rows of
pearls. Shoveling coal in the stoke room, cleaning the donkey engines
on deck, the hard-working vacationers grew tan as the boat passed
through the Panama Canal, threaded through the Gulf of Panama,
and headed down the Pacific coast.

When they arrived in Ecuador, the young travelers dropped in on
their friend Freddie Stagg. A few years out of Harvard, he was running

a massive cacao plantation at Tenguel. Stagg met his guests at a bend in the river and tossed them the reins to his horses. The men rode past gangs of workers who scuffed back and forth on drying tables to spread the moist beans beneath their feet. The workers doffed their hats and chanted, *"Buenas tardes, mí patron."* At the Casa Grande, boys removed the Americans' shoes. Two claps and cigarettes materialized in their hands. That night, an old mestizo came to the veranda. He played fandangos while Hadden and his friends had cocktails and discussed "the benefits of paternal aristocratic government."

Their experience of such government had only begun. Earlier, over oysters at the Guayaquil Ritz, the young men had fallen into conversation with a stranger who turned out to be the secretary to the president of the Guayaquil & Quito Railway. The president invited the travelers to stay at his villa when they left Tenguel. Hadden and his friends spent their next several afternoons screaming down mountains on the railroad's private handcars. They felt like children on an endless roller coaster. On their longest journey, they rode in the car of the American minister—"a soap box orator and a rum hound," Hadden reported to his mother. The train climbed until its passengers had a clear view of Mount Cotopaxi, one of the world's highest volcanoes. "Traveling at such an altitude," one of Hadden's friends reflected, "we felt ourselves on equal terms with the Gods."

Arriving in Quito, the exalted Americans learned that their railroad patron had arranged for them to meet the president of Ecuador. José Luis Tamayo ushered the young men into his office, dismissed his secretaries, and began to talk privately about his liking for American girls. Ecuador, he said, badly needed foreign investment. Might Mr. J. P. Morgan be interested in floating a loan? Hadden liked "Don Looie" and he filed a report for the *World*. Soldiers clicked their spurs, clanked their swords, and led the president's guests to the secretary of war, who said they simply must witness the military at work. The tourists agreeably accepted the invitation but didn't give it another thought.

The next morning Hadden and his friends were awakened by a loud knock on the door. Military officials were waiting outside. Quickly, the ROTC men threw on their old Army gear and piled into the back of a black Cadillac. When the motorcade arrived at the Army's officer school, to their surprise the shavetail lieutenants were asked to mount a podium and conduct a review of the national Army. Soldiers paraded by, stepping in the German style. "Theoretically that is beautiful, Colonel!" remarked the Bald-Headed Sergeant of Battery B. "But don't you think it is a bit impractical now that Germany has been defeated before all the world?"

The Army officers hosted dinner parties in honor of the Americans. Hadden, who had studied a Spanish vocabulary book on the boat ride over, sprinkled his conversations with a few choice phrases. He soon discovered the fastest way to procure a round of drinks: loudly damning Peru. "The speeches! The songs! The toasts!" he wrote his mother. "In Peru, when we get there, it will be:—'To hell with Ecuador!'"

When he reached such uproarious heights, Hadden could be all but unbearable. He brainstormed constantly, spun out get-rich-quick schemes, and fired off letters. Since Hadden seldom felt tired, he had to keep moving. If his ship put in for any length of time, he would get off at once, if only to run headlong down a sand dune. "If a man could get one of these Peruvian sand-dunes to Coney Island & had an elevator to get people to the top, he could make much money," Hadden reasoned. All the while he talked and drank. "Red wine for breakfast! Red wine the last thing before turning in every night!" Hadden wrote his mother. "I have a pleasant 'edge' on from one day's end to another."

Finally one of Hadden's friends refused to go another step. The travelers shipped back, working on the donkey engines again, and Hadden's thoughts returned to the idea. He decided the magazine must be completely impartial. It must take no sides. The notion failed to captivate at least one of Hadden's friends. "I strongly recommended his starting a magazine of opinion—rather than trying to cover all sides of the news," Morris Phinney recalled. The wanderers returned to America just in time to attend the Harvard-Yale football game. They swaggered into the event, swinging Ecuadorian walking sticks and sporting waxed mustachios. Hadden later shaved off the sideburns but a trim mustache remained.

While Hadden was traveling, Luce was suffering a crisis of confidence. He arrived in Chicago playing the part of a dapper businessman, planning to woo the woman he loved and settle into a promising career. But jobs were scarce. The economy, shortly to expand, was in the midst of a postwar contraction. Despite the unfortunate timing, Mrs. McCormick did her best for her favorite boy. She invited Luce to stay at her Lake Forest estate and asked her son to find him a job.

One morning, a Rolls-Royce pulled into the circular drive. Luce climbed into the back of the limousine and sat next to Harold McCormick, chairman of the board. When they arrived at Harvester, Luce noticed how clean Harold's office appeared and how awkwardly he behaved, almost as if he hadn't been there in months. Harold sat down in a swivel chair and called up the president of the company, Alexander Legge, a former cowboy with a genius for mathematics hired by the family to run the firm. Legge walked into Harold's office and spread lengthwise across the scion's couch.

"Well, you know," Harold said, "Mama has always hoped that Henry . . ."

"If Mrs. McCormick wants us to do it, we'll do it," Legge said. "But now, Luce, do you want us to do it? If we take you on, you know, we have to fire somebody else."

No, Luce replied, he did not want that.

Desperately short of funds, Luce moved in with Cully Sudler, who was living with his parents on the Gold Coast. Luce needed any job, preferably one in Chicago. The most attractive of the available options was journalism. Mrs. McCormick's friend Victor Lawson owned the *Chicago Daily News*. He arranged for Luce to meet with his editor, Henry Justin Smith, an idealistic champion of the press. Smith told Luce that he wasn't hiring, but Luce returned several times. Finally Luce begged for a broom to sweep the floors. "Well," Smith said, "it just so happens Ben Hecht says he needs an assistant."

Ben Hecht, who later became one of the most prolific screenwriters in Hollywood, wrote "1001 Afternoons in Chicago," a column that spread across the entire back page of the newspaper. Hecht championed the spirit of the working class and captured the feeling of the streets. Chicagoans would phone him to suggest bizarre neighbors worthy of a feature. Hecht, swamped in notes and leads, needed a legman to track down these snake charmers and punch-drunk boxers, confirm their identities, and ask them a couple of questions. Hecht would spin the rest from his imagination.

For a somber, conservative Ivy Leaguer with grand ideas and no experience, it would be a blessing to work for a gifted writer from a

humble background with a taste for the bizarre. But the combination
didn't take. Luce thought Hecht's work was insignificant if not spuri-
ous. Hecht thought Luce lacked instincts; he was liable to bring in
stories about lemonade stands and traffic jams. "This fellow is much
too naive," Hecht told Smith. The columnist recommended that Luce
be fired. Instead the editor transferred Luce to the city room and gave
him a job as a reporter. "I'm fired, Hurrah," Luce wrote his parents.
"Yes, inside of ten days, I've lost my first job, and got another."

The work of reporting failed to interest Luce much. He spent his
time courting Hotz, taking her to dinner, loaning her books, and giving
her drafts of his articles when he ought to have handed them in. The
sweethearts attended church, the theater, and the ballet; they danced
at the grill of the Blackstone Hotel, home of the "smoke-filled room"
where Harding was selected for the nomination; they motored out to
Lake Forest to take tea with Mrs. McCormick. At night, the couple
stayed up late, playing duets at Lila's piano and talking about books
and politics. "We talk all things from the gods on Olympus down to our
own selves," Hotz wrote in her diary. "I take him 'home' and he me!!"

With his Oxford clothes and affectations, Luce made a strange addition to the city room. Chicago reporters were hard-boiled. They took
pride in getting their hands dirty and scoffed at the white-collar word
"journalist." One Saturday, Luce dressed up for a date with Hotz, only
to realize that he had left a book for her on his desk at work. Luce ran
back to the office and grabbed the book. Just as he stepped into the
elevator, his editor walked in. Smith looked Luce up and down—tweed
suit, gloves, cane—and said nothing. The old elevator shuddered down
to the lobby. Just before Smith left, he cast Luce a withering glance. "Ah,
Luce," he said. "A journalist, I see."

In November of 1921, Smith was compelled to cut his staff. The
editor told Luce he would have to go. The harsh news dismayed the
cub reporter, who had recently taken a punch in the face from a rival
newsman while covering the sensational disappearance of a freshman
at Northwestern University. The story was front-page news because it
appeared the boy could have died during a hazing ritual. Luce thought
he might have drowned. A year and a half later, when the boy's bones
were found buried in sand under a pier near the campus, Luce realized
he could have kept his job if instead of relying on the police he had

hired a boat and searched for the body. But it hadn't occurred to Luce to chase after the story. After he cleaned out his desk, Luce asked his editor if he had any final advice. "Get out of newspapers," Smith said.

Luce told Hotz he would have to leave Chicago. They danced until morning that Thanksgiving. Hotz took a poignant drag off Luce's cigarette, where her lips met his fingers for the first time. Two days later, Luce visited Hotz. They walked out on a tree-shaded point and stared over the lake toward the lights of the Chicago Loop—the same place, brighter now, that had so shocked and enchanted Luce upon his arrival in America. When Luce returned home for the night, Sudler noticed lipstick on his face. It did not take any particular reporting ability to realize what Luce affirmed with a delicate smile. He and Hotz had secretly become engaged.

Hotz's stepfather, a South Side financier, opposed the match. He considered himself a "judge of men" and noticed that Luce left his laundry on the floor. Ever more aware of the gap between his ambitions and his means, Luce felt a bit lost. He considered a job offer from the American Radiator Company. "Happiness is not always in an opera box," he explained to his parents, "yet opera boxes cover a multitude of life's little irritations." To his mother he admitted, "I suppose I shall get out of journalism."

And then the mail came with an envelope from Briton Hadden. It contained a letter from their college friend Walter Millis, which Hadden had read and passed along. Millis was working at the *Baltimore News*. The editors liked his work and wanted two more just like him. Anyone recommended by Millis would get a job in the city room, a fine salary, and the chance to move up. Luce had received a similar letter a few days before, but Hadden put the offer in a new context. "If we are ever going to start that paper," he scrawled, "this looks like our chance."

Luce scheduled a talk with Mrs. McCormick, who was feeling ill and spending time in bed. Her haggard face lit up like the sun when Luce kneeled at her bedside. He always helped her to make out his words by speaking directly into her ear. Mrs. McCormick bought a train ticket for Luce, who rushed to New York to meet Hadden and soon wrote Smith that he wouldn't be getting out of journalism after all. "I hope you will restrain any tendency toward Rabelaisian laughter," Luce added. "And what makes it worse is that two of us are showing signs of pernicious insanity and will probably undertake a new publishing venture in a few months."

Finally it was settled—a strange and powerful friendship had found an object worthy of all its epic restless vitality. Hadden had often felt bored without a giant dream to chase. Now all that nervous energy would be lashed to Luce's will, all that creativity driven toward a goal. At times Luce had considered himself a rival to Hadden, but Hadden tended not to think of their relationship in that way. Immersed in dreaming up new plans, Hadden needed someone to ground the project and drive it toward completion. Luce was his man. "Brit took Harry along because he thought he could be useful," a cousin of Hadden's later wrote. "He was splendid on details, a good planner . . . a promoter, where Brit was a creator. Brit was very fond of Harry."

As much as Hadden wanted to work with Luce, it was probably Luce who needed Hadden more. Launching a magazine alongside Hadden appeared to be Luce's last, best chance to set a path toward wealth and power. Luce had always sought to influence more than educate, while Hadden was moved by the goal of informing people as never before. But once he had Luce near at hand, Hadden could flex that old ability to inspire his friend and steer him toward the greater goal. Keen to social nuance, Hadden felt something of which Luce largely remained unaware. Together, they had the potential to be great.

5

Time Will Tell

WHEN THEY MET AT Penn Station to take the train down to Baltimore, each sporting a thin mustache and carrying a cane, Hadden and Luce looked more like college boys than editors. Between them, they had little more than a year's work experience and a few thousand dollars in savings, all of it Hadden's. But in the next few months, powered by a dream, a rivalry, and a great deal of nicotine, they would invent a magazine of startling originality, find wealthy benefactors to invest in it, win the support of a Wall Street financier, and by the age of twenty-five begin one of the greatest success stories in the history of American journalism.

Hadden chattered as the train chuffed south. He was selling Luce as always, ratcheting up his confidence, hyping the *Baltimore News* as a "small city paper" that would leave them time to hatch their plan. When they arrived at the newspaper, the cub reporters saw a great whirring press visible through plate-glass windows—publisher Frank Munsey's attempt to get workers to buy his newspapers. Soon the newest hires were writing a good chunk of the evening edition and competing to see who could get more lines on the front page. Luce found his feet as a reporter when he brought in some scoops about the Catholic Church. Hadden made print on his first day and ultimately won the contest.

Each afternoon, Hadden and Luce would head to the top floor of a dilapidated mansion, where they shared rented quarters with Walter

Millis. The young men spent their nights chain-smoking and discussing the idea. "People talk too much about what they don't know," Hadden would say. His favorite example was the problem of "war debt." Every American seemed to have an opinion on the matter, but few could say how much money the various European countries owed the United States. It was easy to see why: newspaper editors rarely listed such basic facts, though the papers printed so much else.

Instead of blaming Americans for their ignorance, Hadden and Luce began to discuss the obstacles that had arisen in their lifetime to prevent people from informing themselves. The main problem, they thought, was not a lack of information, but too much. In 1870, there were fewer than six hundred daily newspapers in America; by 1900, there were more than two thousand. In 1885, just twenty-one magazines reached a hundred thousand people or more. In 1905, there were more than 159 such magazines. The expansion continued, aided by cheap postage and fast presses. After the Great War, more newspapers and magazines than ever blared from the crowded newsstands.

For the first time, millions of Americans were getting information from the movies and the radio. In November of 1920, a small station in Pittsburgh broadcast the news of Harding's election. Just two years later, the Department of Commerce would extend licenses to more than five hundred radio stations. In a few more years, one in ten people would own a radio set. The movies had spread from the nickelodeon theaters into giant cinema palaces. A thriving film colony in Hollywood was producing pictures for ten million fans, who would increase to a hundred million by the decade's end. Americans had eagerly entered the electronic era. They received more information in more ways than any people had before.

And there was one more voice competing for Americans' attention: advertising. After the war, corporations encouraged consumers to purchase expensive goods on the installment plan. The dispersal of credit to millions of workers created a vast consumer market. As households bought their first automobiles, washing machines, and phonographs, companies plastered the streets with billboards. The magazines, newspapers, movies, radio stations, and billboards were breaking down regional and cultural boundaries. In cities across the nation, Americans were participating in a vibrant new national culture.

The newspaper and magazine editors, radio and film producers, and advertising pitchmen reached their audience by entertaining them. This began on a wide scale during the late nineteenth century, when publishers reached out to a mass audience by turning the newspaper into a spectacle—part drama, part freak show, part soapbox oration. The Hungarian immigrant Joseph Pulitzer built a vast audience for the *New York World* by adding clever headlines, arresting pictures, and "human interest" features. Pulitzer's imitator and rival, William Randolph Hearst, crossed the line into sensationalism. The blaring headlines and teary-eyed descriptions of Hearst's *New York American* seemed closer at times to fiction than to fact.

The rise of news as entertainment vastly increased the power of magazines. Between 1903 and 1910, the editors of the illustrated national magazines, including *Collier's, McClure's,* and Hearst's *Cosmopolitan,* published the work of the "muckrakers," investigative journalists who unmasked society's ills. Lincoln Steffens's report on municipal corruption, Ida Tarbell's history of Rockefeller's oil monopoly, and Upton Sinclair's exposé of the meatpacking industry created a national groundswell for political reform. Congress passed laws regulating child labor and patent medicines. President Wilson signed the Federal Reserve Act and helped create the Federal Trade Commission. Women won the right to vote. Finally temperance activists succeeded in amending the Constitution to outlaw the manufacture, transportation, and sale of alcoholic beverages. At midnight on January 16, 1920, Americans took a gulp—and began to think the progressive movement had gone far enough.

Now the national magazine publishers were abandoning investigative reporting in favor of photographs and fiction. The publisher Cyrus Curtis reached millions of readers across the nation through the *Saturday Evening Post* and the *Ladies' Home Journal.* The *Post*'s cover illustrations, including some by the young Norman Rockwell, created a joyful, vibrant image of America. But the saccharine entertainment inside the cover could never satisfy people with an interest in the news. On December 17, 1921, the *Post* ran a single news story: an essay by Isaac F. Marcosson on Europe's attempts to recover from the war. The rest of the magazine's hundred pages consisted almost entirely of romance stories. Week after week the *Post* pandered to its readers with celebrity fiction and sentimental poetry.

Hadden and Luce noticed that the few publishers who dared to bring serious news to a large audience were gaining readers and prestige. Adolph Simon Ochs, who published the *Chattanooga Times*, had bought a controlling interest in a failing Democratic newspaper, the *New York Times*, at the turn of the century. Since then, the *Times* had steadily acquired a following by reporting the news fully and in proper terms. During the war, Ochs and his editors sent a cohort of reporters to Europe. Their exhaustive coverage of the cataclysm helped turn the *Times* into the one place where readers could find, as the newspaper's slogan went, "All the News That's Fit to Print."

Though the *Times* came closer than any other newspaper to being the paper of record, it had no national printing or distribution network. The newspaper's readership consisted almost entirely of New Yorkers. The *Times* was a storehouse of information, invaluable to those who had the time and ability to sift through it all. But the newspaper's organization, if there was any, was difficult to determine. And the long sentences of its reporters defied the average mind. Thousands of people skimmed through the *Times* each day, and some had to admit that they did so with a vague feeling of duty. Many came away remembering little.

People wanted to learn the news more quickly now. The pace of life had picked up dramatically since the beginning of the war and publishers who satisfied the demand for quick, accessible news were scoring successes. In 1919, a Chicago publisher, Joseph Medill Patterson, had moved to New York and launched a tabloid newspaper, the *Daily News*. Splashed with sensational photographs and draped in leering headlines, the *Daily News* made appealing subway reading. Within a year a million people were turning to the tabloid for expert coverage of ghastly crimes and celebrity scandals.

The best evidence that people were looking for condensed news reports was the success of the *Literary Digest*, a weekly news summary printed by the encyclopedia publisher Funk & Wagnalls. One of the most popular magazines in America, second only to the *Saturday Evening Post*, the *Digest* often featured a homely illustration on its cover: a matron offering the reader a Thanksgiving turkey; red-coated girls feeding nuts to squirrels. Each week the editors of the *Digest* attempted to summarize the news. Instead of telling what happened in their own words, they sampled thought across the nation by reprinting the homespun truisms of provincial papers. The *Digest's* editors had a weakness for wacky stories, rib-ticklers, and ephemera. They spilled pages of ink on American elections while making no attempt to bring readers news from every continent. Far from a digest, the result was a hodgepodge. Nearly a million people read it each week.

The astounding success of such an ill-conceived ragbag showed that people no longer had the time to pause and reflect, to comb through the news and make sense of it. They needed someone to do this work for them, but no publisher was filling the need. The Hearst papers, tabloids, and illustrated magazines printed readable but vapid entertainment. The *Times*, on the other hand, printed a goldmine of information, buried beneath a mountain of ponderous verbiage. The broad national audience—people who went to the movies, listened to the radio shows, and kept the *Saturday Evening Post* on their coffee tables— had no place to go to read the major news from around the world.

Hadden and Luce realized the nation needed a new type of publication: something that condensed the most important news from the *New York Times* and supplied it to the national audience that read the *Saturday Evening Post* in a simple style that could rival the entertainment value of a Hearst newspaper. The nation needed a publication that actually achieved what the *Literary Digest* attempted. Hadden and Luce hoped to create a weekly report that would summarize and explain the news in a comprehensive, objective, and entertaining manner.

In discussing their project, the young men talked of how Pulitzer, isolated on his yacht, had stayed informed with the help of a private corps of secretaries. Hadden and Luce began to think of themselves as public secretaries. Their magazine would be so simple that even a clueless debutante could appear smart at a cocktail party after reading it for half an hour. Unlike most publishers, Hadden and Luce would not simplify the news to the point of triviality or pander to a mass audience. Rather, they sought to create a periodical that the educated upper class could instantly grasp and the rest could reach up to. The magazine would be that rare combination of style and substance, a mass-market phenomenon that appealed to people's better instincts and elevated their intelligence.

The budding newsmen did not then notice the dramatic expansion of their potential audience. By the start of the 1920s, the vast wealth created by the Industrial Revolution had transformed American society. Between the magnates at the top and the factory hands near the bottom, a group of white-collar businessmen had arisen in the cities—particularly in the Midwestern industrial centers such as Chicago, Cleveland, Pittsburgh, and Detroit. At the turn of the century, when Hearst and Pulitzer grappled to dominate the newspaper business, only half a million Americans held college degrees. By 1921, that figure had doubled—a small increase of immense import. America was developing a middle class. And this emerging group would be interested in reading precisely the type of magazine Hadden and Luce envisioned.

In a nation of strivers, the middle class raced faster than any previous generation. Hot in pursuit of the American dream, they spent their weeks shuffling paper in brand-new skyscrapers. At week's end they went home, beaten down and battered, to cherish a day of recreation, a concept all but foreign to their fathers and grandfathers. In the movie houses, they laughed when Charlie Chaplin stumbled and got a little choked up when Douglas Fairbanks got his girl. They chuckled when their children entered endurance contests to see who could dance the longest, but in a way such contests mimicked modern life. The point was to get in the grand game of capitalism and compete for the prize.

Members of the new middle class passionately wished to better themselves. They thirsted so deeply for advancement that large numbers of people paid to learn techniques of self-improvement. Toward the beginning of the decade, many devoted themselves to the psychological phenomenon of mind training. A Frenchman named Émile Coué traveled the nation giving lectures to packed audience halls on his breakthrough technique of "self-mastery through conscious autosuggestion." Coué convinced millions who bought his books that they could improve their lives if they sat in front of the mirror each morning and intoned a series of lessons. "Every day, and in every way," America said, "I am becoming better and better."

Self-improvement was more than a passing fad. In the modern era, the burgeoning middle class saw knowledge rather than physical skills as the path to power. Men who had not had the opportunity to attend college enrolled in correspondence courses. They hoped to learn how to write the dynamite letter that would help them find a better job. Men who had those jobs rifled through H. G. Wells's best-selling book *The Outline of History.* They looked for the obscure fact that might impress the boss and launch them on the path to promotion. The most popular self-improvement programs and products held one technique in common: condensation. People who hoped to get ahead felt they had to learn more rapidly than ever.

The glittering rush of news and entertainment so enraptured middle-class Americans that they wanted to imitate and acquire it, to grasp and hold a part of what was new. Facts were a form of status; people bought them up and wore them like a raccoon coat. College students who had ascended from working-class or rural roots gleefully joined in the cultural activities that had eluded their parents. In the great Midwestern schools such as Michigan and Wisconsin, middle-class men and women rooted for their football teams more loudly than Yalies ever had. Thousands and thousands of people, stadiums full of them, chanting and waving, laughing and drinking, wished to participate in the new national culture. All they lacked was a guide.

By relating world news in a fresh, clever voice, the magazine Hadden and Luce hoped to create would directly appeal to this growing audience. The plan the young men developed closely followed the ideas Hadden had voiced on the train ride to Texas. Each week they would sift through the newspapers, select the most important subjects, and compress a week's worth of news into short, entertaining stories. Taken together, all of these stories would provide a condensed world report. By distilling events in the simplest terms, Hadden and Luce hoped to make serious news widely accessible for the first time. They were positioning themselves as arbiters of import, twentysomethings with uncommon judgment who would proclaim to the world what was news.

As Hadden worked on questions of prose and style, Luce bent his mind to the logistical problems of what type of publication they should create, how it would be printed, and how often. The partners soon confirmed that they were talking about making a magazine since neither had the money to buy a newspaper press. But the magazine they envisioned would act more like a newspaper because it would offer news rather than commentary. Realizing they had invented a hybrid, Hadden and Luce coined a new word for their creation: the "news-magazine."

Hadden titled their magazine *Facts.* Most magazines took a side; they offered an opinion on the news. Hadden attempted to convince Luce that the real public service lay in helping people to make up their own minds. Though temperamentally better suited to argue than to inform, Luce gradually worked up excitement for Hadden's proposition. "True, we are not going out like Crusaders to propagate any great truths," he wrote his father. "But we are proposing to inform people—to inform many people who would not otherwise be informed; and to inform all people in a manner in which they have never been informed before."

In one crucial respect, however, the young men would gladly fail to inform their audience. When the *Digest* quoted the newspapers, it credited them for the report. The resulting mess of attributions—"argues," "reports," "according to"—made the *Digest* slow reading. Worse, the *Digest* sounded doubtful, since each bit of news arrived with a reservation. Hadden and Luce realized most people didn't care where information came from; they simply wished to know what was most important, most interesting, and most entertaining. Unlike the *Digest,* the news-magazine would sound definite. It would tell stories collected from the newspapers without reference to the source. To the average reader it would appear as if the news-magazine's editors had reported their own stories, when in fact they would be reprinting old news and selling it for five times the price. This could cause some controversy.

A few years before, the Supreme Court agreed with the assertion of the Associated Press that a rival news organization broke the law by selling A.P. reporting as its own. Hadden and Luce did not plan to steal the news, however. They would rewrite a week's worth of events within a single story, provide context and perspective, and in the end change the newspaper content so completely as to make it their own. Besides, by the time their magazine came out, the newspapers it relied on would be used for wrapping fish. The young men ran their plan by Melville E. Stone, the former general manager of the Associated Press. "By the time you print it, it won't be news," he agreed. "Go ahead; you won't be harming anyone."

The newspapers, a paste pot, a typewriter, and a pair of shears were all Hadden and Luce needed to get started. Each afternoon they would cut up the *New York Times* and separate the articles into topics. Once they had a week's worth of news on a story, they would extract the main events from a dozen odd clippings and rewrite the news in their own words. Hadden would cut the stories to the fewest words possible and inject phrases from the *Iliad* that struck him as active and fresh. Finally, he and Luce would type the stories into columns and paste them onto sheets of paper. The "magazine" looked crude, but in essence it would not change for half a century.

In February, the budding editors showed their work to their former writing professors, John Berdan and Henry Seidel Canby, who had come to Baltimore for a meeting of the Modern Language Association. Hadden's abrupt writing style provoked strenuous criticism from Canby, who thought it was "positively atrocious." He urged Hadden to develop a style that was condensed but not "telegraphic." Years later Canby would recall being assured—by Luce, he thought—that the style was intended to shock and could easily be discarded. But Berdan grasped the significance of Hadden's attempt. He was trying to compete with movies, magazines, radio shows, and billboards. "You're writing for straphangers," Berdan agreed. "You've got to write staccato."

At the end of their lunch, Hadden and Luce asked Canby if he thought they should go ahead. "Have you got any money?" Canby asked. Not personally, his old students said, but they knew people who had quite a lot. "Can the donors afford to lose it?" Canby pressed. Hadden and Luce considered their wealthy friends—and decided they had funds to spare. Canby advised the young men to quit their jobs immediately, move to New York, and launch their magazine. Within the hour they walked to work and resigned. The Baltimore editors shook their heads. "All predictions," a reporter recalled, "were of certain and swift failure."

Hadden and Luce took the train to New York and moved in with their parents. Luce sent a letter to Cully Sudler, who immediately left Chicago for New York to sign on as business manager. The three old classmates worked in the Luces' apartment near Union Seminary, with Luce's little brother eagerly running out to buy pencils and cigarettes. After a month, it seemed that the idea warranted an office, and Reverend Luce helped the aspiring publishers rent a room in an old brownstone on East 17th Street.

The young men climbed a spindly staircase surrounded by walls so heavily repainted that the surfaces had acquired the consistency of cheese. At the front of the room was a wall of windows so filthy that they hardly let in light. Soon the room was furnished with two large worktables and three chairs from a Lower East Side junkshop. Sudler sat at one table, and Hadden and Luce faced off across the other. In the middle of the floor, they placed a large copper soap kettle. It would be their ashtray. Hadden hoped to fill it all the way up.

The kettle hadn't filled with more than a couple of cigarette butts when Hadden and Luce decided to scrap the soporific title of *Facts.* They wracked their brains for something crisp yet dignified, but no one could come up with anything. They decided to quit for the weekend. According to some accounts, Hadden had brought to the office a bound volume of an old British magazine edited by Edmund Yates in the 1880s. The title of this magazine, spread across the cover in large capital letters, was TIME. Half dead from exhaustion, Luce was riding the subway home when he stared glassily upward at an advertisement with the same word in the title. Luce tested the word on Sudler, who liked it, and the following Monday Luce tried the title out on Hadden. "That's it," he said.

Hadden and Luce sat down at their typewriters to hammer out a prospectus. For a half hour, there was silence. Finally Sudler, amused to see his friends stumped, banged out what he understood of their idea—"*Time* is a magazine devoted to the time which business men and women can afford to spend in getting the news." They were on their way. For the next few weeks Hadden and Luce faced off across their table and fired copy back and forth as they drafted and redrafted their prospectus. They wrote long into the night six days a week. Each afternoon, they would take a break for tea, a habit Luce had picked up at Oxford. "I had to provide the damn crackers," Sudler recalled.

The prospectus the young men thrashed out remains one of the most significant declarations of publishing principles in the history of American journalism. "People are uninformed," it proclaimed. Instead of blaming reporters and editors, Hadden and Luce enumerated the many quality magazines and newspapers, then posed a novel question: Considering the profusion of excellent reading sources, why did people remain so ignorant? They answered: "NO PUBLICATION HAS ADAPTED ITSELF TO THE TIME WHICH BUSY MEN ARE ABLE TO SPEND ON SIMPLY KEEPING INFORMED."

Brashly, they proposed the solution:

T I M E is a weekly news-magazine, aimed to serve the modern necessity of keeping people informed, created on a new principle of COMPLETE ORGANIZATION.

T I M E is interested—not in how much it includes between its cover—but in HOW MUCH IT GETS OFF ITS PAGES INTO THE MINDS OF ITS READERS.

Hadden and Luce proposed to get the news into their readers' minds by creating a kind of information assembly line. They would read dozens of newspapers, magazines, and journals from around the world. From hundreds of thousands of words, they would distill the "essence" into two-dozen pages. The magazine that resulted would cover all areas of human endeavor, from politics to religion, science to music. Each story, no longer than four hundred words, would be written in "simple, straightforward language."

The young men believed a great deal of ignorance resulted from people being too shy to ask questions. Newspaper editors assumed their readers knew more than they actually did. Reporters, zealous to report the details of the day before, failed to place the recent news in context. As a result, the newspapers confused readers who came late to the story. Hadden and Luce decided to err on the opposite extreme—to write for the person who knew nothing. They would start each story from the beginning. They would introduce every newsmaker. They would illuminate complicated events by briefly relating the context first, then telling the most recent happenings. Intellectual readers would consider *Time* simple. But the vast majority of readers would be able to read the magazine and begin to understand a confusing world for the first time.

Not only would Hadden and Luce distill the news to its essence, they would help people grasp information by placing it within an intellectual framework. Unlike the front page of a newspaper, on which unrelated stories sat side by side, *Time* would categorize the news into departments such as National Affairs, Foreign News, The Arts, The Professions, and Sport. The editors of the *Literary Digest* had made an attempt in this direction by breaking the first part of their magazine into two sections: foreign and national news. But the rest of the *Digest*, though charming, remained pitifully disorganized. One of its largest categories was "Birds, Beasts, and Trees." Another category, "Miscellaneous," at times comprised nearly half the magazine.

The publishers of *Time* would extend the principle of organization to its logical extreme. The magazine would categorize all of human endeavor. National Affairs, for instance, would include sections on Oil, Prohibition, and Women, while Professions would include sections on Business, Medicine, and the Law. Each week readers would be able to look to *Time* for regular information updates. If they kept the magazines and filed them away, readers could conceivably build an index of the important news on every subject. But even if they threw the magazines in the trash, *Time*'s precise organization would still give readers a mental construct that would help them to stay informed.

Hadden and Luce hoped to radically alter the way people understood the world outside their front door. Just as the assembly line had altered industrial production a decade before by dividing a job into a series of discrete tasks, *Time* would alter people's thought processes by dividing all that happened into discrete categories. A great deal of work would be required on the part of *Time*'s editors to break the news down, but the resulting whole would be so much easier to grasp that it would actually appear to be simple. "The one great thing was simplification," Luce later said. "Simplification by organization, simplification by condensation, and also simplification by just being damn well simple." Often a brilliant idea seems obvious after the fact. Soon nearly every magazine and newspaper in America would attempt to compress or categorize the news. It took *Time* to shift the paradigm.

If *Time*'s founders had stopped there, few people would have wanted to read their magazine. But *Time* would entertain as well as edify. All his life Hadden had endeared his friends and acquaintances to the world around by noting their peculiarities, nicknaming and razzing them, and describing their physical quirks. Now Hadden and Luce proposed to treat public figures in the same way in order to pierce the facade that kept them hidden and unassailable. "General Wu . . . and Nikolai Lenin are something more than stage-figures with a name," the prospectus asserted. "It is important to know what they drink. It is more important to know to what gods they pray and what kind of fights they love. *Time* will tell." Suddenly newsmakers would appear before readers on a human scale, and the news they made would seem accessible.

By proposing to tell the news through the personalities who made headlines, Hadden and Luce gambled that they could make important news fun to read. To attract a large audience, they would have to disregard Hadden's goal of attaining pure objectivity in favor of a form of storytelling that would inevitably shade the news with subjective impressions. From the moment of its birth, then, *Time* blurred the boundary between news and opinion. Hadden insisted that the magazine would have no editorial page, but he agreed to two indices at the back of the magazine, "We Point with Pride" and "We View with Alarm," in which the editors would pithily express their viewpoints. "Complete neutrality on public questions and important news is probably as undesirable as it is impossible," the prospectus explained.

The rest of *Time* would print all sides of an issue, while "clearly indicating" which side the editors favored. Hadden and Luce promised to hold "respect for the old, particularly in manners," and to take an "interest in the new, particularly in ideas." They would take the "statesman's 'view of all the world,'" and would distrust government increases in both size and power. Still they would strive to report the news without partisan bias. *Time* was "not founded to promulgate prejudices, liberal or conservative," the prospectus proclaimed. "'To keep men well-informed'—that, first and last, is the only axe this magazine has to grind."

The young publishers would begin by aiming *Time* squarely at the one million Americans with college degrees. But the magazine would be simple enough to appeal to many more. At the end of their prospectus, Hadden and Luce stated their ultimate ambition: "Because it has no political axe to grind; because it presents the facts; because its style is brief, clear, interesting; because its news is organized so that a mind trained or untrained can grasp it with minimum effort;—*Time* should appeal to every man and woman in America who has the slightest interest in the world and its affairs." Over dinner at their friend Lewis G. Adams's apartment, Luce would say that he didn't care if New Yorkers read *Time* as long as people read it from coast to coast. Hadden, when drinking, would occasionally predict, "We're going to be much greater than William Randolph Hearst!"

Hadden and Luce showed their prospectus to Samuel Everitt, the treasurer of the Doubleday, Page publishing house and a family friend of the Luces. Everitt liked the boys. He directed the publisher of *World's Work*, the company's monthly business and foreign policy journal, to help them in any way he could. Soft-spoken W. H. "Doc"

Eaton took his job seriously. "I spent a full afternoon with those fellows going over their first dummy, discussing their editorial philosophy," he recalled. "They certainly were intense about the whole thing, and Hadden seemed to be driving every minute of the time. But it didn't have a professional look to me. I told them I didn't think they'd have a Chinaman's chance."

But the aspiring publishers kept stomping back to Eaton's office in Garden City, each time farther along, each time better informed. Eaton began to think they were smart young men. Finally Hadden and Luce asked Eaton how they ought to go about attracting subscribers. By then Eaton thought of the young men as his protégés. In an act of extraordinary generosity, he taught them the secrets of soliciting through direct mail. Eaton then broke the cardinal rule of publishing and gave them a list of several thousand of his own subscribers. Eaton would come to regret his choice in 1929, when *Time* put his magazine out of business. "Looking back afterward, I was sorry," he said.

Hadden and Luce often spent their evenings at the cold, gas-lit apartment of Samuel Meek, who had admired them since he was their managing editor on the *Yale Daily News*. Meek, who had gone into advertising, flatly told his friends that few people would subscribe to a magazine published by a couple of cub reporters. To compensate for their inexperience, Meek suggested over dinner, they might consider seeking the support of "prominent men." Hadden liked the idea because he had always planned to test every aspect of the magazine against "able journalists of the Swope type."

And so they hit the phones. They set up meetings with journalists, financiers, and professors. Not every luminary warmed to the idea of condensing the news. In Baltimore, H. L. Mencken invited *Time's* delegation into his backyard and listened intently, a cigar jammed between his lips. Though he seemed to respond favorably, he did not ultimately endorse the plan. The president of Harvard was enraged by the idea of simplifying the news. "He thought the whole thing was disgusting and disgraceful," recalled the writer John Franklin Carter Jr., who solicited the man's support on behalf of Hadden and Luce. But many "bigwigs," as Hadden called them, understood the need for a magazine like *Time*. When Hadden returned from a successful meeting, he would stick a little piece of paper to the wall—a quote from the journalist Walter

Lippmann, or the former assistant secretary of the Navy Franklin Delano Roosevelt, or the author and journalist Hendrik Willem van Loon.

Several months later, Eaton helped his protégés draft a subscription offer. Hadden and Luce plastered the circular with the testimonials they had gathered, printed it at the cost of seven hundred dollars, and mailed it to a hundred thousand people. If the test mailing failed to attract interest, they could quit with no harm done. A few weeks later, Hadden and Sudler opened their rusty black mailbox to find three postcards from readers replying favorably to the offer. Six thousand people ultimately requested trial subscriptions—twice what they had expected.

The returns on the subscription offer were strong enough to merit setting up a corporation. Again Hadden and Luce met with Samuel Meek, who was well-connected in the business world. Meek told his friends to talk with his brother-in-law, John W. Hanes, who had recently floated a large issue of R. J. Reynolds Tobacco stock for C. D. Barney & Company. Hadden and Luce trekked to Wall Street, but Hanes told them it would be foolhardy to compete with the *Literary Digest*. "Forget it, and save your money," he said, and sent them away.

They soon came back, Hadden with a look in his eye Hanes would never forget. "We're not going to take your good advice," Hadden said. "We can run a better magazine than the *Digest* and we're going to do it." He began to spin out the concept of *Time*. Hanes liked Hadden's moxie. "Hadden was damned convincing. He could have been a corset salesman," Hanes recalled. "Certainly Luce was there, too. They made a good team. But Luce wasn't much of a talker. He thinks faster than he can talk, you know, and sometimes it gets garbled up. But all the time, Hadden would be in there, selling, selling. He just had what it takes. He was intelligent, he was enthusiastic, he was willing to work and work hard. He was the whole ball of wax rolled into one."

Hanes gave Hadden and Luce the most important piece of advice they would ever receive: to keep control of the company. "How the hell are we going to do that if we haven't got any money?" Hadden snapped. Hanes drew up a plan for two kinds of stock, preferred and common. Preferred would pay dividends to investors sooner, but only the common stock would carry the right to vote on company affairs. Investors would receive one share of common stock with a purchase of two shares of preferred, but most of the common stock would remain in the hands of the company's founders. Hadden and Luce would each keep 2,775 shares—a total of 55.5 percent, giving them control of the company. One friend of Hadden's told him the plan didn't seem fair. "Fair or not, we're going to get away with it," he said.

Publishers told the young men it would take a million dollars to launch a magazine. They decided to raise a tenth of that—ten thousand dollars each from ten wealthy friends. Luce wrote his father that a man who put some money into *Time* would get more fun out of it than "out of a new car." But things weren't so simple as that. Many of their friends had money, but their fathers controlled the funds. What a pity, the old men said, that such bright, hardworking young men were attempting the impossible, forever sealing their status as black sheep in the Yale family, and eliminating the possibility of later raising money for some worthier venture. The few who took an interest offered to invest only as majority stockholders.

Hadden and Luce worked relentlessly—writing letters, calling friends, making trips to Pennsylvania, Connecticut, and Massachusetts. They offered almost anyone they knew the opportunity to invest, with two exceptions. Luce would not ask for money from Lila Hotz or Mrs. McCormick. The prospectus passed through so many hands that it grew dog-eared and stained. Stretching for prospects, Hadden and Luce approached the management of the *Literary Digest.* "They just laughed at us," Sudler recalled.

The constant rejection took its toll on Luce. Here he was, a Bones and Oxford man, going door to door, hat in hand, just as his father had always done. Reverend Luce had started out with big dreams, too—big dreams that went unfulfilled. Now the son's soul ached with the burden of past indignities and future hopes, first among them the intense desire to marry a wealthy girl. Each night when he came home, tired and pining for Hotz, Luce would get out his pen and write her a letter. Falling into bed, he would insist to Elisabeth, who had stayed up to serve him a hot meal, that he must be awakened early in the morning. He couldn't afford to be a minute late. "Oh, Harry just had the burden of the world on him in those days!" his sister recalled.

Again it was Hadden, the chief mystic and go-getter, the public presence and enlivening spirit, who kept the dream alive. He leavened Luce's spirits with a sense of humor and gamesmanship by calling the prospectus his "groining iron," the ultimate tool for bringing men to their knees. "Hit him in the groin!" Hadden would yell before he and Luce left for a meeting. "Let's groin him!" If Luce stuttered while giving the pitch, Hadden would wait patiently for his partner to stumble through. When they scored an investment, Hadden would come back grinning and announce to Sudler that another man had just been groined. If a meeting went poorly, Luce would leave feeling bitter and dejected. "So we lost one fish," Hadden would say. "Let's go get us another fish!"

Hadden's spirit was infectious. When he visited John Hincks in Bridgeport, Hincks's younger sister, Mary, was so enraptured that she decided to spend her personal savings to purchase two shares. Sudler, too, was carried away. Though he joined the effort as Luce's companion, Sudler quickly came to admire Hadden, and to realize that "this whole *Time* idea was his." Sudler thought of Hadden as a creative genius. "If Brit had lived he would have been one of the great men of our time," Sudler later wrote. "He was interested in everybody. His mind was tireless, and he had an almost unparalleled drive coupled with a strong personal discipline. . . . In fact, as Harry will be the first to admit, it was Brit who was the colorful figure of *Time*."

As the months dragged by and little money trickled in, ultimately the pressure mounted on Hadden and Luce to adjust their stock plan. Fund-raising on their preferred terms might never have continued except for a Skull and Bones connection. Their club mate Harry Davison, who had followed in his father's footsteps by joining the firm of J.P. Morgan, purchased forty shares and passed the prospectus along to the senior partner Dwight Morrow. One of the most respected businessmen in America, Morrow asked if the fundraisers would see him on Wall Street.

When Hadden and Luce told Morrow about the controversy over their stock plan, he agreed that they ought to control the company. It was their idea, after all. Morrow decided to match Davison's purchase of forty shares—a nominal investment considering the size of Morrow's pocketbook, but one that carried great significance. In a single pen stroke, the endorsement of a powerful financier helped two recent college graduates keep control of a company that might easily have been pried from their grasp. One *Time* editor later wrote that Hadden and

Luce were saved by "the wave of Morgan's magic wand." It wasn't so plain as that, but three years later Morrow made the cover of *Time*.

In June of 1922, Hadden and Luce attended the wedding of their Bones friend David Ingalls to the Standard Oil heiress Louise Harkness. The *New York Times* covered the reception at the Harkness estate on West Island, which attracted many of the wealthiest members of New York and Cleveland society. Louise herself could have gone a long way toward funding *Time* if she had pawned the diamond and sapphire brooch pinned to her dress. But her wedding hardly seemed the time to approach her.

Finally feeling stymied, Hadden and Luce decided it might help to bring a few more people onto the team. Hadden contacted Wells Root, a recent chairman of the *Yale Daily News*, who was looking for a reporting job. Hadden introduced Root to Swope at the *World*, where Root soon began working. And Root, in turn, agreed to freelance for *Time* when the magazine went into publication. In the meantime, he would keep his eyes peeled for wealthy friends who might like to invest.

Hadden also contacted his cousin John Stuart Martin, who had just finished his junior year at Princeton. A sophisticated and romantic figure, as well as a self-destructive one, Martin had lost his left arm in a childhood duck-hunting accident. Fiercely competitive, he remained the consummate sportsman, and a deadeye with a rifle. Years later, when a Peregrine falcon flew past his office window on the fifty-second floor of the Chrysler Building, he would grab his 20-gauge shotgun and kill the bird in midair, then retrieve it from the roof of a nearby tenement. Martin had a sharp gaze and a deep, mellifluous voice. A member of Ivy, Princeton's most exclusive eating club, he had just been elected the editor of the *Daily Princetonian*.

Having recently acquired a Marmon roadster, Martin suggested to Hadden that they ought to spend the summer driving across the country, stopping at country clubs, where they would sell shares to their friends while hitting the links. In Buffalo, the cousins met Hadden's old Hotchkiss friend Shorty Knox at the bar of the local club. Knox, a Woolworth's heir, immediately agreed to invest and promptly asked his friends if they would like to have a drink. Hadden groined him anyway. But in Erie and Detroit and Chicago and Cleveland, the cousins ran into the same old problems. "Now look, boys," their friends' fathers would say. "Another magazine, a little magazine like this—what's the point? Just go look at any magazine counter. Aren't there enough magazines?"

In Cleveland, Newton D. Baker, President Wilson's former secretary of war, frankly told Hadden and Martin that he would gladly help fund their magazine—as long as *Time* supported the League of Nations. Hadden badly wanted Baker's contribution, but not at the cost of creating a partisan publication. "*Time* will be eminently fair to all sides of great questions," Hadden replied. That was not enough for the spectacled lawyer, who endorsed the project but refused to invest. The roadster-riders made it back to New York, well summered and practiced in golf, bearing pledges worth only several thousand dollars. Cully Sudler, frustrated, decided to drop out.

And then their luck changed. Wells Root had talked about *Time* with his friend William Hale Harkness, who had recently inherited a fortune from his father, the deceased Standard Oil shareholder William Lamon Harkness. William invested five thousand dollars and spread word to his sister, Louise, then living near Harvard with her husband David Ingalls, who was studying law. When Hadden and Luce came to call on the couple, their Bones mate Ingalls laughed off the idea and refused to invest. The *Literary Digest*, he said, was too good to beat. But Louise invested five thousand dollars and showed the proposal to her mother, Edith Hale Harkness, who asked to meet the two young men.

On a hot day in August of 1922, Hadden and Luce knocked on the door of the widow's apartment on East Sixty-sixth Street, just around the corner from Central Park. The suite of rooms was decorated in the Victorian style, every wall lined with blue brocade. Mrs. Harkness, in her sixties and hard of hearing, her back a bit tired and her hair gone white, asked the boys to sit down and trained her ear trumpet in their direction. Hadden and Luce began to explain their project. "That will do boys," she said. "Put me down for twenty thousand." A moment later they were blinking in the sunlight, bona fide publishers at last.

In the end, *Time*'s founders raised $85,675 from sixty-nine friends and acquaintances. Forty-six were Yale graduates, fourteen of them Bonesmen. The largest investors were the members of the Harkness family, who acquired 35 percent of the corporation's preferred stock. The shares Hadden and Luce sold would build fortunes, pay for educations, and fund charity endowments. The Bonesman Frank Peavey

Heffelfinger called his summer home in Minnesota "the house that *Time* built." Harry Davison never made a better investment, though he had plenty of opportunities at J. P. Morgan. When he died in 1961 his small investment in Time Inc., combined with several investments of a similar size made since, had grown to seven million dollars—the largest source of funds in a large estate.

Of far greater significance was the fact that the first magazine to make sense of the news for the nation would soon be brought to life. Hadden and Luce expressed the power of their project by selecting a Latin motto: *De omni re scibili et quibusdam aliis*—telling all things known and some other things, too. The company was incorporated at the end of November with Hadden as the president and Luce as the secretary and treasurer. They agreed to trade those titles every year. As for who would do the editing, Luce knew Hadden "had to have" that job, but in theory they agreed to rotate it. They flipped a coin to see who would edit first, and Hadden won the toss.

6

Long Shot

LUCE ESTIMATED THAT HE and Hadden were taking a "ten-to-one shot." Publishers, noting the young men's paucity of experience, their lack of muscle in the market, their small cash reserves, thought the odds were longer than that. But despite such obvious disadvantages, Hadden and Luce had one major factor in their favor. They were armed with a revolutionary idea of how the news should be told—an idea so radically different from what had come before that it stood a chance of shattering the old consensus, ushering in a new mode of journalism, and creating a different kind of public conversation.

In order to succeed, *Time* would have to be unusually well written. This presented a challenge. Such Yale friends as Walter Millis and John Franklin Carter Jr. believed joining *Time* represented too great a career risk; they decided instead to keep plugging along at established newspapers. Hadden's cousin John Martin was still at Princeton. After he graduated, he planned to spend the next year in England, where Albert Victor Baillie, the dean of Windsor, had invited the dashing collegian to stay with his family. Instead of bringing in young stars, then, Hadden was forced to hire a collection of cub writers with no experience and little more talent. Only one, the recent Yale graduate Manfred Gottfried, would stay at *Time;* he ultimately rose from paper-marker to managing editor. Gottfried was enthusiastic. When slicing the newspapers, he would get down on the floor and tear them apart with the shears. But Hadden thought Gottfried's writing lacked style.

Hadden bent over his writers, working them seven days a week, heavily marking their stories or struggling to rewrite them. After heading out to see Swope or Lippmann, he would return in an irritable mood, urging his young writers to grasp at something they couldn't quite clutch, something even Hadden couldn't yet envision in all of its aspects. Hadden pushed his writers to enliven the news with detail, to focus on character, to take an angle on the story. "Gee, that's *good* good!" he said of one story by Gottfried. "A little bit editorial, but damn good!" The staff put out numerous weekly typewritten mock-ups and two practice issues, identical to a real magazine except Hadden and Luce did not distribute them. When the first practice issue went to the printer in late January, Hadden drove himself so severely that he wound up phoning in the final corrections from his bed. But he managed to get the issue out, and there was something in the writing he liked.

The staff moved into a one-room office near Fifth Avenue. On the weekends, the heat was shut off, so the boys huddled over electric heaters and typed away in their overcoats. Hadden, subsisting on baked beans and cigarettes, worried constantly about his staff. He had no one at all to write Foreign News. Again Hadden got in touch with John Franklin Carter Jr. and begged him to come work for *Time*. Carter still didn't want the job since he was writing for the *London Daily Chronicle* in Rome. But he mentioned the offer to a friend he had recently joined at Monte Carlo's roulette tables who claimed to have experience as a foreign correspondent. Hadden wired back to send the man over.

A couple of weeks before deadline, a little man with a wooden leg and a big mustache sailed to America to accept the illustrious position of Foreign News editor for *Time*. Thomas John Cardell Martyn was the son of a British soldier who had died in Rhodesia. Martyn had lost his leg in the war as an aviator for the Royal Air Force. He thumped around suavely somehow, a skilled billiards player with a touch of class, or so it appeared to the young Americans. Martyn spoke fluent French and German, and though he had little journalism experience he knew quite a lot about European politics. A strange little man, all in all, he would later break with *Time* and found *Newsweek*. He was met at the boat, rushed to the office, and told to start typing.

It was late February and freezing. Messenger boys scrambled in and out. Hadden tore through the office—strewing about paper, pencils, instructions. Luce mapped out the company's budget at a little desk in the corner of the room. He tugged at his hair, tensely, nervously, his head bent low, all but deaf to the hubbub that surrounded him. When he finished his projections, the first budget of the company that would one day grow into the world's largest media conglomerate optimistically projected revenues of $155,000—the same amount Herbert Bayard Swope had lost to Samuel Goldwyn that year in a reckless evening at the poker table.

A printing executive, invited to the office, was soon frightened off. There wasn't anywhere to sit. All the writers were running about. The company didn't have any letterhead or a credit line or even a reputation. Finally a small firm based downtown agreed to print the magazine. They offered Luce a 5 percent discount if he would settle the bill for the first issue before sending the second to press. The American News Company, which distributed magazines to newsstands nationwide, agreed to take five thousand copies. Hadden and Luce set a deadline, postponed it, and settled on a date in early March. For two tweeks the staff worked maniacally, hammering out their first issue. When finished, they had compressed a wide variety of news from around the globe into twenty-six pages.

Just after midnight on the first Tuesday of March 1923, Hadden and Luce took a taxi to Eleventh Avenue. In the small press shop of the Williams Printing Company the young men wrote and cut, pasted and pinned, until finally they had the stories down on the galleys. The first issue rolled off the press just before dawn. It had rough-cut edges and a slightly blotchy cover and it was just small enough to be folded twice and fitted into a pocket, as Hadden had dreamed of doing since childhood. Luce, having spent his time on printing and production matters, finally had a chance to flip through the magazine before nodding off to sleep. Half an hour later, he awoke with a realization. "What I had been reading wasn't bad at all," he recalled. "In fact, it was quite good. Somehow, it all held together, it made sense, it was interesting."

Staring out from the cover was the rustic face of "Uncle Joe" Cannon, who was about to announce his retirement from the House of Representatives after serving for a record-setting twenty-three terms. A short cover piece described the former Speaker as running America's "homely democracy" with the help of "homely democratic symbols—Uncle Joe's black cigar and thumping quid." *Time* carried a wealth of news from every continent and summarized just about every aspect of the American political scene, including the work of the last session of Congress, the important cases soon to be discussed by the Supreme Court, and the annual costs of Prohibition. The stories were brief, often just a paragraph or two, written in prose so terse as to edge toward epigram. Together they provided the nation with its first comprehensive, organized world report.

Back at the office, a team of debutantes hired by Hadden began mailing out the magazine. Luce sent a press release to Edward L. Bernays, a young nephew of Sigmund Freud who had launched a career as an independent publicity agent. Bernays, who would later become known as the father of modern publicity, forwarded the release to the newspapers. The next morning the *New York Times* announced *Time*'s debut. The newspaper noted that "a hundred prominent men are listed as original subscribers."

Time's founders passed the next few days nervously, wondering what their friends would think of the magazine. Strangely, they didn't hear from anybody. Hadden was well underway on the second issue when finally a few friends began calling the office to ask why the first issue hadn't arrived yet. Puzzled, Hadden and Luce retraced their steps. They soon discovered that the debutantes Hadden had hired to label the magazines had gotten their piles mixed up. Some of *Time*'s subscribers had received three copies of the first issue, while many had received none at all.

Despite all the hard work, the first issue of *Time* was a failure. It was read by nine thousand people, barely a third of what it would take to break even in the first year of business. In virtually every city but New York the magazine lingered on the rack. The circulation dipped in the next few weeks as a hundred readers a day canceled their trial subscriptions. Writers and secretaries came and went quickly, never giving their jobs much of a thought. "Look—is this a permanent job?" asked one recent graduate of a local women's college upon being hired to replace a secretary who had quit. "I wouldn't know," Hadden's secretary replied. "This thing may fold any day."

Over the next several months, Hadden and Luce gradually built an audience among college students. Magazines were sold one at a time—at Wellesley by Luce's sisters, at Princeton by star athletes assembled by John Martin, up and down the Eastern seaboard by Dave Keep, a Williams senior who peddled *Time* from dormitory to dormitory and often escaped with the campus police fast on his heels. Hadden asked his female friends to fan across Manhattan's streets, run up to newsstands, and inquire for a copy of *Time*. When the news dealers handed the girls the *New York Times* instead, they would shake their heads and ask again for "*Time,* the weekly news-magazine." "Nevahoidovit," the news dealers barked. Hadden hustled to newsstands and told dealers he had a magazine to show them that was completely different from anything else. If the dealers liked it, he would ask them to take a couple of copies and share them with their dear readers. "Who could resist such fine lads," one dealer recalled years later.

Gradually *Time* gained a following among the young and modern set. College students kept the magazine on their coffee tables, circled favorite phrases or surprising facts, and quoted them to friends. A single issue would make its way through several sets of hands. Years later, one longtime subscriber in California recalled that he first heard about the magazine from a budding artist who traveled West in search of "material." She was tall and thin with a shock of red hair, and she said everyone in her crowd was reading *Time*. When the artist returned home, she sent her new friend a subscription form. Several weeks later he received a harbinger of the new day dawning in the East. "It was then printed on a sort of drawing paper," he recalled, exaggerating only a little. "The edges were not cut sharp but were ragged as if wetted and pulled apart on an irregular line."

With little cash coming in, some weeks the Time Inc. bank account dipped close to zero. Luce, shirttail loose and tie askew, scribbled figures on a pile of paper as he delved into the intricate business of publishing. When his secretary found that *Time* couldn't cover its debts for a few days, she would send out checks without Hadden's signature. By the time the bank discovered the error, the company would be able to afford the expense. Luce often stayed up late, worrying about whether the magazine would survive. "My spirit is within a camel's straw of total wreckage," he wrote Hotz. "Business looks dashed poor." But no matter how bad things looked after a long day's work, Hadden never lost his confidence in tomorrow. And each new day, when he bounded into the office, he almost seemed to carry in the morning.

Hadden encouraged his business team to come up with new ideas rather than simply follow industry practice. "Publishing seems to have a lot of set rules," he said. "Let's see if all these rules and regulations make sense, before we follow them." Most magazines charged advertisers at a linear rate, twice as much for a full page of space as for a half page. Advertisers paid at the same rate no matter how much they bought. Hadden thought this system made little sense, because an advertisement placed next to an article would attract more readers. *Time* increased the price of smaller ads and offered advertisers a discount for buying in bulk. The method became the industry standard.

The advertising manager, Robert Livingston Johnson, bowed and scraped his way into executives' offices, offered them free subscriptions, and, when they turned him down, smiled broadly and sent the magazine to their secretaries. "You fathead!" Hadden teased. At industry conferences, no matter the topic at hand, Johnson would jump from his seat to make the first comment, preceded by the phrase, "Johnson of *Time*." He was desperate to make a fortune so he could go into public service, and he would later rise to become the president of Temple University. Gradually Johnson succeeded in making the advertising agencies aware of *Time*, but in its first months the magazine survived on the dollar bills readers sent in with their subscriptions.

Time's ingenious subscription offers were beginning to have an effect. "We pay the freight!" a typical letter promised. It included, of all things, a self-addressed and stamped postcard. The idea was the brainchild of Roy Edward Larsen, the son of a Boston newspaperman whom Hadden and Luce had hired as their circulation manager. At Harvard, Larsen was the business manager of the most illustrious collegiate literary magazine, the *Advocate*, where he somehow managed to turn the first profit in memory. He decided to work with Hadden and Luce on the advice of Samuel Everitt. "They are a couple of awfully strong-minded people," Everitt warned. But he thought perhaps Larsen could stabilize the productive but violent partnership of *Time*'s two founders. Larsen wore his hair in a slick side part and dictated at double speed. His executive assistant later captured him in *The Man in the Gray Flan-*

nel Suit, a satirical novel on the model American executive. For the moment, Larsen's gray suit pants were wearing so thin that his secretary took bets on how long they would last.

Half a year into publication, *Time*'s circulation began to rise rapidly. As the magazine gained readers, printing and distribution costs rose, but advertising revenues failed to rise along with those costs. Only fourteen companies were advertising in *Time,* and they had bought their space earlier in the year. Now they were reaching extra readers without paying for them. The magazine's growth, though longed for and celebrated, was quickly depleting the company's cash reserves.

Stretching for a solution, Johnson asked Larsen if it might be possible to predict *Time*'s circulation growth. Larsen thought the idea was worth a try. He guessed that *Time*'s readership could grow from just under nineteen thousand readers to thirty-five thousand by the following year. Johnson charged advertisers at the higher rate, and Larsen pushed to meet his guarantee. If he failed, *Time* would have to give the advertisers a refund. The gamble paid off: Larsen met his promise and the practice of setting a circulation guarantee, also known as a "rate base," spread throughout the industry.

Word of *Time* began to emanate from the Eastern seaboard. Excitement spreading west among the set of people who read books by F. Scott Fitzgerald and wore shirts by Coco Chanel. In towns across the country, independent solicitors eagerly hawked *Time* because Larsen offered them a higher commission than the *Digest* paid. Businessmen began to develop a taste for *Time*; its time-saving frankness appealed to them. Some peculiarly devoted people read every word; they called themselves cover-to-cover readers. "We made a hell of a thing of it," Luce recalled. "In the early days you could read it from cover to cover in one hour, so in a way you could hardly do anything else but read it from cover to cover. Nevertheless, this gave us a great peg to sell our advertising."

In the summer of 1923, *Time* moved to a seedy neighborhood surrounding the vast Edison electric plant on the East Side of Manhattan. The area was home to gashouses, a public bathhouse, and an old factory—the Hupfel's beer brewery on East Thirty-ninth Street. The brick loft building took up an entire block and was rented out to a variety of clients including used furniture dealers and a gun repair shop. Hadden and

Luce leased most of a floor for a hundred and eighty dollars a month. The writers brought along battered tables as desks and the advertising salesmen nailed up beaverboard partitions. "There was no heat in the other place," one writer recalled. "This place had heat and light."

Hadden began to discover his editing voice. He coaxed his writers to weave the news into an entertaining story. Though he rewrote their work as little as possible, occasionally he found it inevitable. More often he would hand back a piece and ask the writer to try again. "Let all stories make sharp sense," Hadden would say. "Omit flowers. Remember, you can never be too obvious." Most of Hadden's writers failed to meet his standards. He fired several who later became famous, including Louis Bromfield, whose novel soon won the Pulitzer Prize. "He drools," Hadden said. John Thomas, a friend of Luce, sailed for France after Hadden fired him, and soon wrote *Dry Martini*, a smash success. He would die of acute alcoholism in 1932. Hadden wanted journalists, not novelists. He began to shape the magazine into a coherent whole.

To make sense of the world would be a difficult task for a twenty-five-year-old editor in 1923. The Great War had left widespread social and political upheaval in its wake. The fall of the old imperial powers had led to wars and revolutions across the globe. In Russia, Lenin had suffered a stroke and little-known Joseph Stalin was maneuvering for control of the Communist Party. In the Middle East, the collapse of the Ottoman Empire had resulted in a scramble for territorial control. France had occupied parts of the German borderlands as a result of the Treaty of Versailles. Warlords were struggling over the fate of modern China.

America, too, was rapidly changing. Laborers were striking for their rights. Blacks were migrating North. In the South, white vigilantes were maintaining the old order through lynching. A few women's rights activists, having won the right to vote, were opening a birth-control clinic in New York. Prohibition had resulted in the rise of the Mafia and gang warfare in the major cities and a culture of lawbreaking everywhere else. A new generation was on the rise, creating modern literature and jazz, spreading fashions through film and radio. A fight was on between reformers and traditionalists.

Hadden's youthful viewpoint and his broad definition of what made news helped him to illuminate the times. *Time* depicted the rise of Christian fundamentalism, introduced the chromosomal theory of sex differentiation, discussed the rise of the broadcasting companies, and briefly told the history of the Masonic Order. *Time* printed feature stories on the scientists discovering new vitamins and minerals, on the doctors inventing modern surgical techniques, and on the archaeologists unearthing human history. Hadden called them "The Diggers." In the summer of 1923, the nation was swept away by the pop song "Yes, We Have No Bananas." Flappers, reveling in the carefree spirit of the times, sang the words aloud just to sound nonsensical. *Time* readers knew the song was a band conductor's ode to a New York fruit merchant.

In August, President Harding made a much-publicized trip to the West Coast, where he died, suddenly, unexpectedly, and at the height of his popularity. The President's body was carried to Washington on a train. Newspaper editors splashed the news across their front pages and great crowds lined the tracks to salute the man of "peace and prosperity." *Time* stood out from the hysteria with a candid description of Harding's funeral: "A hymn was sung, a few chapters of Scripture read, a prayer offered, another hymn—and the casket was carried into the vault of the cemetery, where it will rest until a mausoleum can be built. A bugler stepped forward and blew 'Taps.' The mourners departed."

Soon Congress discovered that a member of Harding's administration had leased government oil reserves to political allies in exchange for gifts and loans. The scandal of Teapot Dome, the name of a Wyoming oil reserve, evoked lengthy disquisitions from newspaper editors. Hadden outlined the news in a few columns. He headlined the story "A Stench." One subscriber in Massachusetts began underlining favorite passages and showing the magazine to his friends. Somehow an issue ended up in the hands of a mother, who couldn't help exclaiming over its plain statements and occasional cheek. "Its slogan was 'Curt, Clear & Complete,' and the reporting was exactly that," the subscriber recalled, "a bit shocking to a lady of Victorian background not accustomed to having a spade called a spade, at least in print!"

In a time of disillusionment with moral improvement projects, when the American rejection of the League of Nations made people feel they had marched up the mountain one too many times, *Time* captured the modern viewpoint by cutting public figures down to size. No sooner had Harding's vice president, Calvin Coolidge, taken the oath of office in his father's Vermont farmhouse than *Time* told readers about his morning meal: "Gods have ambrosia for breakfast. Kings, presumably, have tarts. Presidents, New England Presidents, have whole-wheat and whole-rye cereal." Such a detail would seem trivial if printed in the *New York Times*. In the comparatively empty pages of *Time*, the President's diet came to represent his disciplined simplicity.

Within three months Hadden had moved such details from a minor section entitled "Political Notes" to the first page, where he summarized the President's activities in a column called "Mr. Coolidge's Week." Instead of highlighting the President's most important actions, the column gave a blow-by-blow account of his day. *Time* reported that the President's pets ran away, that he kept a seashell on his desk, that he exercised in the morning by riding an electric hobbyhorse. Counting the number of words Coolidge made in his public statements, *Time* determined that he spoke in a "mincing gait." Many thought the column disgraceful; one reader compared it to "neighborhood gossip in a country newspaper." But the column slyly illuminated Silent Cal, a small man for a time when Americans believed in small government.

Over the next several years, *Time*'s coverage of the White House would grow more detailed. By 1929, readers could turn to *Time* and find a map of the White House, including the precise location of the First Lady's bathtub. Such trivialities had always struck reporters as unimportant and inappropriate. But Hadden realized that details helped people to imagine events and comprehend great figures on a human scale. The *Chicago Journal of Commerce* later commented that *Time* gave the reader "the information that he wants, even when he does not consciously know that he wants it."

Instead of prizing the high-minded ideal, Hadden sought to discover the modest truth at the heart of the matter. He was firmly a member of the postwar generation, who prized fact over argument and preferred the cutting put-down to the sweeping declaration. It wasn't that Hadden had no points of view; he had many personal predilections, which he freely injected into *Time*'s pages. Hadden sided with the underdog, the person whose social role was to care for or comfort another. He loved his mother above all, and hence *Time* loved all mothers. Animals were another favorite. Once, when the newspapers began to devote stories to the hunting treks of American scions through the African safari, Hadden called in a writer and ordered him to do the whole story from the point of view of the animals. "We're for the lions every time!" he shouted. "We're for the lions!"

Hadden based his few policy positions on a sense of fairness and practicality rather than on partisan grounds. Story by story, fact by fact, he railed against Prohibition, an impractical law that was costing money and causing crime and injury. He also stood against racial rule in the South. Hadden ran chilling accounts of lynchings that provoked splenetic outbursts from white Southern readers. He angered them further by mentioning blacks in *Time* just as he mentioned whites: with the respectful title of "Mr." When a white reader, Barlow Henderson of Aiken, South Carolina, accused *Time* of issuing a "flagrant affront to the feelings of our people," Hadden replied, "Would Mr. Henderson himself care to be styled plain 'Henderson'?" In a time of disillusionment with partisan argument, Hadden's willful insistence on stark facts struck readers as radical and exciting.

It took time and collaborative effort to cull and interweave such facts in a brief, entertaining report. *Time* stories took little time to read, but they put the news in context by supplying the historical and anecdotal background information that the newspapers lacked. The writing improved dramatically in the summer of 1924 when John Martin returned from England and joined the staff. He soon convinced Hadden to hire another of his cousins, Niven Busch, who had dropped out of Princeton after his father, Briton Busch, lost his fortune. Hadden started his cousins on Milestones, the column listing births, marriages, divorces, and deaths. Soon they were writing humorous stories for several departments. Hadden called them his "red rovers."

The writers could polish their stories to a finer gloss than newspaper reporters because Hadden hired a team of girls to do research. In the first days of publication, *Time*'s writers had lacked the time to search for the entertaining and revealing tidbits Hadden wanted to print. Casually, without fanfare, he hired a girl, Nancy Ford, who took trips to the library and checked the magazine before it went to press. When Ford, exhausted, lost the will to go on, Hadden hired Ruth Ogg. A few months later she suffered a breakdown and was confined to her bed. Hadden decided to hire two girls. When they complained about the workload, he glowered and said, "One used to do the work of two." "Did she die?" they teased, not knowing how close they had come to the truth.

Soon there were three women in the office digging through newspapers and books in search of revealing details. Then there were four. Hadden tried to hire girls who appeared to be in robust health. He offered them seventeen dollars a week. "That's it," he would say, grinning widely. "You may be worth a million, but we can't afford any more!" Hadden began to call the girls "researchers," a title more commonly used to describe laboratory scientists. Because Hadden could hire two researchers for the price of one writer, the research department dramatically cut the size of the Time Inc. payroll.

The women knew they were making less than the men, but they liked the work. *Time* was exciting and fast-paced. The girls who could keep up were brilliant and aggressive, capable of working long hours, skilled at digging up facts. They typed, researched, interviewed, and wrote. Some helped to edit. And it was always surprising what an old man might tell *Time* when he heard the voice of a young woman on the line, asking such intelligent questions so sweetly and nicely. Hadden thought of his girls as a secret weapon; no other publication had such smart, diligent women, and no other publication contained such crisp, scintillating facts.

Some of the girls fell in love with Hadden. They mothered him, bantered with him, gave him cigarettes, and loaned him money when he was broke. Hadden noted the debts in his black notebook and always paid them. During *Time*'s first Christmas, the girls bought Hadden a little wooden duck with a tail that opened and shut. Hadden was touched. He kept the duck on his desk, and the girls kept it full of Lucky Strikes. "Hadden paid no attention to any of these dames," John Martin recalled. "He was just boom-boom-boom Hadden; just cannons, cannons, cannons all day long."

But Hadden did have an eye for one of those dames, a beautiful brunette with a face "right off a candy box." Deborah Douglas was a wealthy girl from Minneapolis who had recently graduated from Vassar. She had a mop of wavy brown hair, hazel eyes, and a vivacious smile. Her beauty was natural: she had a clear complexion, and she did not wear makeup. Douglas had been a star actress at Miss Spence's School before taking up journalism at Vassar. Carefree and creative, she wrote poetry and believed she had a talent for predicting the future through her dreams. She shared Hadden's love for animals.

Much like Hadden's mother, Douglas had no pretense about her. She was gentle, warm, and sincere. She had always been popular, not because she made herself the center of attention, but because she met people with a warm smile and a kind word regardless of their social status. Despite her easygoing attitude, Douglas shared Hadden's passionate dislike for people who seemed puffed-up or phony. She had a lively sense of humor and was attracted to brilliant, irreverent men. The girls in the office whispered that Hadden was "sweet on her." Before long Hadden and Douglas were seriously involved.

Partying in New York, hip flask in hand, watching football in the Yale Bowl, attending marathon bicycle races, Hadden slowly attained a degree of public renown. He stayed out late, still with that glow about him that had always attracted followers. "Hadden could go anywhere and do anything and didn't give a damn," his secretary, Dorothy McDowell, recalled. "He would get invited to debutante parties and wouldn't show at all, or would arrive at midnight in a dirty old sweater. . . . Luce would have given his eyeteeth to get into some of these places."

Luce sat in a small office, scratching out figures with a big green pencil on a pile of cream-colored paper and twisting a forelock of hair. "For cripe's sake!" he told a salesman who had spent eighty cents on a breakfast. "Do you think *Time* can exist if you spend all this money?" Writers who had seen quite a bit of Luce in the company's founding days now saw him rarely—except at night, when he swept the floors. Quietly, Luce kept an eye on the Religion column. He sometimes covered a story in Law or reviewed a book he had recently read. He groused about Hadden's unruly habits, the need for more "system."

Time was not "the fortunate recipient of any overnight popularity," as Hadden admitted in the company's first annual report, but the magazine acquired thousands of new readers by the end of 1923. Lila Hotz's stepfather realized that his daughter's beau had prospects after all, and he finally consented to the marriage. Lila admitted that Luce was poor by her lights, but she told her mother it would be possible to cut costs. She planned to start by giving up expensive indulgences like the fresh strawberries she loved. Mrs. Hotz rented a Fifth Avenue apartment for the young couple, then spirited her daughter to Europe to shop for furniture and antiques. Luce, annoyed to no end, extracted the walnut columns from customs as Lila and her mother strolled through France.

The wedding confirmed aspects of Luce's personality that had given his family pause since his social arrival at Yale. When Mrs. Luce wrote Emmavail that her brother knew "the real from the false in life" and would not become "like the *idle* rich," she almost seemed to be reassuring herself. Neither would be able to attend the wedding. The night before leaving for Chicago, Luce sat on the edge of his iron bed frame and wondered if he was making a mistake by marrying so soon. "The question did not seem to disturb him deeply," Manfred Gottfried recalled. "He was always fond of philosophical questions."

The New York newspapers carried notices of the wedding, with Hearst's *Evening Journal* calling Lila "a member of the swagger younger set in the Windy City." Deborah Douglas took the magazine to press that week as Hadden left to usher at Chicago's Fourth Presbyterian church. It seemed at the time to be one of the most beautiful weddings that had ever taken place. The walls of the church were lined with red brocade imported from France, the bridesmaids clothed in lavish dresses and silver turbans. "Very swagger," a newspaper remarked.

Lila carried a bright orange wreath to the altar, where Reverend Luce assisted in reading the vows. Afterward, on Lake Shore Drive, Hadden and the rest had a separate Skull and Bones wedding, where they muttered the incantations that ushered Lila within their fold. The young couple ran through a shower of rice to a nearby hotel. After a short vacation at The Homestead in Hot Springs, Virginia, where Lila caddied for Luce on the golf course, they arrived on Fifth Avenue just in time for the New Year. A thousand-dollar check awaited them, and a note from Lila's mother: "This is for strawberries."

Hadden ought to have switched jobs with Luce during 1924, for that had always been their agreement. Instead Hadden stayed in the editor's chair. He would remain there with rare exceptions of a week or two for the next three years. As *Time* found its voice, Hadden had the opportunity to plan for the company's future. He began to dream of new projects that would expand *Time*'s readership to a national audience. Despite Luce's best attempts to trim the budget, Hadden was beginning to reveal an expansionist tendency, a mad obsession to keep creating.

With the help of Roy Larsen, Hadden began exploring the promotional potential of radio, which was quickly moving out of the garage and into the living room of the average American. One of New York's most popular radio stations was WJZ, later to become the central station of NBC's Blue Network. Hadden developed a show for WJZ based on a quiz an old Hotchkiss history teacher had given his class. It was called *The Pop Question Game.*

Each week Hadden would write questions based on the news in the current copy of *Time.* On Thursday afternoons, the day before *Time* began to arrive, Hadden and Larsen would head to the WJZ studio at Aeolian Hall. "A pop question game, invented by *Time,* the weekly news-magazine, will now be played," Hadden would say. "Eleven questions, based on news of the week, will be asked. After each question will come an interval of ten seconds. After each interval will come a correct answer. The object of the game is for you to shout out the correct answer before I do. . . . Are you ready? Then play the game!"

The show evolved as Hadden tinkered with the script and finally crafted a snappy introduction. "Take pencil and paper in hand," he would say. "Are you ready? We will now *pop* the question." Listeners would race to write down their answers as Larsen banged three notes on the chimes. The show spread to more large stations, including KDKA in Pittsburgh and WGY in Schenectady. The *Herald Tribune* called it one of the greatest innovations of radio's short history, adding that it "tickled the vanity of the intellectual and awakened the interest of those less quick-witted." What began as a form of promotion for *Time* would develop into one of the most widely used, successful formats in broadcasting—the quiz show.

In 1924, *Time* also invested in a second publication, the *Saturday Review of Literature.* The Yale professor Henry Seidel Canby had started the magazine as a weekly supplement of the *New York Evening Post.* Canby and his editors formed one of the most influential literary circles in the land. But when Cyrus Curtis of the *Saturday Evening Post* bought the paper, he announced plans to popularize the literary supplement and let go of its staff. The supplement was not losing money; it had been a modest success. Roy Larsen suggested setting it up in a new format, and Hadden and Luce were eager to try.

They found a majority investor in Thomas Lamont, the J. P. Morgan partner who was part of the consortium that had sold the *New York Evening Post*. *Time* published the new magazine and took a 10 percent ownership stake. Canby's team created a logo of a phoenix rising from the ashes; they would influence the tastes of American readers for decades. A favorite columnist was Christopher Morley, who came to the brewery twice a week to do his writing. He usually began by smacking a whiskey bottle against the table until the cork popped out. For the rest of the day, he would sit in his office telling stories, tapping his pipe against the heel of his shoe, and filling the office with smoke.

Hadden shocked the editors of the *Review* with his barbaric shouts and habit of throwing books about. Yet he disliked the chatter of the *Review*'s frequent guests, such as the poet Leonard Bacon, who would walk through the office volubly reciting his own verse. Incensed by several visits from a jovial man named Captain Bone, Hadden finally nailed a notice to the wall: "Unseemly hilarity in one office causes disturbance in all. In future, will all editors receiving visitors in their offices bear that in mind." The *Review* staff laughed, agreeing that Morley was the loudest of their crowd, but Hadden topped even him in total noise produced.

Somewhere between the quiz-show listeners and the readers of the *Review*, Hadden and Luce were creating a new type of American audience. It was not an audience for romance stories. *Time* covered a wide range of difficult subjects for a growing professional class. If the magazine were to become a mass medium, it would do so by elevating and expanding the range of people's interests. More readers were beginning to take *Time* as a form of self-improvement. Traveling through the Midwest on his first business trip, Larsen was shocked by the number of congratulations he received. He realized the magazine was beginning to develop a national audience, and it would soon spread far beyond the urban East Coast.

With success in sight, Hadden grew more intense. He seemed consumed by the magazine, worked incessantly, and rarely talked about anything but the news. The girls who admired Hadden from afar found, when they tried to edge closer, that they couldn't get through to him; they couldn't grasp his intentions or find access to his emotions. He seemed wild, consumed by unknown passions, temperamental and prone to extremes. Many came to feel more comfortable admiring him from afar.

Hadden had fallen deeply in love with Deborah Douglas, and they had grown close during *Time*'s second year. Douglas came for dinner at the Hadden home in Brooklyn, where all of the other guests were married couples. Hadden's friends heard that he and Douglas had become engaged. "There was an understanding of some sort," Luce recalled. But Douglas wasn't set on Hadden. A more conventional suitor had arrived in the form of Dick Tighe, a blond, blue-eyed member of Skull and Bones. In St. Paul, Minnesota, Tighe's friends thought he would make a good governor one day.

As Hadden and Tighe competed for her affections, Douglas searched her soul for answers. Her time in New York had become raw and disorienting. "It was very stormy, the whole thing," her second husband, the actor Bob Aden, later said. "Brit meant a great deal to Deborah, and it was not easy for her to make her mind up." Finally the pressure was too much to bear. Douglas quit *Time* and went home to her family. Hadden traveled to Minnesota and asked Douglas to marry him. She refused. Soon thereafter, Dick Tighe moved to Minneapolis to take law classes at the University of Minnesota. Douglas married him in September of 1924. Hadden heard the news late at night while taking *Time* to press. He walked off alone and did not return for two hours.

Douglas married into a family with a history of depression. Tighe's grandfather had committed suicide; though the family history is murky, it was said that he had jumped from a train. In 1928, Tighe's father was found dead in his home after he shot himself with a revolver. Tighe inherited the family curse and quickly descended into alcoholism. He was found in his garage in 1938, dead of carbon monoxide poisoning. Douglas soon fell victim to alcoholism. In 1954, a year after her son's suicide, she swallowed a lethal assortment of pills. Shortly before her death, she remarked that anyone she had ever loved had been taken away from her.

Hadden and Deborah Douglas would never speak again. Later it seemed that Hadden lost an aspect of his emotional ballast—whatever source, unnoticed but ever present, that had kept his emotions stable and upright despite his manic lifestyle and consuming interest in the news. At times it seemed that he was trying to outrace the creeping feeling of melancholy that had occasionally dogged him in his last year at Yale. He began to spend more time alone, wandering through

Grand Central Station, where he enjoyed watching the teeming rush of humanity move about him.

When the stress of the office bore down, Hadden would grab his cousin Niven Busch to play baseball in Central Park. A policeman would often try to kick them off the ball field, which was reserved for boys. Rail-thin Busch would plead to the officer that he was only eighteen, while Hadden, a ball's throw away, would cover his mustache with his mitt. Busch could tell by the brightness of Hadden's eyes that underneath the mitt he was "giggling with insane glee." After a cold shower, Hadden would return to the office brutal and exuberant. "Office girls who were always trying to make him figured he had a dame someplace," Busch recalled, "but this was not the case." The love of Hadden's life, more now than ever, was *Time*.

By the end of its second year, *Time* had acquired a paid circulation of seventy thousand subscribers. College students lingered in the mix, but more *Time* readers were progressive young businessmen. *Time* had spread across the nation by acquiring eighteen thousand readers in the Midwest, five thousand on the West Coast, and two thousand in the Mountain states, as well as six hundred in Alaska, Puerto Rico, and Hawaii. *Time*'s founders were beginning to realize they had only begun to tap into the vast national appetite for news.

The year ended with a pleasant surprise. Haggard and unshaven, Luce confided to his partners that the company had turned its first annual profit—$674.15. Around the same time, a researcher excitedly reported that she had just seen someone reading the magazine on the subway. "I never see anyone reading it," Hadden growled. But the sighting was clearly big news. All of a sudden a low-budget magazine written in a former brewery by a scraggly gang of recent college graduates was turning into the surprise success of American journalism.

7

Ballgames

Time ARRIVED IN MAILBOXES over the weekend. To reach readers on schedule, the magazine had to be printed early Tuesday morning. The editorial staff worked hardest on Saturday and Sunday. On Monday, while the rest of the city began its workweek, the staff at *Time* raced to finish up. The odd hours suited Hadden. He drove his writers and researchers relentlessly four days a week, then left them free for most of the others.

The workweek began each Thursday morning at nine when Hadden charged into the brewery. He rushed wherever he went, chest puffed out, shoulders erect. With his cane he whacked at walls and doors. He was always pinstriped within a dark Brooks Brothers suit with a hat slung low over his brow. He was neat, almost fastidious—nails closely clipped, mustache cut short, hair parted to the side. In the wintertime, he turned up his coat collar and breezed in quickly, looking almost like a burglar. With his dark hair, sharp gaze, and broad shoulders, he made a striking presence.

The brewery had a freight elevator run by a mustachioed European gentleman who intensely disliked picking up passengers. He was usually slow to respond to Hadden's call, and a series of thumps would echo through the building as Hadden kicked the metal door. Once he reached the third floor, Hadden would march straight to his desk. He kicked aside anything that lay in his path. If he appeared to be nursing a hangover, the office boys would lower their heads. But most of the time Hadden would be in a grand mood. Bursting into the room, he would roar with laughter, tell stories, and dictate memoranda before he even sat down and took off his hat. If a secretary said good morning, he would say, "It's always a good morning. Don't have to say anything about that."

Hadden's office was the biggest on the floor and it served as the newsroom. Hadden sat in the back corner of the room at a gigantic rolltop desk large enough to form a private work space. Every morning the office boys would top the desk with a row of Hadden's giant red pencils, twice the size of normal ones with great soft lead. At the back of Hadden's desk, his secretary, the head researcher, sat at a smaller desk in front of a long row of floor-to-ceiling windows. Beside her were four battered tables where *Time*'s vaunted research staff sat: three girls, more or less, depending on how many had recently quit. A nearby bookshelf held a beat-up set of the *Encyclopedia Britannica,* bought at a discount from a writer who needed cash.

Above Hadden's rolltop, a piece of beaverboard caught the debris that fell from the ceiling when the furniture salesmen upstairs rearranged their merchandise. Hadden would sit under the canopy, take off his jacket, don his green eyeshade, and spread out the morning newspapers. For the next several hours, he would read through the news and chuckle over the previous day's follies. "Good guy," he might muse, coming upon a newsmaker who had acted gracefully the day before. More often he would cackle with delight and yell, "Phony!" Tearing out the article, he would scrawl an instruction to a writer. "Gott: Let's blatt this guy. BH." Coined by Hadden, the word meant to excoriate or rebuke.

Occasionally Hadden would spot a story that recalled to mind something he had read a few days before, and an innocuous news item would suddenly take on significance. "Holy Grail!" he would yell, or, "God's teeth!" He would call over a writer who specialized in writing stories with angle or humor, such as Niven Busch. While the writer listened, Hadden would recall from memory all the newspaper stories the writer ought to read. Then Hadden would dictate the thrust of the piece. Later, if the writer couldn't find the newspaper stories, he might come back to Hadden, who would shut his eyes in concentration and put his hand to the side of his face, as if viewing the newspapers in his mind's eye. "Have another look," he would say. "I think you will find it at the bottom of column four on page eight."

If Hadden were clipping a major story for the Foreign News or National Affairs section, he might write a short note about his ideas for the piece, or, on rare occasions, dictate a memorandum to his secretary. Hadden would then attach his note to the newspaper clipping and place the assignment in a wire basket that he kept on top of his desk. His secretary would assign the topic to a researcher, who would read through the previous week's newspaper stories and mark the relevant stories in red pencil. The researchers would take the newspapers to the office boys, who sat in the opposite corner of Hadden's office by the trash, where the rats came out at night.

The office boys were about fifteen years old. They idolized Hadden, who hoped to become a role model to them as Swope had been to him. Most of the boys had earned their jobs by passing a quiz with questions written by Hadden: "Who is Andy Gump?" "Where is police headquarters?" "What is the capitol of Wisconsin?" But the head office boy, Joseph Kastner, had his bright red hair to thank for his job. He had come looking for work at the same time as so many other eager boys that the researcher abandoned the quiz and simply pointed at the redhead. Receiving the newspapers from the researchers, Joe and his workmate would clip the marked stories with a pair of shears and file each set of clippings in pigeonholes by their desk, one hole per story. There it was, all the news of the week.

Occasionally a young man with wild eyes would pop into Hadden's office, grab some clippings from the pigeonholes, and dash back to a smaller room opposite the telephone. Separated from Hadden's office by a partition, this long narrow office had three chairs and a window at the end. The first chair contained Manfred Gottfried, the second usually John Martin, and the third, by the window overlooking Thirty-ninth Street, Thomas J. C. Martyn. When Martyn walked to his desk, the man in the second chair would have to pull in his chair and suck in his stomach to let his friend pass by.

The writers roomed together in cheap, linoleum-floored apartments, sometimes with nothing but an old stove and a couple of iron bedsteads. They were all under thirty with no idea of what they had yet to learn. To hell with it—they simply scrawled, smoking cigarettes, chewing gum, guffawing when they got in a good line. They wore British tweeds to the office; the smart dressers wore derbies and carried canes. Their style of dress revealed their attitude toward reporting. In those clothes, they would never go muckraking in the streets. They viewed themselves as storytellers, not hunting down the facts but culling and arranging them, shaping the narrative, painting the big picture.

While the writers worked on their stories, Hadden would hunker down at his desk, burrow through the news, and dictate memoranda. He never spoke with members of the staff aside from the writers; instead he communicated by note. When a thought came to him—it could be on Manfred Gottfried's late arrival or a problem with a reader's subscription—Hadden would yell it at the top of his lungs. Dorothy McDowell would have to type a memorandum, even though she sat so close to Hadden that it would have been just as easy to talk about it, or to hit him over the head—"something I often wanted to do," she said. A heavy smoker, Hadden lit up with great haste, took a few quick puffs, and forgot about his cigarette as fast as he had lit it. He threw his matches into the wastebasket without shaking them out, and his secretary often had to put out fires.

The writers knew when Hadden liked their work because the partition between their offices did not reach all the way to the ceiling. Hadden would laugh violently when pleased with a story. Often his shoulders shook convulsively. If particularly pleased, he would bound out of his seat, drop by the writers' room, slap a fellow on the arm, and give him a loud belly laugh. If he disliked a piece, Hadden would try to give the writer a clearer idea of what he wanted and ask him to try again. If the writer still couldn't get it to Hadden's satisfaction, he would hand the assignment to someone else. If there had been no competition before, now all of a sudden there it was, a new rivalry.

In the middle of the brewery was the circulation bullpen, where a worried man named Mr. Lindeman supervised a department of female assistants who handled requests for subscriptions. The girls teased Lindeman, which heightened his sense of embarrassment. He was a taskmaster, and some of his girls were absentminded. One Irish girl would respond to his frequent reprimands by leaning forward and allowing a mammoth breast to slip from her blouse. "With a little squeak, she would push it quickly back," Joe Kastner recalled, "having in the meantime caused Lindeman's eyes to swell out of their sockets and having driven everything else from his mind."

Nearby the circulation girls worked the young advertising salesmen, who saw themselves at the vanguard of a publishing revolution. They worked late hours in their cramped office. Not having any files, they simply nailed their papers to the partitions. When the salesmen made their first phone calls, their prospects often thought they were speaking with the *New York Times*. "There's no 's' on it," the salesmen would say before launching into their pitch. The salesmen knew the writers closely. They drank together and played golf. The salesmen admired the writers and realized a bit of controversy helped to push the product. The writers knew the salesmen needed hot copy to sell space in the magazine, and there was plenty of hot copy to go around. All agreed with the salesman Howard Black that "real good journalism sells."

Luce's office measured six feet by ten feet. It was large enough for two desks, one for him and a small one adjoining it for his secretary, Katherine Abrams. Together they handled all of *Time*'s accounts. Abrams was not familiar with double-entry bookkeeping. She kept a list of expenses and the company stamps. If a writer needed to mail a letter, he came to Luce's office and asked for postage. If a researcher needed to make a phone call from the library, she came to Luce and requested a nickel. New researchers gradually discovered that Luce controlled *Time*'s purse strings when he tiptoed through Hadden's office, tugged them on the sleeve, and asked, "What are you doing?" They had better have an answer; Luce was always trying to decrease the size of Hadden's research staff.

The writers had a light day on Thursday since the weekend newspapers would supersede much of the news reported on Tuesday and Wednesday. Manfred Gottfried would straggle in late having already read the newspapers, a habit he acquired when the President died during Gottfried's day off and he learned about it much later from Hadden. Thomas J. C. Martyn, the only writer with a family, would often work at home on Park Avenue, where his two little girls spoke nothing but French and his wife lounged about, smoking cigarettes on the divan.

After work Hadden would bring some friends to his favorite speakeasy, a Czech bistro on Third Avenue. "It was really the most horrible-looking place, really ghastly, with a terrible stench of beer!" recalled Luce's sister Elisabeth, who often came along. Hadden would give the secret knock and a man would come to the door and peek through the slit. Recognizing Hadden, the man would quickly open the door and usher him upstairs to a corner table. The one-armed bartender would drop by to say hello to his pal John Martin, and the two of them would brag about all the things they could do with one arm, while Hadden laughed and made fun of them both.

Hadden and Martin were usually surrounded by a couple of girls. They both had an eye for vibrant women, and Martin especially attracted them with his falcon gaze. Libby Holman liked to come along. A struggling Broadway dancer, she would soon hit it big in her bullfrog voice with the torch song "Moanin' Low." Hadden often invited one of his favorite stockholders, Mary Hincks, a stunning blond with an austere face. The group would drink from teacups and play Twenty Questions, or sometimes Hadden would brainstorm get-rich-quick schemes. His friends would attack his outlandish ideas, and Hadden, delighted, would craft elaborate replies. "He *loved* to laugh," Wells Root recalled. "He loved to tell humorous stories and get a big laugh out of things."

From time to time Luce would drop by the speakeasy. He seemed ill at ease. Hadden's friends tended to dislike Luce; they found him a cold and stilted conversation partner. "He was always a very sainted person, a very consecrated fellow on anything you were talking about, but always just like chilled steel—cold as ice," John Martin recalled. "Oh, a little smile here and a little chit-chat there, perhaps, and always this high titter. It told me something about Harry's character that when he laughed he tittered like a girl." Luce felt bored by the speakeasy talk. He never heard any big ideas or political argument—just a bit of gossip about who had the best bootlegger, or perhaps a string of silly jokes, interrupted by raucous, drunken laughter. Once Luce stopped in to find Hadden and his friends pulling chairs out from under each other's legs. Luce soon left.

On Friday, a few threadbare freelancers would straggle into the office. They wrote more than a quarter of the magazine each week.

The poet Stephen Vincent Benét, in his owlish round glasses, and narrow-nosed John Farrar, the editor of *The Bookman,* might drop off their literary columns, the only signed pieces in *Time.* Hadden would rush the researchers off to the public library to scrounge for details that the writers could weave through their stories. The writers would phone Henry Cabot Lodge Jr., *Time*'s stringer in Washington, for unpublished details about politicians. His title was "The Department of Silly Questions." By the end of the day, Hadden would know what he wanted in *Time* and the work could begin.

Over the weekend, while their friends golfed and partied, the writers undertook a long three days of work. They pulled the bulk of their information from the thick weekend editions of the *New York Times.* All weekend the men in the gun repair shop below *Time*'s offices tested their weapons, including rifles, pistols, and powerful shotguns. The writers worked to the tune of the fusillade—hundreds of thousands of words, scrawled by hand on yellow foolscap, cut by Hadden, pecked into form by the researchers on their typewriters. Saturday at dusk, the men would head to the Yale Club for dinner, while the women, who were not allowed inside, stayed in the office eating cheese and crackers. After the writers returned, they would scribble late into the morning.

Hadden would read through his staff's work as fast as they could hand it in. To watch Hadden edit was to watch Babe Ruth at bat: a man in his element. He wriggled at his rolltop desk; he thumped and scuffed and uttered oaths. He fidgeted, flexing his arms and grinding his jaw as if limbering up his mind with his muscles. When he concentrated, he locked his face in a scowl. If a story failed to meet his standards, he would scuff his feet and let out a low grumble or chuckle—a kind of symbol of the roars he would have been willing to emit if the story had truly pleased him. As the weekend wore on, he grew intense.

By Sunday, Hadden and his staff would be racing to finish the issue. The writers would compose their stories in longhand on yellow foolscap. The researchers, who had worked until midnight the night before, would type the stories up without stopping for lunch. Manfred Gottfried and Thomas J. C. Martyn would write as much as two thirds of the magazine. Twenty years later, it would take dozens of editors, writers, and researchers to handle the same departments. Wells Root would visit *Time* on his day off from the *World* and race through three or four departments in a single afternoon. "You wrote a story and it was run, with very minor amendments, or thrown in the wastebasket, which was where it belonged," Elizabeth Armstrong recalled. "You had a feeling that you were building something. . . . It was *my* department and no one else was fussing with it."

When a writer finished an article, he would hand his newspaper clippings back to his researcher along with his story. The researcher would check the piece against the documents—marking facts with black pencil if they came from the newspapers, red if they came from a book. If she could not confirm a fact, she would mark it with a green dot. Hadden would not print "greened" lines. The checking system worked so well that it spread throughout the industry. Late on Sunday night, Hadden's secretary would proofread all the copy and give it to Hadden, who would read through it, too. If he caught a mistake, Hadden would leave a comment in the margin: "Nonsense!"

Monday was the hardest day. The staff "worked like hell," one researcher recalled. The writers would update the major stories through the day, first with the morning papers, then with the afternoon papers. Hadden would design the issue and keep tinkering with it. Throughout the day he would assign late-breaking news to writers and ask the girls to research details. Hadden's secretary would check the stories for veracity and grammar, order photographs from the news service, supervise the researchers in checking facts that had earlier been "greened," and call the printer about changes to the issue. Late in the afternoon, she would hand all the copy to Hadden, who would head to the Yale Club.

The girls would rush to stuff the week's research into a couple of suitcases, so they would have the work on hand when questions came up later that night. They would top off the suitcases with notes, phone numbers, *Who's Who*, the *Britannica* index, the almanac, the dictionary, and *Time*'s editorial scrapbooks. The office boys would lug the suitcases down to the street, hail a couple of taxis, and yell upstairs for the girls. Hearing the boys' voices wafting through the windows, the girls would run around frantically, digging for newspaper clippings they had decided to bring along at the last minute. Finally the brewery door would swing open, and the girls would burst out, clutching bags and books, and scramble into the waiting cabs.

The taxis would lurch downtown to a dingy neighborhood near Greenwich Village, where Luce had found a cheap printer in a loft near Tenth Avenue. It was known as "Death Avenue" because freight trains trundled down the middle of the street. A group of men on horseback called the "West Side cowboys" tried, often unsuccessfully, to clear people off the tracks. The typesetting room was dusty and cavernous. Stacks of newsprint lined the walls and rats scampered about the floors. Printer's paste gave the place an acrid aroma, and all was lit by a ghostly blue light.

Scurrying inside, the researchers and office boys would see Hadden looking cheery in his green eyeshade, perhaps with a shot of liquor under his belt. Alongside Hadden would be the writer assigned to late-night duty that week, often Manfred Gottfried. By the end of the work-day, Luce would scramble downtown, too. With everyone assembled, the show could begin. By morning, the staff of four women, three men, and two boys would crunch the news of the week into twenty-six pages.

The staff would gather around Hadden, who usually sat in a tall chair at the head of a stone-topped table by the Linotype. An eatery around the corner would send over a stack of fried egg sandwiches, always soft and runny, and a big growler of coffee. While the office boys cooked the coffee on the lead melter of the Linotype, Hadden would tilt his eyeshade to shield his eyes from the glare of the naked lightbulbs. Grabbing the copy and a bunch of giant pencils, he would tuck a couple of spare nubs behind his ears and begin to circle wrong facts and fire out questions. His growling and snapping reminded John Martin of a "suspicious watchdog."

As he worked with his tiny staff around him, barking questions, compressing words, or eliminating them entirely, Hadden seemed to have found his place in life. Luce thought of him as a showman running a "great game" or an "act," and orchestrating all the writers and the researchers to play their chosen part. The crowd gathered around Hadden couldn't help feeling that they were working with a significant figure. "Hadden had a way of looking directly at you and challenging you with his questions that was almost hypnotic," Agnes Cowap recalled. He was "dynamic—a tremendous character." Luce, she said, was "a quieter, more serious type, less dynamic than Hadden. He gave an impression of integrity and quiet efficiency."

The researchers would cut the long newspaper galleys down to *Time*'s smaller size. Hadden would lay the stories down on the galleys and fit them together. Something would always be too long or too short, and the late-night man would strive to save the most interesting material as he added a line here or took one out there. Hadden would pin the stories to the galleys. Finally he would place the pictures on the page, and the staff would compete to coin captions. Hadden wanted each caption to attract readers with easy laughs, and yet to suggest a hidden meaning.

As deadline neared, people grew manic. The researchers would spin around in search of papers as they struggled to find precise answers to Hadden's constant questions. In desperation, a girl would make a late-night phone call. If she couldn't get an answer, Hadden would have to figure out a way to work around the problem. The late-night man would struggle to beat long sentences into submission or to coin a shorter caption. Hadden and Luce would read over the proofs, often with "considerable argument," one freelancer recalled. It was "helter-skelter confusion," Wells Root said.

By midnight everyone would be covered in ink. For the moment the magazine was finished, but the last job had yet to begin: bringing *Time* up to the minute by adjusting the stories with news from the early morning papers. Hadden would run out to get the bulldog editions. He would return in a jaunty mood, holding giant pots of baked beans. He was always "rather gayer," Joe Kastner recalled. "We never could prove it but we were sure he had found a speakeasy." For the next few hours, subsisting on the baked beans Hadden brought in from that secret place the office boys never found, the little staff would rewrite the magazine for the final time. The fastest typist would type the final copy in makeshift columns. Hadden would read over the work and a researcher would hand it page by page to the operator of the Linotype machine.

The Linotype was seven feet tall, six feet wide, and ungodly loud. Its operator sat at a keyboard in front. As he tapped the keys, the machine would assemble a row of metal molds. The machine would pour hot lead into the imprints, which created a row of type in reverse. The end result would be a heavy metal plate. The operator would hand the plate to the printer's foreman, who would run off thousands of copies. Occasionally late-night newsbreaks would force Hadden to resend a page, and he would beg a researcher to go talk with the burly man. "Hell, you're a girl!" Hadden would say. "They can't kill you!"

On difficult nights, Manfred Gottfried might declare that next week the staff would have to find a new whipping boy; he would not be coming back. Other times, too exhausted to kick up a fuss, he would lie down on a table and sneak a couple of winks while he waited for Hadden to approve the last pages. Early in the morning, Hadden would send the magazine to bed. When the final page went to press, there would be a crazed feeling in the air. Hadden and Gottfried might be dumping printer's pins out the window and yelling, "Heads below!"

It was Tuesday morning at four A.M. Four days later the words the tiny staff had culled and wrote and checked and pecked would inspire conversation in living rooms across the country. In a couple of hours those words would come off the press—hot to the touch. Nobody cared. A writer would call a cab for the office boys, who would lug the research suitcases back to the office. Hadden would take the girls to the train station, the whole group walking down the middle of the street so as not to get mugged. The writers would step out, blinking, dodge across the West Side train tracks, and settle down to a mug of bootleg beer at a waterfront eatery. Hadden would shortly join them. "It's a terrible issue!" he would say. "But that's a whacker of a Channel swim story, anyway."

The men would have a party until dawn broke, sleep through Tuesday, and enjoy a lazy Wednesday away from the office. On their days off, they had no one to play with but one another. Hadden would take trips to Westhampton or go golfing in Westchester. On the ride home, there would be silliness and clowning. Hadden and Larsen might be arm in arm in the back, singing, "Around her neck she wears a yellow ribbon." Nothing could be further away than Thursday, when Hadden would walk into the office and find on his desk a fresh copy of the latest issue, with all the mistakes circled in red by his secretary. "It was like signing your own death warrant," Dorothy McDowell said.

Writing for *Time* was tough but exciting. Veterans of Hadden's staff would remember the long nights as a giant adrenaline rush filled with moments of laughter and friendship—the high point of their lives. "In your young twenties, your late twenties . . . nothing is too much," John

Martin recalled. "This is why people can fight wars in the years between twenty and thirty, I expect. We fought—they weren't wars. Hell! They were ballgames. To quote Hadden, they were ballgames."

The stress and effort, the low pay and long hours, the arguments and deadline pressures all later merged in the minds of old *Time* hands as a part of the magic of the place. Briton Hadden, the writers and researchers agreed, was a prince—although they had many an argument. "Whether you killed yourself or not," Elizabeth Armstrong recalled, "one thing the job was, in the old days, was fun." The final bit of fun arrived on Wednesday morning. That was when the writers hopped out of bed, bellied up to a nearby newsstand, and saw their own words staring back at them.

8

Timestyle

ON TUESDAY, MAY 5, 1925, the city editors of the *Chattanooga News* received an unusual phone call from Robinson's drugstore in the small town of Dayton, Tennessee. "This is F. E. Robinson in Dayton," the man drawled. "I'm chairman of the school board here. We've just arrested a man for teaching evolution."

Having read in the newspaper that the American Civil Liberties Union would pay for the defense of anyone who tested the state's new antievolution law, a group of Dayton boosters had convinced a twenty-four-year-old schoolteacher named John Thomas Scopes to stand trial. After his informal "arrest," Scopes left the drugstore to play a game of tennis. The Democratic warhorse William Jennings Bryan, a firm creationist, volunteered his services to the prosecution, and the renowned criminal defense attorney Clarence Darrow offered to defend Scopes—setting up a showdown between science and religion. More than two hundred reporters traveled to Dayton to witness the "Trial of the Century."

Stephen Vincent Benét dropped by the brewery to find Hadden in a pensive mood, fingering his mustache and pondering biblical apocrypha. Thrilled to have an audience, Hadden immediately began telling Benét that even before Noah had built his ark people were building the first public libraries, at least according to certain Irish antiquarians. "Hell, that's nothing," Hadden went on. Another historian had managed to catalog every single one of the books in Adam's library. "Is that a fact?" Benét asked, trying to be polite but glancing toward the exit. "Absolutely," Hadden said. "Fascinating stuff, isn't it? For instance, did you know that one historian did a lot of figuring and arrived at the conclusion that Adam and Eve were created on a Friday a little after four o'clock in the afternoon?"

As he beat a hasty retreat, Benét realized what made Hadden such an effective editor. The man was interested in everyone and everything. He took a visceral delight in hearing information and in telling it. Just because the vast majority of scientists had accepted the theory of evolution, and Hadden himself was naturally suited to go along with them, that didn't mean he wouldn't take a look at the evidence on the other side. Quite the opposite—Hadden's enchantment with the strangeness of people and their passions led him to take an interest in what was happening in Dayton.

Sitting in the brewery, Hadden and his writers delved through dozens of daily reports filed by newspaper reporters from cities across America. *Time*'s staff read through the procedural motions, the feature stories on the townspeople of Dayton, the commentaries filed by celebrity journalists like H. L. Mencken of the *Baltimore Evening Sun,* and especially the *New York Times,* which provided its readers with daily transcripts of Bryan's long speeches. A typical *Times* story began: "The 'heresy' of evolution was denounced with all the vehemence of which they were capable today by William Jennings Bryan and Attorney General A. T. Stewart in the greatest debate on science and religion in recent years, the feature of the day in the trial of John Thomas Scopes for teaching evolution." The story was sensibly written, but far from engaging.

Time's report summed up a full week's newspaper coverage to compress all the interest of the trial into a single page. The story pictured the beginning of an average day in Dayton as citizens awoke to the screeching of the sawmill. They proceeded down Dayton's main thoroughfare, where men peddled sausages called "hot monkeys." A bookseller beamed as he surveyed his makeshift signs: "HELL AND THE HIGH SCHOOLS," "GOD OR GORILLA." Outside town, hidden beneath some bushes, a crowd of "exhausted Holy Rollers" slept off "a night's orgy of insane gesticulation." But the village policeman was sane and reasonable, and so seemed Judge Raulston, who announced in court, "I want you gentlemen from New York, or any other foreign state, to always remember that you are our guests."

The town baked in the summer sun. Great crowds of "gaunt farmers, their wives in gingham and children in coveralls," bounced toward the courthouse in ancient buggies and automobiles, to be met by "smirking, gabbling cynical minions of the press." William Jennings Bryan walked the streets in shirtsleeves, "an impressive pith helmet covering the bald, pink dome of his head." Entering the drugstore for a sundae, Bryan met "freckle-faced young Teacher Scopes, in his blue shirt and hand-painted bow-tie, grinning with bashful curiosity at passers-by." Later, in court, Darrow toyed with his purple suspenders, chewed a plug of tobacco, and sized up his opposition. "The State of Tennessee has no more right to teach the Bible as the Divine Book than it has the Koran," he proclaimed. "This is as brazen and bold an attempt to destroy liberty as was ever seen in the Middle Ages."

Though Hadden and his writers compiled their report from the newspapers, the story they created amounted to more than the sum of its parts. It illuminated the carnival atmosphere of Dayton as the two Americas, one urban and secular, the other rural and religious, joined a fierce conflict that would continue through the century. *Time* reached mailboxes on July 20, 1925, the day a defiant William Jennings Bryan agreed to take the stand for the prosecution, and the crowd grew so vast that the judge shifted the trial to the courthouse lawn. Shaking his fist at Darrow, Bryan argued that if the Bible said it was so God could stop the earth from moving and Jonah could be swallowed by a whale. Later on the stand, trapped by contradicting statements elicited by Darrow, Bryan allowed that perhaps not everything in the Bible should be taken literally. The crowd howled.

As they read the strange account of Bryan's embarrassment, readers could look to *Time* for an image of the man and the scene. But if they subscribed to the *Literary Digest*, they would find nothing at all on the Scopes case. The *Digest* editors had led off that week's issue with "Building Against Earthquakes," a dense two-page report. "Will Man's indomitable spirit find a way to frustrate even the earthquake's fury?" the article began. "There are indications that such a hope is not in vain."

The next week, three days after Scopes was found guilty, the *Digest* made the trial its lead story. "Amazement seems to be the dominant emotion evoked in Europe, in Great Britain, and in the United States by the now world-famous trial," the magazine reported, "which, in the opinion of William Jennings Bryan, marks the beginning of a 'duel to the death' between evolution and Christianity." Other stories that week included "Struck by Lightning—Yet Saved," a whole page with pictures, and "Sells Silk Stockings to Eskimo Belles," the tale of the Western Hemisphere's northernmost storekeeper, who observed of Inuit women, "Sometimes they wear garters that make the Aurora Borealis ashamed of itself."

Compared to *Time,* the *Digest* lacked an instinct for what made news and for how it should be told. The magazine's stories were long, stacked with quotes, confused and incomplete. The *Digest* lacked a cohesive style. Its sense of humor, uninspired and old-fashioned, fell upon sexism as a last resort. Its days as one of the most popular magazines in the country were numbered. And not only the *Digest* failed to keep pace with *Time.* By 1925, there wasn't an editor in the country, not even Swope himself, who could match Hadden's comprehensive grasp of world news combined with his clear-eyed sense of organization and his ability to weave the facts into a story.

The same week he beat the *Digest* on the Scopes case, Hadden brought his readers a portrait of dark-haired George Gershwin, the twenty-six-year-old composer who had shocked the world with his jazz concerto, *Rhapsody in Blue.* Gershwin's face stared out from the cover. *Time* reported on his rambunctious upbringing in a Brooklyn tenement and his occasional run-ins with the law: "He skinned his knees in the gutters of this street; he nourished himself smearily with its bananas; he broke its dirty windows and eluded its brass-and-blue clothed curator. When he was 13, his mother purchased a piano."

Time also found space that week to discuss the impact of the death of the progressive leader Robert La Follette; to report the percentages, categorized by race, of American women who worked, to name the new member of the President's Tariff Commission. The Foreign News department ran a full account of the debates in the House of Commons, the House of Lords, and the French parliament, as well as an update on the war in Morocco. More stories came in from Italy, Czechoslovakia, and

China. In the back of the magazine, the Science department reported that Dr. Alexander Hamilton Rice had heard a strange noise during his expedition to the Brazilian rain forest. It turned out to be a radio blasting a transmission from KDKA in Pittsburgh.

It was just another week for Hadden and his writers. They rarely failed to print a wide-ranging selection of stories laced with humor and insight. In each issue there would be something to interest the average reader—a book review, a feature on an artist or an opera singer, a piece on a medical invention. Hadden had little competition from other magazine editors since few placed a premium on paring down and organizing all the news and telling it in a lively way. As a result, *Time* became the one publication to help the upwardly mobile American with an interest in the world understand events and trends that the newspapers discussed at random.

People did not have to be educated or wealthy to read *Time,* but they had to be curious about the world around them. Hadden did not hope to reach everyone. He derided tabloid readers as "gum-chewers," mindless masses who chomped for a moment on whatever seemed sweet and easiest to read. When the bodybuilding champion Bernarr Macfadden released a New York tabloid, the *Evening Graphic,* Hadden ridiculed it under the headline "Hardly a Newspaper." The story featured an amusing description of the tabloid readers Hadden hoped never to reach: "Gum-chewers, shop girls, taxi drivers, street sheiks, bummers, idlers took one look, recognized it as their kind of publication, fished out two pennies each, bought, read."

At the same time, Hadden deplored the elitism of editors like Harold Ross, who released the first issue of *The New Yorker* in February of 1925. Ross circulated a prospectus stating that the magazine would not be edited "for the old lady of Dubuque." When Hadden took a look at the first issue, with its front cover of a socialite in a top hat peering through a monocle, he called over his cousin Niven Busch. "Just look at this goddamned magazine," Hadden said. "Goddamn it, the old lady from Dubuque is smarter than they are. Dubuque is a great place and just as sophisticated as New York. There's your angle and make it plain the magazine won't last." Busch invented an old lady from Dubuque and sent her a copy of *The New Yorker.* "The editors of the periodical you forwarded are, I understand, members of a literary clique," she replied. "They should learn that there is no provincialism so blatant as that of the metropolitan who lacks urbanity."

At the center of Hadden's project was a sense of faith in the intelligence of the average person. Hadden believed that even an isolationist American who rarely considered ideas or events outside his small circle would wish to learn about the world if it could be made interesting and relevant to him. Although *Time* had begun by reaching the younger set of upper-class readers who subscribed to *Harper's, Scribner's,* and other "quality" magazines, by 1925 *Time's* readership was expanding to people who simply wished to get the news they could not find in their daily papers. They were turning to *Time* because Hadden made the news fun to read.

Hadden had not set out to create a new style of writing. But faced with the necessity of crunching down all of the week's news into twenty-six pages, he quickly developed a hatred of wasted words and hackneyed expressions. If a writer handed in a story that said "in the nick of time," Hadden would hand it back saying "in time's nick." Taking a second look, he would slash the whole phrase, reasoning, "If the rescue was made, obviously the hero was in time." Fiendishly trimming excess verbiage, Hadden quickly stripped the sentence down, cut extraneous clauses, and used only active verbs. He banned inconclusive words like "alleged" and "reportedly." Heroes in *Time* were never talented; Hadden called them "potent."

Freed of the excess baggage, *Time* ran at a frenetic pace. Politicians hurled oaths and inkstands. Protesters bounded and leapt. Dancers chirped and kicked on the stage. When they grew into starlets, their eyes gleamed and glittered. Newsmen scurried after the starlets, cursed, and exploded their camera flashlights. Surprised by a bold statement, the newsmen went pop-eyed. The world, in *Time,* seemed almost to spin out of orbit.

When Hadden began to toy with the sentence, he opened the door to invention. Writers, inspired, laughed as they tried out effects. Innovations gathered steam as Hadden sanctioned one device or backed off on another. Soon the terse magazine acquired exhibitionist ticks. An article on the circus discussed "Seven Ringlings ringing"; a report on the Vatican noted a "woeful wagging of heads." As Hadden's cousins John Martin and Niven Busch gained Hadden's confidence, they filled the magazine with humor. By the fall of 1925, when the Sport department described the football back Harold "Red" Grange as writhing through "seas of grasping moleskin-flints with a twiddle of his buttocks and a flirt of his shin-bone," Hadden had turned from simplifying the news toward bringing the news to life.

Gradually, Hadden began to act as a modern-day bard who sang to his readers the histories of the kings. Homer was his hero and guide, and Hadden kept a copy of the *Iliad* on his desk at all times. "Under no circumstances is it to be removed from the Editorial Rooms," he wrote on the bookplate. Hadden used an 1873 translation by Theodore Alois Buckley, packed with action and loaded with athletic phrases. He admired battle sentences like "blood-red death and stern fate seized his eyes," as well as colorful expressions, like Agamemnon's comment to the timid Menestheus: "Then it is pleasant to you to eat the roasted meats, and to quaff cups of sweet wine." Hadden underlined his favorite passages and jotted them down inside the front cover. He filled nearly twelve pages with exclamations, oaths to the gods, metaphors, and even uses of the subjunctive tense.

Closely cribbing from the *Iliad,* Hadden gave dash to *Time*'s stories by editing them into Homer's backward syntax. A typical sentence ran: "To Versailles (150 years ago) swarmed empurpled princelings, intent on an implicit mission of state." Hadden also made use of Homer's compound adjectives to create vivid descriptions in few words. Strikers marched through *Time*'s pages, "stern-faced, set-lipped." Railroad billionaires, "bullet-headed, thick-jowled," munched their breakfast bacon. Politicians, "steely-eyed" or "iron-jawed," struck the pose of the *Iliad*'s great statesman, Agamemnon, king of men. Hadden trained his writers to convey force. Readers sped through the magazine.

Hadden had another purpose for Homeric style besides making *Time* easy to read. He wanted his readers to grasp the importance of the people they read about and commit the facts to memory. Since he lacked the space to get too deeply into history and context, Hadden used the Homeric epithet to tell readers what they needed to know about newsmakers in just a few words. Every figure discussed in *Time* had his own tag line, even the "famed poet William Shakespeare." A frustrated reader wrote in to ask what was next—"onetime evangelist Jesus Christ?"

Hadden soon moved from literally defining a news figure to a subtler type of writing. He began to use the Homeric epithet to convey the character and appearance of public figures. When he called the Russian revolutionary Grigory Zinoviev the "bomb boy of Bolshevism," Hadden symbolized the radical's role in creating party doctrine. Most of *Time*'s readers had no idea who Zinoviev was, but they knew about British statesmen like Winston Churchill. Hadden glamorized his portly vigor with the expression "ruddy as a round full moon." Suddenly Churchill stomped onto the American stage, a grand, heroic figure heralded by an operatic theme song. Announced by such sweeping, athletic phrases, newsmakers seemed powerful, glamorous—larger than life. Like the gods of the *Iliad*, they towered above mere mortals.

In imitation of Homer, Hadden portrayed politicians, businessmen, and university presidents not as staid officials but as inspiring heroes and hilarious buffoons. The grand men marched through the world and shook the ground with heavy steps. "See how he bows right and left, this gangling fellow, as lean as a lariat, in the old suit and the cracked shoes," *Time* remarked of the comedian Will Rogers. "His under lip protrudes like the point of a vulgar joke. His jaws move perpetually, up and down, chewing insult, chewing fancy, chewing humor, chewing gum." In the age of black-and-white photographs and silent film, Hadden's energetic portrayals helped readers to imagine newsmakers.

Having placed public figures on a pedestal, Hadden found new narrative possibilities. He could, for instance, knock them down. *Time* published items about politicians fighting on the golf course, losing their swimming trunks in the ocean, and singing lewd songs to their children. While the newspapers printed posed photographs, Hadden realized that a candid picture could be more revealing. For years a startling image of the fascist dictator Benito Mussolini glared at readers from *Time*'s pages. "His eyes rolled with fury," the caption cracked. Even a reader who knew nothing of Mussolini could grasp that Hadden thought he was a no-good guy. If a public figure phoned *Time* to protest, Hadden would chirp, "Cameras cannot lie."

When a newsmaker earned Hadden's ire, he would ask his writers to invent an epithet or a nickname. Hadden picked on oddballs and extremists like the *Evening Graphic* publisher Bernarr Macfadden, who continued to attract ire from Hadden by doctoring photographs and publishing false news. Hadden disapproved of Macfadden's tendency to publish sexually revealing photographs and of his equally sexy instruction to his fans. An early proponent of weight lifting, Macfadden advised his readers to love their bodies. Hadden asked his writers to coin a nickname for his nemesis. Niven Busch came up with "Body Love," a name Macfadden never lived down.

Readers cherished the predictable comfort the epithets provided. When they opened *Time,* they felt a bit like children returning to a favorite storybook. *Time*'s epithets grew more daring by the year: first Hadden took on the mayor of New York, then a few financiers, and finally several senators. *Time* dubbed Senator Henrik Shipstead of Minnesota "the duck-hunting dentist." James Thomas Heflin of Alabama, a rotund racist who occupied entire sessions of the Senate with invective against the "Catholic conspiracy," was known to *Time* readers as "'Tom-Tom' Heflin, who mortally hates and fears the Roman Pope." If *Time* stopped using the epithet, readers would beg to see it again. By showing they understood the joke, they proclaimed their belonging to Hadden's elite circle of the young and urbane.

Far from feeling troubled by the possibility of abusing the power of the pen, Hadden exulted in it. He asked his researchers to comb through reference books in search of public figures' embarrassing middle names. Most people knew of the pioneering automaker William Durant; beginning in 1926, *Time* readers knew him as William Crapo Durant. There was something so intimate about revealing such a small detail. To John Martin it seemed like his cousin was undressing great men "in Macy's window." Middle names, like nicknames and epithets, provided Hadden a coy method of demeaning unsavory characters. Once a writer, confused, asked Hadden what angle to take on a piece about the hated owner of the *Saturday Evening Post.* "Listen," Hadden said. "Do you happen to know what Cyrus Curtis' full name is? It's Cyrus Hermann Kotzschmar Curtis, by God! We can't leave a name like Kotzschmar lying around, can we? Let's find some damned excuse to get it in the magazine."

Time's use of middle names, nicknames, and epithets presented an irony. Hadden, who had spent his life proclaiming his desire to impart only the facts, was impishly influencing his readers' views. At first he tended to impart only character judgments. But there could be no fine line between the personal and the political. When he coined a teasing phrase, Hadden gave himself the power to twist the news by subtly defining a newsmaker in his readers' minds. A sign of *Time*'s slide toward bias emerged as early as 1923 when the magazine referred to the "socialist-sophist Upton Sinclair."

Engrossed in entertaining his readers, Hadden stepped away from his childhood goals of fairness and accuracy. Writing for *Time* was an act of caricature. When Hadden and his writers grew lazy, their epithets and descriptions conveyed only surface features. American politicians had strong chins and straight noses. Brits were dandy and suave, Asians blank-faced and inscrutable. *Time* described one Chinese statesman as "a thick-set, oval-faced Chinaman with eyes like pinpoints of black steel." Hadden's frequent use of racial and national stereotypes revealed the superficiality of his writing style, a style that was itself a form of stereotype—a shorthand capable of illuminating the underlying reality but equally capable of misrepresenting it.

By exalting the newsmaker—a person who mattered simply because he made print—Hadden distorted the news. *Time* glorified great men, and a few women. The powerless made it into Hadden's pages as anonymous members of frightening crowds or in the Miscellany column, where Hadden printed short stories of people hacking each other to bits or being mauled by animals. By focusing on the people in power, *Time* ignored all but the most direct causes for change. Social and economic issues were too difficult to dramatize, and Hadden disdained theory of all kinds. Because *Time* seldom discussed the causes behind events, the magazine often took a superficial view. But Hadden believed people who read *Time* remembered it and learned more in the long run.

Beside his copy of the *Iliad,* Hadden kept two more tools that helped him to bring the news to life: a thesaurus and a small black notebook. Hadden delighted in forceful words and fresh expressions. When he heard one, he pounced. "That's a knockout word," he would say, chuckling and trying it out in various intonations. He would jot the word down in his black notebook and inject it into conversation. Within a few months, he would fill up several notebooks. From time to time he would tear out the pages and pull writers aside to show them his treasured expressions. The writers would inject their stories with Hadden's language and a new phrase would flower in *Time*.

Hadden had a predilection for funny words that led him to print slang and apply archaic words in new contexts. The prince of Monaco was a deep-sea diver, but *Time* called him a "bathysophical enthusiast." Those who supported Prohibition were known as Drys; *Time* called them the "adherents of aridity." One *Time* story on a swimmer trailed by a shark referred to the water as the "pellucid blue." By sprinkling the magazine with a few difficult words, Hadden subtly flattered his readers and invited them to play an ongoing game. Those with large vocabularies could pat themselves on the back, while the rest guffawed at *Time*'s bright boys and looked the word up.

Conservative readers accused *Time* of making a mockery of the English language. That was precisely the point. Hadden liked words that made him laugh. He used "poltroon" for coward, "tatterdemalion" instead of ragamuffin. He called a politician with strong opinions a "bastinado," a reference to the form of torture that involves lashing. Hadden called a university a "musnud," the word for a pillow sat upon by an Asian potentate. The usage was so inventive that the *Oxford English Dictionary* cited it in its later editions. By taking the stiff dignity out of English, Hadden made the news accessible to average Americans, even as he expanded their vocabulary.

Often Hadden toyed with words in order to refine a concept. When an idea or theme emerged from *Time*'s pages, Hadden would issue a word hunt, and the writers would race to find a novel term. Some of the terms they found altered the American lexicon. Seeking a new word to describe an honorary degree, Hadden chose "kudos," the Greek word for magical glory. He later expanded his use of the word to describe any acclaim a person might receive for an achievement. Hadden also employed a clever term for opinion makers. Such men thought themselves to be wise, so he called them by the name of his old Yale prankster group: "pundits." Luce involved himself in Hadden's game by selecting a word to describe a wealthy industrialist. When Commodore Perry opened Japan to the West, he had negotiated with the *taikun,* a general who controlled the country in the name of the emperor. Since then, Americans had often called a person endowed with power but not office a "tycoon." Luce popularized the term by applying it to a business magnate.

Hadden and his writers also invented words in order to save space. The term "news-magazine" had begun as a compound noun. In 1927, when Hadden eliminated the hyphen, he coined a new word for a new type of news medium. Other neologisms proved less successful. A senator from Arkansas would castigate his enemies, often with sarcastic wit. *Time* called him a "sarcastigator," but the term failed to stick. Writers attempting to sound lettered would denote a person's past title or station as "erstwhile." Hadden outlawed that word in favor of "onetime," which remains in use today. Cleverest of all was *Time*'s word for a prominent society figure. At Hotchkiss such a boy was known as a "social light." *Time*'s compression, "socialite," soon entered the dictionary.

Within a few years of founding the magazine, Hadden began to codify his innovations in a stylebook. Toward the end of the stylebook, he wrote two lists, "Forbidden Phrases" and "Famed Phrases," which commanded writers to use certain words often and others never. Under the heading "Unpardonable Offenses," Hadden listed the failure to print a person's nickname. Middle names, he advised, must be included if "little-known," "comical," or otherwise significant. Hadden redrafted the stylebook every few years. This was necessary. A phrase that seemed fresh one year, once copied into the black notebook, could quickly reach hackneyed status.

Hadden never wished to create a single style. He simply hoped to push his writers toward tight, active prose. Five years after *Time*'s founding, G. Bernard Riddle, an Indiana advertising executive, warned *Time* that magazines and even advertisers were copying its "scintillating, crisp" style, and soon it would no longer be original. "Let not Subscriber Riddle, acute, observant, fear for '*Time*'s Typical Style' because he scents plagiarists, pirates, copycats," *Time* replied. "*Time* has created no set, wooden 'style,' which could be aped, but instead strives toward that future medium of expression in which words shall be best fitted to deeds." A few rules never changed. Toward the end of his life, Hadden listed them on the front of his stylebook: "Be specific." "Be impersonal." "Appear to be fair." "Be not redundant." "Reduce to lowest terms." Hadden wrote his favorite last: "You cannot be too obvious."

Having invented a new writing style that made each sentence entertaining and easy to grasp, Hadden and his writers began to toy with the structure of the entire story. Most newspaper writers tried to tell everything in the first one or two paragraphs. By printing the most important facts first, they destroyed the natural narrative of news. Hadden trained his writers to act as if they were novelists. He viewed the whole story, including the headline and caption, as an information package. Some parts of the package provided little information; they grabbed readers, teased them, and encouraged them to move on.

The *Time* story followed a plot line. It opened with a bit of tension: the criminal marking time in his cell on the last day of his life; the teenage sensation waiting in the wings of the Metropolitan Opera as the crowd began to buzz; the swimmer coating her body with grease as she prepared to leap into the ocean. Crisis arose: the appeal was denied; the singer stepped into the spotlight; the swimmer grew faint, buffeted by angry waves. And then, resolution: mounting the gallows, the criminal confessed; romancing the spotlight, the singer burst into an aria; reaching the shore, the swimmer became the first woman to cross the English Channel.

Hadden edited the entire magazine to create a sense of suspense. His headlines never gave up the story; instead they tantalized readers with titles like "Sea of Revolt," "Place of Prodigies," "Flowers Wilt." Opening sentences began at a cosmic level: "Stars twinkle, the moon beams." Or they began at the most minute: "The long Presidential forefinger extended itself." Often the start of a story took the tone of a tale told around a campfire: "Out of Russia, weird and mystic land . . ." A story on Italy would coyly begin with the image of a dog howling and scratching at a spot in the forest floor. Carabinieri would prance by, capes flowing and swords rattling, to discover the object of the dog's intrigue—a murdered government minister. *Time* writers called this style of introduction the "blind lead."

Hadden entranced his readers by giving them a front-row seat at history's stage. Sitting in their cubbyhole of an office, *Time*'s three staff writers dug through the *New York Times* to find the details buried deep within that symbolized the story. When Winston Churchill lost a close election, *Time* described the cigar dropping from his mouth and falling to the floor. When Lenin died, *Time*'s story, "Cold Death," showed the mourners shuffling past his tomb in air so cold that sparrows fell dead from the trees. By skillfully employing such narrative detail, Hadden and his writers managed to paint a word-picture in their readers' heads. In the era before television, no news organization gave people a better feeling of how history looked and sounded.

At times Hadden's writers moved from a novelistic style to that of pure pulp fiction. "A great storm arose. Heaven tipped crazily, the long seas towered and swept by," *Time*'s report on a shipwreck related. "A woman shrieked, seeing the portholes burst. The vessel groaned, feeling downward for her grave on the cold sea-floor. The Black Sea flung its folding mountains on and on toward land and the winter gale hissed a dirge for the works of man." A reader congratulated *Time* for the piece and Hadden took a bow by reprinting it in the Letters column.

The freedom to pluck the choicest news nuggets from several conflicting accounts, interweaving them into one masterful spectacle of delights, led *Time* writers down the road toward fakery. When a *Time* story on a big-game hunt described monkeys swinging from the mangrove trees, an alert subscriber informed *Time*'s editors that swamp trees did not exist in the high plains of Nairobi. But Hadden never prevented his writers from spinning a yarn. When a Mexican cowpuncher saved the daughter of Mexico's president from a runaway bull at a rodeo, *Time* guessed at his thoughts: "Ah, such a daughter. Hair and eyes blacker than a moonless night; a pale, inscrutable, beautiful face from which no amount of contact with the shallow Americanos would erase the stamp of primitive womanhood. There was such a girl once in a bar at Tia Juana, a girl to wring your heart in the dusk."

Drawn to human drama, *Time* had the potential to emphasize the most sensational aspects of the news. Hadden relished train robberies, plane crashes, and knockouts. He filled the magazine with royal processions and often emphasized conflict, a habit made plain by a recurring headline format: "Wells v. Bigelow," "Atheists v. Chaplains," "Fish v. Oyster." Many *Time* stories expressed a ghoulish delight in human suffering. When a hurricane ravaged Miami, *Time* puckishly reported, "People drowned like trapped puppies to the frivolous dirge of tinkling glass." Miami's city manager protested *Time*'s tone. But when the newspapers in Florida were dedicating pages to murder trials, Hadden was bringing his readers news from around the world.

In his effort to break the news down to its fundamentals, to make the people behind the news more memorable, to shock, amuse, and attract new readers, perhaps Hadden oversimplified things a bit. A tight focus on plot, ignoring the historical forces and political conflicts shaping events, made it difficult for the reader to determine why a news event had happened and what was at stake for the parties involved. Hadden's reliance on a small set of narrative techniques made one *Time* story sound much like the next. Heroes and villains strode through the world—raising voices, slamming fists, firing guns. They were portly or wiry, firm-chinned or beady-eyed, mannequins in an endless procession of action.

Time's audience happily read along, picking up true and false impressions, a circumstance that shocked and frightened more sophisticated observers. The media critic Marshall McLuhan later called *Time* a "nursery book in which the reader is slapped and tickled alternately. It is full of predigested pap, spooned out with confidential nudges. The reader is never on his own for an instant, but, as though at his mother's knee, he is provided with the right emotions for everything he hears or sees as the pages turn." But providing readers with emotions was exactly what Hadden tried to do; he wanted them to see and feel the news.

Some readers found *Time* amusing but wished it would explain the significance of events. "Your magazine deals with personalities," a New York reader wrote in a letter to the editor. "I am interested in the forces that make people act. P.S. Please cancel my subscription." But for each reader dissatisfied with Hadden's shallow treatment of serious subjects, another reader admired his frank avowal to impart facts and laughs without heavy moralizing. For each reader who thought *Time* lacked the appropriate background information, another would have turned away if forced to read a sentence more. Anyone could grasp *Time*, but not without effort. Each issue of the magazine arrived packed with information and required curiosity and thought.

The writing style Hadden developed came to be known as Timestyle. Critics focused on the backward locutions, epithets and nicknames, but there was much more to it than that. Hadden inspired his readers with the magic of the news. He captivated them with the personalities behind the news. He hooked them by building suspense and weaving the news into a story line. Taken together, the many stories Hadden told formed an epic tale that brought Americans closer to events than ever before. Hadden helped the nation envision each event as part of a grand and ongoing drama—tragic and comic, momentous and farcical, painful and inspirational. It all added up to a true tale about the way people lived.

With his sharp sense of humor and taste for the ridiculous, Hadden made the perfect spokesman for the hip-flask generation. His terse, upbeat sentences expressed the exuberance of the Jazz Age; his sly wit struck readers as decisively modern. His pose of casual sophistication seemed sensible to war-weary readers who looked upon moral reform with skepticism, while his roguish pose attracted the young. Thus *Time* became their mouthpiece. All the college students who dropped by one Cleveland mother's home talked about *Time*. "Do you realize," she asked, "that you are the paper of the rising generation?"

The elders understood as much. Some worried that Hadden's stylistic revolution augured an abrupt decline in civility and a withering of intellectual standards in public debate. "My chief quarrel with you," Yale president James Rowland Angell wrote Hadden, "is that I get terribly fed up with the apparent forced effort to get rhetorical effect by grammatical inversion, and I tire very much of an under-current of the 'smart Aleck' tone of some of your writers. I dare say that this impatience reflects the inevitable late Victorian age, to which unhappily I am obliged to admit that I belong, and younger readers probably find piquant and stimulating what to me is at times rather nauseating." But Angell added that success itself proved Hadden's instincts right.

As *Time*'s circulation ticked upward, letters to the editor poured into the office. Several readers attacked *Time*'s "catty" tone, its "air of 'smarty' self-consciousness." One reader wrote, "I am an even-tempered man, but, by God, when I read such tripe, I swear a blue streak and kick my favorite dog." Others begged Hadden to stop writing backward before he destroyed the English language. "Why do you prefer going around Robin Hood's barn every trip instead of in the front door?" asked a reader from El Paso.

For each reader disgusted by *Time*'s violations of convention, another thanked *Time* for enlivening serious topics. One reader complimented *Time*'s "unequaled faculty for condensing a great bulk of news into a few lucid paragraphs. And your knack for puncturing bull bladders by clever and oblique hits and subtle passes adds spice to your splendid talent." Another praised *Time*'s "nonchalant and indifferent manner of treating a man's religion as if you are referring to his ham and eggs of the previous breakfast." A third thanked *Time* for serving up "a mental cocktail."

Amused by the piles of letters he kept receiving at the office, Hadden decided to print a batch. Letters became the magazine's most entertaining department, a strange brew of outrage and delight. Cranks wrote in to catch *Time* making mistakes. Hadden printed the letters under nonchalant headlines, and the next week new cranks wrote in to attack the old ones. Once a letter writer returned from vacation to find that *Time*'s readers had ganged up on him for a grammatical error. He promptly wrote a second screed, which Hadden printed under the mocking title "Home Again." Hadden told his writers he wanted *Time* to resemble a Roman circus: there should always be five fights going on at once.

Many of the letters Hadden printed made it clear that people were reaching up to *Time*. The magazine encouraged them to learn about places they had never lived, ideas they had not yet grasped, phrases they had not yet mastered. "*Time* is the most radical, most conservative, most damnable, most altruistic, most agnostic, most religious, most international, most national, most communistic, most democratic, most social, most socialistic, most hated, most lovable, most suppressive and most newsy magazine published," one such reader averred. "Thereby it is self defense that I hand you herewith two years' extension to my subscription."

Hadden had not invented Timestyle alone, but he was the moving spirit. Writers coined words and phrases. Hadden culled the results into a coherent whole. It was his voice that spoke forcefully through each page. Certainly Hadden could not have created *Time* and made it popular without a strong partner to help manage business affairs. But without Hadden there would have been no magazine. "Luce is the smartest man I ever knew, but Hadden had the real editorial genius," Luce's secretary, Katherine Abrams, said. "He was warm and he was human and he had what Luce lacks, an instinct for people."

Reading *Time,* Hadden's old Hotchkiss classmates recalled his swift tongue and chuckled over the public figures getting the Hadden treatment. Hadden's friends detected his attitudes in the magazine, they recognized his fascination with people, and they heard the inflections of his voice. "Hadden talked like what people thought Timestyle was," one writer said. Or, as Cully Sudler later put it, "Brit *was* Timestyle." It was Timestyle that made *Time* popular nationwide, and therefore it was Hadden who made *Time* a success. "I don't think Luce could have done it," John Martin later reflected. "It took a unique, funny, bizarre character like Hadden to create this funny thing."

In only a few years, Hadden had transformed journalism into something new and ushered reporting into the world of national entertainment. To be sure, he had built upon the work of others, just as his own work would inspire much to come. But of all the journalistic stylists, Hadden was the most revolutionary. Had he never created Timestyle, reporters doubtless would have sharpened their prose. But perhaps no editor could have touched on such a wide range of subjects with such facility and wit, or cast such a precise focus on the personalities in the news, or cemented such a firm bond between a news organization and a nation. It took a genius to do that.

9

Burning Both Ends

IN JUNE OF 1925, the *Boston Globe* printed a long story on the group of "boys" transforming the world of journalism. The caption under Hadden's picture read: "Who Realized that Busy Men Would Appreciate Reading a Magazine of Skillfully Formed Synopses." Luce's face, printed below Hadden's, was captioned: "Another One of the Organizers of *Time*."

Those within the company knew Luce was more than an organizer; he was a partner in *Time*'s creation. But they thought of him as a publisher rather than as an editor. Some writers never approached Luce except to shake a fist at him and demand a late paycheck. Once Niven Busch, who was always running short of cash, threatened to punch Luce in the nose if he didn't reimburse Busch for some expenses Luce had taken his time approving. "You can't do that," Hadden advised his cousin. "If you hit Luce, you might hurt him. I don't want you to hurt Luce. I need him."

Hadden and Luce often shouted at each other in front of their staff. "They used to fight bitter," Wells Root recalled. "If you hadn't worked with them and known them well, you would bet that they were going to tear each other's heads off." The next moment they would be pals again, lunching at the Yale Club, restlessly waving their napkins in the air to attract the waiter's attention. When they talked about business, Hadden barking out ideas and Luce coolly analyzing them, *Time*'s founders formed a fascinating contrast—as Manfred Gottfried put it, a "strange and wonderful pair."

To all it was clear that Hadden and Luce were deeply devoted to one another. They remained inextricably linked since each provided the ultimate test of the other's creative process. "I once asked Luce why they argued all the time," his secretary, Katherine Abrams, said. "Luce said that was the wonderful thing about it. Hadden was an awfully hard guy to convince. Whenever Luce had an idea, he would first try it out on Hadden. If he could finally convince Hadden, then he knew his idea was good."

Because Hadden so rarely revealed his inner feelings, Luce never quite knew where he stood with his partner. Luce desperately wished to find out what Hadden thought of him, and occasionally Luce would ask their mutual friends if Hadden had ever dropped a hint. Finally one friend passed along the single comment Hadden repeatedly made about the unusual bond. "It's like a race," he would say. "Luce is the best competition I ever had. No matter how hard I run, Luce is always there."

It was a strange kind of tribute, based more on respect and strife than liking and support, but it was the highest compliment Hadden could ever give. Easily bored, he thrived on competition and argument. Luce was the only man Hadden ever knew who could consistently satisfy his need for a challenge. Luce took the comment to heart. "If anyone else had said that, I might well have resented the implication that the best I could do was to keep up with him," he said decades later. "Coming from Hadden, I regarded it, and still regard it, as the highest compliment I have ever received."

But it was Hadden who made most of the decisions at *Time*. He was the "original," as Luce and others called him, and he let no one forget it. Hadden not only respected Luce, he deeply admired him. "He's a business genius!" Hadden would say. But Luce didn't want to be a business genius; he wanted to share in editing the magazine, and he wanted to have an equal say in the company's affairs. Since *Time*'s founding, Luce, who disliked the bustle and estrangement of New York life, had several times suggested moving the magazine to another city. He even went to Washington to negotiate with printers. But Luce eventually agreed with Hadden that the organization remained too young and rickety to be uprooted. The staff stayed in New York, and Luce continued to feel that Hadden's voice counted most.

It agonized Luce that he wasn't much respected in the office. "Everyone who knew Briton Hadden loved him," Roy Larsen's secretary, Polly Groves, recalled. "You couldn't love Henry Luce. You admired him, but you couldn't love him." Beneath the cool exterior, Luce dreaded the condescension of Hadden's cousins and the quiet forbearance of secretaries who politely waited as Luce stuttered through dictation. Luce blamed himself for failing to excel at the verbal interplay his coworkers prized. Once Thomas J. C. Martyn's wife traipsed through the office in an afternoon gown, smoking a cigarette and saying to the girls, "Oh, come, don't tell me you work!" Luce would have liked to put her down, but his tongue was tied. "Oh dash it," he wrote Lila. "I wish I weren't a second-rate man."

The lingering asymmetry in Luce's partnership with Hadden began to contribute to a creeping sense of animus. It pained Luce more than he let on that Hadden did not seem to respect the importance of the business side. Once *Time*'s founders were in the middle of a meeting when their acquaintance Stanley Rinehart called to place an advertisement for Doubleday, Page, the company that helped put *Time* on its feet. Failing to recognize Rinehart's voice, Hadden shouted that the office was closed and slammed down the phone—an act that lost *Time* the account for a while. Luce later claimed that when he took a turn as editor he would return to his desk to find the company in disarray. "Hadden was downright allergic to business," Manfred Gottfried said. "On occasion, when he was expected to take care of business matters, I believe he plain goofed off."

Luce believed he could improve the magazine if he ever got hold of it for more than a week. Although Hadden printed exceptional writing, he had some notable blind spots, particularly in Foreign News. Hadden's disregard and occasional contempt for business and his frequent recourse to humor made Luce think of his partner as reckless. Luce recognized Hadden's brilliance, but he thought Hadden lacked an understanding of the dollar and a sense of limits—especially when he attacked public figures. Luce admired public figures. He wanted to be one, and he thought Hadden was endangering the chance of that happening. Luce believed Hadden took unnecessary risks.

A few times a year, Luce would talk Hadden into trading jobs for a week. Luce would tell Katherine Abrams to keep an eye on Hadden and make sure he didn't spend all the money. Dorothy McDowell would keep an eye on Luce's trash because he had a habit of throwing copy away by mistake. Luce found Hadden's editorial sanctum to be a strange and brutal place. One Sunday Luce was taking a turn at editing when Niven Busch came by to do some writing. Finding the door locked and the elevator man asleep, Busch grabbed a spoiled turnip from the street and threw it at the upstairs window. The turnip broke through the window and hit Luce in the back of the head. The office girls jumped and rushed to his aid. "Are you hurt, Mr. Luce?" they asked. "I think so," he said, but when they picked the bits of glass off him they found he had not been hurt at all.

Gradually, the writers and researchers discovered that Luce was a talented editor—not as creative as Hadden but brilliant in his own way. Luce had an organized mind and a talent for performing surgery on a story. Even his hands moved like a surgeon's, with sharp slashes of the fingers, whereas Hadden swung his whole arm through the page. "Luce was the best pencil editor I ever saw," Dorothy McDowell recalled. "I never saw a man who could so make something out of a disjointed, poorly organized thing. . . . He was not as good an idea man as Brit, but he sure could operate on a manuscript." Nevertheless, Luce's chances to edit were few. Hadden would shortly send Luce's secretary a note, asking her to confiscate the editorial files on Luce's desk and send them over to Hadden, who would pick up his regular duties the following week.

At Yale, where students believed few women could ever match the intensity of the bonds formed inside the society tombs, Hadden and Luce seemed to have reached the heights of male friendship. But a boyish understanding sealed by competitive ritual was apt to be supplanted by more supportive relationships with women. Luce began to grow beyond Hadden as he settled into married life.

Lila's kindness and attentiveness provided Luce a welcome respite from his days at the office. Feeling that he had a home for the first time since he had left Weifang for boarding school, Luce reveled in having a woman attuned to his needs. When Lila went to Massachusetts to vacation with her mother, Luce kept her informed of every mundane detail of his welfare. "Huge supper," he wrote. "Chicken, by gosh, all to meself." Lila would be pleased to hear her husband was getting by without her, and Luce left her no doubt that he valued her. "Am very ineloquent but continually in the thought of you, my darling," he closed. "Not only do I adore you; I depend on you for everything."

The Luces had learned of love through English sonnets and popular songs. Their letters and poems to each other expressed a placid innocence. "On the branched wings of love I ride, / For thou dost every kind of love ignite," Lila wrote her husband in one poem. Sex was a simple business. Luce later said he "simply did it and then rolled over and thought about *Time*." On August 20, 1924, Lila wrote the smallest of cursive sentences in her private diary: *"Madame, je suis en train de faire un enfant!"*

By 1925, with *Time* barely in the black for the first time and Lila expecting her child in the early spring, Luce felt happier than ever before. On his day off, Luce delighted in staying home and reading or taking Lila to the museum. Twice a month on Wednesday nights, the Luces would host small dinner parties. They invited men from *Time*, women from Spence, people Luce wanted to question on topics of interest, and others who impressed him for their cleverness. Luce drove the conversation. If small talk came up, he would appear disgusted for a moment, then quickly change the subject. At first the Luces served only ginger ale since neither of them liked to drink. But they soon realized such occasions demanded spirits and found themselves getting to know the bootlegger. "We were merry," Lila recalled.

Lila's skills as a hostess and dancer—she was especially gifted at the Viennese waltz—raised Luce's personal standing among Manhattan's social elite. Judge Robert L. Luce, a distant cousin and supporter of *Time*, playfully acknowledged his younger relation's rise in an admiring poem for the couple:

> *Who is the man who holds the reins,*
> *Where Wealth or Fashion entertains,*
> *And needs no funds but just his brains?*
> *Why, Harry.*

Judge Luce titled the poem "At the Tomb of Napoleon," a reference to the place where the young couple had begun their romance. He dedicated the poem to Luce, whom he called Napoleon's "spiritual successor."

Few men at *Time* felt so impressed by Luce's Napoleonic drive for power and influence. Hadden tended to hire self-assured and expressive people, and wealthy ones. Working alongside Luce, such men sensed in him a limitless drive, inspired by a basic neediness and social uncertainty. They couldn't help laughing at Luce when they had the chance, especially since he often frustrated them by winning so handily in the end. "Harry went around as far as he could git," John Martin said years later, tightly grasping the one advantage he had left. "Those of us who never had this what you might call vacuum in our background, or inferiority in our social ceiling, never seemed to need to find the rungs on the social ladder the way he did."

Hadden still socialized with the Luces from time to time. Lila appreciated Hadden's spontaneity and in March of 1925 she noted in her diary that she had gone to an "impromptu theatre party of Brit's." Despite their occasional moments of closeness, the childhood rivals were growing apart. While Luce was growing into adult concerns and acquiring a new sense of self-worth, Hadden seemed to be escaping further into the refuge of a lingering adolescence. "Harry at all times was thinking about the outer world, where Hadden wasn't," John Martin recalled. "Luce was much more instinctively a social animal than Hadden. Hadden was pretty damn antisocial, really."

After the emotionally draining breakup with Deborah Douglas, Hadden became entangled in several flirtations with close friends. Many thought of Hadden as a genius, and some seemed to love him. Hadden toyed with some and acted awkwardly around others, always with the same result. The flirtation would wind down, replaced by a platonic friendship. "With his small-boy quality, he engaged the sympathy of almost every woman," Manfred Gottfried later wrote. "However, too much of the quality apparently prevented them from thinking about him as a husband. The gals he wanted would not marry him. I gather he became rather frustrated on this score."

The debutantes on the New York party circuit had a tendency to throw themselves at Hadden, who would show up at parties looking like the conventional Yale suitor, then shock the society girls by making odd and unpredictable answers to their questions—an attempt, it almost seemed, to cut off the possibility of a conversation. The girls, starved for eccentricity of any kind, would want to get closer to this strange and mysterious figure. Hadden would pick a debutante from the crowd, shower her with affection for a few weeks, then cut her off, leaving her shocked and wounded.

Finally he began to date another *Time* researcher, Elizabeth Brown. A blue-eyed brunette, she had grown up near Hadden in Brooklyn Heights, attending Packer, the sister school to Poly. She would later model sporting fashions for Abercrombie & Fitch. Brown seemed to be a fine match, but Hadden told his cousins that he didn't want to marry yet. He feared a girl might try to blackmail him down the aisle. "He was even more terrified among respectable women than whores," Niven Busch recalled. "He thought of women as calculating and cynical and behaved in the same fashion toward them." Having given his heart once only to be disappointed, Hadden now seemed frightened of betrayal. He often said to Busch of women, "You can't trust them."

It seemed unusual that such a good-looking, muscular man could outstrip the highest expectations of success yet fail to find a girl to marry. It seemed more unusual that a virtual sex object, eagerly approached by dozens of girls at parties and mooned over by more in the office, would become so saddened by his first breakup that he would refuse to take subsequent girlfriends seriously. Hadden was always quite secretive about his love life, and his failure to settle down caused a great deal of speculation from people who knew or wrote about him. "Brit . . . was the most manly guy on earth," Cully Sudler recalled. "And we always used to speculate if any girl would ever get Brit." Twenty years after Hadden's death, the nature of that speculation had changed. People began to wonder whether Hadden was gay.

The speculation upset Roy Larsen and other close friends of Hadden's, who had seen him date numerous girls and preferred to think he eventually would have married. They did not want to talk about the issue in the open, and so it lingered on. In 1964, Luce assigned Robert T. Elson, his former London bureau chief, to write a history of the company. When Elson interviewed most of Hadden's inner circle of friends, several of them brought up Hadden's sex life. "Hadden was not a woman's man, and he paid no attention to women until much later in his life," John Martin told Elson. "If you want a digression on Hadden's sex life, I know all about it. I don't know whether this comes into the book or not. I think some part of it should."

But Elson did not wish to discuss Hadden's sexuality. He worried that if he dug too deeply he might discover something he did not want to know. "Hadden was by no means a homo," Elson told Martin when they met to discuss *Time*'s history three months later. "In our day that never came up. Now that comes up all the time." "That's it," Martin agreed. "It comes up all the time." Elson expunged the record by deleting portions of the interview transcripts that dealt with Hadden's sexuality. As for the tapes themselves, the company's archivists threw them away.

After the breakup with Deborah Douglas, Hadden began to drink more often. A few drinks helped him break past his shyness and forget his troubles. For a man who loved to skirt the rules, drinking held the attraction of being illegal. A night out was always an adventure: the speakeasies spread through Manhattan, with their codes and customs, rotgut moonshines and exotic cocktails, were like foreign countries to explore.

Hadden knew where to find the speakeasies on Second and Third Avenues. He knew their secret knocks and code words, and when he walked through the door the owners would greet him by name. "When thoroughly enjoying himself he was often thoroughly taciturn," Niven Busch recalled. "He would pour down one stiff drink after another, showing little effects. Narrowing his eyes and flexing his jaw muscles, he would sit in a corner, winking and glaring around. Sometimes it would turn out later he thought some woman particularly attractive. Yet his liking would never be apparent at the time."

Hadden's cousin John Martin was also turning into a heavy drinker, as was Hadden's brother, Crowell. None of them lacked for drinking companions. "In those days," Elizabeth Armstrong would recall, "everybody went to parties and everybody had too much to drink." Hadden was not a "bad drunk." He didn't cause scenes or act cruelly toward others. But considering how hard he worked during the day, his friends considered his nightlife reckless. "I worried about his abusing his physique so—drinking much more than he needed, because he was very entertaining with much less," Luce's sister Elisabeth recalled.

"And you just had a feeling that he was just burning that candle much too hard. It burnt both ends."

In addition to the heavy drinking, Hadden routinely engaged in other habits that couldn't fail to take a toll on his health. Often he would go for long stretches without eating. When he finally stopped for a meal, he would order double portions of everything, slice his food up hastily, and devour it until he felt glutted. He averaged five hours of sleep a night, seven if he needed a long rest. His body began to show the stress. His hair, like Luce's, was sparse in front. His face, once chiseled, began to look bloated. His cheeks bulged, making his eyes appear hooded and squinty. He grew stocky—the result of too many four-hotdog dinners at the ballpark, too many rounds of whiskey at night. "He worked too hard," Manfred Gottfried said. "His nerves began to frazzle—or perhaps they had always been frazzled."

The tension between *Time*'s founders worsened as they realized that they had made a potentially fatal misjudgment. Encouraged by the quick growth of 1924, when Larsen managed to double the magazine's circulation from 35,000 to 70,000 readers, Hadden and Luce had set the goal of reaching 110,000 people by January of 1926. In the previous year, they had managed to expand without spending additional money. But as *Time*'s circulation rose in 1925, they began spending more to print the magazine and mail promotion circulars to potential new readers. In the first four months of 1925, the postage costs for these efforts alone rose to more than $24,000. *Time*'s total promotion budget climbed to more than $45,000, an increase of more than $7,000 over the previous year. The high costs of the sudden expansion rapidly depleted the company's cash reserves.

By the end of the winter, the young publishers realized they would soon be out of capital. They decided they would have no choice but to refinance the company by selling more stock to investors. It would be a risky move, diluting their position as majority stockholders of the voting shares, and bearing the potential to spread ugly rumors of impending demise throughout the industry. But if they didn't issue more stock, the company would die. Quietly, Hadden and Luce put together a stock issue. They approached their original investors privately so as not to arouse public suspicion that Time Inc. lacked sufficient funds. Together they paid a call on Mrs. Harkness, who immediately thrust a check for $25,000 into their hands. Luce's secretary would never forget the look of wonderment on his face when he came back from the meeting. "She likes me!" he exclaimed.

The refinancing brought Time Inc. additional capital of $64,125. But Luce wasn't entirely satisfied. He continued to think New York was the wrong place to print *Time*: too expensive and too far from the burgeoning national audience. Although *Time* went out Tuesday morning for weekend arrival, the magazine had a long way to travel. In the Northeast, *Time* often arrived in mailboxes the following Monday—sometimes on Tuesday or Wednesday. In the Midwest and West, by the time the magazine arrived the date on its cover had often passed, and much of the information inside the magazine was nearly two weeks old. Such slow delivery could cripple a magazine that purported to deliver the news.

The young publishers knew they would speed up *Time*'s delivery by several days if they could somehow manage to get the magazine classified as a newspaper. While magazines traveled second class, the newspapers traveled as quickly as first-class mail in special sacks labeled "Newspapers." *Time* contained more news than the average paper. Its case to be classified as one improved in January of 1924 when Postmaster General Harry S. New issued Order No. 99, defining newspapers as publications in which "the leading and major feature is the dissemination of timely news of interest to the general public, whether published daily or weekly." Certainly *Time* met that definition. In February of 1924, Roy Larsen sent the postmaster of New York a letter petitioning for the status of a newspaper. But the New York office submitted the proposal to Washington, D.C., without offering an endorsement. The Postmaster General turned down *Time*'s request within two weeks.

As Hadden and Luce began the difficult climb toward a circulation of a hundred thousand, they began attracting more readers from the Midwestern and Western states. Dozens of subscribers wrote in to thank *Time* for making them feel better informed than ever before. Dozens more complained of how belatedly the magazine materialized each week. "My copy has not yet arrived," wrote Charles H. Titus from far-off Walla Walla, Washington. "I would appreciate having it regularly as it contains material invaluable to me in my work."

Luce believed he could solve *Time*'s delivery problems and improve the corporation's financial position by moving the office to a central distribution point. In the Midwest, Time Inc. could afford a better printing arrangement and a larger office, and the magazine would reach most readers several days sooner. While the New York post office would continue to pay little attention to *Time*, in a smaller city Luce and Larsen might be able to arrange better treatment. Luce liked the idea of living somewhere besides New York. Ever since his days at Hotchkiss, he had dreamed of having an American town to call his own. Perhaps Luce discussed the idea with Hadden. No one recalled his doing so.

In March of 1925, Hadden abruptly announced to Luce that he was going on vacation. Hadden's girlfriend, Elizabeth Brown, was leaving for Paris. Hadden would meet her there. Brown had big hopes for their time together. She and Hadden were intimate, and she hoped Hadden would propose to her. Hadden, nervous perhaps, decided he needed a companion on his venture; he asked Roy Larsen to come along. Shocked, Luce worried about running *Time* single-handed—just as his wife was preparing to deliver her baby.

On Friday, March 13, 1925, Hadden joined the Luces for dinner. They split a couple of lobsters, talked about the old days in the Yale reserves, and discussed Hadden's upcoming trip. "Very gay," Lila wrote in her diary. The newspapers that day reported that the Chinese Nationalist revolutionary Sun Yat-sen had died. On Sunday, Luce arrived at the office to help edit the next issue. He soon discovered that an office boy had misfiled the press clippings on Sun, and Hadden had forgotten about the story. Luce raced into the editorial chamber and demanded to know how the father of modern China could die and *Time* would have nothing to say about it. Summoning up her courage, Elizabeth Armstrong stepped up to take the blame for the mistake and offer an apology. "Sorry!" Luce yelled. "This is a matter of her being fired."

Hadden covered Sun's death in the March 23 issue, and Luce backed off on his threat. But tensions were brewing at *Time*. As he prepared to leave town, Larsen sent renewal letters to subscribers and a trial mailing to potential subscribers. The returns on both came in unexpectedly low. With advertising revenues failing to pick up, Luce continued to believe Time Inc.'s financial situation looked grim. The research staff was in disarray since Hadden had just hired an unemployed actress he had met at a party. Nobody told her what to do, and for a few weeks she stayed on, useless, as Hadden begged Dorothy McDowell to fire his friend. Finally McDowell capitulated. Hadden's last memorandum said, "Do you mind waiting until I get on the boat?"

On his last day, Hadden installed Manfred Gottfried in the editor's seat. "See that Luce doesn't meddle," Hadden instructed. He left Dorothy McDowell and Elizabeth Armstrong with dozens of ideas and tips. "I won't have reached the Statue of Liberty before Harry Luce is trying to break down the staff," Hadden said. "Don't you let him." He left for Le Havre on the SS *Paris*. A few minutes later, Luce called in McDowell. "We've got to cut down on the staff," he said. "We only need two researchers." McDowell replied that she and Armstrong would be the ones to leave; they certainly wouldn't stay and do the whole job alone. Luce's face flushed. "We'll say no more about it," he said.

On board the *Paris*, Hadden and Larsen discovered that they had become public figures. Though they slept in second class to save funds, they spent most of the trip in first class attending a series of parties. When the boat neared France, they decided they would have to repay their new friends by hosting a party of their own. By the time the boat reached shore, Hadden and Larsen had seventeen cents between them. They continued to party on credit and at sunrise checked into the Hotel Louvois. Just before turning in, Hadden wired Luce. He asked for the transfer of $1,500 in Time Inc. funds.

Hadden picked an unfortunate time to send Luce his request. The toilets in the women's bathroom had recently clogged and overflowed, flooding the floor and staining the furniture in the store below. When the store threatened to sue *Time*, Luce began to worry about losing thousands of dollars in fines. His mood worsened on April 30, 1925, when he received the company's latest financial statements from John H. Schnackenberg & Associates, an auditor on Madison Avenue. There it was in red ink: Time Inc. had lost $1,958.84 over the previous four months. The company had subscription revenue in the bank and new capital to draw upon. But it could not operate at a loss forever. Something had to be done.

Suddenly, Luce decided to fix Time Inc.'s financial problems once and for all by moving the company to the Midwest. While Hadden was abroad, Luce traveled to Cleveland and solicited an offer from the industrial printer John Penton. Estimating that *Time* could save twenty thousand dollars a year by printing off Penton's press, Luce signed a contract with Penton and rented office space in his building. When Larsen returned from Europe before Hadden, Luce convinced his circulation manager to support the move. Without alerting the board of directors, Luce set up a separate corporation, Time Inc. of Ohio.

In Paris, Hadden took a tour of the French sewers with a couple of American girls. After a night out, he visited the Chambre des Députés, where an important debate was underway. "He slept soundly," a friend recalled. It wasn't long before Elizabeth Brown went home to quit her job at *Time*. She later said she had wanted to marry Hadden, but he had broken things off.

Hadden trod on to England, Austria, and Czechoslovakia, where he met President Masaryk, then rode through town in the president's private motorcar. "Received salutes and hat-doffings all the way," Hadden wrote his mother. When he came home, the burden of two years' work seemed to have lifted from Hadden's shoulders. He bounded to his desk and let out a whoop. "Gee, that's great," he said, waving the change from a twenty-dollar bill his secretary had left on his desk. "That's all the money I have in the world."

Then he found out what Luce had done in his absence. Estranged more than ever, the childhood rivals went to the Allerton House, a bachelor hotel on Thirty-ninth Street, where they argued it out away from their staff. Hadden felt it would do *Time* irreparable harm to be removed from the nerve center of New York. But that wasn't what injured him most deeply. It shocked Hadden that Luce could make such a large decision without contacting Hadden first. Neither had done that to the other before, and Luce's action struck a severe blow to their partnership.

In conversations with the rest of the staff, Hadden defended his partner's judgment by asserting that the economies in the move were justified. But Hadden was deeply distraught by Luce's betrayal. His emotions were shaken, and at times they washed over him. Hadden knew Cleveland was far removed from the advertising executives on Madison Avenue and all but devoid of news sources. As the advertising manager, Robert L. Johnson, protested, "You can't rewrite the Cleveland *Plain Dealer*." Johnson and Hadden argued for hours about the move, with Hadden vehemently defending a decision he secretly did not support. Finally Johnson tried to walk out. Hadden grabbed him by the scruff of the neck and whipped him around. Shaking his fist in his friend's face, Hadden growled, "If you ever agree with me when you don't really agree with me, I'll kill you!"

Hadden and Luce agreed to move to Cleveland by the end of August. The decision precipitated a massive breakup. The advertising staff stayed behind in New York and set up an office with the *Saturday Review* editors, who shortly parted ways with *Time*. The only researcher who agreed to make the move was Ruth Flint, who had a crush on Hadden. Joe Kastner, the redheaded office boy, desperately hoped to remain with *Time*. One morning Hadden pointed his cane at Kastner and said, "Joe, you come to Cleveland and we'll pay you twenty-five dollars." Kastner decided to stay in New York, but he later went on to Yale and came back to the company as an editor. Hadden raised his salary for the last two weeks and got him a job as a copyboy on the *World*. John Martin also took a desk at the *World*, where he would serve as *Time*'s one-man New York bureau, a job that consisted of reading through the *New York Times* and sending his rewrites to Hadden.

The move left *Time* without a Foreign News editor once again. Thomas J. C. Martyn had a young family to feed and he was incensed when Hadden and Luce refused to pay his moving expenses. Martyn quit and sold his five hundred shares to *Time*'s founders—a deal that cost him a fortune. Though Martyn remained close to Hadden, he grew increasingly bitter toward Luce in the next several years. In 1933, Martyn would launch *Newsweek*, saying he hoped to "run Harry Luce out of business."

The rest of the staff, from the founders down to Luce's loyal secretary, would have to move over a single weekend. Since they couldn't afford to pay for moving expenses, Hadden and Luce tacked a letter to the wall announcing that everyone was fired. Those who made it to Cleveland would be hired back. Luce sent his wife and son to Chicago, where they would stay for a few months while he found a new home. Hadden bought an old Chevrolet to make the trip west. Just before leaving town, he drove by the corner of Forty-second Street and Fifth Avenue. Some day soon, he promised his auto, they would return to that very corner and rejoin civilization.

10

Hammer and Tongs

THE STAFF SCRAMBLED WEST and checked into the musty boarding-houses lining Euclid Avenue, a loud, muscular road crisscrossed by trolleys and choked by exhaust. Cleveland's central thoroughfare was once known as "Millionaires' Row." But the city barons had long since left the four-mile stretch of shady lawns lined by Italian palazzos, French chateaus, and Romanesque revival castles. Now half the houses were torn down. The rest were caked in soot and overshadowed by construction cranes and steel-girded buildings. Cars ensnared the street in traffic and drowned voices in honking horns.

Nestled on the southern shore of Lake Erie at the cross section of east and west, Cleveland was naturally positioned to become an industrial powerhouse. During the Gilded Age, the city had earned a name as the center of the iron ore industry, the hometown of Rockefeller, and the birthplace of Standard Oil. Since then, Cleveland had grown into a center of manufacturing where car and plane parts were made, and a national hub of commerce where the great ships and trains passed through, leaving profits in their wake. The city had doubled in size since the Great War as hundreds of thousands of Southern share-croppers and Eastern European immigrants arrived in search of jobs.

The old families who had built Cleveland were leaving the city to build suburbs. In Shaker Heights and Cleveland Heights, the upper class maintained a tight-knit community much like that of the Gilded Age. Though not as powerful as before, they remained a force to be reckoned with in Republican politics. The Western Reserve families, descendants of the original settlers who had come to Cleveland from Connecticut, eagerly welcomed Yale men—especially Bonesmen. Among Cleveland's upper class, a particularly good time meant lunch at the club followed by a trip to the sauna, where bloated old men lay festooned in white-towel cocoons. Social rounds to the opera or the orchestra were dictated by habit, lubricated by courtesy, and deadened by a sense of propriety. "It was Luce's idea of Heaven," one *Time* editor later wrote. "It was Hadden's idea of Hell."

Luce envisioned himself quietly raising a family and becoming a prominent local businessman. He picked an apartment by the old Lake View Cemetery, not far from Shaker Heights. Lila painted the master bedroom pink, stenciled flowers over the wainscoting, and created the perfect bedroom for the baby. The Luces christened their child with the dynastic name of Henry Luce III. Luce proudly reflected to his parents that the boy already had the bland sense of humor of a British earl. "Well, I think all my efforts are now centered around a vision of you and me having a good time for a mighty long time sometime," he wrote Lila. "Of course one has visions of a more (perhaps) Lewie nature. One imagines oneself famous. One even imagines oneself powerful."

Hadden bridled against Cleveland's small-town atmosphere and worried about its effects on *Time*. He couldn't find any good writers in Cleveland, and he couldn't convince many to leave New York. Having turned down one girl who had flunked his current events test, he soon found himself sending her a second wire: "COME TO WORK." When the singer Libby Holman came to town, Hadden pressed her into service. After a few minutes she yelled, "The hell with all this!" She threw *Who's Who* at Hadden's office. Just at that moment Hadden opened the door and caught the book square in the chest. He fell onto his back. With few reliable staff members, Hadden did much of the work himself. He drove himself harder than usual, often working through the night and occasionally catnapping at his desk.

The move sapped the corporation's cash reserves. Luce opened an account with Cleveland's Central National Bank, but there was little to put in it. As the days shortened and the first cold snap arrived, *Time*'s founders wondered if the company would outlast the winter. Luce tried to sound an optimistic note to his wife, but he was worried. "*Time* is (or seems) very close to making a lot of money, and yet . . . also so far away from it," he wrote. "A well established magazine can make barrels of money. And then again lots of magazines drag on a futile existence making none. Which is *Time* going to be. Which? Which? Which?"

Hadden and Luce had faced dark days before, but always together. Now they were drifting apart. The tension between them finally burst into view on Thanksgiving, when Luce invited the staff for dinner. The maid cooked a large turkey and the researchers expected a cheery affair, but Hadden sat sullenly, hardly saying a word. He perked up only once, when someone remarked that John Martin was driving to Cleveland and was probably only a hundred miles away. "That's a hundred miles better off than we are," Hadden said. Toward the end of the meal, Luce ceremoniously rose to carve the last bit of turkey. "Now I know the girls will have more," he said in his best businessman's tone. "Pig women!" Hadden cracked. He retreated into silence.

In December, Luce received a phone call from the manager of Cleveland's Central National Bank. The Time Inc. bank account had dwindled to less than two thousand dollars. As a personal favor, the manager offered Luce an overdraft to help survive the lean winter. Luce and Larsen labored over a Christmas subscription letter that threatened to be their last. Larsen mailed it out, and for weeks *Time's* founders waited, wondering whether readers would rise to the call. "Things have got to pick up such a hell of a lot within the next two months if we are to continue swimming!" Luce wrote Lila. "But we are all working at it hammer & tongs. At last Brit has realized that he can't play the funny boy—he is scared stiff. Roy is working like a Trojan. I never thought of Roy as a genius—but maybe genius is only hard work."

In January, hundreds of new subscription requests poured into the office. Larsen happily got to work billing his new subscribers, but he was soon shocked to receive complaints from readers who claimed they had already sent in their five dollars. Looking like he was about to burst into tears, Larsen raced into the circulation bullpen. He spilled all of the garbage cans onto the floor, then rifled through the trash on his hands and knees. The money was not to be found. Soon Larsen learned that some of the girls he had hired to handle the Christmas rush were graduates of a nearby reform school.

Despite the theft, Time Inc. weathered its first major crisis and emerged stronger. The magazine's circulation increased to 107,000 readers—just shy of the goal Hadden and Luce had set the year before. The cash reserves swelled to nearly forty thousand dollars by the end of January and never dipped perilously low again. Back in New York, Johnson reported a breakthrough. Not only had his salesmen doubled the annual advertising revenues, they already had two hundred thousand dollars in orders on the books for 1926. Time Inc. finished the year with a loss of nearly twenty-four thousand dollars, largely due to the cost of the move, but prospects for the next year looked bright.

In January of 1926, Hadden and Luce began making *Time* the chief news source for many Midwestern readers. Unlike readers in New York, who felt burdened by the voluminous newspapers, most readers across the Midwest were desperate for serious news. The move to Cleveland improved *Time*'s standing with Midwesterners because the magazine arrived in their mailboxes a day sooner. *Time*'s founders had a plan to improve upon that record. They hoped to finally convince the postal service to handle *Time*, though second-class matter, with the expedition of a newspaper.

No other general-interest magazine managed to be classified as news, but *Time* had a uniquely strong case. Luce and Larsen prepared a study that contrasted *Time*'s contents over several months with those of the *Literary Digest*. Luce joined Cleveland's chamber of commerce, which backed the plan, as did the local post office. Shepherded to Washington by John Dempsey, a Yale graduate who had made partner at Cleveland's major law firm, Hadden and Luce met with Senator Theodore Burton, a resident of Cleveland's Cuyahoga County. The senator sent them directly to the Postmaster General's office. A few days later, *Time* was reaching cities across the country by the end of the week, several days in advance of the *Literary Digest*.

As their geographical reach expanded, Hadden and Luce grew aware of the potential to reach a wider audience than they had previously imagined. They had always assumed that people nationwide felt inundated by news and entertainment. As they began to read the

Cleveland *Plain Dealer,* they realized that even strong local newspapers provided little national and world news. Outside of the big cities people were hungry for information, and a publication that made national and world news understandable could become widely popular. The young men began to ponder how they might turn *Time* from an urban magazine into a news medium for the nation.

Enthusiasm for *Time* began to spread as Hadden and Luce raised their gaze beyond their former East Coast confines. With the endorsement of Cleveland's business leaders, the publishers planned a series of promotional tours that took them to chambers of commerce in places like Toledo, Grand Rapids, and New Orleans. *Time*'s founders would announce in advance of their arrival that they planned to give their audience a "surprise." Business leaders would turn out in large numbers. When the room filled, the dashing visitors would shock their hosts by whipping out giant cue cards and pencils and announcing the start of a "skull test."

Great crowds of businessmen sat like diligent schoolchildren, fat pencils poised at the ready. The youngsters asked them questions: "Who is the oldest justice of the United States Supreme Court?" "In round numbers, how much money does France owe the United States?" "In which state did Sinclair Lewis locate his imaginary village of Gopher Prairie?" The men would scratch their heads and wiggle their pencils. One local wise man would win a free subscription, but most would write down the wrong answers. The young men would shoot them down, the newspaper reporters would howl, and the next day's paper would feature a front-page story on the clever young editors.

Lila Luce told her husband she preferred it when Hadden traveled and left Luce in town to edit the magazine; she missed her husband when he went away. Luce coolly replied that he liked giving speeches. He was gaining control of his stutter, warming to the role of a public figure, and feeling increasingly frustrated that Hadden rarely let him edit the magazine. Every few months, Luce would "fight his way back" into the editor's chair, the researcher Faith Willcox recalled, not because it would "do the business any good, but because he felt each needed the experience on the other side." But Luce never managed to edit for more than a couple of weeks. Willcox recalled, "Hadden and Luce really had to argue it out."

Almost in compensation, Luce began to assume the role of proprietor. He became *Time*'s public face at the opera, the orchestra, and the charity drive, in part because Hadden refused to show. "He was the *Time* representative," the Cleveland hostess Katherine Halle recalled. "He was very ceremonial in those days." Luce also began to abrogate for himself some of the paternal rights of the chief executive. When he visited the advertising office in New York, the secretaries had to rush about to smooth his path, even going so far as to remove an executive from his office so that Luce could work alone. "We have to handle Mr. Luce with kid gloves," one secretary warned another.

Fully ensconced among Cleveland's suburbanites, the Luces danced at the country club and joined the Harknesses and Hannas on the dinner-party circuit. The matrons of Cleveland practically fell over themselves in the rush to admit Lila to their arts groups. When Lila went to a benefit luncheon for the Cleveland Orchestra, the president of the Women's Auxiliary grabbed her by the elbow and ushered her to a seat by two of Cleveland's leading ladies, Mrs. Newton D. Baker, the wife of Wilson's secretary of war, and Mrs. Andrew Squire, the wife of the city's top law partner.

Lila was adept at social maneuver and cagier than she let on. Arriving in Cleveland, she had written her mother a letter describing the town's "social bugs." By the following winter, she had become one herself. After the Luces attended a party held by a less-established, artistic crowd, Luce praised his wife for the radiant elegance that never ceased to open doors for the young couple. "Harry says I rose to the occasion like a cake of yeast in the oven; eyes sparkled, lips wittified, feet almost kicked," Lila wrote her mother. "And OF COURSE, of all the places we have been to, this was the only one which did not represent lots and lots of money."

The Luces did not attend Hadden's parties, which acquired a reputation for prodigious drinking and a royal mad brand of humor. Hadden had moved into an old apartment far from Shaker Heights and close to downtown. The cupboards overflowed with ketchup and molasses, toilet paper and toothpaste, since Hadden, believing a house could never have enough supplies, had run out to buy everything at once. Eagerly preparing the place for his penniless roommate, Niven Busch, Hadden bought an extra-large mattress, which turned out to be too big for either of the bedrooms. Busch slept in the kitchen. A singer he was dating soon moved in.

Hadden launched a sandlot baseball team, the Crescent Athletic Club. The players wore ludicrous green uniforms designed by Hadden himself. The Crescents, mainly Ivy League sports stars, traveled through Cleveland's outskirts to do battle against teams of union men. Hadden would bring along a keg of beer. He missed a lot of pop flies but he was visibly delighted after one victory when an old country woman introduced herself. Angrily, she demanded, "What do you city fellers mean by coming out here and doing this to our boys?" Hadden loved running the team, and he told his friends that one day he would buy a New York ball club. "When I get my baseball team, the first thing we do is open the gates and let all the kids in free, see?" he would say. "Then, when all the kids are in and provided there's still some room left, we begin to sell tickets."

Hadden limited his social contacts to an inner circle of suitably nonconformist friends, including his cousins, his ball team, and several would-be girlfriends, who often got together to drink bootleg liquor, play games, and crack jokes. Hadden's friends would remember the years they spent with him in Cleveland as a rare moment when he brought together a tight clique of fast-moving people and linked their lives by the golden thread of his charm. They had a sense of themselves as an elite group of charlatans putting one over on their stodgy friends and relatives. Prohibition gave everything the heady air of adventure, and Hadden, with his knack for throwing parties, remained the social ringleader. His partner in crime was John Martin's wife, Mimi Bushnell Martin.

Five-foot eleven with deep red, curly hair and widely separated brown eyes, Mimi reminded men of the women in Titian's paintings: she had a ravishing and seductive presence. She had first heard of John Martin through her elder brother, who had roomed with John's brother at Yale. Finally meeting John on the Cunard liner *Berengaria* while returning from a year at a Parisian finishing school, Mimi fell passionately in love. A stormy romance began on the boat, and the couple married in Manhattan's Old Trinity Church after Mimi discovered she was pregnant. When she arrived in Cleveland with her baby boy, John Martin had already begun philandering. Soon Hadden and Mimi had formed a close bond.

Hadden and Mimi shared a wicked sense of humor and were constantly pulling pranks on each other. In the Martins' house, they hosted elaborate parties. Hadden, who took unusual pride in his ability to observe with all his senses, would set up experiments to test his friends' sense of smell and touch. He would spread some commonplace foods on the kitchen table, blindfold his guests, and lead them down the line as they poked the objects with their hands or bent over and sniffed. "What *have* you got a hold of?" he would say, theatrically, as the party broke into laughter. Hadden would crown the winners with ridiculous medals and ribbons. Then they would go head-to-head with the all-time champion—Hadden himself. "He didn't want any game that he couldn't win at," John Martin said.

Martin realized his wife was spending more and more time with his cousin. Hadden chided Mimi for her expensive French furniture and her upper-class affectations. Entranced by her great eyes, so widely separated that Mimi had difficulty finding a pair of sunglasses, Hadden called her "Beady Eye." Mimi called Hadden "BH." Wildly fond of her cousin, she often seemed closer to him than to her husband, and she would stay up late listening to Hadden's brainstorms. One day Mimi and Hadden paired off their friends and sent the couples on a treasure hunt snaking through the Cleveland speakeasies. While everyone else hunted, Hadden and Mimi spent the day together.

With most people Hadden behaved quite casually, but where Mimi was concerned he obsessively observed the conventional routines of birthdays and christenings. As Mimi's second pregnancy advanced, Hadden became entranced by the notion that throwing a party for a newborn child would bring good luck. An hour after the Martins' daughter, Barry, came into the world, Hadden rushed over to the Martins' house with yards of gaudy bunting. He draped the house until it looked like Little Italy and rang up his friends to come greet the newborn child. Mimi would later describe the night as a magical moment of closeness and camaraderie, one of those times that seemed to stretch out and define an era. The next week, a phony copy of *Time* appeared on Mimi's doorstep, identical to the real issue except for an item in the Milestones column: Born, to Mrs. and John S. Martin, Book Editor of *Time,* a daughter, Cleva, in Cleveland.

John Martin had no reason to feel jealous of Mimi's affections; he had women on the side. But he often groused about Hadden's tendency to keep his desk piled high with work, a tactic Hadden devised to keep Martin from drinking. Martin could be nasty when in his cups. Once, in a cantankerous mood, he threatened to quit *Time* and head to the Sargasso Sea. Roy Larsen instantly volunteered to buy Martin's stock, and Martin would have closed the deal, but Mimi threatened to divorce him if he did. "*Time* stock is no good. It pays no dividends," Martin protested. "I believe it's good anyhow, because I believe in Brit," Mimi said. Martin's reply was surprisingly bitter. "Oh, you're always sold on Brit," he said.

Mimi separated from John for a while and took the children back to New York. One night Hadden drove to the city, arriving late at night. Not wishing to awaken his mother, he went to Mimi's apartment, where they stayed up all night, talking. Mimi knew Hadden's visit appeared improper and she begged Hadden not to pull any pranks in her new building. She knew from experience that he was apt to spend fifteen minutes riding the elevator just to aggravate the doorman. Hadden promised to be good. A few minutes after he left, the doorman knocked on Mimi's door and handed her two of the dirtiest dollar bills she had ever seen. "Madam," he said, as if speaking to a woman of the night, "the gentleman said to give you these." Mimi called Hadden in a rage. He burst out laughing, delighted to have angered her. "Have you ever seen such dirty dollar bills?" he guffawed. "I had to walk into twelve stores to find them." Finally Mimi began to chuckle. "Wasn't it funny?" Hadden went on, sounding almost like a little boy. "It wouldn't have been funny if the bills hadn't been beat up. You *are* laughing, aren't you?"

Hadden's social life was growing wilder. By 1926 he had grown into a full-blown alcoholic. No one viewed him that way at the time; *Time's* writers had yet to witness the ravages alcohol addiction would work on their friends and family over the next two decades. The trouble was also hard to spot because Hadden continued to do productive work. No matter how much he drank, he still slept only five hours a night, and still pulled long days in the office. But Hadden poured down drinks easily with no sense of limits, and his behavior when drunk was growing reckless.

Like many young men of the time, Hadden had a makeshift distillery. Once, when Christopher Morley visited Cleveland after publishing a book, Hadden became terribly excited about throwing a party for a literary hero. The occasion required spirits. Unfortunately, Hadden's filtration system failed, and his fresh batch of gin came out full of charcoal. Nervously, Hadden poured the black liquor into dark green cups, hoping no one would notice. The ruse worked until Dave Ingalls sauntered in late and poured his drink into a clear cup. "Is *this* what we have been drinking?" Morley declared. He stomped out. Fortunately Hadden hadn't run out of liquor entirely, at which point he was known to serve a demon cocktail of one part gin to five parts Angostura bitters. It was not a recipe for long life.

At night, Hadden would head out to the speakeasies, where he surveyed the scene with a glint in his eye, pouring down drinks almost without noticing it—no cocktails, just whiskey or gin. Hadden and Niven Busch would compete to spot people who looked like George Folansbee Babbitt, the dull American businessman of a popular Sinclair Lewis novel. Hadden left his license plate dangling from his car so that friendly motorists would honk their horns and warn him that it was about to fall off. "Babbitt!" Hadden would yell, scoring a point. He drove recklessly, sometimes crashing into lampposts. "He didn't give a damn about fenders," John Martin recalled. "He just drove that Chevy and he said, 'Cleveland! I don't want to live here, but I'm living here, so you'll have to put up with me.'" Hadden called his car Leaping Lena.

Hadden remained at heart a joyous little boy with simple pleasures and rascally impulses. Friends would drop by his apartment in formal attire to find him in a rumpled old suit, insisting that they go to a Cedar Avenue rib joint. He liked to take his friends to the circus. Once, at the end of the show, some performers walked out dressed as "living statues," waving an American flag. Hadden bolted from his seat and cracked out a salute, hollering, "Old Glory!" Everyone around jumped up to join Hadden in a huzzah for America. He sat down instantly, grinning from ear to ear at having stoked the crowd's small-town patriotic impulse. "He was bored," one friend recalled. "And he loved—in a naughty way—to make the average citizen look like a boob."

Hadden had developed some odd customs like showering several times a day and refusing to use a bar of soap that anyone else had touched. He held an active dislike for masseurs, doormen, overly formal waiters, and anyone else who reminded him of pampered living. He loved cabbies, however, and had developed a number of rituals revolving around taxies. After hailing a cab, he would ask the driver, "Who's your favorite ballplayer?" If the driver didn't say Babe Ruth, Hadden wouldn't get in. If the ride went well but wasn't quite long enough for a good fare to build up, Hadden would let the cabbie circle the block a few times before pointing out his office. "That sign there," he would say vaguely, "isn't that the Penton Building where we're going?"

Instead of a cigarette kettle, Hadden now kept a giant pot of pennies on his coffee table. He waited—"like a sleuthing cat," one friend recalled—for his guests to ask about the pot. Hadden would smile cagily at those in the know and tell the fresh initiate that one day he would probably find himself dead broke, but as long as he had a pot of pennies in the living room he could always get a cab ride home. He explained it all in dead earnest as if only amateurs and fly-by-nights would fail to take such precautions in life. "Hadden didn't have an adult point of view on anything," the researcher Faith Willcox recalled.

At least one writer thought Hadden was beginning to lose control of himself. "I still remember working late one night in the writers' office in Cleveland," Manfred Gottfried recalled. "Suddenly there were long and prolonged growls from the next room, then heavy pounding noises. Brit was sitting in his chair, with a piece of copy in front of him, and stamping his feet on the floor. He had found something in a piece of copy, something that did not conform to his stylebook, and he was venting his wrath. In part, this was due to the condition of his nerves and, in part, it was no doubt done to attract attention. On other occasions, I knew him to gnash his teeth."

The fundamental feeling of loneliness that had occasionally depressed Hadden since college returned to him more often now. Though the partners who founded *Time* had little in common, Hadden always considered Luce one of the few people who could understand his concerns. They still shared moments of fellowship. At the end of the week, they could be found side by side in the printer's room putting the magazine to bed, both stained with ink, Hadden slashing with his giant pencil and Luce quietly twisting a lock of hair. Once Mimi Martin asked Hadden why he would want to work with someone so different from him. Hadden answered, "I'll bet you that a British general would rather talk to a German general than to an ordinary person of his own nationality."

But Luce was asserting himself more and more often, and Hadden, feeling threatened, began antagonizing his partner. Hadden relied on Luce to do the work he wanted nothing to do with—to cut costs, to fire staff members, to soak up anger and frustration. On payday, Hadden would barge into Luce's office and yell so loudly that others could hear, "Are you going to sign my check today, or am I going to go hungry?"

Hadden's increasing eccentricity baffled Luce, but it seems the two never discussed their personal problems. Hadden remained a mystery to his partner. Decades later the fact remained evident when Luce struggled to describe for his corporate historian the change that came over Hadden in Cleveland. "He got very troubled," Luce told Robert Elson. "He was reckless and . . . he'd stay up very late. He got to drinking." After wrestling with the problem, Luce asked Elson, "Can you give any explanation as to what was sort of biting him, you might say?" After all those years, he still didn't know.

No longer on friendly terms with Luce, Hadden sought companionship among Cleveland's small circle of bohemians. He enjoyed the company of Jerome Zerbe, a Yale student who later became a pioneering society photographer and a pillar of New York's gay establishment. Hadden also became close with Jerome Zerbe's older sister, Margot. Like Hadden, Margot despised intellectuals; she was known to say of her finishing school, "it sure finished me." They seemed well suited to each other, and they went on a few dates. When Margot visited the office, Hadden would sidle up to her and ask if she would like to go "coon hunting," a base phrase for necking. Margot would laugh and refuse. She may have been willing to go on more dates, but Hadden never asked.

Roy Larsen eventually asked Margot out, and they were married in the summer of 1927. The Larsens and Hadden remained closer than ever, and Margot, an acerbic woman with rarely a kind word to say, always had the highest praise for Hadden. Margot Larsen would outlive her contemporaries. In 2003, she was living in a nursing home, lucid at times but no longer capable of answering direct questions. When Margot's children threw her a small party on her hundredth birthday, an elderly man approached and decorously announced that he felt honored to have known her. "Oh, don't go away and leave me," Margot replied. "Are you thinking about your boyfriend?" her caretaker asked. "Yes," Margot said, "Briton Hadden."

At a party Hadden met a boyhood friend of Jerome Zerbe's named Winsor French, the stepson of Joseph Oriel Eaton, a prominent Cleveland industrialist. French was flamboyantly gay, though people simply called him effeminate. Having dropped out of Kenyon College, he was trying to begin a writing career, but he had recently flunked Hadden's current events test. French told Hadden a quiz was no way to hire anybody; there were geniuses walking around who couldn't identify a single obscure head of state. Hadden hired French immediately and gave him the title of chief of research.

Hadden told French to sit outside the editor's office with nothing on his desk, not even a pencil or a piece of paper. "Executives should never work. Only give orders," Hadden said. French dared not disobey. He became Hadden's court jester, summoned to eat twice a day, to be a fixture at parties, to tell jokes and keep Hadden in touch with Cleveland's upper class. French would show up for work in the afternoon, always with a fantastic excuse. "I never did learn what French's duties were," one office boy recalled. "He seemed quite a character to me, an East Side lad, with his pansy-like mannerisms and his soprano voice." French's impression of Hadden in that year revealed how much he had changed. "He was shy, a rebel," French recalled.

Hadden was also working closely with the Foreign News editor, a recent Yale graduate named Laird Goldsborough. Short and overweight with long dark hair that flowed over the back of his collar, Goldsborough was partly lame due to a childhood hip ailment. He limped along with the help of a cane, sweating profusely. He was also hard of hearing. At parties, where the din made it difficult to hear, Goldsborough would find a friend, trap him in a corner, and lean in quite close, enveloping him within a pungent aroma as he whispered stories into his ear—stories Goldsborough and no one else found funny. Goldsborough wrote like a silkworm, spinning out a story from start to finish almost without stopping. When he came up with a particularly delicious phrase, he would pause to savor it, purring like a cat, then read it aloud and cackle.

An admirer of aristocratic lineage, Goldsborough followed the lives of the European nobility and particularly delighted in gossip about the British royal family. He had heard rumors that Edward, the Prince of Wales, was leading a wild social life. Hadden had always published news of celebrity divorces in the Milestones department, but he considered most royal gossip too tawdry for the news pages. Goldsborough found a way around that problem by creating the phony character of Mary Elizabeth Robinn, a spinster who wrote letters to the editor about the prince's latest sensational exploits.

Hadden and Mimi Martin would get together to dream up new Robinn scenarios, and Hadden would pass them on to Goldsborough. "Goldie would chortle," John Martin recalled. "And he could imitate a crotchety female of a certain age more delightfully than anybody you can imagine." Readers eagerly ganged up on Robinn; one called her a disappointed virgin. "The noun 'virgin' is not one which gentlemen or ladies employ, in any other than a religious connection," she replied. "You may rest assured that my married or unmarried state, as the case may be, is not a subject upon which I shall stoop to satisfy curious vulgarians."

The phony letters awakened *Time*'s readers and inspired them to write in about their own pet subjects. Even Hadden's mother got into the game. "Don't speak of 'early U.S. furnishings,'" Mrs. Pool wrote her son. "It is 'early American furniture' for it was here long before the colonies were U.S." Hadden beamed. He immediately published the letter, replying, "Original Subscriber Pool cannot be refuted." By opening the magazine to outside attack, Hadden cleverly increased his readers' loyalty. In the midst of the Robinn brawl, a minister from rural Ohio wrote that he had enjoyed his first four copies of *Time*, including the "frontal attack, rude and discourteous," of the Letters page. "More power to ye, Mr. Editor," wrote the Reverend Angus E. Clephan. "I'm wid ye."

As the magazine grew more popular, advertisers finally jumped on the *Time* bandwagon. In Detroit, known as the "graveyard" by advertising executives because the automobile accounts were so tough to obtain, Robert L. Johnson worked a canny bit of salesmanship. He advised a Pontiac executive to take out half as much space as he would have liked. *Time* readers were wealthy, Johnson said; they would only buy a Pontiac as a second car. The story of Johnson's honesty spread through Detroit, and the automakers began to think of him as a consultant rather than as a salesman. Lincoln, Rolls-Royce, Packard, and Cadillac all began advertising in *Time*.

As *Time* approached national prominence, its founders began to clash over the magazine's editorial direction. Hadden had a habit of running brutally honest articles about *Time*'s own advertisers. When Johnson came back to the office crowing about having won the International Mercantile Marine account, Hadden ran a story calling the president of the company "pop-eyed." Johnson recalled, "It's true. He was pop-eyed." Hadden gained readers by acquiring a reputation for honesty, but he also lost some large accounts. Once Johnson cried on Mimi Martin's shoulder, begging her to rein in Hadden. Dry-eyed, Johnson lobbied with Luce and Larsen for a change in policy. Thousands of dollars in profits were on the line, millions perhaps—and the support of wealthy businessmen, whom Luce worried about offending.

The matter came to a head when Fisher, a luxury wooden autobody maker, signed a large contract with *Time*. Soon after the magazine began running Fisher's advertisements, the automakers held a convention in New York. Several automakers introduced luxury steel models that rivaled the wooden models for appearance and beat them on safety. Niven Busch filed a report from the convention that began with a romantic description of a steel Mercedes that "made the rest look shoddy." He concluded the piece with a quote from Edward S. Jordan, a respected automobile executive, who said that in accidents involving wooden cars "it's the splinters that kill."

Fisher had bought a full page in the same issue. The advertisement depicted a grove of trees and emphasized Fisher's use of high-quality hardwood. The company called up Luce to cancel its contract, as did Cadillac, which, like Fisher, was owned by General Motors. Luce, enraged, thought the article was "colossally stupid." He took the train to Detroit for several nervous meetings with men from the advertising agencies. "You can imagine my sentiments," he wrote Lila. "Big man at the breakfast table, trying to put up courage to face a good hard spanking by a few damn advertising men!" Cadillac soon came back to *Time*. But Luce always claimed that the article "completely ruined us in Detroit."

By the spring of 1926, Hadden and Luce had reached an impasse. A phony letter here or there couldn't endanger the magazine, but Luce felt that blatant jabs at advertisers would attack its lifeblood. Hadden believed he was upholding the standard of fairness and impartiality, and he resented attempts to favor *Time*'s advertisers. He bore a grudge against Luce for the move to Cleveland, and his bitterness and disgust for the city seeped back into his perceptions of his partner. Each had little access to the other's thoughts since they rarely talked. But every few months they discussed one matter that grew more urgent to Luce by the day. When would he get to edit? He had waited three years.

Finally Hadden agreed to switch jobs with Luce for the unprecedented length of six weeks. "Luce is pleased because he considers himself a journalist at heart," Hadden wrote William V. Griffin, a member of the board. "Hadden is delighted because he sees a possible avenue of escape from Cleveland."

Between trips to New York, Hadden had a chance to reflect upon what he had created. He lined the walls of his Cleveland office with every *Time* cover, signifying a growing consciousness of his achievement. He also asked several mentors if they had any suggestions. "I feel as tho Mr. Rockefeller should suddenly demand my advice upon financial matters," John Berdan replied. "The style irritates people almost to madness, but they continue to subscribe and bring their friends."

Toward the end of March, a letter for Luce arrived at the office in a large, white envelope stamped "Confidential." Robert Maynard Hutchins, who had graduated from Yale a year after *Time*'s founders, had accepted a position as the school's secretary. Hutchins offered Luce an honorary master's degree at the next graduation ceremony. He would receive his kudos at the tender age of twenty-eight. Luce gave the letter to Lila as a birthday present. "The matter is to be kept strictly confidential until the hour of the ceremony," she wrote her mother. "I think that Brit must be getting the same honor, as to the world, they are twins in achievement."

Actually, the authorities at Yale had not offered Hadden an honorary degree. In June of 1926, Luce slipped out of Cleveland without telling Hadden where he was going. At the graduation ceremony in New Haven, Yale's president praised Luce's "precocious intellectual abilities" and conferred upon him an honorary degree for the achievement of *Time,* "whose success has surprised even the optimists." Hadden found out about the award by reading the next morning's paper. When Luce came back to Cleveland, he walked into Hadden's office and announced, "Well, I've wiped your eye."

The awarding of an honorary degree from Yale provided *Time* its first formal public recognition. For Luce to step forward alone—at the alma mater, no less—struck Hadden as the ultimate betrayal. The action shattered Hadden's trust in Luce and left him feeling deeply wounded. He was "so mad it nearly killed him," Mimi Martin recalled. Hadden drove to New York to confide in his closest friends. They could tell he was angry that Luce had accepted the degree and offended that Luce had not told him about it beforehand. But what grieved Hadden most was the way Luce had robbed his soul, standing on stage and taking credit for ideas that had moved Hadden since childhood. "God knows," Hadden said, "the newsmagazine was my idea."

Hadden's friends wondered how Yale could stumble so badly, grievously injuring the relationship of its two young stars. They wondered if powerful Yale alumni had heard the rumors of Hadden's nocturnal libations, or if the board, believing they could honor only one man, had simply decided on the man with the Phi Beta Kappa key and the Oxford pedigree. One member of the Yale Corporation claimed that Luce had lobbied for the degree. Whatever the cause, it seemed cruel for Mother Yale to spite a favorite son. "We all felt that Yale hadn't investigated closely enough," John Hincks later said, "or they would have realized that the genius in back of *Time* was Brit, not Harry."

Twice now, Luce had exceeded the bounds of fairness and respect governing his intense competition with Hadden. Though Hadden could be a tough competitor, he had never been a ruthless one. Luce, on the other hand, could be moved by pride or moral certitude to break ties of honesty and loyalty thought to have been immutable—and to do it in ways so inexplicably cruel as to leave people shaking their heads, mystified. People could only assume, as Thomas J. C. Martyn later put it, that the action "took the measure of the man."

The controversy didn't much trouble Luce, who had stood on stage to be commended and received a hood to match his academic gown. Perhaps he did not realize that in order to gain this moment of ceremonial commendation he had sacrificed the most important friendship of his life. Hadden told his cousin Niven Busch that Luce had "double-crossed" him. For several months afterward, Hadden refused to speak to Luce. They communicated only in writing.

11

Hot Stuff

SOON AFTER LUCE RECEIVED his honorary degree, Hadden's friend Stuart Heminway visited him in Cleveland. Heminway asked Hadden how he liked the town. "I have been here forty-four weeks and have been to New York thirty-six times," Hadden said. Heminway asked how Luce was doing. Hadden said he had absolutely no idea. "What, don't you two see anything of each other anymore?" Heminway asked. "The less I see of him the better I like it," Hadden said.

In public, Hadden put the best face on things, writing a story for the house magazine of the Cleveland chamber of commerce about how much help the city had provided the young company. "*Time* is here to stay," he concluded. "*Time* likes Cleveland." Privately, he expressed a different attitude. "We think we're hot stuff here, big frogs in a small puddle," he would say. "But what the hell are we? A bunch of kids, deafened by adulation. We sit at dinner parties with people twice our age and they listen to us. We think we're some punkins. We must get back to New York where we have competition and can't get smug."

Back in the editor's chair in the second half of 1926, Hadden began to fill the magazine with more jokes and pranks, often poking fun at rural America. He invented a new phony correspondent, George Zweiger of Chillicothe, Ohio. "What's West Virginia but Ohio's coal bin?" Zweiger wrote *Time*. "Just a dirty disheveled stretch of mine dumps, scraggly mountains, filled with a bunch of ignorants that only know enough to swing picks and drink moonshine." West Virginian readers wrote *Time* to attack Ohio, and newspapers in both states spread the controversy. Reporters in Chillicothe tried to track down Zweiger, but they weren't able to find anyone by that name. Newspaper reporters called the office, wondering whether *Time* had manufactured the controversy. Hadden, in a panic, ordered his researchers to destroy the files. From then on, *Time*'s phony correspondents tended to live in large cities, making Hadden's hoaxes more difficult to detect.

Realizing that a scandal could provide free publicity for *Time*, Larsen encouraged Hadden to attack a variety of towns across America. They stayed up late at night plotting their targets. In the next several months, *Time* ran a report on political corruption in Indianapolis, covered a newspaper battle in Denver, and made fun of the only skyscraper in Greensboro, North Carolina—a town *Time* called "second-rate." Larsen checked the circulation figures in those areas the following year and discovered that the readership had increased between 50 and 100 percent. "The numbers speak for themselves," he wrote Hadden. "What we have done in Winston-Salem, Denver, and Indianapolis, we can do in hundreds of cities and towns throughout the country." "Noted," Hadden wrote back. "This important point is well taken. Will cooperate. BH."

Hadden's attacks on small-town and rural America earned *Time* the hatred of book-burning preachers, Prohibitionists, and a good number of Southerners who disliked reading about lynchings. "I would not want your propaganda sheet even if it came free of charge," wrote a chiropractor from Lebanon, Missouri, after reading "A Snake in the Grass," an article about *Time* in his Baptist newspaper. "One thing this country needs is publications that stand four square for American ideals." Hadden must have chuckled over the letter; it was pasted into the company scrapbook.

Each denunciation piqued the interest of upwardly mobile college students and businessmen who identified with *Time*'s lambasting of rural authority. People disgusted by the simplified portrayal of their block or town always seemed to believe the picture painted of their neighbor. When a Cedar Rapids newspaper interviewed J. Melvin Hutchinson of the Cedar Rapids Savings Bank, the reporter asked the executive which magazines he liked to read. "*Time*," he answered. "It is curt, clear and complete in its presentation of the week's news." His picture showed the typical *Time* reader, a dapper man in a tight-fitting sport coat.

Journalists and university professors were beginning to think of *Time* as a major magazine. One of Hadden's idols, the Hearst editor Arthur Brisbane, began reading *Time* regularly after his face appeared on the cover. In the fall of 1926, he mentioned the magazine in a column. Harvard's President Lowell, who had scoffed at the notion of paring down the news several years before, took a sudden interest in *Time*'s story about him. "I showed it to the president myself," a Harvard student wrote Hadden, "and he was frightfully tickled, although he tried hard not to show it and declared that he didn't think his voice was high-pitched in the least."

Advertising sales were rising dramatically. Hadden and Luce wisely pumped their profits back into the magazine. They increased its size first to forty-four pages, then occasionally to fifty-two. They also switched to a thick cover paper with a sheen that was more attractive on the newsstand. The company finished 1926 with a profit of just over $10,000, closing a record year in which advertising revenues rose to $240,000 and the average circulation climbed to 111,000 readers. "After that," Roy Larsen recalled, "it was simply a matter of growing as fast as we could." Instead of sending their investors an early dividend, as they might have felt pressured to do, *Time*'s founders allowed their coffers to swell and saved funds for their first promotion efforts.

For all of *Time*'s success attracting subscribers and advertisers, the magazine had yet to gain widespread attention because of its anemic newsstand sales. Small, black and white, and printed on cheap paper, *Time* had little chance of attracting those who hadn't already heard of it through word of mouth. Only thirty-five hundred of America's sixty thousand newsdealers carried it. Though a low public profile increased the magazine's appeal to its devoted following, Hadden and Luce would have to crack the newsstand audience to acquire a place in the center of public life.

They started to talk about the problem in the office. The advertising team thought about it. Finally Robert L. Johnson asked a newsdealer for his thoughts. "What you need on the cover," the dealer responded, "is pretty girls, babies, or red and yellow." Pretty girls and babies seemed out of the question—for the moment anyway—and yellow perhaps seemed a little gauche. But a splash of red would be feasible and quite in keeping with the appearance of the magazine. In the New York office, where Johnson related his story to the advertising team, Hadden's Westhampton friend Philip Kobbé grabbed a crayon and a copy of *Time*. He drew a bright red border around the outside. "That's it!" Hadden said. *Time* was about to go color.

The red-bordered cover of January 3, 1927, represented a visual improvement over its black-and-white predecessors. It also brought in $1,400—in the form of a bold yellow advertisement. The back cover featured an apple-cheeked girl leaning her head into an Atwater Kent radio: "Here is Radio's greatest thrill—a touch of your fingertips and the ONE Dial finds anything on the air within range." Newsstand sales began to climb. The red-bordered cover epitomized *Time*'s American identity and sold it to readers much as the sight of a roadside diner could sell a slice of warm apple pie. It would be as a consciously American magazine that *Time* would rise to national prominence.

In the beginning of 1927, Hadden finally agreed to switch jobs with Luce for a longer stretch of several months. Luce doubted whether Hadden would have the appetite for the physical and financial aspects of printing such as buying the paper, contracting with the printer, and balancing the budget. But the switch turned out to be just what the company needed. Luce, though a talented juggler of the financial books, was not much of a strategist compared with Hadden. No sooner had he settled into his new job than Hadden hired several production assistants to handle the more onerous and repetitive tasks, freeing his hand to develop a strategy for long-term growth.

Aside from creating *The Pop Question Game*, Hadden and Luce had never thought much about how to promote *Time* to readers and advertisers. Hadden believed a fresh promotion campaign would boost *Time*'s revenues and awaken advertisers to the potential of reaching a national news audience. He asked Phil Kobbé and Dave Keep, the Williams graduate who had started by selling *Time* to college students, to brainstorm ideas with the Cleveland advertising firm of Fuller, Smith & Ross. Hadden wanted to do something as shocking on the business side as he had done with the magazine itself. "To stay in this business, you

have got to stick your head out the window and yell once in a while,"
he told his team. "Doesn't matter what you say, just stick your head out
the window and yell."

The idea of what to yell ultimately came from the advertising salesman Howard Black, a hard-drinking, redheaded Irishman who had been
fired from numerous jobs and was living on tomato juice when *Time*
hired him. More of a listener than a talker, Black had the salesman's gift
for close observation. He discovered that he could impress advertising
executives by showing them a list of the Harvard, Yale, and Princeton
Club members who subscribed to *Time*. When Black showed the list to
a buyer for the firm of Barton, Durstine & Osborn, the man replied,
"What you're trying to tell me is that you have a readership of young,
up and coming men." Black went back to the office and proposed that
Time stop talking about how busy its readers were and start talking
about their buying power.

Dave Keep and Phil Kobbé designed a handsome booklet that would
promote *Time* to advertisers as the best way to reach the "Young Executive." They titled the booklet "This Class-Ridden Democracy." Sprinkled
with clever writing and pictures, the booklet made a compelling case
that *Time*'s readers existed on the leading edge of America's cultural
and economic growth. Who read *Time*? The Young Executive did. He
belonged to the top 5 percent who earned each year one third of the
national income. Wealthy, powerful, informed, and energetic, the
Young Executive golfed and went on vacation. An informed consumer,
he spent his money freely and paid attention to what companies said
to him. He was a man advertisers wanted to reach, and *Time* had him.

In developing such a vivid picture of *Time*'s audience, Hadden and
his team created a modern approach to marketing a magazine. Hadden
intertwined elements of mockery and flattery in his approach. In meetings with advertising executives, he cracked that *Time* was building a
tremendous following among "young nincompoops." Far from taking
offense, the advertising executives saw Hadden as the spokesman for
a rising generation. They began recommending *Time* to their clients,
and advertising revenues climbed to nearly $415,000 in 1927. By the
end of the year, *Time*'s advertising salesmen, who worked on commission, were making more money than Hadden and Luce. Driving to the
office in their sports cars, wearing the latest in jackets and ties, golfing

on the weekends with their brand-new clubs, they were living, breathing paragons of *Time*'s nincompoop fan base.

As he grew familiar with Madison Avenue, Hadden realized that the large advertising firms dominated one of the most dynamic and revolutionary sectors of the expanding consumer economy. Advertising and promotion techniques were changing as rapidly as any aspect of American commercial life—and to more lasting effect. Young pitchmen had broken into the advertising industry and invented a fantasy world that stimulated people to buy products they had never dreamed of needing. Hadden admired the talent of the new pitchmen, but he believed the record of their achievement was mixed.

At its best, advertising added a touch of romance and poetry to people's lives and helped them feel more attractive, powerful, or mysterious than they really were. Copywriters, casting aside the habit of the hard sell, instead worked to summon up the subconscious urge to buy. The makers of the Jordan sports car made their mint by implanting positive associations with just four words: "Somewhere west of Laramie." Below the headline, a dashing young man rocketed along in his convertible, free for a moment from the busy world. People began buying Jordan sports cars to share in the feeling of liberation.

For every lyrical Jordan advertisement, there seemed to be three advertisements that made people feel more ugly or smelly than they really were. The king of insidious suggestion was Listerine, the mouthwash maker. Listerine was originally formulated as a surgical antiseptic, but by the Great War people were gargling with the amber liquid instead. After the Armistice, Listerine's makers hoped to create a larger market for their mouthwash. They finally struck gold by popularizing the word "halitosis," which encouraged people to think of fetid breath as a medical condition.

Listerine's most effective advertisement was headlined "OFTEN A BRIDESMAID, NEVER A BRIDE." It featured the picture of a lonely girl next to the following paragraphs:

Edna's case was really a pathetic one. Like every woman, her primary ambition was to marry. Most of the girls of her set were married—or about to be. Yet not one possessed more grace or charm or loveliness than she.

And as her birthdays crept gradually toward that tragic 30 mark, marriage seemed farther from her life than ever.

She was often a bridesmaid but never a bride.

That's the insidious thing about halitosis (unpleasant breath). You, yourself, rarely know when you have it. And even your closest friends won't tell you.

The rise of Listerine provided a sign of just how much control the advertising industry could exercise over people's lives merely through positive or negative suggestion. All of a sudden, Americans felt insecure about their breath.

Hadden decided the world of modern advertising was worth a closer look. He would provide that look, and promote *Time,* too, by printing a circular and sending it free of charge to three thousand advertising executives. Punning on the expression "Time and Tide wait for no man," Hadden named his circular *Tide.* The lead story reviewed *The Sword Arm of Business,* a new book by Theodore F. MacManus, a pioneering advertising executive who now declared, "The making of money is cheapening." Another story listed the contradictory claims made by rival toothpaste makers, including Colgate, one of the first companies to pay for a large block of back covers in *Time.* "God help you," one reader wrote Hadden, "with the criticism that will be yours." Hadden gleefully printed the letter in a house advertisement for *Tide.*

The circular caused such a stir in the industry that Hadden decided to keep publishing it once a month. He hired a single employee to help put the magazine out: Ed Kennedy, a young advertising copywriter with dirty fingernails and a penchant for reciting poetic verse. Hadden's secretary recalled Kennedy as a "wonderful elfin genius." He would shortly rise to become *Time's* chief business writer, before descending into alcoholism and dying toothless and broke in a Philadelphia men's shelter. Hadden liked taking his new writer to baseball games, where Kennedy shocked Time Inc. board members with behavior so atrocious that decades later Dave Keep refused to discuss it.

Together Kennedy and Hadden studied the persuasive tactics of America's pied pipers of commercialism. In an age when *Forbes* and the *Magazine of Business* featured soporific essays such as "Henry Ford on Progress" and "Mark Sullivan on This Business Age," *Tide* provided the first frank discussion of advertising ethics and tactics, often creating controversy. The business publisher William A. Forbes called *Tide* "the most original and constructive movement in advertising circles in a decade." Still it seemed odd for *Time*'s business manager to be printing a magazine that criticized his potential targets. It would never have happened if Luce had allowed Hadden to remain as editor of *Time*. "Harry was better at the business management and liked it better, and Brit hated it," John Martin said. "I mean, thus you have *Tide*, which kids the whole idea of advertising, see?"

Controversial though *Tide* may have been, it succeeded as *Time* had in attracting attention to the company and moving toward profitability. Soon *Tide* had five thousand subscribers, each paying a dollar a year. The magazine did exactly what Hadden intended: it made advertising executives aware of *Time*. One month after *Tide* came out, the trade journal *Advertising & Selling* included *Time* in a list of successful new advertising mediums. *Time*'s editors, the trade magazine said, had "leaped from Yale classrooms to handle the news with smartness and sophistication. And its readers follow their pranks with the same mixture of pride and impatience with which a parent regards an incorrigible young son."

Time remained a subscription-based magazine. The few thousand copies that sold off the newsstand amounted to only 5 percent of the magazine's paid circulation. But the red-bordered cover gave Larsen something to sell. With Hadden's encouragement, Larsen began to increase *Time*'s newsstand presence, and soon he was selling ten thousand copies off the stands each week. In 1927, Larsen and Hadden took out advertisements in newspapers and ran promotional quizzes in the magazine. They hoped to double *Time*'s newsstand figures by the following year.

Though Luce had entertained doubts about leaving Hadden alone on the business side, in just a few months Hadden had transformed *Time*'s business plan from that of a small, insignificant magazine to that of the first news medium consciously marketed to a national audience. *Time*'s readers were wealthy, educated, obsessed with status, as revealed by their delight in poking fun at the rural and uneducated, and fanatically interested in learning and improving. They were intelligent and curious about the world around them, and they loved a good joke or a bit of ironic flavor. They were devoted to *Time,* so devoted that they thought of the magazine as a status symbol and carried it about.

Time's circulation had stabilized just above a hundred thousand readers, but thousands more were out there—perhaps millions. Now the company had the coffers to pursue them. Hadden, Luce, and Larsen knew that in order to blanket the nation they would have to turn *Time* from a more or less cult phenomenon, much talked about but less often seen, into a recognizable brand. What type of image *Time* should project to its potential readers would become the chief source of contention between Hadden and Luce, who was quickly adapting the magazine to his purposes.

Editing was tougher than Luce had imagined. Even with his wife arranging his meals and picking him up from work late at night, he would have to spend an entire day recuperating each week. Once he became so exhausted that he ran a fever. But Luce proved to be a brilliant editor. He could take an article Hadden might have rejected, read through it quickly, make a few quick flicks of the pencil, and suddenly it would be ready for publication. The result might be less brilliant than the rewrite necessary to satisfy Hadden, but it would also be more incisive, and it would take on the fundamental questions at the bottom of the issue. Luce's editing had only one major drawback. "The trouble with Harry," Elizabeth Armstrong later said, "is that he hasn't any sense of humor."

The writing in *Time* was improving dramatically. John Martin was now writing National Affairs. Late in 1926, Manfred Gottfried had sold his 450 shares back to Hadden and Luce and left for Italy to write a novel. A touch of wit went missing, but that may have been because Niven Busch, sick of Cleveland, had returned to New York and started freelancing for *The New Yorker.* The editor, Harold Ross, heard that Busch came from *Time* and called him into his office. "I wish you would do something for me," Ross growled. "Find out who was the stinker who wrote that snide article about *The New Yorker.*" "I did," Busch said. Ross gave him a job.

Time's back-of-the-book departments were acquiring depth, especially the coverage of science and medicine. This was largely due to Myron Weiss, a Harvard student turned typesetter and proofreader who had worked for the medical corps during the war. Weiss delved into academic journals to find stories the newspapers covered only haphazardly. He had a knack for explaining arcane details with engaging language. Reporting on an experimental brain operation at Johns Hopkins, he told his readers to imagine a tumor as a "sloppily rounded corn fritter." After reading the story, a doctor complimented *Time* for contributing to public knowledge of science.

The magazine changed in a greater way under Luce's watch. Hadden instructed his writers to tell both sides of an event. As storytellers, they could take creative license in shaping the facts and impart the news with their sense of how things looked and felt, but they were not to take partisan political positions. Like Homer, they should find heroes and fools on both sides of the story. Hadden's writing style nevertheless gave *Time* the power to transmit character judgments and coded values. Motivated by the dream of informing as many people as possible and by the urge to entertain, Hadden largely put his power to use for humorous ends. But Luce had views to impose and he dreamed of becoming a public figure. Unwittingly, Hadden had built Luce a podium.

No sooner had Luce taken the editor's seat than he began to twist and distort the news. *Time*'s emerging bias first grew evident in Foreign News. Laird Goldsborough quickly impressed Luce with his writing ability and knowledge of foreign events. He described the vast cast of international statesmen so adeptly that at times he seemed to be a master of puppets, dangling and manipulating a whole set of marionettes upon his wooden stage. In a time when few Americans cared about the warlords fighting over a fractured China, Goldsborough gave the warlords nicknames and identified them by their peculiar backgrounds and reputations. Luce would later say that if any American readers understood the Chinese civil war they probably read about it in *Time*— quite a high compliment from an old China hand.

The editor and his foreign news writer struck up a friendship. Goldsborough, who badly wished to be loved, almost seemed to look up to Luce as a more glamorous and attractive version of himself. Finding in Luce an eager conversationalist, Goldsborough began to stroll into the boss's office to ask for his take on a story or invite him out to lunch. On Saturday, as the staff prepared their final articles, Goldsborough would ask Luce if he had any final reflections. Luce, more accustomed to weary forbearance from writers, valued the budding friendship. "I kept in very close touch with Foreign News via Goldsborough," he recalled. "Whatever views I had . . . or whatever views he had . . . we would talk about it."

With his sardonic sense of humor, Goldsborough had a keen eye for the kind of trivia readers had come to expect from *Time*. He manipulated narrative details to convey his opinion without stating it plainly. The more freedom Luce gave Goldsborough, the more he used Timestyle to brand public figures. "Goldie was like an old fat lady sitting there in his office," John Martin recalled, "and he had these people sized up so much better than we did that we learned to say, Well, I guess Goldie thinks that this new premier of France or this new character on the German scene or in Italy is not to be applauded. Why, then we'd let Goldie pull off some of his little, snide inside punches."

Time had always championed the cause of capitalism and democracy, but the "statesman's view of things" implied a certain judiciousness. Hadden, apolitical at heart, did not wish *Time* to bow to extremism from any direction. When Mussolini began to outlaw his political opposition, he violated the democratic sentiment that ran strong in Hadden, who portrayed Mussolini as a tin-pot dictator, petty in thought and ferocious in deed. But Goldsborough believed that whatever his faults "Il Duce" represented a bulwark against the threat of socialist revolution. Luce proved receptive to his viewpoint.

Goldsborough began to praise the fascists as bold leaders, while he described Communists as evil and irreligious, with sallow mugs, cold eyes, and cruel expressions. "Behind the relentless mask of the Third International, beaked sardonic visages relaxed in a sour smile," a typical *Time* story ran. Sanctioned by Luce, Goldsborough would control nearly every word printed in *Time*'s Foreign News section until their falling-out in 1940. Goldsborough would then work in counterespionage with the Office of Strategic Services, a precursor to the CIA. In 1950, wearing a bowler hat and carrying a cane, he would jump to his death from *Time*'s office building.

As Luce began to transform *Time* into a bullhorn for his political views, he also began to receive acclaim. Hadden, though known in New York society, had never sought printed publicity. Not only was he shy, he had the journalist's urge to keep the story on the news rather than on himself. But no sooner had Luce begun to edit *Time* than a column about him appeared in a Cincinnati newspaper. It lingered almost romantically over Luce's jutting chin and steel-blue eyes and called him the "sharpshooter of the magazine world." Luce was building a public record of the time he spent as an editor.

Despite Luce's increasing experience, a huge story could fall at his feet and he would hardly seem to recognize it. Perhaps the biggest story of the century in column inches and hoopla began on the morning of May 20, 1927, when Charles Lindbergh entered the cockpit of his single-engine monoplane. A foolhardy yet photogenic young man, he was determined to fly solo from New York to France. *Time* reported:

> At 7:52 a.m. he was roaring down the runway, his plane lurching on the soft spots of the wet ground. Out of the safety zone, he hit a bump, bounced into the air, quickly returned to earth. Disaster seemed imminent; a tractor and a gully were ahead. Then his plane took the air, cleared the tractor, the gully; cleared some telephone wires. Five hundred onlookers believed they had witnessed a miracle. It was a miracle of skill.

When he touched down at Le Bourget the following evening at 10:22 P.M., Lindbergh became the first mass-media hero.

The story was so important that Myron Weiss checked the Aviation department as it came off the press, just to make sure it looked all right. At the last minute, Weiss came running wildly from the pressroom, face and hands covered in black ink. "Jesus!" he yelled, waving his arms. "They've put an 'h' on Lindbergh!" Everyone panicked for a few moments until someone realized that was exactly how Lindbergh spelled his name. On the cover of *Time* that week were King George V and Queen Mary of England, who had just received a state visit from the president and foreign minister of France. Lindbergh wasn't royalty and Luce wasn't sure if he would always be around. "It may be true that heroes are made, not born," *Time* commented the following week. "But it is a fact that many a hero has unmade himself."

Luce remained as much proprietor as editor. He was glad to receive an invitation to join the Rowfant Club, an elite group of aesthetes and collectors of first editions. Lila wrote her mother that the victory was especially sweet because the same club had blackballed Roy Larsen. (He later got in.) At the country club, Cleveland matrons insisted on a spin around the dance floor with the celebrity editor. "Very sticky," Luce wrote Lila after one party. "Only had time to dance with about 7 dames which are already on the semi-duty list." In the office, he completed his cheerful immersion in suburban life with a promotional booklet entitled "A Tour Through *Time* Colony," featuring pictures of happy suburbanites enjoying their shiny cars, large houses, and green lawns. These were not nincompoops in Luce's view. He was one of them. He belonged.

Dinner parties at the Luces' place grew from eight to twenty places, the guests ever more illustrious. Luce worked tirelessly to attract industrialists and philanthropists, whose increasingly frequent visits gave him an inner thrill. "I've just this minute, on the brink of defeat, captured the great Len Hanna!" he wrote Lila, cresting the wave of a social coup. "Ah, what a glorious thing to be a Leonard Hanna." The cycle would feed on itself for the rest of his life as Luce climbed higher and higher, past Leonard Hanna and on to presidents and generals, seeking inclusion within ever more elite circles of influence, yet never quite feeling that he had become a "glorious thing" himself.

Hadden continued to head east most weekends, sleeping on the train to rest for the revels ahead. When Luce's secretary, Katherine Abrams, quit *Time* to move back home, Hadden reacted despondently. "I wish I were going too," he said. "If I have to stay on here much longer, I'll commit suicide." During one visit to New York, Hadden spent the weekend at Howard Black's house. Just before they went to a baseball game, Hadden asked Black to come with him while he placed a down payment on an apartment in Tudor City. "Why a New York apartment if you're in Cleveland?" Black asked. "We're coming back to New York," Hadden said. Idly at first, he began thinking about what type of magazine he might like to create next.

With a modest profit in the offing for 1927, Luce finally felt he could afford to relax for a moment. He and Lila planned their long delayed honeymoon, a six-week trip to Europe. They sailed for France in June and toured through Switzerland and Burgundy before heading to Paris. There they met the former *Time* freelancer Archibald MacLeish at his coldwater flat on the Boulevard St. Michel. Seeing Luce for the first time in years, MacLeish had an impression of an awkward, uncouth youth, "good bread but unleavened." MacLeish asked Luce what he thought of the wine country. "Vézelay was beautiful, but that hotel," Luce said. "There was only one bedroom and Lila had to sleep on the floor."

When the couple arrived in London, Luce turned ghostly white. "I feel terribly sick," he told his wife. "You take care of the baggage." His illness turned out to be a reemergence of the dormant malaria infection he had contracted as a child. Lila took a flat on Cork Street and hired two servants. Luce was forced to stay in bed for a month. As Lila nursed her husband to health, a barrage of wires began arriving at the hotel from Cleveland. Hadden was arguing in his headstrong way that the company must return to New York.

From Luce's perspective, it could have been worse. He had his detractors in the office. Now that Luce was out of town, John Martin was suggesting to his cousin that he ought to buy out Luce's stock and go on without him. Perhaps Martin did not yet realize the extent of Hadden's emotional attachment to Luce. Instead Hadden wrote a letter to the board of directors: "*Time* has reached a point where it is possible for us to consider entering into some other publishing venture. No new venture can well be entered into, however, unless both the Editor and the General Manager are on the job in New York."

Leery of an irrevocable decision and no doubt aware of the tension brewing between *Time*'s founders, the board gave Hadden permission to close down the magazine's Cleveland operations. By the time Luce returned home, the decision had been made. The editors and writers would return to New York in July. "I could have perhaps said, 'No such thing,'" Luce recalled. "But I knew it was impossible, that he was psychologically so determined to get back to New York that there was no use arguing." Roy Larsen sided with Hadden, agreeing that Cleveland was a backwater. "It was inevitable," Larsen later said. "We just couldn't operate out there."

Luce contracted with the Chicago printing firm of R. R. Donnelley & Sons. Old T. E. Donnelley was a Yale man, excited about *Time*. He traveled to Cleveland to negotiate with Luce and agreed to a novel system of production. The magazine would be written and edited in New York, then sent to Chicago by a combination of airplane and telegraph, and finally printed on a giant press by the same company that printed the *Encyclopedia Britannica.* Luce and Donnelley signed the deal on the last day of August. The newspaper horoscope that day predicted success for those entering into business deals, especially those related to publishing. They pasted the horoscope to the contract. "The offices of *Time . . .* are to move back to New York," *The Bookman* commented, "and so passes another brave attempt to break the editorial ring of the metropolis."

It would be a triumphant return. *Time* had stood at the doorstep of insolvency after the move to Cleveland. Little more than a year after the company almost went bust, Hadden and Luce stood poised to double their revenues and quadruple their advertising income. Time Inc. was not yet greater than the Hearst empire, but already it was more significant. Hadden and Luce were cobbling together upwardly mobile readers who would form the core of the national media audience in years to come. With money in the bank, a solid relationship with a quality printing press, and the creative impetus of New York to draw upon, the young publishers would have every opportunity to launch a new magazine.

It remained to be seen what each hoped to create from the opportunity for expansion, and whether they could maintain their friendship long enough to agree on a common course of action. Hadden and Luce still hardly spoke, and each knew little of the other's thoughts. For the moment, however, the future looked bright—for Hadden anyway. On his last night, he threw a party at the Rowfant Club. "A phenomenal dinner," Winsor French recalled, it "broke all the bylaws." The next morning Hadden quit the club and left for New York.

12

Man of the Year

THERE WAS EVIDENCE OF prosperity at 25 West Forty-fifth Street, where *Time*'s new office sat directly across from the Harvard Club and one flight below *The New Yorker*. Hadden and Luce had the word T I M E printed in gold leaf on the glass office door. Just inside, a young receptionist smartly operated a small switchboard. The board of directors raised the salaries of the founders to ten thousand dollars a year, and they began to spend money more freely. "They are now a national magazine," observed Manfred Gottfried, who had just returned to town, "and have to live up to their place."

Time's growing audience spread across America. In the corridors of power, sixteen U.S. senators subscribed, and in Hollywood Adolphe Menjou was seen carrying a copy—an action that curried no favor with Hadden, who soon dubbed the star actor "Dandy Menjou," "he of the cynical eyebrow and curling lip," who "wears fine clothes to hide his scrawny shanks." The New York press, which had always treated *Time* rather snobbishly, began to pay attention. When a *Herald Tribune* columnist printed a friend's jesting account of his typical day, it included the activity, "reads *Time*, says it annoys him." Hadden's cadences had spread to many a college campus. The members of the Princeton Quadrangle Club called *Time* "as popular here as ice cream."

Hadden and Luce knew they would soon be wealthy men. Quietly, they began trying to buy out their small investors, though not Hadden's favorite, Mary Hincks. Unfortunately nobody wished to sell; even Manfred Gottfried, having given up his common stock, fiercely held the forty shares of preferred his parents had bought for him in the earliest days of the company. Luce watched the ledgers closely, imagining what all the new advertising accounts would do for his lifestyle, but advising Lila not to spend anything yet. By the beginning of October, Luce realized he would soon hit a new milestone. "I will be in a manner of speaking a millionaire before I've finished being thirty—in other words I'll only be a year late!" he wrote Lila. "Got to catch up somehow!"

Hadden, by contrast, seemed to miss the old feeling of struggle. One night, while drinking with Dave Keep, Hadden put away a few rounds and began to get raucous. "Listen, Dave, mark my words well," he said. "Some day, *Time* will have a quarter of a million circulation." Keep was nonplussed; it seemed obvious that the magazine was well on its way to having many more readers than that. Mystified that he had failed to start an argument, Hadden shouted all the louder. "Mark my words!" he yelled. "Mark my words well!"

Hadden continued to run the magazine with an appreciation for inspiration and whim. Some writers composed their stories at home, others in a speakeasy across the street. There were six writers now, and a new one joined the team when Hadden hired a high school dropout from Pottsville, Pennsylvania, who had attracted Hadden's attention by writing several letters to the editor. John O'Hara arrived at *Time* in a moth-eaten raccoon coat and bearing a letter from the Yale employment bureau, though he had never gone to college. Shortly to become a famous novelist, he spent his free moments jotting down bits of narrative, which he promptly dropped into the wastebasket.

Although Niven Busch had left for *The New Yorker*, Hadden encouraged his cousin to contribute a story or two. Hadden also hired Niven's younger brother, Noel Fairchild Busch, who began by reviewing books and later wrote the cinema column. When an office boy arrived for his first day of work, he saw the Busch brothers in the lobby, playing miniature golf with their canes and some discarded cigarette butts. "I want you to pay attention to those Busch boys," Luce advised a new writer. "They're a couple of cheap Broadway sports and they don't know anything, but they can write the stuff."

No one in the office had any illusions about what made *Time* so successful. It was the writing style. "Mad as I get with Brit—unbelievably disagreeable as he is most of the time, I could never leave this job because it is an inspiration to work for the man—and you simply can't help admiring him and being fond of him," Winsor French, who had traveled east with the company, wrote his friend Katherine Halle in Cleveland. "He is a genius. . . . *Time* is certainly the absolute expression of everything that he stands for, down to the letter Z. . . . The damn magazine is his mind, his personality—his very existence."

Taking a female reader's suggestion, Hadden launched a new department called Fashions, a guide to modern living that reported on new ideas and movements in architecture, furniture design, cooking, and home improvement. The section obviously attracted women, and at first male readers bridled against the change. They were soon won over by *Time*'s intelligent treatment of fresh subjects such as posture chairs, the rise of foreign ingredients in American cooking, and a German building constructed entirely of glass. Everett Jackson, a Massachusetts reader who at first protested the section's creation, soon wrote a second letter to compliment the department's "spicy newsiness."

Some couldn't see the news value in lifestyle subjects. One grumpy reader complained that *Time*'s article on colorful kitchen implements had emboldened his wife to ask for every household gadget known to humankind—or "man," as he put it. "I will cancel her subscription," wrote A. E. Rivington of Louisville, Kentucky. Hadden gleefully printed a radical response from Sarah Goodwood of Detroit: If the Mr. should cancel the subscription, then the Mrs. would be justified in canceling the marriage. Fashions soon disappeared from *Time,* but the department would return in several guises through the decades. The women's subjects Hadden explored would spawn entire categories of magazines about cooking and homemaking as well as building and design, beginning with the Time Inc. magazines *Architectural Forum* and *House & Home.*

While Fashions increased *Time*'s female appeal, another section gave the magazine a new allure for readers of the gum-chewing variety. "Names Make News," the column began. "Last week the following names made the following news." A short list of newsmakers followed, along with descriptions of what they had done in the previous week. Readers liked the section, and over the next few years it would evolve into a basic gossip source for people who preferred not to realize they were taking an interest in celebrity trivia. Decades later, when *Time* executives brought tabloid fodder into the mainstream press by launching a magazine about celebrities, the editors took the name of Hadden's small department as their title. It was called "People."

While arguing for the return to New York, Hadden had written the board of directors that his reporters ought to start doing some original reporting instead of taking everything from the newspapers. In the second half of 1927, Hadden's writers began to stretch beyond the clippings, introduce their own ideas, and write longer stories: *Time*'s first feature pieces. One story on an opening session of the Senate, likely written by John Martin, took readers inside the chamber to show them the stentorian Senate clerk whose voice volleyed through the room, the aged parliamentarian who padded onto the floor, inspected his pen nib, then left, and the freshman senator who entered amid allegations that he had stolen the election. *Time* compared the senator to "an ostler at his master's wedding, awkward but proud, mortified but grinning, sheepish without shame." One reader complimented the magazine's "nose for character."

Hadden had never dedicated much space to writing about the person on the cover of *Time*, who simply happened to appear in one of the news stories each week. But readers loved the cover portraits by S. J. Woolf, and when the artist traveled to Europe in the spring of 1927 his fans loudly protested his absence. One reader even suggested that the artist ought to stop "galavanting" around the continent and get back to work. When Woolf returned to America the following fall, Hadden assigned him numerous covers and began to experiment with assigning feature profiles to go along with them.

Soon *Time* abounded with idealized portraits of news figures like Hearst, whose furrowed brow contrasted so comically with his doubtful smile. "William Randolph Hearst is called an attractive man," *Time* reported. "His is a great, tall, 220 lb. figure with long arms and big hands. His eyes are bluish grey, and it is said, not very kind. He is quiet, almost bashful, and possesses quantities of that illusive thing called personality." The story traced Hearst's rise to prominence, then outlined his latest predicament in a burst of Timestyle: "The terrible tabloids have out-Hearsted Hearst and now the morning field in screams and scandals is dominated by the *Daily News*."

Hadden was beginning to mature as an editor. He was focusing on ideological and economic issues as he had never done before. On the tenth anniversary of the Bolshevik revolution, Hadden began his coverage with a view of the parade wending through Moscow: "Caucasian cavalry dashed by, their gleaming sabers at salute, their long black capes flowing behind. . . . Then came the Turkoman cavalry at a sharp trot, wearing their huge black shakos and great ponchos." The following page discussed the changes in education, divorce law, price controls, and trade that had occurred since the fall of the czar, with contradictory interpretations from the *New Masses, The Nation,* and Alexander Kerensky, who had been forced out of power by the Communist coup.

Finally the story introduced *Time*'s readers to a bilious little man who would shortly grow into a grand and monstrous character on history's stage: "He is distinguished by a well-shaped head surrounded by a shock of black hair, just beginning to grey. He has a silky black mustache. His eyes are black, and rarely is there a gleam of merriment in them. His facial features suggest cruelty—a hard mask of oriental ruthlessness." Joseph Stalin was his name.

In October of 1927, Hadden devoted several columns to the election of Victor L. Berger to the chairmanship of the Socialist Party of the United States. The story segued into a primer on the basic tenets of socialism. To help his readers distinguish one political ideology from the next, Hadden asked his readers to imagine a color wheel with each color representing a different political stripe. *Time* named celebrities who belonged to each category, from the true blue of J. P. Morgan to the fiery red of the executed radicals Sacco and Vanzetti. As for Berger, Hadden decided that he wasn't really red; he was pink. The piece ended: "Red footstools, red neckties, intentionally crude cartoons, stuffy parlors and garrets, late hours, morose arguments, 'long-haired men and short-haired women,' dirty fingernails and a strange courage, are among the peculiar properties of Socialism."

The breadth and sophistication of Hadden's latest efforts far surpassed his earlier work. But Luce and Larsen wished he would cut down on the offbeat humor. By the fall of 1927, Hadden was printing

up to six columns of letters each week, interpolating his own corrections, apologies, and counterattacks, and castigating his writers with
a "thorough-going rebuke" when readers found a mistake. One oft-
rebuked writer was Peter Mathews, a fictional member of the masthead. Hadden used the letters section to give readers a stake in *Time*.
He invited them to vote on the color of the cover or on a proposal
for a news column about checkers—invitations that sparked further
outbursts.

Hadden's most outlandish correspondent was a phony one: Morris
"Al" Epstein Jr., a loudmouth from Brooklyn who closed each letter with
the observation, "They all lay down sooner or later!" Readers eagerly
corrected Epstein's sloppy grammar. Epstein reached full flower when
he submitted a diatribe against *Time*'s gentlemanly Sport department:
"Bowling on the green!! Who called *that* a sport anyhow? It sounds like
old ladies' stuff to me, rolling little balls on the ground and not even
socking anything with them!" Epstein was forced to "lay down" when a
Time reader wagered that he could do better on the first try at bowling
than Epstein could at golf. "Dealing in facts, *Time* must admit the existence of gambling in the fabric of this world," Hadden replied. "*Time*
sanctions the challenge." But Epstein refused to compete and soon
thereafter he vanished from the magazine.

Time remained the place to hear the full-throated call of the average American moron, expressing his prejudices with confidence and
joy. Subscribers enjoyed reading such letters and tried to take a broad
view of the phenomenon. "As for the letters you print!" one reader
wrote Hadden. "Of course one really doesn't care a hoot about your
awful cover, or your late proposed checker column, or the other stock
subjects; your red-blooded American or Americanne makes the most
naïve spectacle of himself when he essays literature via his subscription
to *Time*. Therefore I and my friends, grateful, honest, give a trio of
tremulant yoicks for *Time*. Long may it wave!"

By baiting his readers into argument, Hadden was creating a bizarre
brand of humor. Luce and Larsen worried he would push *Time* toward
those who enjoyed laughing at the middle class—a wealthy, elite audience. When Larsen received a letter refusing *Time*'s latest subscription
offer on the grounds that a "professional intellectual" magazine did not
appeal, he warned Hadden that too many cracks could cap *Time*'s audi-

ence and curb their ambitions to blanket the nation. "It sounds dangerous to me, especially in view of the fact that *Time* has only one purpose—to make money," Larsen wrote. "There is more money to be gotten out of Babbitts of a higher grade than out of the so-called intellectuals. God forbid that we should become their mouthpiece!"

As the economy heated up, Hadden's dislike for puffery and his delight in expressing contrary viewpoints led him to print a few articles that poked fun at business. In September of 1927, he chose to lead the business section with a short piece entitled "Pure, Green Greed." The story quoted the answer of Charles R. Flint, the father of trusts, to a reporter who asked what kept him going year after year. "Pure, green greed," Flint replied. "Greed, and greed alone, is the reason for a man's wanting to swell his wad million after million." Such stories were not mere jokes. They reflected Hadden's point of view, which ran counter to Luce's. "Hadden wanted business, and especially Big Business, to be frequently taken over the knee and spanked like an ill-mannered brat," recalled Noel Busch, who often wrote Hadden's business column.

Larsen believed *Time* wasn't nearly as comprehensive as it used to be. Although he had begun by printing eighteen departments every week, by the summer of 1927 Hadden was printing only ten to fifteen departments and leaving out news that didn't interest him. Larsen was soliciting new subscribers by sending them a copy of the magazine alongside a brochure called "The Newsmagazine Idea." Impressed by the circular, one man in Groton, Massachusetts, opened the magazine to the National Affairs section. Hoping to find a summary of the week past, he learned instead that Mrs. Coolidge liked the circus. Larsen wrote Hadden that it seemed misleading to promise readers all the news from around the world only to offer under the heading of "France" a brief story on "a street fight over a tipped-over banana cart."

A conflict was emerging over what type of magazine *Time* should become. Hadden believed it would be possible to reach a vast national audience without sacrificing the note of flippant urbanity with which the project had begun. He continued to publish the stories he would like to read, perhaps not considering that his tastes had changed. His connection with his readers was kinetic, and as evidence he could point to *Time*'s high renewal rate. But Larsen believed that if Hadden hoped to attract several hundred thousand and perhaps even a million readers he would have to edit for a broader audience.

Eager to make *Time* acceptable to a wider public, Larsen began sending Hadden weekly reactions to the magazine that pointed out offensive letters, attacks on public figures, and instances of blatant neglect of serious news. In the fall of 1927, Larsen warned Hadden that more subscriptions expired during September and October than during any other time of the year. To offset the impending losses, Larsen was launching a massive subscription drive. He planned to market the magazine as a teaching aid for schoolteachers. "May I ask a favor?" he pleaded. "Will you try to make the September and October issues the purest we have ever issued?"

A few weeks later, Hadden ran a story in the Education section about little boys and girls punching their teachers in the face and kicking them in the shins. He titled the article "Little Rebels." Larsen sent Hadden another memorandum, begging him to stop intentionally disrupting *Time*'s circulation efforts. Hadden scrawled "quite right" at the top of Larsen's memorandum and asked him to take a look at the following week's Education section. The lead story that week stated that parents were wasting their money by sending their children to college. It began, "One-sixth of the college population should be sacked."

Luce was growing frustrated with the constant battles. "This Hadden-Luce yoke is certainly galling," he wrote Lila. "His intentions are okay—But the differences between us are so great—However I don't see any way out which seems better than struggling through with it. Perhaps if I made up my mind to include mentally in our budget 'Hadden nonsense, $50,000—or $100,000 per annum' it might be conducive to peace of mind! Of course, this letter should be torn up pronto."

After Luce proposed restraining his partner with an editorial constitution, Hadden promised to be "18 department conscious" and began to fill Letters with serious debates. Larsen, mollified, wrote Hadden of the December 5 issue: "I find nothing in it which any sane and normal Babbitt or bigwig could possibly object to." It finally seemed as though Hadden and his partners had struck the perfect compromise. They would expand their readership by trimming back the wildest excesses and continue to discuss a wide range of topics while maintaining a humorous edge.

When 1927 came to an end, *Time* posted another small profit despite the cost of the return to New York. Advertising income had risen to $414,000 for the year. The magazine was attracting 138,000 readers a week, and Larsen was guaranteeing advertisers 180,000 for the next year. In the distance, he could see a shining figure: 200,000. Revenues were rising so quickly that Hadden and Luce anticipated making their first large profit in 1928 and sending investors their first dividend. And they were about to create an annual feature that would take its place alongside the Coca-Cola bottle and the Campbell's soup can as one of America's most enduring icons.

It happened, paradoxically, because the last week of 1927 was unusually dull. The President lit the capital's Christmas tree, of course, and Chiang Kai-shek broke off his relations with the Soviet Union. The pope named a couple of cardinals in Rome, and the Hungarian composer Béla Bartók made his American debut. Nevertheless, it seemed at the time to be a light news week; no subject presented itself to the editors as especially worthy of cover treatment. When they held a meeting to select a cover subject, an editor suggested a novel idea. Why not ignore the past week and highlight instead the individual who most influenced events in the previous year? It seemed obvious who that would be.

In the six months since his solo flight across the Atlantic, the aviator Charles Lindbergh had received cheers around the world as a hero of almost Christ-like significance. Flying through the clouds in *The Spirit of St. Louis,* the boy from Minnesota triumphed for a moment over the horror of war, over the cynicism of Prohibition, over weakness, fear, and indecision. Tall and clear-eyed with a shy smile, he represented America's self-image—moral, daring, optimistic. He flew into the future linking countries and people, an apostle of understanding and peace. On his return to the United States, he was greeted in New York by a ticker tape parade so crowded with confetti that people could hardly see. His face appeared in just about every newspaper, on souvenirs, in movie houses, and on postcards. It was the most ubiquitous face ever seen in the United States—but it had yet to grace the cover of *Time.*

Normally *Time* readers appreciated the magazine's refusal to be carried away by blind adulation, but by the end of the year it no longer seemed possible for a mainstream magazine to continue in such a vein. People were cheering Lindbergh as the hero of the century. As a phenomenon, if not as a man, he had risen to historic significance, and readers were clamoring for his face to be placed on the cover. *Time* did not have to idealize Lindbergh in order to view his flight as the major news event of the year. By acceding to their readers' demands, the editors could compensate for a slow news week while correcting an embarrassing oversight. "The boys felt pretty ingenious about getting around the problem," the chief researcher Mary Fraser recalled.

It so happened that S. J. Woolf had drawn a portrait of Lindbergh in the American embassy just six days after his arrival in Paris. Lindbergh had agreed to autograph the picture, which gave it a commemorative feeling appropriate for the last issue of the year. Underneath the picture, Hadden and Luce printed a clever caption: "THE MAN OF THE YEAR." Skipping over Lindbergh's accomplishments, the story began with a picture: "Height: 6 ft. 2 inches. Age: 25. Eyes: Blue. Cheeks: Pink. Hair: Sandy. Feet: Large. When he arrived at the Embassy in France no shoes big enough were handy."

The Lindbergh story marked a major turning point for *Time.* By elevating the young Minnesotan to a rare and high throne, the edgy little upstart cast aside its sneering humor and embraced the values of mainstream America. To be sure, there were still some who suspected a hint of disrespect in *Time*'s use of colloquial detail to register a hero in the American memory. "Let me tell you, *Time,*" wrote Grace Gordon Cox of Boston, "there will never be a man on your staff big enough to 'stand in Lindy's shoes!'" But another reader, J. Montrose Edrehi of Pensacola, Florida, wrote that his heart soared when he saw the cover. *Time,* he realized, had saved its best for last.

13

Geniuses

AN ATTRACTIVE COPY OF *Time* rolled off R. R. Donnelley's sixty-ton press early in the new year. The magazine had a modern look, with larger paper and lighter print. The colors were crisper and, since Donnelley's could print two colors at once, the magazine took half the time to print. The editor could send his copy to Chicago on Sunday night and telegraph late-breaking copy throughout the following day with the knowledge that his words would arrive in subscribers' hands by Friday. That man was Henry R. Luce, who finally insisted on taking a full year in the editor's chair.

Descending to the ground floor in the rickety elevator, Winsor French asked Noel Busch how he thought the new editor would change the magazine. "How in hell would I know?" Busch said. "I've never even seen the bastard." Just at that moment French jabbed Busch in the ribs. The elevator had stopped at a lower floor and a somber figure was stepping in, his faced cloaked by a gray felt hat. No one talked the whole way down. Finally the elevator stopped and the man walked out. "Well," French said, "You've seen the bastard now." It had not dawned on Busch that this strong and silent figure could be Luce since he hardly matched the meek man of Niven's description.

The change French expected came quickly. As more advertise-ments flooded in, Luce increased the magazine's size, which gave him the chance to print more news. The curiosity that made Luce such a voracious and tireless traveler also made him a unique editor. Luce had a tendency to fill an entire page with background information, thereby turning a simple story into a takeout on a region. Under Luce's editorship, *Time* occasionally took the tone of a geography lesson, complete with detailed maps. Although his sense of humor differed from Hadden's, Luce could be whimsical in his way. Instead of printing only the names of several South American countries, he began to print "A=Argentina," "B=Brazil," "C=Chile."

Unlike Hadden, Luce interpreted events for his readers. *Time*'s cover on January 16, 1928, featured a portrait of Calvin Coolidge on the eve of his trip to Cuba, where the President planned to meet with the leaders of several Latin-American nations at the sixth annual Pan-American Congress. Luce took the opportunity to expound on the theme of American empire:

> Britannia is said to have ruled the waves of all the oceans. Other powers have been content to rule a sea apiece. Rome was the Mediterranean's master. The Kaiser ruled the Baltic. Mussolini claims the Adriatic. To every sea its Caesar—to the Caribbean the mighty U.S.

A simple story about a meeting, which Hadden would have covered by highlighting the key participants, was transformed into a feature piece on an entire region. The context Luce supplied helped readers to grasp the meaning of events, but so much interpretation also threw the news into a world of subjectivity.

Luce tried to widen *Time*'s appeal by tempering its inclination to shock. Hadden, helped along by Wells Root and Noel Busch, made a habit of printing insulting movie reviews. The most recent movie review column edited by Hadden called Hollywood's new fare "insipid," "vulgar," and "interminable," and insulted the actress Maria Corda, the famous Helen of Troy, as "a pretty little blonde girl with an affected way of showing her teeth." Angered by *Time*'s elitism, a Floridian reader suggested the magazine should view films from the perspective of the people in the audience. Hadden had always scoffed at such complaints, but Luce replied that he would heed the criticism.

Readers were shocked by the sudden change in *Time*'s temperament. Several attacked *Time* for pandering to "commonplace and commercial" interests. "Do not, *Time*, cease to tell the truth in art as your
reviewer sees it," wrote Edward P. Goodnow of Boston, "until you cease
to tell the truth in news." But Luce wanted to sell magazines, and if he
had to hawk some mediocre movies in order to do so, he was willing to
make the concession. The next issue's reviews complimented terrible
movies as "blithe, casual, flippant, almost constantly entertaining." In a
peroration reminiscent of Luce's days on the debate team, one review
stated: "Scarcely any period of 30 seconds passes without supplying
new and highly legitimate grounds for laughter."

Luce was willing to make such compromises in order to increase
Time's bottom line. When one of *Time*'s largest advertisers, Walter P.
Chrysler, finally grew tired of being ridiculed for his middle name of
Percy, he threatened to pull his advertising out of the magazine. Luce
agreed never to mention the name again—except once a year, just to
prove that *Time* could. Editorially, the decision seemed insignificant,
but it showed Luce's early compliance with the needs of his advertisers
and his less than total allegiance to the principle of fairness.

Whereas Hadden took an interest in and was amused by eccentric
people, Luce admired people in positions of power. Instead of printing
outlandish letters from phony correspondents, Luce printed "serious
point-making letters," as he called them, from public figures. "Frankly,
I haven't criticized the editorial content of *Time* for a long while simply
because I have found little to criticize," Larsen wrote John Martin in
June of 1928. "The things which particularly gripe me in the magazine—moron letters, nigger boot-licking, unnecessary sex appeal, digs
at bigwigs—have one and all been eliminated, at least to the degree to
which we can eliminate them."

Marriage and fatherhood gave Luce confidence while making him
less intellectually adventurous than he had been in college. He did
not shy away from impressing his conservative moral standards on the
staff. Walking through the office one Sunday, Luce noticed that the
writer Alan Jackson was wearing an Easter cutaway and accompanying
regalia. Assuming Jackson had just come from church, Luce congratulated his writer for making the right choice. Jackson, amused, decided
not to tell Luce the truth. He had worn his Sunday suit to the office

only because he went to church so infrequently that he felt he ought to get some use out of it somehow.

The writer who most identified with Luce's cultural conservatism was Laird Goldsborough, who shared Luce's respect for aristocracies of all kinds, whether of intelligence, breeding, or wealth. Goldsborough was rising to a position of authority in the office. Though he was sick in mind as well as body, his very instability helped to give him a kind of tyrannical authority possessed by no other writer. "He stuck by himself," Elizabeth Armstrong recalled. "If he didn't like what was being done with his material, he would have a nervous breakdown on Saturday night and no one knew whether he would come back or not."

Goldsborough held crude and stereotyped attitudes; one article he wrote referred to Asians as "slant-eyed poppy-landers." But he wrote evocatively. In a typical week, he could skip through power struggles in Moscow with asides on vodka and caviar, flowing into a poetic description of the exile of Comrade Trotsky: "Twenty minutes past nine was the historic hour. Sullen but docile Russians had slowly gathered, drifting in to the number of 1,500. Now they waited, massed before the great railway terminus at Moscow, shuffling and shivering beneath cold stars, but ready to shout, 'Long live Trotsky!' and then 'Farewell! Farewell....'" After hooking readers on the narrative, Goldsborough would tell them his opinion: "At Moscow who remains? Paramount is Nikolai Lenin, lying embalmed at the Kremlin, a lifelike, strangely magnetic effigy of himself, an idol wondrously potent among groping, uncertain Russians. In the Idol's name rules Josef Stalin, like most high priests a perverter of original doctrine."

Time was growing one-sided under Luce. In previous years Hadden took care to compensate for his personal judgments of news figures by quoting conflicting press interpretations of events. Sometimes Hadden even quoted socialist papers. Luce, by contrast, privileged his own viewpoint. When the secretary of the navy doubled the number of Marines fighting the Nicaraguan revolutionary Augusto Sandino, Luce quoted several different opinions—but he noted that a general in the Marines held the "mature" view: "Every American who is proud of being an American should be proud of the American Marines in Nicaragua."

Whereas Hadden often poked fun at business culture, Luce essentially agreed with President Coolidge's maxim that the business of America was business. In the spring of 1928, as the stock market continued to shoot upward, Luce dramatically increased the size of the business section. Soberly, *Time* warned that workers investing their salaries might be putting their savings at risk. "The 'public' had finally come in, tardily, clumsily, 'at the top,' as always," *Time* reported. "It astonished nobody, because 7,000 tickers are now hypnotizing greedy eyes in 40 states, leaving scarcely a middle-sized town from Maine to California where citizens may not actually see their savings bank with-drawals dance past their giddy eyes in strange, cryptic abbreviations three minutes after passing their checks to the broker."

All through the spring of 1928, Luce and his writers watched the hyperactive stock market, but they also took care to cover trends within the larger world of business and industry. Luce ran an illuminat-ing feature piece on Sosthenes Behn, the press-shy financier who put together the telephone and telegraph conglomerate IT&T. Luce also ran a piece on Peggy Cleary, a successful investor who nearly became the first woman to hold a seat on the New York Stock Exchange. The article, "Skirts," observed that the new breed of woman was on the verge of breaking into yet another smoky men's club. *Time* believed Cleary had the necessary "firmness of jaw possessed by exquisite, mer-ciless croupiers who rake chips on Monte Carlo's greens." What was more, *Time* added, "Miss Cleary is pretty."

Luce thought of industrialists as public figures and hoped that if he covered them as such perhaps they would behave in a more public spirit. Fascinated by the powerful new American economy, Luce began searching for writers who could enliven *Time*'s business reporting. John Martin, recalling that Scottish bankers preferred hiring classics stu-dents to men with technical backgrounds, advised Luce to simply hire a good writer. Martin recommended a Princeton friend who happened to have majored in classics. Parker Lloyd-Smith soon quit his job at the *Albany News* and came to work for *Time*. "So down came this fellow . . . who still looked like a woolly lamb," Martin recalled. "Sort of no chin and fuzzy head of hair, and these great big girlish eyes, a rather sharp nose, and a prissy little mouth—but oh, boy! What a keen bébé!"

A sweet, dashing man, Parker Lloyd-Smith had always taken the female roles in prep-school plays. Women found him attractive, while classmates at The Hill School and Princeton joked about his effeminate manner. They would be shocked, in September of 1931, when he committed suicide by jumping off the roof of his building. A poetry and art lover, stylish to the point of being foppish, affected in speech, Lloyd-Smith developed a fluid style. For the first time, executives began to look to *Time* as a source for business news. When *World's Work* asked Julius Klein, the director of the Bureau of Foreign and Domestic Commerce, which magazines he enjoyed reading, Klein said he relied on *Foreign Affairs*, *Living Age*, and, for "business and economic journalism," *Time*.

The 1928 presidential election provided Luce the opportunity to step into the public spotlight while testing *Time*'s storytelling methods on a national story. The campaign season began with a shock when President Coolidge, having served barely four years since President Harding's death, released a laconic statement: "I do not choose to run for president in 1928." The humorless country lawyer would return home to Massachusetts to whittle wood on his front porch.

Several Republicans made plans to run for the office. The front-runner was Herbert Hoover, who had risen to fame during the war by leading a commission that brought food to the starving people of Belgium. He had then led the government's efforts to help those displaced by the Great Mississippi Flood. The Democratic house was divided. The rising urban wing of the party championed New York's Al Smith, a charismatic Irishman who had risen from the Lower East Side to the governor's mansion and there passed a series of progressive reforms. While Hoover called Prohibition a "noble experiment," Smith called it a stimulus for corruption.

Smith was one of *Time*'s original subscribers. The majority of the writers supported him, and it was thought that Hadden did. Luce was repelled by Hoover's high starched collar and found him lacking in Rooseveltian charisma. "The country can now afford anything except moral leaderlessness," he wrote in a note for a speech that he delivered in Rochester, New York. For the first time in his life, Luce found himself disagreeing with his father. Reverend Luce, a Republican by long-standing habit and principle, supported Hoover for religious reasons, too. Though far from a fundamentalist, Reverend Luce adamantly supported Prohibition. Luce told his father that the law perversely encouraged people to drink. He wrote a check for $100 to the Smith campaign.

Luce covered the 1928 election exhaustively, beginning a tradition that would distinguish *Time*'s election coverage for decades. Many issues featured up to six pages on the race. The coverage, breezy and laden with minutiae, tended to focus on appearances more than platforms. Hoover had a portly build, chubby cheeks, and buckteeth, as well as workmanlike habits, an engineering degree, and a history of building dams. *Time* called him the "Beaver-Man." Like a beaver, Hoover was efficient, the magazine estimated, but he lacked that mystic core required to "satisfy as a popular leader."

Time dubbed Al Smith the "Brown Derby" in honor of the hat he had worn since young adulthood. Smith's rise from poverty was a dramatic one, and the magazine made use of its human interest in describing the governor's youth: "He could dance jigs and recite and he thought he could sing. He wore fancy waistcoats, a red necktie, tight trousers and a trig brown derby. He grew tall and quite handsome. He was blond, eager, jocose. They always called him Alfred." *Time* guessed that Smith could win with the help of his "wide smile, throaty laugh, instant humor, lowly origin, the tilt of the Brown Derby." Or perhaps he would lose due to "spittoons, chewed cigars, damp shirt-sleeves, profanity."

Here was a new kind of press, focused entirely through the prismatic lens of personality. In later years, for better or worse, more newspapers and magazines would mimic *Time*'s approach by covering the question of who would win more than the political issues at stake. For the moment, *Time* stood out in style and substance. When Al Smith called Herbert Hoover "Candidate Hoover," the *New York Evening Post* observed, "He sounds like *Time*." The *Evening Post* sounded like *Time*, too, calling Smith "jaunty, jolly, cocksure" and describing his speech as a "stern-browed challenge to his dastardly foes."

The star writer who had likely coined the nicknames for Hoover and Smith was John Martin, who was writing thousands of words each week and almost single-handedly building a persona for the magazine. In 1928, he went to the Republican convention, reporting for *Time* in print and on the nascent NBC radio network. Delegates and reporters, discovering Martin represented the magazine, would parrot back to him their most cherished epithets. Since radio remained a phantom medium, Martin was surprised that so many people heard his voice on the airwaves. "Scarcely a day has passed since June 14 without an echo from it," he wrote Roy Larsen. "We ought to arrange to 'horn in' on these national hookups more often."

Not yet twenty-eight years old, Martin was a top-notch correspondent. Of all *Time*'s talented writers, he was the best at cobbling together anecdotes from several sources. When Hoover was nominated by his home state of California, Martin seemed to stand in the whole hall at once, noticing and recording the slightest detail: "The sputtering, hissing Klieg searchlights played down on a tall, dark, ministerial figure grasping the high lectern with both outstretched hands. . . . Writer H. L. Mencken took off his coat, revealing a cocoa-colored shirt and loud suspenders. . . . As the noise continued, Will Rogers' lower lip stuck farther out. . . . Last to quiet down was a quartet of harmonizers accompanied by a fat man with an accordion." When transposed to television, Martin's style of narrative reporting would turn politics into a spectator sport.

The Democratic convention, six weeks later in Houston, proved more dramatic. Several decades had passed since an urban candidate had won the Democratic nomination over the party's rural, Southern base. The convention hall was too stuffy for some humors, as *Time* wryly reported in an account of a debate between several Democrats over Prohibition: "Senator Tydings at one juncture found it necessary to call Bishop Cannon an utterer of falsehood. Senator Glass told Senator Tydings he was behaving 'indecently.' Senator Tydings leaped at Senator Glass, had to be held."

Smith's rise to the nomination empowered the party's urban wing, but Smith would not win the nomination without the helping hand of the former Democratic vice-presidential nominee Franklin Delano Roosevelt. The convention hall went silent as Roosevelt, having recently survived a life-threatening bout with polio, struggled toward the podium. "With his limp and cane and the stretch of suffering on his face, he might have made an appeal to the audience more emotional than any of the other speakers," *Time* reported. "Instead, he held himself erect and delivered what all critics agreed was the most intelligently well-bred speech of either of the big conventions. . . . Compared to the common run of nominating effusions, Mr. Roosevelt's speech was as homo sapiens to the gibbering banderlog."

Once again the *Time* eye was everywhere at once, simultaneously positioned on the convention floor and in the governor's suite in Albany. *Time*'s description of Smith's reaction to Roosevelt's speech hinted at the emerging rivalry between them:

> Candidate Smith fingered his watch-chain, bit his cigar, blinked at the ceiling, took out the cigar, stared at the ceiling. The others sat rigid, occasionally stealing looks at him. During the directly personal part, about his "kindly heart" and understanding of "the average man," Candidate Smith looked overheated, troubled.
>
> ". . . Victory is his habit—the happy warrior, Alfred E. Smith," came the last words, then the crashing applause. Puffing hard at his cigar, Alfred E. Smith left the room.

No other publication could reveal so much information through the subtlety of gesture.

While *Time* excelled at describing the surface features of personal rivalry, the magazine paid little attention to the subterranean shifts that can drive the direction of a political campaign. By the time of Smith's July nomination, the Southern and Western states were immersed in a sea of "literature": pamphlets and broadsides accusing Smith of being a drunkard and womanizer who planned to take his directions from the pope. *Time* responded to each charge as it came up. "Is Governor Al. Smith a drinking man?" a Des Moines reader asked. *Time* replied, "Candidate Smith, like many another U.S. statesman and politician, enjoys an occasional cocktail and highball, relishes a stein of cool Munchener beer. Candidate Smith is no alcoholic, no inebriate. . . . Unless all who drink are drinking men, *Time* would not classify him as a drinking man."

By the fall, thousands of anti-Catholic "campaign cards" were spreading through the South and West. *Time* noted that the cards were handed out by civil servants, "unauthorized by the Republican National Committee but undeterred," and printed an example of their prose:

> When Catholics rule the United States
> And the Jews grow a straight nose;

When Pope Pius is head of the Ku Klux Klan,
In the land of Uncle Sam—
Then Al Smith will be President
And the Country won't be worth a dam . . .

Such infantile poems doubtless amused *Time*'s editors, but Luce and his team underestimated the depth of prejudice in the land, and the extent to which political forces were capitalizing on society's basest impulses. In the end, *Time* missed the big story of the election.

As Election Day neared, the anti-Smith forces reached a crescendo of vitriol. Finally Hoover accused Smith of being a socialist. Smith clambered aboard a train and traveled through New England—Boston, Rhode Island, Hartford, New Haven. Adoring crowds mobbed him at each stop. "Swarming imps were everywhere, all yelling and grinning, a few tying to the Derby's car tin cans which other imps snatched off, pummeling the tin-can-tiers," *Time* reported. "Pandemonium dinned from incessantly sounded motor horns, blared from brass band, split the welkin with shrieks of 'Al! Al! We're for you, Al!' While Mrs. Smith beamed and threw kisses by the hearty handful, the Governor seemed to grow at last almost awed with the frenzied multitudes. Like a magician's wand his small brown hat seemed literally to conjure cheers. He was supremely happy, but perhaps amazed."

The excitement of the crowds transfixed the nation, with some seeing the makings of a popular movement. But no one knew whether the crowds would translate into votes. The cover of *Time*'s election issue showed a sea of faces. "THE PEOPLE," it was captioned. "Is it a great beast?" Luce printed a map of the nation that labeled various regions with flippant descriptions: "Anti-Saloon Land" across Indiana and Missouri, "Cracker Land" in northern Florida, and, on Lake Erie, where the bootleggers traveled, "Rum." The issue also included a scorecard. "Let subscribers preserve this copy of *Time*," Luce instructed. "On Election Day, having cast their votes, taken their holiday, dined and turned on their radios, let them use the blanks below for predictions, wagers or alert tabulation."

On Election Day, *Time*'s editor turned the crank for Smith—the first and almost certainly the last time Luce would vote for a Democrat. Hadden arrived at the office wearing a Hoover button. "It's easier this way," he said, explaining that his family always voted for the Republicans. Most of the nation broke for Hoover, who won in a landslide. The following week, *Time* beat the *Literary Digest* by analyzing the election results state by state. Jauntily, *Time*'s writers mused over a few factors that may have hurt Smith: "spitting on floors, rough voice, vulgar accent." But it was he who had stirred the crowds. As for Hoover's fate, *Time* reported that on the morning of the election Mrs. Coolidge had found a black cat crossing the White House lawn.

By the end of the election season, *Time* was reaching 188,000 readers. Larsen guaranteed advertisers a circulation of 220,000 for 1929 and 300,000 for 1930. Newsstand sales had jumped from 12,000 to 25,000 copies, and *Time*'s founders expected to reach 30,000 newstand readers in the following year. Luce had printed *Time*'s first sixty-page issue, then its first sixty-four-page issue. He had run a color portrait on the front cover. The company's profit after taxes was more than $125,000, a figure boosted by a 20 percent increase in advertising lineage and full-page advertisements from Kodak, Graybar Electric, GM, Chrysler, Lincoln, and Rolls-Royce. Even wayward Fisher Body returned to *Time*. The company took out three full-color back covers—just as Luce ran a laudatory profile of the Fisher Brothers. Most brilliant of all were the Camel ads with their dapper college boys smoking in the football stands, arm in arm with their fur-fringed girlfriends: "Camels—so mellow, mild and unfailingly good." Robert L. Johnson, having promised a million dollars in advertising revenue during 1928, would beat his prediction by a hundred thousand dollars.

Time was leading a shift in the way the nation thought about the news. The magazine's tight focus on plot, its relentless attention to personality, its colorful method of physical description, and its clever, entertaining style were all finding their way into the newspapers. So were *Time*'s neologisms. The *Saturday Evening Post* referred to Knute Rockne as the "famed Notre Dame football coach." *Town Talk* began referring to itself as "The Southern Newsmagazine." The *Colorado Lookout* published an entire issue in Timestyle, with a note at the top: "apologies to *Time*."

Some newspaper editors, especially older ones, believed the magazine had cheapened and popularized their profession. When *Time* teased Cincinnati as a drooping town run by Procter & Gamble's "knights of soap," the hometown paper lashed back. *Time*, it said, was a "gargoyle of the new urge, which finds its inspirations in the drone of saxophones, the beat of drums and the flash of a pert flapper's underpinnings." But by 1928 people were growing accustomed to saxophones and flappers. *Time* was the magazine for the moment, a badge of sophistication and style, and a new kind of mass educator for the middle class. One California columnist went so far as to recommend *Time* to his readers as "a university to a busy world."

Luce had added depth and sophistication to Hadden's achievement. They had always cooperated in that way. Beaming with pride in Luce's work, Hadden told friends that he had received tons of angry letters during the election season—almost the same number from cranks on the left as from cranks on the right. This was proof, he thought, that *Time* had played it straight. Listening to Hadden talk about Luce, Mimi Martin realized her friend felt a real and permanent love for his partner, despite the tension that lay between them. They were speaking again, though only occasionally, and when talking with others Hadden coldly persisted in referring to his partner as "Mr. Luce."

Surely they shared a strange and tense partnership, yet it had always been an effective one. They had succeeded together against the longest of odds, and most observers preferred to think that somehow they belonged together—cosmic twins and opposites, linked by madness and daring, who together saw things others couldn't notice. Seeing Hadden and Luce for the first time in a while, the Yale professor William Lyon Phelps wryly recalled predicting that they would fail. "I was absolutely correct," he maintained. "There was just one thing I overlooked. You both are geniuses."

14

Oliver Twisting

Time's EDITORS WERE GROWN up now and beginning to raise families of their own. John and Mimi Martin had taken an apartment on Park Avenue. The leading advertising executives were living in the suburbs. The Luces were renting a townhouse in Turtle Bay, where they socialized with the violinist Efrem Zimbalist and other members of café society. The Larsens soon moved nearby, and the Luce and Larsen children would later become neighborhood playmates. Hadden didn't appear to be headed for this world. Every few months he would take an office girl on a weekend love binge, and sometimes he would even propose marriage. A few days later he would break it off.

Hadden purchased a three-bedroom spread in a cooperative building at 25 East End Avenue. The Hadden home was a motley ménage, free-spirited, egalitarian, and exceedingly crowded. Hadden usually had two friends living with him, including William J. Carr, a young attorney and friend from Yale, and Thomas J. C. Martyn, who had separated from his wife. There were also a couple of cats; Hadden enjoyed taking in strays. Evening guests came in and out constantly, including the singer Libby Holman and Luce's distant cousin Judge Robert L. Luce, who would brighten when Holman launched into one of her harangues. The roommates took their meals together, served by a Chinese cook. Once a week each of them would give a dinner party, which the others were free to attend.

Hadden believed any group could have fun together if properly lubricated. He tested his pet notion by inviting a ludicrous mix of people to his parties. Dreaming up his latest guest list with the help of Mimi Martin, Hadden would chuckle over each possibility: a minister, a ballplayer, a Japanese whore. No one was too strange for Hadden. He only required each guest to be a leader in his or her chosen field.

At the start of his social experiment, Hadden would coax his guests into conversation, push liquor into their hands, and, if all else failed, gather them in the living room to sing. Puffing out his chest like an orchestra conductor, he would grandly wave a German schnitzel-bank pointer for comic effect. If the group grew bored or fractious, Hadden would duck unseen into the kitchen, and several minutes later the phone would ring. Gravely explaining that he was needed at the office, the editor would rush out the door.

Hadden was drinking a vile brand of Scotch that he purchased for forty-five dollars a case when everyone else was paying ninety dollars. His friends refused to drink it. Often he recited a favorite poem:

> *He is not drunk who from the floor*
> *Can rise again to drink some more.*
> *But drunk he is who prostrate lies,*
> *And who can neither drink nor rise.*

Hadden drew a silly cartoon of a chubby man enacting the words of the poem, had the picture copied, and sent it to several friends. Most of them wished Hadden would lie prostrate more often and rise to drink again a little less frequently. "Hadden was drinking too much for his own good," Luce said. "I knew that."

A regular at P. J. Moriarty's Third Avenue speakeasy and the original "21," Hadden especially loved big places with a large dance floor that afforded space for pranks. He would steal a dance with a girl, prep-school style, in order to provoke a fight with her date. Once, in a speakeasy with Niven Busch, Hadden spotted a man who resembled the boxer Kid McCoy, who had recently been sent to San Quentin for killing his girlfriend. Hadden pointed the man out and yelled, "Dat's him! Dat's the moiderer!" The proprietor rushed over and begged Hadden to quiet down before a murder was committed again.

Friends and rivals at Hotchkiss, Hadden *(right)* and Luce *(left)* formed a "strange and wonderful pair."

During the Great War, Hadden and Luce edited the *Yale Daily News*. When the board of 1920 posed for a portrait, Hadden sat in the center with Luce at his right-hand side.

In 1925, the *Boston Globe* credited Hadden with the idea for *Time*.

The same story called Luce "another one of the organizers."

Hadden *(right)* with his writers *(from left)*: Manfred Gottfried,
John S. Martin, Thomas J. C. Martyn, Niven Busch.

Hadden and Luce
with Cleveland's city
manager, reading
the first issue of *Time*
to be printed in
Cleveland.

Time's most brilliant writer, the one-armed John Stuart Martin, had a mellifluous voice and a way with women.

Circulation manager Roy Edward Larsen spread *Time* across the nation, partly by helping Hadden to spark local feuds.

Luce fell in love with the wealthy Lila Hotz atop Rome's highest hill.

Hadden went through stormy times with Vassar graduate Deborah Douglas.

His closest friend was his cousin's wife, titian-haired Mimi Martin.

Office wags called Hadden "the Terrible-Tempered Mr. Bang."

With Hadden, one idea led to three or five. He and his editors pepped up a slow news week by naming Charles Lindbergh "The Man of the Year."

Hadden in his editing regalia: shirtsleeves, green eyeshade, big pencil.

Hadden spent several nights in jail for getting into drunken brawls or for disorderly conduct. It was a kind of sport for him. Once a taxi driver tried to extort Hadden and his Yale classmate Henry Thorne. They simply paid the usual fare and walked into a speakeasy. When they left the speakeasy, the cabbie was waiting outside along with several of his friends. The men knocked Hadden out cold and left him lying in the gutter. Hadden was still unconscious when the police arrived, so the authorities asked Thorne for his friend's identification. Thorne had just made up a couple of false names when Hadden suddenly revived. With an air of patrician dignity, he roared from the gutter below, "Officer, he's not telling the truth. His name is Thorne; mine is Hadden."

One of Hadden's old childhood friends, Rice Brewster, approached an editor of *Time* to ask if something could be done about Hadden's drinking. Nothing was done, and the fear of causing Hadden pain prevented Brewster and several others from directly confronting Hadden. "We wanted to stop him from throwing things away," Brewster later said. But as for bringing it up with him, "you just couldn't." Brewster would live to regret that choice.

The wild, contrarian nature that attracted people to Hadden was acquiring a darker edge. At times Hadden seemed to be proving an inner vision of himself as doomed to be misunderstood. His snarl, always evident, had grown extreme, and his old Yale friends often found themselves defending Hadden to those who hadn't known him long. His bouts with melancholy seemed increasingly severe. "Brit was a lonely fellow," Niven Busch recalled. "Many fellows admired and deeply liked him, as I did, and were grateful to him for his help, extended generously to all. But though he seemed to return their feelings and to extract a sense of comradeship from being with them, he could never lose himself sufficiently to feel that they were truly friends."

Stories about Hadden's temper circulated through the office. There were rumors of his arguments with the ancient elevator at 25 West Forty-fifth Street. It didn't hold many people, and when it filled to capacity on a high floor it would simply speed to the lobby without stopping. Hadden would become so enraged at the sight of his employees whizzing by him that he would shout and beat at the gates. Office wags nicknamed Hadden "the Terrible-Tempered Mr. Bang" after a fearsome character in a comic strip. Those who didn't know him thought he was fierce and brutal. "I always thought that was a show that he was putting on," Luce's sister Elisabeth said. "It finally got to be such a constant behavior that it may have become part of his character."

The generous and politic leader of the Yale democracy seemed to have faded into the past. He was overshadowed by a grim successor—restless and irritable, impolitic and intemperate. "When he was not working on *Time* he wanted desperately to have a good time, and yet nothing seemed to give him solace," John Hincks recalled. One night Hadden went out with Hincks and their old Hotchkiss friend "Ep" Herman to the little underground bars in the Village. They closed down place after place, and each time Hadden's friends said it was time to go home, but Hadden pressed for just one more place, just one more drink. Finally the bars shut down and still Hadden could not bear to stop moving. It was two in the morning when he dragged his friends to Bryant Park to play a frenzied game of tag.

Inevitably, Hadden's friends went to bed, and he spent his nights on a solo trip to dawn—pushing past midnight through those lonely hours when the world lay asleep and he alone, exhausted by life but wired inside, faced the old inner demons that had haunted him since college. He was a geyser of ideas, spewing forth plans and dreams, jokes and stories, and beneath it all a vague but palpable feeling of anxiety. Often he phoned Winsor French, who would dutifully get up to listen to Hadden's babblings, regardless of the hour. Finally one night French called the police, who arrested Hadden in the Village for disturbing the peace and possession of bootleg liquor.

Hadden took to calling French the "office boy." When French asked for a raise, Hadden replied that his pay would not be increasing and he could "take it or leave it." One day French walked into Hadden's office and saw a note on his calendar for Friday at 2 P.M. It said, "Oust French." French walked in at the appointed hour and announced that he was quitting. Hadden roared so loudly that French thought his boss could have been heard down the block. "He took me for a two-hour lunch of martinis, during which he talked about nothing except baseball and possible candidates for my former job," French recalled. "It was impossible to get mad at him. The man had the kind of charm that could bring birds from the trees."

On his days off, Hadden spent his time at a club for city youth, where he taught some boys how to put out a newspaper. On the weekends, he would take the train to Connecticut to see Mary Hincks and her husband, Duke Dusossoit, who would toss a baseball with Hadden on the wide, green lawn. Hadden said he would like to live on a farm but he couldn't bear to leave Manhattan. He joked that perhaps he would move to Central Park. When Hadden visited Howard Black in Riverside, Black's children recognized a kindred spirit and invited Hadden to come play with them. Hadden's chest swelled with pride as he walked them along a stone wall that seemed extremely high to ones so young. Spending the evening with Bob Johnson in Stamford, Hadden would tug off his boots to warm himself by the fire, stare deeply into his friend's eyes and ask, "How are you today? Are you all right? You look lousy." He seemed at such times a bit lost himself. "Oh, he was a character. I really loved him very dearly," Johnson recalled. "Harry was married and Roy shortly was married, and Brit was lonely. Brit loved people, you know. . . . Brit was very sentimental."

One of Hadden's girlfriends lived in Westhampton. Late on Friday, Hadden would call Niven Busch and they would drive to the old Westhampton Hotel. If all the rooms were booked, they would cover themselves with rugs and sleep in the lobby. The next day they would golf and swim, or hit some baseballs around, and Hadden's eyes would grow bright again. "At least half a dozen girls in Westhampton thought they would marry Brit," Busch recalled. "They would get me in a corner and talk seriously, trying to pump me as to his habits and with whom he was sleeping. They wanted to discover what secret source caused the pent-up violence of his nature and his fascinating disdain for humankind. I never could give them much information since I did not know myself."

The saddest part of Hadden's desolation was that he could feel so alone while so many people loved him. Friends and family admired his tremendous energy. Now it seemed as if he was turning it against himself. The playwright Thornton Wilder, who had traveled in parallel with Hadden at Yale, occasionally crossing paths since, never could figure out what lay at the root of Hadden's "explosive kindness and finally that energy bent in a sort of big scale generous self-destructiveness." Wilder wrote that Hadden was "never small, never less than magnanimous, but somehow out of joint with his task, and visibly burning himself up. But always a prince."

Hadden felt particularly restless because he lacked a magazine to edit. Since childhood, he had rarely known that feeling for long. With John Martin's help, Hadden turned *Tide* from a free circular into a regular monthly magazine with a bright blue cover, a list of subscribers, and advertisements of its own. The cousins planned each issue in a single thigh-slapping meeting and wrote the articles almost immediately. "It cost me two weekends, turning out this copy apart from what I took home," John Martin recalled. "That's how lucubrative we were in those days. I could turn out copy, and good copy." Hadden's secretary, Elizabeth Robert, would paste the stories into columns, make the photo cuts, and send the magazine off to press. "Almost overnight, it was written, submitted and approved," she said.

When Lucky Strike created an advertising campaign featuring celebrities who encouraged people to "reach for a Lucky instead of a sweet," Marlboro launched a rival campaign featuring the names of deceased celebrities. One advertisement entitled "What Famous People Would Have Said About Marlboro" invented a quote from Napoleon: "Always before a famous battle I calm my nerves with a Marlboro." Hadden asked his secretary to find out what type of tobacco Napoleon really smoked. Elizabeth Robert discovered that Napoleon had smoked only once, when a Middle Eastern ambassador gave him a fine oriental pipe. Unable to get the pipe to work, Napoleon cried out, "Devil take it!" A friend managed to get the pipe going, but the smoke disgusted Napoleon. "Take the beastly thing away!" he commanded. "Oh! What filth! I shall be sick directly!" After that, Napoleon always called smoking "a pastime for sluggards." No doubt Hadden's article displeased Marlboro's ad men, but it provided a service to readers.

Tide exposed a culture of consumption predicated on low ethical standards that allowed companies to encourage thoughtless behavior or even lie about their products. Hadden and Martin noticed that the makers of one luxury car, the Reo Flying Cloud, encouraged people to speed; that the makers of Deodo encouraged their customers to skip bathing and instead shake on a little deodorant powder and walk out the door; that the makers of Phillips' Milk of Magnesia encouraged people to "over-indulge" because they could always take a spoonful of medicine. Hadden dubbed this type of ad the "Cloven Hoof" because it encouraged a devilish impulse.

Once Hadden, in a brainstorm, observed that companies were increasingly telling clients who had already bought their products to throw them out and replace them with new ones. "Are you a 4-Belt man?" asked a small belt company in Rochester, New York. The W. G. Clark cigarette lighter company encouraged customers to buy a lighter for every room of the house. Hadden dubbed this tactic Oliver Twisting after Oliver Twist's famous demand at supper: *Please, sir, I want some more.* "I think it was perhaps the first real, frank discussion of advertising that there'd been," Roy Larsen later said. "*Tide* was a real feather . . . in *Time*'s cap."

Nevertheless, *Tide* continued to cause problems for *Time* by occasionally criticizing *Time*'s own advertisers. Johnson blamed *Tide* for jeopardizing *Time*'s advertising accounts. "I thought *Tide* was a very dangerous magazine," he recalled. "I really put the heat on Brit pretty badly. But Brit loved that little book—he thought it was a wonderful idea." Hadden knew that Luce also disapproved of *Tide*'s cynical view of the business world. In fact, Luce was pressuring his partner to get rid of the magazine. When an advertising salesman told Hadden that his client had complained about a rough article in *Tide*, Hadden said, "Don't worry, because we're going to stop it any way."

It was time for *Time*'s founders to capitalize on their fanatical following. With circulation climbing, ad revenues skyrocketing, and readers suggesting the creation of a second publication, *Time* seemed poised to expand into new ventures. Hadden had taken a few stabs in that direction by launching a second magazine and a radio show, but those were small projects. Now Hadden and Luce were ready to develop something on the scale of *Time*. The choice of an undertaking would determine much about the company's future, and Hadden, Luce, and Larsen were all dedicating their thoughts to the question.

Hadden believed it would help to know more about his audience's buying habits. He asked Dave Keep to draft *Time*'s first reader survey—a pioneering idea in the days before focus-group testing and statistically accurate opinion polling. Dave Keep wrote *Time*'s readers a list of questions about their buying habits. He titled it after one of the questions in the survey: "Do You Own a Horse?" Hadden laughed, grabbed his pencil, and drew a silly neighing horse face. He titled the survey "an inquisition" and mailed it to *Time* subscribers. More than half responded to the first solicitation.

The survey results showed that *Time* stood alone among magazines. Thirty-seven percent of *Time*'s readers owned two or more cars; more than 10 percent owned horses. *Time*'s devotees were just as wealthy as the people who read Condé Nast's *Vanity Fair,* the humor magazine *Life,* and H. L. Mencken's *American Mercury*—but there were twice as many *Time* readers. Not only were they wealthy and numerous, they were actively interested in what *Time* had to say and sell. More than 80 percent reported that they read the magazine from cover to cover. And they were eager for something new from the young publishers.

Early in 1928, a young Cincinnati radio announcer named Fred Smith asked Roy Larsen for permission to start a new radio show based on the contents of *Time.* Larsen immediately realized that an innovation was in the air. He asked Smith to quit his job and come work directly for the company. A remarkable burst of creativity followed. In a few weeks, the pair designed a fifteen-minute news summary for broadcast, which they called a "newscast." When thirty-three radio stations agreed to run *Newscasting* each week, the word entered the American lexicon.

No sooner had *Newscasting* gone on the air than a cry rose from the newspaper industry. *Editor & Publisher* attacked *Time* for profiting from the newspaper reports twice, once in print and once over the airwaves. In a bizarre editorial, the trade magazine's editor compared newspapers to a legendary Dutch giant who was bitten to death by many tiny ducks. Hadden swung his red pencil into action. "*Time* has no desire to fight the U.S. press," he quipped in a letter to the editor. "Such a fight would be too much a case of small duck vs. giant." Larsen and Smith got to work on a second show, *Newsacting,* which dramatized the news in scenes with sound effects. By the end of 1928, sixty radio stations across America were playing the show, which spread *Time*'s name beyond its wealthy readership and took the company into the mass market.

Luce was also experimenting with a new idea. Parker Lloyd-Smith's articles for *Time*'s business section had inspired Luce with the notion of creating a new kind of magazine that would capture the epic grandeur of American capitalism. Where others saw only dollar signs, Luce thought of plants, buildings, and trucks. Naming the tycoon was not enough; Luce wanted to picture the fabulous life a corporate executive led, tell of the decisions he made on which other lives hinged, and explain the systems and philosophies that drove commerce. Luce dreamed of a magazine that would write the history of industrial civilization. Stumped for a name, he asked his wife to jot down some ideas. Lila suggested *Fortune*.

In the summer of 1928, Luce began to write down some story ideas. He assigned Parker Lloyd-Smith to work out the concept. Lloyd-Smith visited Luce at his rented summer home in Washington, Connecticut, where they talked about what the magazine should achieve. Their idea soon grew radically far from *Time* and *Tide*. Rather than compressing business news, *Fortune* would expand business itself into a vision of American society. The magazine would conjure a four-color dream of capitalism; it would be a monument to progress, printed on thick cream paper. From the start Luce planned "something gloriously big and *not* like *Tide*," Roy Larsen recalled. "He hated *Tide*. He hated the whole idea, and so did I."

The notion of *Fortune* disgusted Hadden. He ridiculed Luce's concept as "high-class Babbittry." But Luce meant to see the project through, and he would be free to pursue his ideas when Hadden took back the editorship of *Time*. They had hired a recent Yale graduate, Charles Latimer Stillman, as a permanent business manager. Toward the end of the year, Luce took a proposal for a new business magazine to the board of directors. The board overruled Hadden's opposition and permitted Luce to set up an Experimental Department. High in the attic, Parker Lloyd-Smith and his researcher, Florence Horn, crammed into a little room tucked behind a chimney. The makeshift office was just large enough for two people. Hadden pretended not to notice them.

Hadden spent his days in the business office brainstorming ideas for Time Inc. His new executive secretary, a rosy-cheeked Princeton graduate named E. Robin Little, kept Hadden's desk supplied with fresh pencils. Hadden would stick a pencil between his teeth and chew it like a cud, now and then spewing the pulp onto the floor. He would toss around thoughts and chuckle to himself as he considered the possibilities. Every now and then Luce would wander through the business department to ask what Hadden was doing. "Well, he has his feet on his desk and is chewing pencils," Little would say. "Fine, Robin, leave him alone," Luce would say. "He is germinating another idea."

A week later Hadden would call in Little and dictate a stream-of-consciousness memorandum. At times Hadden would dictate to two secretaries at once, each taking down a separate idea. Little would type up the memoranda, including Hadden's observations of the factors that made people "tick." The result would either be brilliant or insane. Little noticed that Hadden's mind had a "vaulting" character: from the slightest stimulus it could spring into the "greatest flights of fantasy and imagination." Decades later, after a long career as a newspaper editor and Pan Am executive, Little called Hadden "one of the most brilliant, perhaps the most brilliant man of his generation."

Hadden jotted down his ideas in his black notebook on a page titled "EXPANSION." The list included magazines dedicated to sports, photographs, fiction, fashion, letters to the editor, schoolchildren, women's and culinary subjects, a radio show, a daily newspaper, and even an American history textbook. Though Hadden never said it in so many words, he was dreaming of a vast news and entertainment company. Each project shared the ambition of engaging people in order to communicate significant ideas. Hearst had tried to create such a company. He had failed as age outstripped his sense of what the public liked to read. It remained to be seen whether Hadden could rediscover his rhythm and find new sources of inspiration in his quest to create new products.

The ideas that first interested Hadden separately appealed to *Time*'s female and male readerships. Hadden put E. Robin Little to work on a concept for a fashion magazine called *Tone*. At the same time, Hadden and John Martin wrote a prospectus for the first general interest magazine to cover the world of sport. Most publishers assumed that people who liked to go skeet shooting would never take an interest in boxing and vice versa. But Hadden thought it would be possible to create a single sports entertainment audience. Over a couple of lagers at Susskind's Restaurant on Lexington Avenue, Hadden shared his idea with Noel Busch, who had started covering hockey for the *New York Daily News*. Hadden told Busch he would launch a sports magazine but for one obstacle. "You've got to remember that Luce is no sports-man," he said, grinding his jaw on a crust of rye bread. "H. R. Luce, no sportsman he."

After he abandoned the sports magazine concept, Hadden finally hit upon an idea that made him feel passionate again. He wanted to tell the news of the week through photographs. Picture weeklies existed in Europe, though those publications ran illustrations as well. In America, photojournalism was a stronger force, and printing tech-nology was improving rapidly. In a few years, several publishers would begin to dream of producing the first mass-market picture magazine. But they had not thought of it yet. Hadden dreamed of a new force others could not yet envision—a force that would shortly transform American culture.

In the prospect of a picture magazine, Hadden finally found a new project worthy of his attention. With Timestyle, he used words as con-duits to place images in his readers' heads; now he saw the potential of giving people the images themselves. Hadden shared his idea with his Cleveland friend Katherine Halle when he took her to watch Yale and Harvard play football just before Thanksgiving of 1928. When Halle asked Hadden what the title would be, he said he liked the name of the old humor magazine—*Life*. Halle noticed that even as Hadden chat-tered away he was burning with fever. She told him that he ought to see a doctor. Hadden said he would be all right.

Luce sensed in Hadden a strange draining away of energies, a list-lessness and boredom with life. As 1928 drew to a close, Hadden began taking mysterious absences from work. Just when Luce grew desperate for him, Hadden would spring into the office, claiming he had spent the week throwing hay on a farm in Indiana. Once, after Hadden dis-appeared for several days, he contacted E. Robin Little and asked him to come to the New York Harbor. Little found Hadden on the deck of a tugboat and acquired the impression that his boss was working as a deckhand. Hadden would return to work full of new observations, plotting new ideas for *Time*. But his claims of vigorous activity seemed preposterous in light of his continual fever. His illness was "mysteri-ous," Noel Busch recalled, "and increasingly serious."

By the fall of 1928, Time Inc. was expanding so rapidly that the office was almost too cramped to put out the magazine. Researchers checking facts would bump arms with office boys slicing up newspapers. Hadden rented several floors in the Bartholomew Building, which was not far from the Chrysler Building, just under construction as the world's tallest skyscraper, and in range of the great cinders spewing from a nearby power plant. Hadden told his friends that he planned to commute to work in a small motorboat—an editor transformed into a sea captain by the means of a yachting cap. The gossip columnist Walter Winchell passed the rumor along to the readers of the *Evening Graphic*.

When the staff moved to the Bartholomew Building in early December of 1928, they found new desks instead of thrift, and a reception room with formal furniture. The editor's office had a door leading onto a small porch with other doors leading to other offices—the perfect means of escape, Hadden cracked, if he needed to run away from irate subscribers. The young publishers left the uppermost floor entirely empty; it would be reserved for expansion. Hadden kicked off the move with an office soirée. He filled the water cooler with bootleg wine and asked the new business manager, Charles Stillman, to mix a bathtub of gin. Hadden was in top form that night, and people talked about how much he would enjoy editing once again.

In private conversations with friends, however, Hadden hinted that he didn't know where he was headed in the coming year. He remained staunchly opposed to publishing a magazine devoted to business, and yet everyone knew how hard Luce was working on the idea. This was no mere personal difference: *Tide* and *Fortune* represented two fundamentally opposite views of the American way of life and of *Time*'s role in covering America. Finally it appeared as if Hadden and Luce were headed for a confrontation over the direction of the company. Dining with Hadden toward the close of 1928, one friend asked him if Time Inc. was really going to publish a magazine that glorified the world of business. Hadden pounded the table with his fist. "If we do," he declared, "it'll be over my dead body."

15

The Final Fight

SHORTLY BEFORE CHRISTMAS OF 1928, Hadden called in sick. His fever had taken a turn for the worse. Nobody thought much of it, least of all Hadden. Each week he would come back to the office in the hopes of feeling well enough to work. By the end of the week he would call in sick again. He just didn't have the energy to go in. At last Hadden stayed home for two weeks straight. Luce's secretary was alarmed. "You better look after Hadden," Katherine Abrams warned Luce, "or he'll be dead."

Mimi Martin came to visit Hadden frequently. One bitterly cold night, walking home from a party, they crossed paths with a black-and-white tomcat. "That's a mighty mean ole cat," Martin said. Hadden disagreed. "That's a mighty *cold* little ole cat," he said, scooping up the animal. "I'm going to take him home." Almost as soon as Hadden set the cat down in his apartment, it started jumping about and throwing fits. Mimi thought it looked a little "mangy"; she didn't like the idea of Hadden having the cat around. But Hadden insisted on keeping it. Later, when he offered the cat a bowl of milk, it lunged at him and clawed his arm.

Around the same time, Hadden began to feel tired and lethargic. He couldn't find his old spirit. He felt he should be able to shake off the illness, but somehow he couldn't do it. Hadden asked Oz Jones, an old Yale friend who had since become a doctor, to give him a checkup. Jones paid Hadden a visit and prescribed several cold medications, but nothing seemed to work. Freddie Benham, Hadden's friend from the *World,* dropped by to find Hadden sad and listless. "What's the matter, boy?" he asked. "I'm not well," Hadden said. "I just don't seem to have any ambition and I feel weak." Finally Hadden phoned his mother and asked her to come over. Mrs. Pool found her son pacing the floors barefoot. She drove him straight home to Brooklyn.

Dr. Pool, a prominent physician at Long Island College Hospital, gave his stepson an examination. Afterward, Pool drove Hadden to The Brooklyn Hospital. Hadden checked in and was given a nice corner room on a high floor. The room had a balcony and a view of some shade trees. The doctors told Hadden that perhaps it would be best if he rested in bed for awhile. When he heard Hadden had gone to the hospital, Luce went to speak with Dr. Pool. Luce told Hadden's step-father that Hadden had felt weak for quite some time; perhaps something could be wrong with his heart. Dr. Pool assured Luce that Hadden was in good hands. The hospital had brought in a heart specialist from Manhattan.

Hadden sat in bed, talking on the phone with friends. He ordered meals from a nearby Schrafft's restaurant which always sent him a giant bunch of grapes. Hadden's nurse would peel the grapes before he ate them. In the first weeks the office boys would drop by with page proofs and Hadden would edit *Time* in bed. It is impossible to know the types of treatment he received or the tests he underwent since most of Brooklyn Hospital's medical records were later destroyed in a ware-house fire. But the hospital cultured more than seven hundred blood samples that year to test for the presence of bacteria. It is likely that Hadden's was among them. William Lohman, the attending physician for the Department of Medicine, diagnosed Hadden with *Streptococcus viridans,* a bacterial strain commonly found on the skin or in the mouth and considered harmless unless it enters the bloodstream.

Hadden believed that his troubles began with the flu. While his immune system was compromised, the cat had scratched him, trans-ferring the bacteria to his bloodstream. Hadden's nurse later said that he had recently had two teeth pulled, an operation that occasionally introduces *Streptococcus viridans* to the blood. Regardless of how Hadden contracted the infection, it was his inability to throw it off that troubled the doctors. They believed Hadden was suffering from "blood poisoning," a severe infection that spreads throughout the body, taxing the entire system and depriving the tissues of oxygen.

In treating such cases, the doctors had few resources at their disposal. The year before, the Scottish scientist Alexander Fleming had discovered that a certain kind of mold called *Penicillium notatum* released a substance that seemed to kill bacteria. But it wouldn't be until the Second World War that doctors would begin using penicillin to cure bacterial infections. Without the aid of antibiotics, people often died of the more virulent strains of strep within a week. Even a *viridans* infection could spread through the bloodstream, traumatize the body, and eventually cause multiple organ failure.

Hadden didn't want his room cluttered up, so there were no flowers there, just a couple of books and the most recent issues of *Time* stacked on the floor by his bed. "What a nice magazine," his nurse said one day as she was tidying up the room. "I started it," Hadden said. Bored and isolated, he spent his days ringing up friends in Cleveland and New York. Libby Holman called. Margot Larsen often visited, bringing along a batch of fresh strawberries. Hadden would have been a model patient except for his fear of anyone coming into contact with his bed. If his mother so much as brushed against it, he would fly into a rage.

Aside from Mrs. Pool, the most frequent visitor to the hospital was Luce, who came every day for about an hour. Hoping to spark Hadden's interest in life, Luce always arrived with reports from the office. He had just named Walter P. Chrysler *Time*'s Man of the Year for 1928. The story called Chrysler a "torpedo-headed dynamo" and made no mention of the hated "Percy." Plans for the business magazine were well underway. Parker Lloyd-Smith was bringing his mock-ups to completion, and Luce was discussing the magazine's layout with the graphic designer Thomas Maitland Cleland. It would soon be time to decide whether to take the risk.

Hadden remained dead set against the idea—a position made evident to the doctors and nurses who were quite shocked by the violently loud arguments that accompanied Luce's numerous visits. After Luce left the hospital, Hadden would act nervous and depressed, and his nurse would have to give him a sedative. "Are you sure Harry Luce has to come by so often?" Hadden's mother gently asked him one day. Hadden said that he was.

By the middle of January, when Hadden called up Katherine Halle in Cleveland, he sounded so faint that she could hardly hear him at all. The doctors injected Hadden with horse serum, hoping the antibodies horses carry in their blood might battle the infection. Instead Hadden came down with serum sickness, an allergic reaction to the foreign proteins that causes systemic swelling, among other complications. Indeed, he also began to suffer from phlebitis, a swelling of the veins that creates pain in the extremities and a sign that his blood was not circulating properly. The doctors believed the bacteria had infected the valves of Hadden's heart, which could no longer pump sufficient nutrients through the body. If the bacteria remained in Hadden's heart and multiplied, he would die.

Hadden was suffering from a high fever and experiencing intense swelling in his legs. The doctors told callers that his nervous condition was "poor." Perhaps he was simply depressed or perhaps his heart was throwing off clumps of bacteria to the brain. On January 19, 1929, Luce sent a letter to his Bones mates about Hadden's health, a step taken only in critical circumstances. "The cause for worry lies in the fact that no improvement has occurred and his vitality is consequently being depleted," Luce wrote. "His morale has naturally suffered somewhat, and it is therefore important that he should not suspect the seriousness of his case." Luce asked his friends to be gentle with Hadden. They should act as if he had a bad case of the flu.

Although Luce and Hadden's family were trying to conceal the seriousness of his condition, Hadden seemed to realize that his body was nearing the end. On January 21, he was forced to miss a triumphant meeting of the board of directors, who voted to distribute the company's first dividend to owners of the preferred stock. After the meeting, Elizabeth Robert dropped by The Brooklyn Hospital to see Hadden and hand over his director's fee, a twenty-dollar gold piece. "Take it back," Hadden said, turning his secretary away. "I wasn't there. Anyhow, I won't get well." The look on his face reminded her of a frightened little boy.

Each day Luce would sit for hours at Hadden's bedside. Hadden's mother glared at her son's partner, and he felt it. He knew she bore a grudge against him for accepting Yale's honorary degree. Mrs. Pool's cold treatment embittered Luce, for he loved Hadden. Deeply worried about his friend, Luce felt compelled to stay by his side. Luce kept coming to the hospital, hoping to help Hadden fight by stimulating his interest in Time Inc. But Luce's attempts to talk with Hadden about the company only further strained their relationship. Hadden's nurse, who heard their arguments from the other side of the door, worried that Luce was exhausting her patient. "She liked Hadden," recalled a journalist who spoke with Hadden's nurse years later, "and she felt that something was wrong with what was going on."

The question of the business magazine may not have been all that Hadden and Luce discussed. Both must have known, as Hadden's health weakened, that Luce would have to consider the future of the company. There were those shares in Time Inc. to think about; Luce could not well run the company without them. "We talked occasionally, I mean in the preceding several years, that maybe we ought to have some arrangement whereby if one of us died the other one would have the right to buy his stock," Luce later said. "But we never got around to doing anything about that." But that was not the story circulating through *Time*'s hallways in later years.

Writers for *Time*, many of them loyal to Hadden's memory, later claimed that Luce asked to buy Hadden's stock—or at least enough shares to ensure Luce's permanent control of the company. If Luce did so, Hadden would have fully absorbed the severity of his case not from his doctors but from Luce. He would have received the crushing news that he was likely to die from the friend and rival who was finally overtaking him. Such a conversation could not have increased Hadden's fond feeling for Luce, but it is impossible to know if it occurred. Luce never revealed what he and his partner talked about during those visits. There was envy between them, and deep misgiving. There was also love.

On January 28, 1929, Hadden received a visit from his roommate, the attorney William J. Carr. Hadden's nurse, Lucy Wolinski, was called in as a witness. Wolinski saw a third man in the room who was most likely Hadden's brother, Crowell Hadden III. Hadden told Carr what he would like to have done with his estate and effects if he died. Carr wrote Hadden's requests in longhand on a legal-size sheet of paper. His cursive grew small and cramped as he neared the bottom of the page. Finally Carr passed the sheet to Hadden. Unable to write his name, Hadden scratched a wavering X. "His mark," Carr wrote nearby.

Hadden entrusted his brother with the management of his million-dollar estate, the majority of which consisted of several thousand shares in Time Incorporated stock. Hadden had only one wish: the entire estate must be left to his mother, who could not sell her shares in Time Inc. for forty-nine years. The request encapsulated Hadden's friendship and rivalry with Luce. Hadden's faith in the long-term value of Time Inc. stock revealed his belief that Luce would make the company a success, even without the benefit of Hadden's partnership. But if Hadden's family obeyed his will, Luce would never gain full control of the company.

A few days after Hadden signed his will, he lay so close to death that his doctors were forced to consider radical measures. A decade earlier, Hugh Young, a doctor at Johns Hopkins, had discovered the power of Mercurochrome as a topical antiseptic. He soon began injecting Mercurochrome into patients with blood poisoning. Some of his patients had experienced miraculous recoveries, and Young reported in the *Archives of Surgery* that one was "well, dancing, and exercising" when last heard from. Autopsies of other patients who had died after receiving Mercurochrome showed lesions on their kidneys and intestines. Hadden's mother decided that she couldn't bear the risk.

Instead Mrs. Pool gave permission for her son to receive a series of blood transfusions. The doctors hoped that more healthy blood would help Hadden's body to combat the bacteria. Dozens of Hadden's friends came to the hospital to have their blood tested. Hadden, experiencing heavy heart palpitations and swelling in his limbs, sat through the procedures with his crooked grin intact. "Hope I don't turn into an Irishman!" he joked when Howard Black arrived to donate. Hadden endured more than a dozen transfusions in all, perhaps as many as twenty or thirty. John Martin reported to the Time Inc. board of directors that his cousin's heart was beating more regularly afterward, his fever had gone down, and he had made a small but definite step toward health.

Luce did not volunteer to give Hadden his blood. Perhaps he held back because of his history of malaria, which can be transmitted through the bloodstream. In the end Hadden asked for Luce. It turned out that Luce had the right blood type. He gave Hadden several transfusions, so much blood that Luce felt physically weakened and his face was left drawn and white. Luce came to see Hadden several more times over the next few weeks. Hadden appeared slightly better, but his mind was rapidly deteriorating. The "extremely sad and pathetic thing," Luce recalled, was that his partner seemed to have forgotten his recent rise to success. One day Luce told Hadden about *Time*'s new promotion campaign, a set of advertisements soon to run in the major American newspapers. Hadden asked how much the campaign would cost, and Luce estimated a few thousand dollars. "My God, Harry," Hadden said. "Are you sure we can afford it?"

It seemed to Luce during his last few visits as if Hadden had forgiven him for their many arguments and recriminations. The tension between them vanished, and suddenly they were whole again, partners and friends. It is impossible to know if Hadden also felt that way. At times it seemed that he wished to say something personal to Luce. Perhaps he wished to mention his will. But Hadden never did so, and Luce felt unable to take the initiative in sparking some kind of closing conversation. "The last time or two that I was there, I guess I knew he was dying and maybe he did," Luce recalled. "It seemed to me that he knew and every now and again was wanting to say something, whatever it might be he wanted to say in the way of parting words or something. But he never did, so that there was never any open recognition between him and me that he was dying."

Luce would have liked to visit Hadden in February, but his family said he was too shaken to receive callers. Lila Luce talked on the phone with John Martin, who stayed in constant touch with Hadden's family and told her that Hadden had written a will. Martin asked Hadden's family if he might like to see Luce again, but they said Hadden was too "indifferent to everything and everybody." Elisabeth Luce's husband, a young corporate attorney named Tex Moore, advised Lila that her husband ought to stay near the deathbed, "just for the looks of it, and for the sake of the organization," even though Hadden would probably be unconscious near the end. "I understand they do not talk any more as if there is any possibility of his pulling through," Lila wrote her husband. "It will be a terrible thing to realize that Brit just is not on earth any more, but maybe knowing it now will relieve you a little of the shock of finding him gone."

On Hadden's thirty-first birthday, the office boys bought him a meerschaum pipe and the finest tobacco they could find. The head office boy visited Hadden and wished him "a quick return to the office smoking that pipe for many long years." John Martin, who was editing *Time* in Hadden's absence, drew a series of cartoons lampooning the *Time* team. It was just the kind of thing Hadden loved, a "thorough-going round of schnitzel-banck" full of cracks about his secretary, the writers, and Luce. On the last page, Hadden was pictured lying in bed and reading the latest issue of *Time*. He looked cross and was saying, "Terrible! Rotten!" Ten days earlier, Luce had overridden Hadden's objections and submitted to the board of directors a special report that called for the publication of *Fortune*. "I am certain," Luce wrote Harry Davison, "that, if Brit had not been taken ill, he would be in agreement with me on this course."

Hadden did not act surprised when his family told him that his condition was serious and he would probably not live much longer. To his nurse it seemed his mind was far away; he wasn't totally connected to the world anymore. But he seemed to summon all of the fight he had left, and for a week he showed steady improvement. On February 26, some friends gathered at Hadden's apartment for a dinner served by Mr. Wu, his Chinese cook. They telephoned Hadden's mother, who said Hadden had suffered a small stomach upset but otherwise was feeling well. It came as a surprise early the next morning when Hadden's heart stopped beating. He died quietly with no friends or family at his bedside.

The news of Hadden's passing began to spread on the morning of February 27 as *Time*'s staff arrived at work. Condolences flooded the office. "UNSPEAKABLY SHOCKED AND DISTRESSED," telegrammed the Yale professor William Lyon Phelps. "Only those of us who knew the real fame for which Brit was pointed can realize the true tragedy of his untimely passage," an advertising man wrote Bob Johnson. "I can't imagine anyone who can begin to take his place." John Martin picked up a pencil and tried to write an appreciation of his cousin, but the experience was too raw. The writers quit work and went to lunch, where they reminisced about their editor. Back in the office, they spent the afternoon fielding reporters' phone calls. Luce wandered the halls, his eyes brimming with tears. Coming across a researcher, he asked, "Miss Spieth, how do you feel?" He looked lonely and lost.

The next day's newspapers mourned Hadden as the greatest journalist of the rising generation. In an editorial titled "A Death Too Early," the *New York Times* called Hadden "an example of the fruits that can be plucked by youth," adding that "his industry, his touch of genius and his character have added a novel chapter to the book of journalism." Roy W. Howard, the chairman of the Scripps-Howard newspaper chain, said, "The death of Briton Hadden robs American journalism of one of its greatest promises." The publisher Paul Block said, "America has lost one of its most brilliant publishers and writers—one who accomplished in a few years what many publishers have tried to do in many years." Emerson Tuttle of the Yale faculty wrote Luce, "You won't find his like again, and doubtless won't try."

Hadden's body was dressed in a suit, placed in an open casket, and taken to his mother's house in Brooklyn Heights. Elizabeth Pool sat with the body through the weekend. Friends and family came to take a turn beside the casket. Mimi Martin was shocked to see someone who had always been so lively suddenly dead. It didn't seem like Hadden at all. The funeral was held at the Holy Trinity Church in Brooklyn. There were ten honorary pallbearers including Luce. A large group assembled—friends, neighbors, the entire staff of *Time*—but it was not a comforting service. The church was dim and dank. The ceremony seemed formal and grim. Of everyone there, John O'Hara recalled, it was Luce who looked the "most beat up."

After the service, Hadden's friends and family proceeded to the Green-Wood Cemetery to gather at the Hadden family plot under a tall oak tree. Hadden would be buried beside his father. Prayers were said and the casket was lowered into the ground. When the groundskeeper bent over to start shoveling, Mimi Martin noticed a split in the leg of the man's pants. She pointed it out to John and they both had a chuckle, agreeing, "Brit would have loved it."

Deeply distraught, Luce returned to *Time* to face a growing pile of condolence letters. "Nothing can ever take the place of Brit's companionship in my life," he wrote T. E. Donnelley in Chicago. Over the next few weeks, Luce asked several of his employees if they would like to go out to lunch. Not knowing why he wanted to see them, they sat there, touched, as Luce reminisced about Hadden for several hours. "I don't know how I'll get along without him," he said. Months later, Luce wrote a friend that nothing anyone could say would ever "mitigate the tragedy." He consoled himself with the thought that the magazine Hadden had created would always honor his legacy. Responding to Langhorne Gibson of the humor magazine *Life*, Luce wrote, "You have expressed our hope that *Time* may always be a fitting monument to him."

Several men were so scarred by Hadden's death as to be left with a deep and inconsolable feeling of loss. John Hincks was wrung out for months; he never stopped missing Hadden. It seemed strange that Hadden would die so young considering that he had been so full of life. "I didn't believe anything could down him. You know his personality gave that confidence to me at least," Peavey Heffelfinger wrote John Hincks a few months later. "Not a day has passed that I haven't thought of him and how much I loved and admired him. Somehow the bottom seems to have dropped out for me. It's the first real loss I have had."

Hadden's friends believed his heavy partying, inability to sleep, and refusal to eat properly had lowered his chances of fighting infection. He worked too hard, drank too much, and refused to take care of himself once he fell ill. *Time*'s writers were forced to agree that a little "Body Love" might have helped Hadden. But that didn't stop them from hating the publisher Bernarr Macfadden, who struck a cruel posthumous blow in a column called "Body Loving," which ended his long-running feud with Hadden. "One of my most caustic critics had to pass on to the cemetery," Macfadden wrote. "A brilliant mind, but lacking balance; and I would say it was entirely because he had not given his body the attention and care to which it was justly entitled."

Whether or not Hadden had loved his body, the cause of his death would always remain a mystery. Over the decades, Luce continued to think about the loss of energy Hadden had experienced before he fell ill. It seemed evident that something was wrong with his blood, especially since Hadden survived for another month after the doctors began giving him transfusions. Luce wondered if Hadden had suffered from leukemia, which deprives the body of healthy white blood cells and can leave it susceptible to infection. But Hadden's doctors ought to have been able to detect leukemia in his blood. Hadden could also have suffered from an unidentified virus that attacked his heart. The possibilities were endless.

Though he hadn't worked on the case, Dr. Pool continued to believe that nothing more complicated than a bacterial infection had caused his stepson's death. When he entered Hadden's apartment to gather his things, Dr. Pool saw the Nasty Mean Ole Cat. It was throwing a fit. Hadden's maid, Olyve, told Dr. Pool that the cat had "scratched Mr. Brit up something fierce." Dr. Pool took the cat to the hospital to have it tested. The laboratory discovered that the cat was seriously ridden with streptococcus, but not with the *viridans* strain. The strain of strep the cat carried would have killed Hadden in less than a week if he had contracted it.

Years later, when Oz Jones gave an interview on Hadden's illness, he held to the original diagnosis. Somehow the *Streptococcus viridans* had entered Hadden's bloodstream, perhaps through a scratch, more likely through the dental operation, or, as Jones guessed, through the sinuses. After entering Hadden's bloodstream, the bacteria attached to his heart. The heart weakened and finally stopped beating. The people most susceptible to this type of blood poisoning are those with a diseased or damaged heart. Jones thought it possible that Hadden's long childhood illness was actually an undiagnosed case of rheumatic fever, which can scar the heart and leave it susceptible to infection. If this were the case, a short course of penicillin would have cured Hadden had he fallen ill just fifteen years later.

More than Hadden's illness, the mood change that preceded it would impress itself upon the doctor's memory in later years—so much so that, when interviewed decades later, he felt compelled to discuss the emotional context of Hadden's downfall. Jones had visited Hadden's apartment frequently during the final year of his life. He had watched Hadden pace up and down, telling everyone within earshot how frustrated he felt. Like many others, Jones had been troubled by Hadden's mental condition. He believed that Hadden was bored to death—"fed to the teeth with his quick success."

16

Burial

ON THE MORNING OF Hadden's death, Luce sent the newspapers a telegram that called Hadden the publisher of *Time* rather than a founder and the first editor. Later that evening, Luce sent the newspapers a short biography of Hadden that claimed the two had alternated "year by year" as publisher and editor—a lie Luce would repeat throughout his life, verbally and in a corporate biography he released to the press. Hadden's friends and family expected his face to appear on *Time's* cover. When the next week's issue came out, they found a short two-column obituary, a page of quotations about Hadden, and a promise that within a year "a book about Hadden will be sent to all who ask." The following week, Luce removed Hadden's name from the magazine's masthead and put his own name alone at the top.

Hadden's mother was shocked and grieved. She believed Luce had done her son an injustice. Crowell Hadden defended Luce by insisting that the magazine had a policy against placing the face of a dead man on the cover. In fact, four years earlier the cover had featured the dead pilot of the *Shenandoah,* a Navy dirigible destroyed in a thunderstorm. Mrs. Pool never accepted the reasoning for *Time's* decision. Despite Luce's efforts to broker a peace, the tensions between him and Hadden's family never diminished. Rumors about Hadden's will were beginning to spread beyond the Bartholomew Building. The will's conspicuous suggestion—that in his last days Hadden had doubted his partner—posed a deep embarrassment to Luce. He soon realized that Time Inc. could not be run under fractured authority. The ownership situation was untenable.

Convincing the Hadden family to give up its voice in *Time*'s affairs would be a tricky matter. No mother would be inclined to break her son's final wish. Crowell Hadden knew the value of his mother's property and Mrs. Pool was not disposed to cooperate with Luce. But Luce was determined to get hold of Hadden's stock. On April 23, 1929, not two months after Hadden's death, Luce made a proposal to the Hadden family. He asked if they would be interested in taking shares of preferred stock in return for their common stock, which carried the right to vote on company matters. "Legally, the trustee can do almost anything he wants to. Sentimentally, he is bound by Brit's expressed desires," Luce wrote Harry Davison. "The will, of course, is a very hasty and imperfect statement of his desires." Luce assured Davison that Hadden's shares would be used to create an employee stock plan. "Incidentally," Luce went on, "I do not seek any greater equity for myself. Possibly in connection with the new magazine it might seem proper to advance my personal interests slightly."

Hadden's family turned down the deal. The following month Luce offered Crowell Hadden a seat on the Time Inc. board of directors. Crowell Hadden accepted the seat. Suddenly Crowell had a new responsibility to consider in addition to his brother's memory and his mother's financial well-being: the future of the company. Luce also got in touch with Wilton Lloyd-Smith, the elder brother of *Fortune*'s editor and an acquaintance of Crowell Hadden. A successful financier, Lloyd-Smith helped Luce arrange a second proposal to the Hadden family. Posting his own Time Inc. stock as collateral, Luce would take out a giant loan and use it to purchase the Hadden shares outright. It may have been Luce or Lloyd-Smith who convinced Crowell Hadden to act in the company's best interest and arrange for his mother to sell her stock. In any case, Crowell came around.

Luce's deal with the Hadden family broke down when the two sides failed to come to terms on the price of the Hadden shares, which were rapidly rising in value. Business manager Charles Stillman, three years out of college, broke the impasse. He solicited a bid from a Boston bank, which pegged the price of Hadden's stock at $360 a share. Luce put together a syndicate to buy out the Hadden family at that price. The company's revenues increased so rapidly in the intervening months that Crowell Hadden tried to raise the price, but Luce held firm. In September of 1929, not a year after Hadden's death, Crowell Hadden sold the syndicate 2,828½ shares worth more than a million dollars.

The deal enriched Luce's closest friends and allies. Luce allowed Wilton Lloyd-Smith, who had made the deal possible, to buy five hundred shares. Roy Larsen bought 550 shares, and Harry Davison purchased three hundred. Charles Stillman, who had saved the deal, purchased a hundred shares and was soon made treasurer of the company. John Martin bought two hundred shares, half of that amount purchased with Luce's knowledge in a separate deal with Mrs. Pool. But it was Luce who took the greatest portion. He bought 625 shares. "Thus ends, we hope happily, a prolonged debate," Luce wrote his parents. "I will own 40% of the stock (instead of about 32%) which makes my interest, for practical purposes, the controlling interest."

Having encouraged the Haddens to make the trade, Luce and his associates would later claim that Mrs. Pool approached them first. They said she hoped to sell the stock because she needed money. In fact, Mrs. Pool was quite wealthy and had no need for cash until the stock market crash of the following month, which would never have harmed her if she hadn't agreed to a deal with Luce. During the Depression, as the price of Time Inc. stock soared, Mrs. Pool lost almost a third of her million-dollar estate. In her last years, after the death of her second husband, Mrs. Pool still managed to keep a Park Avenue apartment and a house in Litchfield, Connecticut. But she could only support her sister Ethel and help to support numerous friends and employees by invading the principal of the Briton Hadden trust. While Luce's heirs would ultimately divide an estate containing more than $109 million in Time Inc. stock, the next generation of Haddens inherited shares worth $2,600,000.

The sale of Hadden's stock marked the beginning of a new era at *Time*. Although Luce had emphasized the need for an employee stock plan when he justified the purchase of the Hadden shares, as it turned out Luce allocated to that stock plan only 158 ½ of the nearly three thousand shares purchased by the syndicate. Adding some other shares to that number, Luce distributed three hundred shares at a friendly rate to several key staff members, including the Foreign News editor, Laird Goldsborough, the chief of research, Mary Fraser, and the advertising executive Howard Black. All remained loyal to Hadden's memory, but they were stockholders now. As business partners in the enterprise, their interests lay with the man who led the company. It was a masterful coup.

In the black notebook found among his things after his death, Hadden had charted a vision for a media and entertainment company. The vision came to pass. Not a year after Hadden's death, Luce launched *Fortune* at the audacious price of a dollar an issue. Luce had dreamed of creating the most beautiful and lavish magazine ever published, a magazine that would depict the economy at its height. When the economy crumbled, Luce went ahead anyway. In difficult times, when many wondered if the nation would ever rebound, *Fortune* scrutinized the American economic system while idealizing the power and glamour of the American way of life. Hot on the heels of that astounding success, Roy Larsen launched the *March of Time* radio drama and newsreel series, which helped to bring national broadcast journalism to the masses, introduced narrative journalism to a wide audience, and spread the *Time* name nationwide.

Luce officially arrived in society eighteen months after Hadden's death when *Vanity Fair* chose Luce to appear in its "Hall of Fame" column, explaining that he had "originated the newsmagazine idea." The author of the story was the magazine's managing editor, a wealthy single mother named Clare Boothe Brokaw. Introduced to Luce at a party a few years later, Brokaw shocked and transfixed the young publisher by launching into a penetrating critique of *Fortune,* then outlining her ideas for a new picture magazine. Luce had not faced this kind of combat since Hadden's death. Intensely attracted, he fell madly in love, asked Lila for a divorce, and married Clare.

Clare Boothe Luce filled the intellectual vacuum in Luce's life left by Hadden's death, and she started her husband on his next great idea. More of a word than a picture man, Luce was initially skeptical when his editors suggested launching the "picture mag" Hadden had dreamed of in the last year of his life. Clare convinced Luce to go ahead. Though Luce barred Clare from the project, his team created a sensational hit. They named the magazine, as Hadden had once suggested, *Life*. The first issue sold out immediately, and the magazine ultimately overtook the *Saturday Evening Post*.

Hadden had developed the formula for turning news into a form of national entertainment. Now Luce elaborated upon that formula on a grand scale. As the legacy of Hadden receded and Luce's own successes multiplied, he became a more confident and substantial person—not a romantic hero, as Hadden had been, but a titan. Dramatically brusque, Luce carried about him an air of confidence and determination. The reach of his mind and the intensity of his drive combined to impress upon people the raw force of a dominant and powerful character. A *Brooklyn Eagle* correspondent who interviewed Luce in his office left dizzied by the editor's manic pace. As remarkable as Hadden had been, Grantland Rice wrote, "*Time*'s other founder is just as brilliant and just as dynamic."

Occasionally it seemed as if Hadden's personality was speaking through Luce, as if Luce understood the importance of the spirit Hadden had spread through the office and was consciously trying to rally the staff in much the same way. Marching back from lunch, shirttails loose and tie askew, Luce would stand in the lobby waving his arms and championing his latest grand idea. For the moment anyway, it seemed to him the greatest thing on earth. Back in the office, Luce would bark out exclamations in Hadden's staccato style. Why were the editors sabotaging his four-color map? Was *Fortune* printed on toilet paper? The piece needed "sex, sex, sex, sex!" Later, leaving the office for the night, Luce would flash his secretary a mischievous grin and tell her he had just been trying to "raise a little hell." Howard Black, who had always thought of *Time*'s founders as perfect opposites, noticed Luce making a conscious effort to take on some of his old friend's personality traits—as if Luce missed the spark Hadden once provided and saw the need to kindle it himself.

As he grew more confident, taking on pieces of Hadden's character, perhaps Luce's increasingly brilliant reputation began to outshine in his mind the fading memory of Hadden. Luce had never felt comfortable with Hadden's influence. The memory of competing with

Hadden, of struggling with him and often following his lead, was in part a memory of weakness. There had been good times, and certainly Luce did not wish to forget them entirely. But he allowed others to forget them. Despite his promise to publish a book about Hadden within a year, Luce did not do so. For several years after Hadden's death, his name made no appearance in the magazine he had created, except in obituaries of his relatives and in an obscure footnote that hinted at his drinking problem.

But the memory of Hadden haunted Luce. And so did the blame of Hadden's friends. Their judgment hung over Luce, the editor Ralph Ingersoll later wrote, "like a choking miasma." Believing that Hadden deserved recognition, three years after his death his friends launched a campaign to create a building in his name for the student paper at Yale. The outpouring of love was remarkable. Nearly three hundred people pledged funds, and the philanthropist Edward S. Harkness, one of the original Time Inc. stockholders, donated a prime piece of real estate in the heart of Yale's campus. Luce would later claim that he was the building's main donor. In fact, he contributed $10,000 toward the $113,000 construction budget, while the Haddens contributed more than $50,000.

In April of 1932, Hadden's friends and family gathered at the Briton Hadden Memorial Building for a ribbon-cutting ceremony. In a touching display of love for his cousin, John Martin wrote a speech for the occasion. Expecting no more than a few choice words, the crowd slowly awakened as Martin began to discuss the originality of Hadden's ideas, and for the first time a large group began to think about how deeply Hadden had transformed American journalism. Roy Larsen recalled, "We realized we were hearing great words about a great man."

When *Time* covered the event in two columns toward the back of the magazine, Mrs. Pool began to think Luce was allowing her son's name to fade into obscurity. "It's too bad you couldn't have seen your way clear to do the thing Brit would have done," Mrs. Pool wrote Roy Larsen. "And after the very poor showing Luce made at his death you had a chance here to redeem that, excused on account of lack of time & space, commented upon by many many people. You have had many weeks to have done this properly, to have paid Briton Hadden the trib-

ute he should have had from his own paper. You may be all very efficient but you have very poor memories; poor idea of what is fitting
when you put in the place of honor, a stupid bishop, instead of the
man who made you all. And this goes especially for Harry Luce."

Behind Luce's back, people still whispered that Hadden, not Luce,
was the true genius behind *Time*. Nine years after Hadden's death, on
the occasion of *Time*'s fifteenth anniversary, the *Washington Post* congratulated *Time* and called Luce a genius. Nevertheless, the paper
noted, it was Hadden, not Luce, who was responsible for the magazine's "refreshing color and verve," which had quite obviously diminished since Hadden's death. In the tight-knit circle of New York society,
people continued to whisper that Luce was not the inventor of *Time*.
Often the talk reached Clare Boothe Luce. "I used to be annoyed," she
recalled. "Harry never was. I never heard him speak disparagingly of
Hadden."

Still it must have been upsetting to Luce that the man who out-
shined him all his life would continue to do so from beyond the grave.
In the thirty-eight years between Hadden's death and his own, Luce
rarely discussed Hadden. In recent interviews, none of the few surviving writers and editors who worked closely with Luce could recall his
ever having brought up Hadden in conversation. Nor could either of
his sons, including his elder son and namesake, Henry Luce III, who
followed in his footsteps by writing for the *Yale Daily News*. Luce was
equally reticent in his writings. In 1940, while drafting a response
to the Yale class of 1920 twenty-year questionnaire, Luce wrote that
Hadden "in fact created" *Time*. But Luce never mailed the response;
he filed it away and sent his classmates a list of his own activities
instead. Once, at a Yale reunion, Cully Sudler lamented the tragedy
of Hadden's death. "Oh, it's all right," Luce said. "*Time* was Brit's
monument, and he done it."

During his career as *Time*'s editor, Luce delivered well over three
hundred separate speeches on a wide range of topics—from the economy and the Constitution to the nation's role in the world and the fate
of China. He even talked about the postwar American building boom.
In many of his speeches, Luce discussed the kind of journalism *Time*
did, and what *Time* stood for—an opportune moment, it would seem,
to reconnect *Time* with the Hadden legacy. But Luce never discussed

the importance of Hadden's ideas or admitted his significance in the birth and rise of *Time*. In fact, in all the hundreds of Luce's speeches stored at Time Inc. and at the Library of Congress, Hadden's name appears only four times—in two talks Luce delivered before a group of his employees, and in two talks he delivered in the last years of his life. On all but one of those occasions, Luce spoke Hadden's name once, quickly, and immediately went on to discuss other subjects.

It wasn't as if Luce didn't like to reminisce. Luce frequently discussed personal aspects of his past and the people who had most influenced him. Luce did so quite movingly and eloquently. Luce discussed his youth in China in seven separate speeches, his parents in four, his experiences in high school and college five times. He talked specifically about journalism at Hotchkiss in one speech, and he talked about his experience of the Great War in another—appropriate points, it would seem, to mention Hadden. Luce did not.

There were numerous moments, over the years, when it almost seemed odd not to discuss Hadden. In 1942, shortly after the attack on Pearl Harbor, Luce returned to Yale to deliver a talk at the annual banquet of the *Yale Daily News*. On the podium, Luce reminisced about heeling the *News* and the start of the Great War. He did not speak of Hadden. Afterward, Luce joined a couple of students at Mory's wooden tables, where they ended up drinking pints until four in the morning. Only then did Luce bring up Hadden, calling him the idea man in the partnership. That night Luce left the impression that he took it as his duty to carry on without Hadden in the dark days of war to come. But Luce would not say so publicly.

Luce thought about Hadden that year as hundreds of correspondents from Chungking to New Dehli to Rio de Janeiro brought *Time* news from around the globe. In July, the producers of the *March of Time* asked Luce to deliver a speech for the nation about the purpose of the free press during wartime. Luce drafted the talk twice, scratching out sentences and writing new ones by hand. In both drafts, he tiptoed around Hadden's name, referring to the "group of us" who started *Time*. But Luce's talk changed radically after he submitted it to the show's producers, chief among them Roy Larsen. On July 9, 1942, Luce delivered his talk on national radio. In the final version, he mentioned the words "my partner, Briton Hadden."

The fact that Luce would write around Hadden's name in a pub-lic address, only to end up making a specific reference to him when subject to the purview of their longtime associate, suggested that some-thing more was at work than a reticence to discuss the past. No one would expect Luce to mention Hadden in every speech of his life, or even in many. But particularly in Luce's later years, as the record filled with stories he told about nearly every aspect of his life, one would expect him to take an opportunity to register Hadden in the Ameri-can memory. One might even expect Luce, Hadden's intellectual soul mate, to go out of his way to do so, if not frequently then in a few sig-nificant moments. But Luce never did so—with one great exception.

In 1943, at *Time*'s twentieth-anniversary dinner party, Luce was asked to discuss the origins of the magazine. It was clear from the way Luce began his speech that he recognized his failure to discuss Had-den over the years. He even admitted, in a rather odd aside, that if asked to explain his neglect of *Time*'s history before a jury he would be found "guilty as hell!" Luce explained that during the busy years of the company's expansion, followed by the frantic years of the Sec-ond World War, he had not had time to consider the past. But he also stated plainly that he planned to interpret the past as he saw fit. "Let the dead past bury its dead," he declared. "Let us live in the present, spend and be spent. If we stop to think, let it be of the future. We have no rear guards: we have only advance patrols, scouting parties, thrust-ing toward the promised land."

Nevertheless, Luce said he intended to speak of the past that night and to answer a question he had often been asked—"How did *Time* really get started?" Luce began to tell the story of how he and Hadden had walked through Camp Jackson together, discussing the idea of "that paper." It was then, Luce said, when their partnership was born. It would have been easy to go on and discuss the fruits of that part-nership and the ideas Hadden had contributed to it. Instead, Luce simply called Hadden a "great stylist" and told the story of how he had once shaved off all of his hair. "Yes, Sergeant Hadden, I couldn't admit it then, but you were one good soldier," Luce said. "Take the salute tonight and know that your caisson *is* rolling along." The same night, Luce delivered an anniversary talk on the *March of Time*, broadcast nationwide over NBC's Red network. He did not mention Hadden.

For the rest of his life, when asked about Hadden, Luce would answer in brief, saying Hadden died just as *Time* was "beginning to see the light." Mentions of Hadden in the pages of the magazine he created grew less common and less accurate by the year. As Hadden's legacy faded, people naturally wondered why *Time* didn't sound more like its editor. *Business Week* commented in 1948 that Luce and *Time* were "as dissimilar as two personalities can be. . . . Luce takes everything with almost equal seriousness, weighing, sifting, deliberating. *Time* is light-handed, iconoclastic, puckish." Unaware of Hadden's lasting legacy, *Business Week* concluded: "But the two identities, contrasting as they appear, are facets of the same man. *Time* is a side of Luce called forth by the magic of the written word."

Twenty-five years after the founding of *Time*, the role of the man most influential in the invention of the newsmagazine had been wiped out. Luce's prominence over Hadden was so complete that most people, even Luce's harshest critics, thought he was responsible for inventing Timestyle. Only a few lonely souls remembered the truth. As one subscriber meekly reminded *Time* in a letter to the editor that was never published: "Briton Hadden was the presiding genius."

People who had been close to Hadden during *Time*'s first years were furious at Luce for his display of ingratitude. The researchers most loyal to Hadden's memory, his girlfriends Deborah Douglas and Elizabeth Brown, noted to their friends that Luce wasn't the genius behind the thing when they worked there. At Yale, where memories of Hadden remained vivid, the majority of Luce's close friends, including members of Skull and Bones and former editors of the *Yale Daily News*—men who otherwise deeply admired Luce, viewed him as the champion of their worldview, and considered him an honored friend—felt that he had buried Hadden's place in history. "*Time* was Brit's idea," John Hincks said. "It had its genesis in Brit's head. The style was Brit's. Brit raised all the money. I am a good friend of Harry's and I know what he has done since Hadden's death, but I don't think Brit has ever had proper credit."

By the end of the thirties, Mrs. Pool had lost all hope that *Time* would ever recognize her son. When in 1940 *Time* asked original subscribers to write in and identify themselves, Mrs. Pool wrote back, "I'll say that I am an 'Old Timer.' Being the mother of Briton Hadden

I. knew *Time* before it was 'journalistically' born. I am *Time*'s Grand-mother. You have done well with my son's brain child and I hope you have not forgotten him."

Well aware of Mrs. Pool's grief, Luce's Yale friends encouraged him to publish the book about Hadden that he had long ago promised. At the invitation of Hadden's old Brooklyn neighbor, Stuart Heminway, who had briefly worked for the company, Luce spent an evening with Mrs. Pool. Hadden's mother gave Luce and Heminway a valuable col-lection of Hadden's childhood letters, stories, newspapers, and pho-tographs. The three agreed that together they would publish a book about Hadden. Heminway started in on the first chapter, but he wasn't able to get far. Luce never picked up the project.

As *Time*'s twenty-fifth anniversary approached, Mrs. Pool met Sam Walker, the chairman of the *Yale Daily News*. Walker talked about their conversation with the outgoing *News* chairman, his friend John G. Rohrbach. The young men spent an afternoon with Mrs. Pool at her home in Litchfield, Connecticut. She told them that "my friend Harry" had long ago offered to publish a book on Hadden. Since Luce had failed, Mrs. Pool had decided to fund the project. "I wouldn't say she was bitter," Rohrbach recalled, "but I think she was very disappointed." The young men left convinced that there was a major book to be writ-ten about Hadden, and that they couldn't write it without the papers stored at Time Inc. On a balmy October day in 1947, they met Luce through his son Henry Luce III at the Yale-Wisconsin football game. Rohrbach and Walker told Luce of their talk with Mrs. Pool.

Over the next three months, as Luce and his editors planned *Time*'s twenty-fifth anniversary celebration, Luce scheduled and canceled sev-eral meetings with the young men. All the while he was working closely with Max Ways, a wavy-haired senior editor who specialized in intellectual topics, to prepare the longest yet account of *Time*'s history. Ways wrote a rough draft that included a narrative of the early days of the magazine. Luce advised him to cut out the "housewifely detail—about red dots, going-to-press and all that stuff" and instead "concentrate mainly on *Time* today." The special issue came out on March 8, 1948. Ways's report went on for ten pages. Hadden's name appeared in two paragraphs.

A week before the story came out, Stuart Heminway had written Luce to encourage him to "pay some tribute to Brit Hadden." Luce wrote back that the Yale students might be the "providential answer." Luce received Rohrbach and Walker on St. Patrick's Day. He greeted them cordially and agreed to read their sample chapter. As the talk progressed and the Yale students watched Luce, they began to realize that their chances of receiving access to Hadden's papers were slim. A book would be written, but it would not necessarily be the type of book the young men hoped to write. "Luce wanted to get it off his agenda. He was sort of shamed into getting a book done," Rohrbach said. "He was very concerned about his own reputation. He didn't want to tell us that, but we both felt that he realized that he was putting himself in jeopardy."

Instead of allowing the Yale students to see the papers Mrs. Pool had given him, Luce gave the project to the writer he had once called a "cheap Broadway sport." In the twenty years since Hadden's death, Hadden's cousin Noel Busch had become a widely traveled foreign correspondent for *Life*, a master of journalistic stunts, and a skilled interviewer who met with everyone from Trotsky to King Ibn Saud. Quick and clever, Busch cultivated the art of writing breezy coffee table fare. He had a reputation for getting facts wrong or fudging them entirely. Reviewers disparaged his first three books. One *New York Times* critic noted "a basic inadequacy of information, a distressing superficiality and a glib delight in sweeping generalizations based on very little evidence."

Busch's wit and style so endeared him to Luce that at one point he had asked Busch to become his executive assistant. Busch had turned down that job. But when Clare Boothe Luce ran for Congress in 1942, he was more than glad to draft a laudatory profile, which the editors of *Life* refused to print. "I came to know Luce as well if not better than I had ever known my late cousin," Busch later wrote. "The consequence was not only a basic liking for him but substantial admiration." Busch's production at *Life* had tapered off since the war, but he continued to make liberal use of his expense account. A committee led by John Shaw Billings, whom Luce had made editorial director of all the magazines, recommended firing Busch. Instead Luce transferred him to the corporate payroll and assigned him to write the book on Hadden.

Busch received exclusive access to corporate files, the aid of past and present *Time* writers and executives, a researcher, two secretaries, and a salary of twenty-five thousand dollars. Uninspired, he relied on his researcher to conduct most of the necessary interviews. The bulk of Busch's own reporting consisted of several visits with Luce at his summer home in Connecticut. If Busch took notes of those conversations, the papers did not survive. Believing his book would have to serve "a positive public relations function" for the company, Busch portrayed Luce as an equal in the founding of *Time*. Though the idea had moved Hadden since childhood, Busch failed to print that evidence, and he studiously avoided the matter of Hadden's will. Hadden emerged as an irresponsible funnyman, a child at heart who would rather have been a baseball player than a journalist, and finally as a drunken miscreant. Busch handed in his draft a little more than five months after he began.

Despite Busch's effort to understate his cousin's contribution, Hadden's genius shined through the story. If *Time*'s early days were to be told, certain elements could not be ignored. The forceful expression of Hadden's writing at Hotchkiss and Yale so clearly presaged Timestyle that, despite all his effort to make light of Hadden's talent, Busch could not avoid depicting an editor so original and compelling that he ultimately threatened to eclipse the Luce legacy. Reading over the manuscript, Rosalind Constable, who wrote Luce and a select group of editors a weekly memorandum on intellectual life and the arts, saw the potential of Hadden's character to attract attention, even if portrayed superficially. "If we aren't too careful," she warned, "Hollywood will pay us half a million for the movie rights."

Subtly, almost conspiratorially, a manuscript intended to enhance the Luce legacy had squirmed from his grasp and now threatened to detract from that legacy instead. It would be embarrassing for Luce to exercise naked power on his own behalf, but like any leading executive he had people who were paid to do that sort of thing for him. After reading the manuscript and suggesting a few changes, Luce passed the work to his public relations team. "I wonder whether Hadden's genius isn't proven almost too well," the special projects executive Calvin Fixx wrote Busch. "As I say, you settled *that* question for me. But you raised another one, namely, the question of Luce's actual contribution in the founding of *Time*."

Luce settled the question in the most straightforward of ways. He gave the manuscript to Roy Larsen. Larsen, in turn, sent the manuscript to the two people who looked out for Luce's interests more than anyone else, Luce's sister Elisabeth and her husband, Maurice "Tex" Moore, chairman of the Time Inc. board. After reading over the manuscript, the Moores suggested dozens of places where instead of crediting Hadden alone Busch ought to write "Hadden and Luce." Busch refused to make those changes. But a greater one was yet to come.

Luce's public relations team didn't trust Busch, and executives including Roy Larsen insisted on reading over the final galleys before the book went to press. As deadline neared, Luce's team tried to convince Busch to scrap the title *Briton Hadden: His Life and Time*, which they called "untruthful." Busch resisted tenaciously, but under intense pressure from John Shaw Billings Hadden's cousin finally agreed to a new subtitle: *A Biography of the Co-founder of Time*. It would be Hadden's fate to go down in history as *Time*'s co-founder, whereas Luce would simply call himself the founder. Both terms were arguably true, of course, but the asymmetry of their use would suggest to the outside observer that Hadden was the second man.

Shortly after the book's publication, Mrs. Pool called up Busch's researcher, Lilian Rixey. "Co-founder is wrong," Hadden's mother said. "He's the founder, not the co-founder. It was entirely his idea." John G. Rohrbach, who had since started work at *Life*, eagerly read Busch's book; he thought it failed to "plumb the depths of what Hadden contributed to the partnership." Niven Busch, who had gladly sent along several pages of notes on Hadden, was deeply disappointed by his brother's work. "I remember him thinking that the book was just way off and didn't do justice to Hadden in any way," Niven's son Jerry Busch recalled. "He felt it was an affront to the memory of Briton." Another of Niven Busch's sons, Terry Busch, later said: "He felt that it whitewashed Luce, that it was a kiss-ass book to Luce."

The book sold poorly. Time Inc. refused to promote it in connection with the twenty-fifth anniversary, despite the entreaty of the book's publisher, Roger Straus. Niven Busch, who had gone into screenwriting and sold his novel *Duel in the Sun* to Hollywood, asked Luce to help make the book into a movie. Luce turned him down. Having controlled every aspect of the book project from hiring the writer to approving the jacket design, Luce proceeded to deny his influence, at one point telling a journalist that the book was not authorized by

Time Inc. When a Yale librarian offered to store Hadden's letters in the school's records room alongside the papers of great journalists, politicians, and public figures, Time Inc. refused the request. Hadden's letters, surviving editing notes and memoranda were folded into the corporate archives and sealed from view.

For the next half century, even though Hadden's family owned his letters, Time Inc. restricted the public's access to these papers without the family's knowledge or consent. Not one person from outside the company was allowed to read Hadden's letters until after Luce's death. Once Time Inc. had collected the record of Hadden's life and work, his story saw little daylight. Political controversy continually swirled around Luce. Many admired him despite *Time*'s biased news coverage for one reason only. As Eric Sevareid later put it on the *CBS Evening News,* "By any accounting, Henry Luce revolutionized journalism in this century. It took a big man to do that." The true story of Briton Hadden bore the potential to undermine Luce's authority as an innovator, thus opening him to political attack. Time Inc. executives left the story untold.

Despite their efforts, the story could have emerged in 1949 when *Collier's* assigned the journalist A. J. Liebling to do a series on *Time.* A brilliant writer with a skill for parsing language, Liebling delved into back issues of the magazine with the help of his researcher, the young writer James Munves. They compiled examples of epithets and physical descriptions of newsmakers that changed by the year along with Luce's political opinions. Walter Winchell reported that Liebling was preparing an eviscerating series of controversial stories—"hoticles," as Winchell called them. Roy Larsen telephoned the president of *Collier's.* Larsen was not one to make threats, and given *Time*'s history of dispatching enemies perhaps no threats were needed. Larsen simply made a friendly offer to endorse the rather optimistic circulation figures *Collier's* planned to report to the next meeting of the Audit Bureau of Circulations. *Collier's* killed Liebling's series within days.

Nevertheless, it still appeared that Hadden's story might emerge. The editors of *Collier's,* saving face, planned a gentler series on *Time.* They handed Liebling's assignment and some of his research to George Frazier, who had written features for *Life* before becoming one of the country's foremost jazz critics. Frazier, though not as intellectually penetrating as Liebling, had a nose for a good scoop, and he soon became interested in Hadden. Frazier also knew James Munves and hired him as a researcher. It was Munves who found Hadden's will at the Surrogate Court of New York County. Discovering that Hadden's nurse had signed the will as a witness, Munves tracked her down in Brooklyn. Lucy Wolinski told Munves the story of Hadden's deathbed arguments with Luce. Frazier, interviewing Luce personally, pressed him about his relationship with Hadden. Luce replied that he hadn't always gotten along with his partner, but he had loved as well as envied him.

Once again, the executives at Time Inc. grew worried. They were especially worried about Munves, who had visited the office announcing, "We intend to rake you over the coals." It was at this point that John Philip Sousa III, the special assistant to *Time*'s publisher, allowed Munves inside his office, showed Munves a file of articles about Luce, locked the file away in his drawer, and told Munves that he would not be allowed to read it. Sousa left the key to the drawer in plain view and announced that he was leaving for the weekend.

Taking Sousa's strange behavior as a coded hint, Munves grabbed the key and read through the entire file of stories. When Sousa returned the following week, he flew into a rage and accused Munves of rifling through his office. High-ranking *Time* editors complained to the *Collier's* team. *Collier's* held Frazier's story, let Munves go, and refused to give Frazier any of his legman's research—sabotaging their work. For yet another decade, the Hadden files sat untouched. Luce's secretary recalled of him during that time, "He never, ever mentioned Briton Hadden."

During the 1950s, as *Life* spread through the land and Luce's power reached its apogee, he did not discuss Hadden in a single speech. And yet, in a 1953 talk entitled "Journalism & Responsibility," Luce found time to claim that he invented "the word news-magazine." Five years later, when Luce returned to Yale to deliver a talk at the *Yale Daily News'* eightieth-anniversary dinner, he recounted the freshman year heeling competition and the story of how Alger Shelden had made the newspaper's editorial board. Luce then told the story of how proud he had felt when his son made the board. He mentioned all of this without once mentioning Hadden.

In June of 1959, Time Incorporated moved into a new skyscraper at Rockefeller Center—the Time-Life Building, forty-eight stories tall with Jet Age furniture, canary yellow accents, and recessed lights, all crowned by a ninety-six-foot sign, flashing "TIME-LIFE." Luce gave a talk upon the laying of the cornerstone, filled with documents of *Time*'s past including the original prospectus. "We honor the honest work done," he declared, "and we remember, not without laughter and not without tears, and always with affection, the men and women who were Time Inc. in other times and places."

A year and a half later, Luce agreed to a rare interview with *Closeup*, a news program aired by the Canadian Broadcasting Corporation. "Could we talk about the beginnings of *Time*?" the interviewer, Barry Harris, asked. "Well, we had, er, my original partner and I had this idea," Luce said. He mumbled Hadden's name so unclearly that the typist who transcribed the recording failed to catch it. The typist left a blank space and inserted a question: "Name?" Robert Crone, the show's producer, forwarded the transcript to Luce. Instead of providing the name, Luce scratched out that portion of the interview.

Shortly before he retired, Luce selected his London bureau chief, Robert T. Elson, to write the authorized history of Time Inc. Elson and Luce, sharing an interest in religion, had developed a close professional friendship. A sober, deeply conservative man, Elson couldn't quite understand Hadden; he viewed his sense of humor as almost cruel. But Elson would have a chance to learn more. Luce invited his writer to Phoenix, where they would discuss the early days of Time Inc. at the Luces' pink house with its vast flagstone patio overlooking the golf course of the Biltmore Estates.

On his first trip, Elson interviewed Luce for three days in sessions that lasted for several hours each. Elson recorded the conversations onto reel-to-reel audiotape. When Elson asked Luce for insight into Hadden's personality, Luce at first sounded stumped. He called Hadden a "most unusual character" and a difficult one to "bring to book." Finally, at the end of the second long day of talk, Luce broached the subject of Hadden's death. He went into a detailed account of the stock sale and the syndicate, adding of Hadden, "I don't know if he even had a will."

Just before closing the interview, Elson returned to the subject.

"There *is* one story," he said. "I haven't checked this . . . that Brit *did* have a will. But this provision was broken. Have you heard that?" There was a long silence, then the sound of ice clinking about in a tumbler. Luce whispered, barely audible on tape: "No, I haven't." Elson spoke more forcefully: "You never heard that story? That there was a will?" A loud thumping began, the sound of a glass or a foot banging against a table. Finally, after another pause, Luce changed his story. "Yes," he said. "It rings a slight bell."

Elson's book, *Time Inc.: The Intimate History of a Publishing Enterprise,* would be published in 1967. The book laid out the barest factual account of Hadden's death and its aftermath—an account that carefully skirted what happened between *Time*'s chief creative genius and the man who expanded the company into a media empire. Hadden emerged as an immature and unpredictable man who relied on Luce's sound, steady judgment. A dozen senior Time Inc. executives, including Luce's son, read the manuscript before it went to press. Journalists hailed the book as a model corporate history.

Luce and his cohorts had compiled Hadden's story, told it inaccurately, diminished its significance, barred public access to the true story, prevented the few enterprising journalists who developed an interest in Hadden from pursuing it, and ultimately succeeded in burying Hadden's role in history. By the end of Luce's life, few people, journalists included, knew of Hadden's importance to the rise of *Time.* Had all of this happened by accident, or was it more or less the way Luce wanted it?

If Luce wished to recognize Hadden, he could have made one simple gesture. Hadden's old friend, the founder of *Newsweek,* once suggested the idea to Luce, though not in the most measured of words. "There is no doubt that it was Brit's genius, and not yours, that is the basis of *your* magnificent success," Thomas J. C. Martyn wrote Luce from retirement in Santos, Brazil. "You might pay him belated tribute by putting his name as cofounder on the inside masthead of *Time.*" Hadden's name made no such appearance during Luce's life. "That would have been Luce's decision to do that," *Time*'s managing editor Otto Fuerbringer recalled. "Nobody else would have."

Luce still loved Hadden, he honored him in his heart, and, at least as it seemed to Clare Boothe Luce's assistant, he missed Hadden more than he ever could say. Though the desire for fame and power ran strong in Luce, so did a strong sense of morality. But the essence of a man's character is tested only when it conflicts with his self-interest. Luce failed that test, and he did not feel right about what he had done. In the final years of his life, as Luce prepared to step down from his post as editor of Time Inc., he had one final opportunity to set things right. Sensing that he might not live to witness the fiftieth anniversary of *Time*'s publication, in 1963 Luce planned a gigantic party to celebrate the magazine's fortieth anniversary. There would never be a more appropriate moment to do his friend justice.

The Party of All Time

ON THE EVENING OF May 6, 1963, more than two hundred reporters arrived at the Waldorf-Astoria Hotel in New York. Correspondents from around the globe and cameramen representing every American television network crowded the lobby and awaited their quarry. When the black limousines glided down Park Avenue, and one by one the passengers emerged—first a dozen, then a hundred, and finally nearly three hundred of the most illustrious people in America—the hotel grew louder and more chaotic, until everyone was immersed in a deafening roar, punctuated only by the flash of cameras. By then Bob Hope was telling his fellow comedian Danny Kaye, "I've been to a lot of these things in my life. But this one—this one is going to be the party of all time."

Packed into two rooms was a crowd of rare achievement. There were clergymen and generals, athletes and intellectuals, artists and politicians. There were opera singers and piano virtuosos, architects and cartoonists, a premier and a president. The greatest boxer of all time was there, and it didn't matter if you thought he was Jack Dempsey or Joe Louis, since both had arrived. So had many of Hollywood's leading ladies, from Rosalind Russell to Gina Lollobrigida, wearing a low-cut gown with a rose tucked between her breasts that quickly attracted a crowd of senators. Among the group were boardroom leaders, power players, creative geniuses, and research scientists without whom the wheels of American life simply wouldn't turn. "Take a good look around, baby," Bette Davis told her daughter. "You'll never see anything like this again."

Here was the face of success itself, the American Dream personified. One executive likened the experience to sitting in the middle of *Who's Who*. For once bank presidents, governors, and even heads of state seemed quite common. "I want you to meet the former president of Mexico," one guest screeched to another. "He's darling." One man was so impressed as to be reduced to a kind of fame-crazed madness. All but unrecognized, he ran from table to table throughout the night, kissing actresses on the back. Rumor had it that he was a scientist who had once won the Nobel Prize.

The roar grew so loud that by seven fifteen, when the dinner gong clanged, no one could hear it. The lights flickered, but nobody noticed because cameras were constantly flashing. Finally a voice boomed over the loudspeaker—"Your attention please . . . your attention *please.*" Tipsy on cocktails and drunk on fame, the guests traipsed to the Grand Ballroom, where red-coated waiters served them Truite de Rivière en Gelée à la Muguette and Baba Anniversaire Flambé Montmorency. It had taken sixteen chefs and more than fifty cooks and kitchen hands a day to prepare the menu, which one reporter called a "gourmet's dream."

In the front of the room, the elite of the elite occupied a three-tiered dais. Gaunt and stooping General Douglas MacArthur, who would offer his reminiscences to *Life* a few months later, was smoking a giant cigar. Bob Hope was scribbling out jokes on cocktail napkins. Mrs. Luce, her hair dressed in the shape of a crown, held a cocktail purse in the crook of her white-gloved arm. With sharp eyes she surveyed the room. Looking over the crowd, the eminent theologian Paul J. Tillich reflected, "In Europe, it would be a group which only royalty could command." But in America the only man who could bring such a group together was Henry R. Luce.

Under the lights that spotlighted the flower-trimmed dais, Luce's leathery face, lined by deep grooves, bore the marks of four decades spent traveling the world, bending presidential ears, writing, speaking, and chain-smoking. His lanky frame, soon to be wracked by lung cancer, had begun to look as wiry as when he was in prep school. His hairline consisted of a gray fringe around the side and a few strands at the top. But the most remarkable aspect of his graying visage remained unchanged: a pair of steel-blue eyes, narrow as slits, framed by two massive, rust-gray eyebrows. They looked, Alfred Kazin later wrote, as if they had been "planted and watered to intimidate subordinates."

Presidents feared this man; senators and congressmen bowed to his will. Five hundred reporters and correspondents curried his favor from thirty-five news bureaus around the globe. He spoke to the nation as a minister would, reaching seven million Americans in *Life*. He preached to the rich and powerful in *Fortune*. He blanketed the nation with *Sports Illustrated, Architectural Forum, House & Home*, a book division, and five VHF television stations. But as immense as his influence had grown, it was the little magazine with the bright red border that remained the centerpiece of his project. When *The New Yorker* printed a cartoon of a man adjusting his tie in front of the mirror, he saw in the glass his face on the cover of *Time*.

And so it was naturally to *Time* that Luce returned at the peak of his career to pay tribute to his success. The theme of the evening would be the American pageant—forty years of history as recorded in the pages of *Time*, represented by the heroes *Time* had championed. More than fourteen hundred people came to the Waldorf that night from around the world and from every part of public life. Two hundred and eighty four of the guests had appeared on the cover of *Time*. The evening's program would consist of simply introducing them. There could be no applause, or the affair would last all night.

But when the band broke into "It's Gonna Be a Great Day," the crowd immediately began clapping. The applause grew louder and more insistent as Luce stood by the podium, tearing off his glasses to peer into the crowd, waving at his friends and employees, jerking his glasses back on again. He moved about like a wind-up soldier. After the invocation, Luce took the podium and waved his left hand. "The point of this party is the people who are here," he barked. "That they should enjoy meeting each other face-to-face, as we hope they have enjoyed meeting each other in the pages of *Time*."

One by one, Luce began intoning the names of the men and women who had made *Time*'s cover. A group of emcees including Henry Cabot Lodge Jr. and Bob Hope aided the editor. As each celebrity stood up to be bathed in *Time*'s spotlight, some for a final time—Eddie Rickenbacker, Ed Sullivan, Thurgood Marshall—the crowd could not help but associate Luce with the story *Time* had told. On and on the list went—Jackie Robinson, Darryl F. Zanuck, George Balanchine—ruthlessly, efficiently, with no pause for the crowd to clap, just a steady, thundering and ultimately overwhelming wave of awe. It was a masterstroke of publicity that summed up *Time*'s position in the center of American culture.

The dinner lasted until midnight. The crowd roared for Milton Caniff, they shook the room for Casey Stengel, they broke into thunderous applause for Jonas Salk, who had triumphed over polio. Allen Dulles smoked his pipe and scraped bread crumbs onto the floor. Carmine De Sapio of Tammany Hall never removed his sunglasses. Ina Claire shed tears onto her pink gauze gown when Helen Hayes introduced her as "one of the bright jewels in the American theater." Vice President Lyndon Johnson praised Luce for selecting cover subjects "on a basis other than beauty." He then raised a toast "to our host and to our country, America, the land of the free."

As the dinner neared its end, the grandson of the man who had long ago funded Reverend Luce's work in China stood to make a speech. It was the portly president of Time Inc., James Linen III, who announced to the party that the President of the United States had sent along a telegram. "Every great magazine is the lengthened shadow of its editor, and this is particularly the case with *Time*," John F. Kennedy had written. "The conception of a magazine which would render weekly reports on every aspect of human action and thought was revolutionary; and, in having the wit to imagine this conception and the capacity to bring it to successful realization, Henry R. Luce has shown himself one of the creative editors of our age." Luce thanked the President for his "most admirable compliment."

On the podium that night, Luce took care to salute Roy Larsen, "the best lifelong partner anybody ever had." He thanked his publisher and his managing editor, "the two men who really run *Time*." He saluted his wife, Clare Boothe Luce, who would have made a "best-selling cover" had she not married the editor. He must also have thought about his old partner. A few days before, while summarizing his career in a talk at Columbia University, Luce had briefly said the words "Briton Hadden." But he couldn't do so on his crowning night. At no point during the evening's program did Luce utter the name of the one man who had made it possible for him to stand before that crowd.

After the dinner, the guests partied until early in the morning. Ginger Rogers danced with Henry Luce III, who had gone to work as a correspondent for the Washington bureau and risen to become the circulation director of *Fortune*. For thirty seconds or so, she danced with Briton Hadden's nephew, Crowell "Pete" Hadden, an advertising salesman who had worked his way up from the mailroom. Gene Tunney, victor over Dempsey in the famous "long count" rematch, was talking about a young boxer named Cassius Clay. "Cassius won't be ready in one or two years," Tunney said. "Watch for him in three." The quarterback Bobby Layne wandered about in a stupor, accosting reporters, "I bet you didn't know I was on the cover of *Time*, did you?" As Roy Larsen traversed the floor, he offered a copy of the Hadden biography to the gossip columnist Hedda Hopper, one of the many guests who had never heard of Hadden. Luce sat smoking cigarettes next to Gina Lollobrigida and a bottle of Bollinger. His eyes gleamed.

Drifting through the crowd were a few of Luce's friends from Skull and Bones. One was Dan Winter, who had known *Time*'s founders since their days at Hotchkiss. Winter's thoughts turned toward Hadden that night. He felt Luce missed his chance to repay his debt of "honor, respect and loyalty to Brit." After the party, Winter would suggest to Luce that it was time to pay his partner a proper tribute. Luce's reply was curt. "Brit's memory lives on, and on nearly all suitable occasions he is referred to as co-founder," he wrote. "The living memory is the best of all memorials."

If on the greatest night of his life Luce had yet to come to terms with his friend and rival, Winter nevertheless sensed a gentler spirit within his mighty schoolmate. Beneath the domineering exterior, a feeling of love and loyalty was slowly working over Luce. In the following four years, having retired from the active editorship of Time Incorporated, Luce would immerse himself deeply in religion and once again find that old sense of closeness with God. During that time, Luce would begin to come to terms with his past. In the spring of 1966, he agreed to an extended television interview, during which he spoke warmly of Hadden and credited him with the impetus for founding *Time*.

In February of 1967, the last month of Luce's life, one of his editors would ask him to write an introduction to the *Time Capsule* for 1923, a little book drawn from the pages of *Time*. Luce would craft a narrative of the night his tiny staff worked until dawn on the magazine's first issue—"with Briton Hadden in command." These were fond words from an aged man surveying his entire life. They would turn out to be the last words Luce would submit for print. He offered them in the spirit of friendship, which was all Hadden ever asked of him.

Hadden had picked a strong partner in Luce, a man capable of bringing dreams to life. Together they had created an American institution. Although Hadden never received proper credit for the crucial part he had played in the rise of the national media, accolades had never interested him much anyway. The idea itself was the thing. Perhaps that was why Dan Winter imagined Briton Hadden looking down from heaven that night, smiling his sideways grin. "Good work, Harry," he was saying. "Good work, Harry—that's swell!"

ACKNOWLEDGMENTS

THIS BOOK BEGAN AT 202 York Street in New Haven, Connecticut, in the Briton Hadden Memorial Building. I spent much of my time there as a junior at Yale when I edited the *Yale Daily News*. On the top floor, Hadden's dusty portrait looms over the wood-paneled boardroom. The painting is dimly lit by an old lamp. Hadden sits in his shirtsleeves and a green eyeshade. He is armed with a giant *Time* pencil. Gazing at Hadden's portrait, I became interested in his expression—a sideways smile that gives his face an air of mystery.

Late at night, after putting the paper to bed, I would sit near Hadden's portrait and leaf through the bound volumes. Flipping through his editorials, I was captivated by Hadden's writing style. Rhythmic, compact, Hadden's sentences practically jumped off the page—much like the impish voice of the early *Time*. If it were true that Hadden's "genius created a new form of journalism," as the plaque in the building's foyer states, I wondered why so few people had heard of him.

I wrote an essay about Hadden for a class on "The Art of Biography" taught by John Lewis Gaddis. The following year, on a whim, I sent the essay to Walter Isaacson, who was then *Time*'s managing editor. Several weeks later, I was surprised to find in my mailbox an encouraging note. I immediately wrote back and asked for access to the Time Inc. Archives. Isaacson, a noted biographer, turned the key that would unlock *Time*'s secret history.

A few months later, having moved to New York and found a job as a production hand at ABC News, I was admitted to the Time-Life

Building at Rockefeller Center. There a three-thousand-pound Mosler fireproof safe contains many of the papers of the corporation's founders, including their childhood poetry and their letters home throughout preparatory school and college. Gradually my access expanded. I was permitted to read memoranda, financial records, and hundreds of interviews with and letters from Time Inc.'s most influential participants, including top editors and executives, Hadden's friends and family, his office boys, even his friend and roommate who later broke with *Time* to launch *Newsweek*.

Time Inc. began collecting oral history reminiscences in 1948 when Lilian Rixey interviewed dozens of people for Noel F. Busch's book on Briton Hadden. Later, Luce appointed a corporate historian, Alex Groner, to run the archives, and a bureau chief and editor, Robert T. Elson, to write the company's history. Luce directed his team to pursue the truth, an instruction followed with intuition and persistence by Celia Sugarman, Roy Larsen's longtime secretary and a talented interviewer. Luce devoted hours to discussing his life and company on audiotape. He meticulously saved his business papers, which were folded into the archives after his death. Most of the papers at Time Inc. have been sealed from public view for fifty years, many for longer. This is the first book by someone who has never worked for the corporation to benefit from unfettered access to the archive.

A new era at Time Inc. began with the death of Luce when *Time*'s editors placed Hadden's name atop the magazine's masthead. I could not have written this book without the help of the corporation. Time Inc. archivist Bill Hooper has dedicated much of his life to preserving and studying the history of the corporation. He contributed his vast knowledge of the collection and made innumerable research suggestions along the way. Pamela Wilson, the former director of the archives, and Diane Francis, the archival assistant, gave devotedly of their expertise and effort, as did Kathi Doak, the director of the Time Inc. Picture Collection. During the four years and more that I researched this book, not once did they ask what I thought or what I would write. It was a rare stroke of luck to work so closely with the dedicated custodians of a major historical collection.

I also feel deeply grateful to the families of *Time*'s founders, who took a sincere interest in this project and contributed numerous insights. Hadden's nephew, Crowell "Pete" Hadden, and his wife, Madeleine, provided permission to read the Hadden papers and discussed what they knew of Hadden's life. Luce's son, Peter Paul Luce, and his wife, Betsy, hosted me at their home while I read through the papers of Luce's first wife, Lila Tyng, and his father, Henry Winters Luce. We talked for many hours over the course of the project, and our conversations contributed mightily to my understanding of Luce. In the last years of his life, Henry Luce III provided access to his father's papers and dedicated several hours to discussing his father.

The families of Hadden's friends and coworkers responded enthusiastically to the idea of telling his story. They are listed under "Author's Interviews." I would like to mention here a few who provided crucial historical materials and recollections. Hadden's cousin Beatrix Miller discussed her memories of Hadden and her brothers. Akiko Busch shared her father Noel F. Busch's unpublished manuscripts on working with Luce. Niven Busch's sons Jerry Busch and Terry Busch, his daughter, Mary-Kelly Busch, Noel Busch's daughter Mary Fairchild Busch, and Niven Busch's former wife Carmencita Cardoza all provided insights on the brothers Niven and Noel Busch. Bob Aden, who has since passed away, discussed Deborah Douglas and shared his memoir on their marriage. Deborah's granddaughter Rebecca C. Morey and Deborah's niece Susan Aguilar also discussed Deborah Douglas and sent me pictures of her. Bob Larsen, Jonathan Z. Larsen, Christopher Larsen, and Margot Anne Simonson discussed their father, Roy Larsen, and Christopher shared with me an essay he wrote on Hadden. Barry M. Osborn discussed her father, John S. Martin, and her mother, Mimi Martin, and shared letters of her father's. Stanley Stillman discussed his father, Charles L. Stillman, and contributed numerous thoughts on Hadden, Luce, and the significance of the Time Inc. achievement. Speaking with the many people who contributed sources and documents to this book was a valuable experience in itself, and I am grateful to all for their time and insight.

The biographer W. A. Swanberg, and to a lesser extent the journalist George Frazier, saved a great part of their research into Hadden and Time Inc. The foremost Frazier expert, journalism professor Charles Fountain, discussed Frazier with me and shared Frazier's papers relating to Hadden. I am grateful to Fountain for taking the time to find some papers that contributed several revealing anecdotes to the story. The writer James Munves recollected working as a legman for Frazier and A. J. Liebling, and sent me the notes he took on his talk with Hadden's nurse, Lucy Wolinski. Munves kept a copy of this interview for more than fifty years; had he not done so, a crucial piece of the story would have disappeared. I am also indebted to the writer James M. Wood, who shared with me the letters of Winsor French to his stepfather, J. O. Eaton, and to the historian Alan Brinkley, who shared with me photocopies of the Lila Tyng and Henry Winters Luce papers that were in his possession.

In the course of researching this book, I visited or received historical materials from about a dozen collections, including the Boston University Archival Research Center, the Columbia University Rare Book and Manuscript Library, the Cornell University Division of Rare and Manuscript Collections, the New York Public Library, the University of South Carolina's South Caroliniana Library, the University of Wyoming American Heritage Center, and the Wisconsin Historical Society. I thank the staffs of these collections for their devoted care of historical sources.

I would especially like to thank the Manuscripts and Archives staff at Yale's Sterling Memorial Library, where I have come to feel so much at home. The university archivist, Richard V. Szary, and the chief research archivist, Judith Ann Schiff, made many helpful suggestions. At the Library of Congress Manuscript Division, where I read the Henry Robinson Luce and Clare Boothe Luce papers, the archivist Nan Thompson Ernst gave generously of her time and provided many helpful suggestions. I also spent an enjoyable week at Hotchkiss, where the archivist at the time, Nighat Saleemi, allowed me to read through the bound volumes of the Hotchkiss *Record* and the *Lit*, and arranged for me to read through the alumni records of Hadden and Luce. The current Hotchkiss archivist, Peter Rawson, has also been extremely helpful.

While I researched the various factors involved in Hadden's death, Scott Podolsky, an instructor in medicine at Harvard Medical School who practices internal medicine at Massachusetts General Hospital, Selim Suner, an assistant professor of emergency medicine at Brown

Medical School, and Richard S. Hotchkiss, a critical care specialist at Washington University, helped me to think about streptococcus and sepsis. The combination of their efforts helped to place Hadden's death in clinical and historical perspective. Cisco Gamez, the media coordinator at the Brooklyn Hospital Center, helped me to locate several useful sources in the hospital's archive.

I feel grateful to John Lewis Gaddis, first for encouraging me to write about Hadden, then for prodding me into the realization that I was far from finished. Several years later, when I returned to the Yale campus to complete the book, I found New Haven as stimulating as ever. I was fortunate to connect with Gaddis Smith, an expert on so much of the history covered in this book. He read the manuscript and contributed many suggestions. I would also like to thank the incomparable combination of John Merriman, Jay Winter, David Brion Davis, and John Demos for inspiring me to write history.

For my opportunities as a journalist, I thank the *Yale Daily News*. It has been said: "The *News* is a cruel mistress." But it is also a loving one, and deeply committed. I would like to thank Susan Zucker and George Thompson for carrying on the institutional history of this special place for more than thirty years. I would also like to thank my friends on the board of 2000 and my mentors on the board of 1999.

My agent, Amanda Urban, took an immediate and enthusiastic interest in the project and championed it throughout, reading through pages whenever I handed them in, and offering encouragement and advice. What a rock she has been. My editor, Terry Karten, never ceased to provide thoughtful comments and critiques; her commitment has been unflagging. My line editor, Danny Mulligan, provided detailed edits on a long manuscript draft. My copy editor, Estelle Laurence, provided a helpful final read. I'm grateful to Roberto de Vicq de Cumptich for his beautiful jacket design. And I'm grateful to Jennifer Smith, Alison Schwartz, and Liz Farrell at ICM for all of their hard work. It's a joy to work with such a steadfast and experienced team.

My fact checker, Herb Allen, spent a month helping to compile the source notes. His ideas and suggestions improved this book in countless places, and his humor and friendship were invaluable. Blair

Golson tracked down the Briton Hadden and Elizabeth Pool files at the Surrogate Court of New York County. He also helped with the source notes, as did Rebecca Dana, Christine Oh, Sophia Emigh, and Mila Dunbar-Irwin. Casey Miner provided her thoughts on the Nettie Fowler McCormick papers. It was fun working with all of them.

Quite a number of my friends and family have made unusual sacrifices and devoted their thinking to this project. I am indebted to Noah Kotch, Holly Martin, Thomas Wexler, Bryant Urstadt, and Amy Taubin, who read the manuscript in various stages and made many suggestions that helped to steer my writing process. Jon O'Neill, Charles Savage, Alex Taylor, Julia DeRouen-Hawkins, Paul Torelli, Michael Miarmi, Jeff Glasser, Emily Nelson, and Ann Treistman all provided invaluable comments and plenty of encouragement, too. Philip Z. Kimball, Robert and Abigail Kimball, Laura Kleinhenz, Trevor Hochman, Kelly Burns, Dale Park, Carrie Elston, James Tunick, Rebecca Friedman, John Mills Pierre, Ames Brown, Casey King, Lawrence P. King, and Michael Case Kissel were all generous with suggestions and support. I feel lucky to have come to know through the years such a wonderful group of people.

I have always had a strong sister in Claudia Wilner, who has been a source of insight since I can remember. This project was no exception; her suggestions helped me to reach numerous breakthroughs, and finally to hone the narrative. This book would not be the same without her contribution. I always returned to my work refreshed after spending an evening with her fiancé, Tom Kozak. My parents, Jeff and Lucy Wilner, have stood by me all my life, particularly during the last several years. They have enriched my life in countless ways. They have provided every kind of encouragement and support. I couldn't have done it without them.

In the course of researching a life, a biographer finally hits a point where he begins to grasp a person in whole. I feel that way about two people. Despite his tremendous intellectual powers and an inner wish to do right by his partner, Luce never told the true story of his relationship with Hadden, though he had every opportunity to do so. But he showed signs of change toward the end. Despite an expressive gregariousness and will to action, Hadden often shrank from emotional contact and honest communication. But he died as he lived, hoping for the best from a friend. They shared in common the struggle toward something higher and better within the self. I hope that both would see the power in their story and discover in its telling the redemption long sought and never found.

—*Isaiah Wilner*
New Haven, January 31, 2006

A NOTE ON SOURCES

THE FOLLOWING SOURCE NOTES are grouped into themes within each chapter. Readers interested in a particular topic may turn to the relevant heading to gain an overall sense of the range of sources used to construct that part of the narrative. Oral history reminiscences are cited in the following format: "Name, date, archive." Letters and memoranda are cited: "Name A to name B, date, archive."

Most of this story resides at the Time Inc. Archives in New York City (TIA). The Briton Hadden papers (BH) include childhood letters, writings and drawings; letters Hadden wrote while traveling between 1920 and 1925; one of Hadden's black notebooks; his copy of the *Iliad*. The Henry R. Luce papers (HRL) include childhood letters, writings, sermons, and speeches; drafts and copies of Luce's letters to people outside the corporation; letters Luce received from friends, acquaintances, public figures, and others. Although Time Inc. holds both the Hadden and Luce collections, the families of the founders retain the rights.

The Time Inc. Archives hold corporate records including annual reports, budgets, business plans, financial statements, memoranda, minutes, stock books, stylebooks, and other documentation of the corporation's activities. The collection includes the Time Inc. papers of Henry R. Luce and Roy E. Larsen, Hadden's surviving editing notes and memoranda, documentation of major events such as *Time*'s fortieth-anniversary party, and research compiled by the Time Inc. corporate history team. These materials are categorized in subject files.

In addition to the subject files, Time Inc. keeps a set of name files on people who came into contact with the corporation. The career of a typical employee may be recorded in several folders: a pictures and biography file; a miscellaneous file that contains correspondence with Luce and other executives; a speeches file; an oral history reminiscences file; and a file of newspaper clippings and other biographical materials collected by the disbanded Time Inc. research department.

The Time Inc. Archives also hold the papers of Henry P. Davison Jr. (HPD), an original investor and early board member who kept his corporate correspondence with Hadden and Luce, and the Publicity files, a collection of company scrapbooks. When quoting newspaper and magazine clippings from the scrapbooks, I have identified the clipping in almost all cases. In the few cases in which I could not identify the clipping, I have noted its provenance.

Several more archives hold important pieces of Luce's story. The Library of Congress Manuscript Division in Washington, D.C., holds 110 boxes of Luce's papers (HRLLOC). This collection includes Luce's correspondence with *Yale Daily News* editors and Hotchkiss and Yale classmates. The collection also includes numerous speeches and talks delivered by Luce, particularly on religious subjects. Though Time Inc. holds an extensive collection of papers detailing the fortieth-anniversary "cover party," the Clare Boothe Luce collection at the Library of Congress (CBL) holds valuable documentation and photographs of the occasion. More information on Luce and Time Inc. can be found in the papers of the biographer W. A. Swanberg (WAS) at the Columbia University Rare Book and Manuscript Library in New York City. Swanberg interviewed Luce's acquaintances and Time Inc. employees, and Swanberg's papers include extensive typed notes of those talks.

Several collections detail Luce's childhood in China and the lives of his family members: the Lila Tyng (LT) and Henry Winters Luce papers (HWL) held by Peter Paul Luce in Englewood, Colorado; the Severinghaus Family papers at the Cornell University Division of Rare and Manuscript Collections in Ithaca, New York (SF); the Nettie Fowler McCormick papers at the Wisconsin Historical Society in Madison (NFM). The Henry Winters Luce papers contain the letters Luce's parents wrote in response to Luce's childhood letters, making it possible to read both halves of the conversation.

Outside of the Time Inc. Archives, the few known sources of material on Hadden's life include the papers of George Frazier (GF), stored at the home of Charles Fountain in Duxbury, Massachusetts, and the numerous drafts by Noel F. Busch of his unpublished memoir *Life with Luce*, stored at the home of Akiko Busch in Lagrangeville, New York (NAB). The Ralph Ingersoll papers (RI) at the Boston University Archival Research Center contain numerous drafts of Ingersoll's unpublished memoir of working with Luce, which includes a chapter detailing what Luce said about Hadden in the years just after his death. Briton Hadden's will was admitted for probate at the Surrogate Court of New York County in New York City (SCNY). Documents pertaining to Hadden's estate are available to the public and can be found under the name of Briton Hadden and that of his mother, Elizabeth Pool.

Throughout this book, the word *Time*, italicized, refers to the magazine. The phrase "Time Inc." refers to the corporation. Hadden, Luce, and their staff traditionally capitalized the names of their magazines. Their competitors tended not to do so. I have capitalized such names only when necessary to provide historical flavor. During Hadden's life, the corporation spelled its name with a comma: "Time, Inc." But the "Inc." shortly came to be considered a part of the corporation's title and the comma was dropped not long after Hadden's death. I have held to the later punctuation because it reflects the way people thought of and spoke of the company.

Several women gave oral history reminiscences to Time Inc. after they married and changed their names. Women in these notes generally appear under the same name that appears in the body of the text. Thus Mimi Martin, who gave reminiscences to Time Inc. under three different names, always appears as Mimi Martin. Mary Fraser, who later became Mary Fraser Longwell, simply appears as Mary Fraser.

Luce's first wife appears in these notes as Lila Hotz, her maiden name, then as Lila Luce, her married name, and finally as Lila Tyng, the name she used after her divorce and remarriage. Lila's mother, Lila Frances Ross Hotz, appears in these notes as Lila F. R. Hotz. Luce's sister Emmavail appears as Emmavail Luce when a child, then as Emmavail Severinghaus after her marriage to Leslie R. Severinghaus. Luce's sister Elisabeth appears as Elisabeth Luce when a child, then as Elisabeth Luce Moore after her marriage to Maurice T. Moore.

A few more names deserve special mention. Luce's mother always spelled her name with a "z." She is noted as Elizabeth R. Luce. Her friend Mary Linen is noted as Mary Linen McWithey after her marriage. Hadden's grandfather is Crowell Hadden. Hadden's father is Crowell Hadden Jr. Hadden's brother is Crowell Hadden III. Hadden's nephew is Crowell "Pete" Hadden. Hadden's mother, Elizabeth "Bess" Busch, is noted as Elizabeth Pool, the name she took after her second marriage during Hadden's childhood. In a few cases a person referred to familiarly in the text appears formally in the notes. Thus the Time Inc. employee Dave Keep appears here as O. D. Keep, and Cully Sudler is noted here as Culbreth Sudler. Hadden's friend Stuart Heminway published a Yale class of 1920 book, *Twenty Years with Nineteen-Twenty,* under the name of C. Stuart Heminway.

Readers may turn to the Bibliography for a selection of the books and publications I relied on in conducting research. I am most indebted to George Wilson Pierson for his durable tome *Yale College*; to Nathan Miller for his thought-provoking account of the twenties, *New World Coming*; to Ann Douglas for her intellectual history of the Jazz Age, *Terrible Honesty*; to Paul Starr for his wide-ranging work on *The Creation of the Media*; to Robert T. Elson for his corporate history, *Time Inc.*

The best source of insight into *Time* is the magazine itself. In the course of writing this book, I read every sentence *Time* published during Hadden's life. To supplement the written record, I interviewed people connected with the history of Hadden, including the children of Hadden's friends and employees, and people who witnessed aspects of Luce's treatment of Hadden's legacy. I conducted most of these interviews on the phone and typed notes onto a laptop computer. I conducted some interviews in person. Many people talked with me numerous times. All are listed on the following page.

AUTHOR'S INTERVIEWS

Bob Aden • Susan Aguilar • Marge Alge • Letitia Baldrige • Thomas H. Black • Akiko Busch • Jerry Busch • Mary Fairchild Busch • Mary-Kelly Busch • Terry Busch • Carmencita Cardoza • Gay Claridge • George Crile • Daniel P. Davison • David Dolben • David Duff • Winslow Duke • Ted Farrell • Dick Feagler • Otto Fuerbringer • Marion Gottfried • Robinson Grover • Crowell "Pete" Hadden • Charles Haffner III • Rosalie Heffelfinger Hall • Bebe Hardwick • Chan Hardwick • John Winslow Hincks • Tony Hiss • Michael Z. Hobson • Peter Hobson • Richard S. Hotchkiss • Seymour Knox IV • Elisabeth Krueger • Bob Larsen • Christopher Larsen • Jonathan Z. Larsen • Stevia Sargent Lesher • Robin Little • Mary Lowman • Henry Luce III • Peter Paul Luce • Gloria Mariano • David Briton Hadden Martin Jr. • Howell C. Martyn • Coralee McInerney • Beatrix Miller • Michael Moore • Rebecca C. Morey • James Munves • Harvey K. Murdock • Barry M. Osborn • Scott Podolsky • John G. Rohrbach • Jonathan Schuyler Root • David Ryus • Shirley Shortlidge • Hugh Sidey • Margot Anne Simonson • Stanley Stillman • Don Stoltz • Selim Suner • Herbert Bayard Swope Jr. • Laurence Tighe • Stirling Tomkins Jr. • Edith Van Slyck • Peter Van Slyck • Sidney Young Wear

ABBREVIATIONS

Time Inc. Archives—New York, New York
  Briton Hadden papers (BH)
  Henry R. Luce papers (HRL)
  Henry P. Davison Jr. papers (HPD)
  Corporate Records and Reminiscences (TIA)

Boston University Archival Research Center—Boston, Massachusetts
  Ralph Ingersoll papers (RI)
  Herbert Bayard Swope papers (HBS)
  Libby Holman papers (LH)

Columbia University Rare Book and Manuscript Library—New York, New York
  W. A. Swanberg papers (WAS)

Cornell University Division of Rare and Manuscript Collections—Ithaca, New York
  A. J. Liebling papers (AJL)
  Severinghaus Family papers (SF)

The Hotchkiss School—Lakeville, Connecticut
  Hotchkiss Alumni Records (HAR)

Library of Congress Manuscript Division—Washington, D.C.
  Clare Boothe Luce papers (CBL)
  Henry Robinson Luce papers (HRLLOC)

New York Public Library (NYPL)—New York, New York

Surrogate Court of New York County—New York, New York
  Briton Hadden estate files (SCNY)
  Elizabeth Pool estate files (SCNY)

University of South Carolina, South Caroliniana Library—Columbia,
    South Carolina
  John Shaw Billings papers (JSB)

University of Wyoming American Heritage Center—Laramie, Wyoming
  Niven Busch papers (NIB)
  Noel Fairchild Busch papers (NOB)

Wisconsin Historical Society—Madison, Wisconsin
  Nettie Fowler McCormick papers (NFM)

Yale University Manuscripts and Archives—New Haven, Connecticut
  Diaries and memorabilia of Paul S. Phenix (YMA)
  Records of the Students Army Training Corps (YMA)
  Reminiscences of Charles M. Fleischner (YMA)
  Picture Collection (YMA)

Privately held collections:
  Henry Winters Luce papers—home of Peter Paul Luce, Englewood, Colorado
    (HWL)
  Lila Tyng papers—home of Peter Paul Luce, Englewood, Colorado (LT)
  George Frazier papers—home of Charles Fountain, Duxbury, Massachusetts
    (GF)
  John S. Martin letters—home of Barry M. Osborn, Locust Valley, New York
    (JSM)
  Winsor French papers—home of James M. Wood, Cleveland Heights, Ohio
    (WF)

Privately held manuscripts and files:
  James Munves files—home of James Munves, Prince Edward Island, Canada
    (JM)
  Noel Fairchild Busch manuscripts and notes—home of Akiko Busch,
    Lagrangeville, New York (NAB)
  Bob Aden manuscript—home of author, New Haven, Connecticut (RA)

SOURCE NOTES

PROLOGUE: DEATH WISH

Hadden's decline: Lucy Wolinski, undated interview, ca. 1950, JM; Oswald Jones, Aug. 9, 1948, TIA; John S. Martin, "Bulletin on Mr. Hadden," Jan. 30, 1929, TIA; Briton Hadden, Last Will and Testament, Jan. 28, 1929, SCNY; Henry Thorne, Nov. 30, 1948, TIA; Winsor French, June 26, 1956, TIA; Niven Busch, "Biographical Notes—Briton Hadden," June 8, 1948, TIA; Niven Busch, Mar. 11, 1965, TIA; Henry R. Luce, Jan. 12, 1965, TIA; Mimi Martin, Aug. 5, 1948, TIA; Mimi Martin, Feb. 3, 1958, TIA; Elizabeth Robert, Feb. 13, 1956, TIA; "Briton Hadden Dies; An Editor of *Time*," *New York Times*, Feb. 28, 1929, p. 20; "$1,028,724 Left by Briton Hadden," *New York Times*, Dec. 30, 1930, p. 44.

Hadden's personality and appearance: Nancy Ford, Feb. 12, 1958, TIA; Culbreth Sudler, Mar. 9, 1965, TIA; Niven Busch, "Biographical Notes—Briton Hadden," June 8, 1948, TIA; Elizabeth Pool, May 10, 1948, TIA; Briton Hadden Photographs file, TIA; Evans Woollen Jr. to Lilian Rixey, Apr. 30, 1948, TIA; Agnes Cowap, Dec. 1962, TIA; George Frazier, *It's About Time*, p. 114, GF; Mimi Martin, Aug. 5, 1948, TIA; Mimi Martin, Feb. 3, 1958, TIA; "Libby Holman Interview with Arlene Francis," WOR-NY, LH; Elizabeth Robert, Feb. 13, 1956, TIA; Mary Fraser to Patricia Diver, June 16, 1939, TIA; Amanda Frank, Jan. 5, 1954, TIA, Amanda Frank, Jan. 30, 1958, TIA; Harold Lateiner, June 14, 1939, TIA; Harold Lateiner, Dec. 6, 1960, TIA; Celia Sugarman, May 3, 1955, TIA; Alice Weigel, May 21, 1958, TIA; Joseph Kastner, undated memorandum, ca. June 1939, TIA; Florence Horn, Oct. 4, 1961, TIA; E. V. Hale, "Recollections of Briton Hadden," June 29, 1948, TIA; Thornton Wilder to James A. Linen III, undated letter, ca. 1949, TIA; Noel F. Busch, *Briton Hadden*, pp. 212, 232.

Hadden's relationship with Luce: John S. Martin, "Briton Hadden as Editor and Co-Founder of *Time*," Apr. 27, 1932, TIA; John S. Martin, Apr. 4, 1956, TIA; Culbreth Sudler, Mar. 9, 1965, TIA; W. Rice Brewster, May 14, 1948, TIA; W. Rice Brewster, Mar. 10, 1965, TIA; Lewis G. Adams, Dec. 28, 1955, TIA; Henry Seidel Canby, June 24, 1948, TIA; Laura Z. Hobson, Aug. 26, 1969, WAS; Dorothy McDowell, July 30, 1948, TIA; Mary Fraser, June 16, 1939, TIA; Joseph Kastner, undated memorandum, ca. June 1939, TIA; Harold Lateiner, June 14, 1939, TIA; Wells Root, Mar. 10, 1964, TIA; Katherine Abrams, June 22, 1948, TIA; Henry R. Luce, Jan. 11, 1965, TIA; Henry R. Luce, Jan. 12, 1965, TIA; Henry R. Luce, Jan. 13, 1965, TIA; Henry R. Luce, Apr. 29, 1965, TIA; Manfred Gottfried, Aug. 16, 1961, TIA; Mimi Martin, Aug. 5, 1948, TIA; Winsor French, June 26, 1956, TIA; Niven Busch, "Biographical Notes—Briton Hadden," June 8, 1948, TIA; John M. Hincks, Apr. 30, 1948, TIA; Thomas J. C. Martyn to Henry R. Luce, Mar. 17, 1966, HRL; Rosalind Constable to Mary Fraser, Nov. 12, 1948, TIA; Noel F. Busch, *Briton Hadden: His Life and TIME*, ch. 9, p. 23, NOB; Noel F. Busch, *Briton Hadden*, p. 42.

Expansion and influence of Time Inc.: Henry R. Luce, Jan. 12, 1965, TIA; Henry R. Luce, Jan. 13, 1965, TIA; Thomas M. Cleland, Sept. 2, 1960, TIA; Florence Horn, Oct. 4, 1961, TIA; Roy E. Larsen, Aug. 28, 1956, TIA; John S. Martin, Apr. 4, 1956, TIA; Charles L. Stillman, July 26, 1965, TIA; George Frazier to W. A. Swanberg, May 16, 1970, WAS; Noel F. Busch, *Briton Hadden*, pp. 204, 221–27; Edward Bliss Jr., *Now the News*, pp. 66–68, 230–44; David Halberstam, *The Powers That Be*; W. A. Swanberg, *Luce and His Empire*; Loudon Wainwright, *The Great American Magazine*.

Hadden's last days and estate: Lucy Wolinski, undated interview, ca. 1950, JM; Ralph Ingersoll, *High Time*, pp. 36–37, RI; Henry R. Luce, Jan. 12, 1965, pp. 40–54, TIA; George Frazier, *It's About Time*, GF; Briton Hadden, last will and testament, Jan. 28, 1929, SCNY; Henry R. Luce to N. L. Wallace, Feb. 27, 1929, TIA; W. A. Swanberg, *Luce and His Empire*, p. 80, WAS; *Time*, Mar. 11, 1929, p. 63; "Briton Hadden Dies; An Editor of *Time*," *New York Times*, Feb. 28, 1929, p. 20; Henry R. Luce to Henry P. Davison Jr., Apr. 23, 1929, HPD; Henry R. Luce to Roy E. Larsen, Sept. 3, 1929, TIA; Thomas J. C. Martyn to Henry R. Luce, Mar. 15, 1966, TIA.

Burial of Hadden's role in history: Noel F. Busch, *Briton Hadden*; *Time*, Mar. 11, 1929, p. 2; *Time*, Mar. 17, 1967, p. 19; Henry R. Luce, Speeches and Writings file, TIA; Henry R. Luce speeches, HRLLOC, CBL; Henry R. Luce, speech at *Time*'s twentieth-anniversary dinner, Mar. 11, 1943, TIA; "The idea that founded an empire," British press clipping, May 19, 1963, Publicity files, 1963, TIA; Culbreth Sudler, Mar. 9, 1965, TIA; *Time*, Mar. 8, 1948, pp. 55–66; *Business Week*, Mar. 6, 1948,

p. 3; "Henry R. Luce, Creator of Time-Life Magazine Empire, Dies in Phoenix at 68," *New York Times,* Mar. 1, 1967, p. 1; "Johnson, in Tribute, Calls Luce 'American Journalism Pioneer,'" *New York Times,* Mar. 1, 1967, p. 33; "2,000 Pay Tribute to Henry R. Luce," *New York Times,* Mar. 4, 1967, p. 27; *The Week,* cover, Apr. 26–May 2, 2002; David Halberstam, *The Powers That Be,* p. 62; Nina Munk, *Fools Rush In,* pp. 4–5; James L. Baughman, *Henry R. Luce and the Rise of the American News Media,* p. 33; "U.S. Stamp Covers *Time* Magazine Co-Founder, Henry Luce," U.S. Postal Service, ca. Mar. 3, 1998; Jerry Busch, author's interview, May 22, 2003.

1. BIRTH

1898: Joyce Milton, *The Yellow Kids,* pp. 79, 218; Peggy Samuels and Harold Samuels, *Remembering the Maine,* pp. 30–60; Edwin Emery and Michael Emery, *The Press and America,* p. 249.

Hadden's birth and family: John S. Martin, Feb. 28, 1956, TIA; *Brooklyn Life,* Feb. 27, 1892, p. 9; *Brooklyn Life,* Nov. 19, 1892, p. 22; *Brooklyn Life,* June 11, 1898, pp. 12–13; *Brooklyn Life,* Jan. 18, 1908, p. 15; *Brooklyn Life,* July 15, 1916, cover; Addison Steele, "The Looker-On," *Brooklyn Life,* May 27, 1905, p. 9; *Brooklyn Daily Eagle,* May 14, 1905, p. 6; New York Health Department Marriages Index, 1895–1901, NYPL; Elizabeth Pool, Aug. 1, 1929, TIA; Elizabeth Pool, Apr. 29, 1948, TIA; Elizabeth Pool, May 10, 1948, TIA; Niven Busch, Mar. 11, 1965, TIA; Clay Lancaster, *Old Brooklyn Heights,* p. 16; Brian Merlis and Lee A. Rosenzweig, *Brooklyn Heights & Downtown,* p. 48; James H. Callander, *Yesterdays on Brooklyn Heights,* p. 131; Beatrix Miller, author's interview, July 11, 2003; Harvey K. Murdock, author's interview, May 31, 2003; Noel F. Busch, *Briton Hadden,* pp. 4, 7, 9.

Hadden's cousins: Jerry Busch, author's interview, May 22, 2003; Terry Busch, author's interview, June 7, 2003; Mary-Kelly Busch, author's interview, June 20, 2003; Gay Claridge, author's interview, Apr. 4, 2002; Beatrix Miller, author's interview, July 11, 2003; Barry M. Osborn, author's interview, Apr. 6, 2002, Sept. 8, 2003; Mary Lowman, author's interview, June 25, 2003; John S. Martin, *A Grab-Bag for My Grandsons,* TIA; "Noel F. Busch, Author and Correspondent for *Life* Magazine," *New York Times,* Sept. 11, 1985; Niven Busch to J. Richard Munro, Mar. 21, 1986, TIA; "John S. Martin, 76, Ex-Managing Editor of *Time* Magazine," *New York Times,* June 21, 1977.

Hadden's early youth: Elizabeth Pool, Apr. 29, 1948, TIA; Elizabeth Pool, Aug. 1, 1929, TIA; John S. Martin, *A Grab-Bag for My Grandsons,* ch. 2, pp. 1–3, TIA; W. Rice Brewster, Mar. 10, 1965, TIA; W. Rice Brewster to Marie McCrum, Mar. 1, 1965,

TIA; Stuart Heminway, undated notes, TIA; Stuart Heminway, May 19, 1948, TIA; Mimi Martin, Aug. 5, 1948, TIA; E. V. Hale to Noel F. Busch, June 30, 1948, TIA; John E. Woolley, Feb. 4, 1958, TIA; Robert Honeyman to Lilian Rixey, Nov. 3, 1948, TIA; Lilian Rixey, "Genealogies from *Rabbits*," Aug. 10, 1948, TIA.

Death of Hadden's father: *Brooklyn Daily Eagle,* May 14, p. 6; New York City Death Records, Kings County, Certificate No. 9265, May 13, 1905, NYPL; *Brooklyn Life,* May 27, 1905, p. 9; Niven Busch, Mar. 11, 1965, TIA; W. Rice Brewster, Mar. 10, 1965, TIA; Elizabeth Pool, Aug. 1, 1929, TIA; Elizabeth Pool, May 10, 1948, TIA; Briton Hadden to Elizabeth Pool, childhood letters, Sept.–Oct. 1915, BH; Briton Hadden, "Bellee's Adventure with a Toad," *The Life of a Rabbit,* quoted in Lilian Rixey to Noel F. Busch, Aug. 10, 1948, TIA; Niven Busch, "Biographical Notes— Briton Hadden," June 8, 1948, TIA; Mimi Martin, Feb. 3, 1958, TIA; W. Rice Brewster, May 14, 1948, TIA; W. Rice Brewster, Mar. 10, 1965, TIA; Robert Blum, Apr. 15, 1965, TIA.

Interest in baseball and games: Elizabeth Pool, Apr. 29, 1948, TIA; Elizabeth Pool, May 10, 1948, TIA; Mimi Martin, Feb. 28, 1956, TIA; John E. Woolley, June 4, 1948, TIA; W. Rice Brewster, May 14, 1948, TIA; W. Rice Brewster, Mar. 10, 1965, TIA; John M. Hincks, Apr. 30, 1948, TIA; Briton Hadden to William Pool, undated letters, ca. 1915, BH; Crowell "Pete" Hadden, author's interview, Nov. 22, 2005.

New York journalism: *Brooklyn Life,* Jan. 23, 1892, p. 8; *Brooklyn Life,* Feb. 27, 1892, p. 9; *Brooklyn Life,* Nov. 19, 1892, p. 22; *Brooklyn Life,* Dec. 3, 1892, p. 9; *Brooklyn Life,* Nov. 21, 1896, p. 18; *Brooklyn Life,* June 11, 1898, p. 13; *Brooklyn Life,* Nov. 11, 1899, p. 9; *Brooklyn Life,* May 20, 1905, p. 5; *Brooklyn Life,* May 27, 1905, p. 9; *Brooklyn Life,* July 15, 1916, cover; *Brooklyn Life,* Sept. 2, 1922, p. 8; Briton Hadden to Elizabeth Pool, Jan. 2, 1914, Feb. 9, 1914; undated, ca. spring 1914, BH.

Hadden's journalism activities: Robert Honeyman to Lilian Rixey, Nov. 3, 1948, TIA; Robert Honeyman to Robert T. Elson, May 6, 1965, TIA; Elizabeth Pool, Apr. 29, 1948, TIA; *Poly Prep,* Oct. 16, 1908, p. 4; *Poly Prep,* May 28, 1909, p. 244; Briton Hadden, *Daily Glonk,* May 5–8, 12, 1913, BH; Mimi Martin, Aug. 5, 1948, TIA; Mimi Martin, Feb. 3, 1958, TIA; Miles Merwin Kastendieck, *The Story of Poly,* pp. 208–9, 235; *Brooklyn Daily Eagle,* June 7, 1925.

Luce's family: Elizabeth R. Luce to Mary Linen McWithey, letters, ca. 1912, SF; Emmavail Severinghaus, July 17, 1969, WAS; Henry Luce III, author's interview, Dec. 27, 2001; Emma Hays to Elizabeth R. Luce, June 24, 1896, SF; Horace Pitkin to Henry W. Luce, June 10, 1896, SF; Luther Davis to Henry W. Luce, June 16, 1896, SF; Oliver J. Kingsbury to Elizabeth R. Luce, June 15, 1896, SF; Edwin C. Lobenstine to Henry W. Luce, June 5, 1896, SF; Margaret L. Eddy to Henry W. Luce, June 22, 1896, SF; Henry W. Luce to "home friends," Mar. 1, 1903, SF; Daisy Rice to Elizabeth R. Luce, June 10, 1918, SF; Elizabeth R. Luce to Mary Wood, numerous letters, 1918–23, SF; Henry W. Luce to Emmavail Luce, Oct. 8, 1916, SF; B. A. Garside, *One Increasing Purpose,* pp. 58–69, 73–75; W. A. Swanberg, *Luce and His Empire,* pp. 15–20.

Mission compound and Luce's birth: Henry R. Luce, "The Christianity of the Missionary," Sept. 10, 1946, HRLLOC; Elizabeth R. Luce to Mary Linen, Nov. 21, 1897, SF; Dec. 11, 1898, SF; B. A. Garside, *One Increasing Purpose,* pp. 79–80; Elisabeth Luce Moore, Apr. 17, 1991, TIA; Henry R. Luce to Elizabeth R. Luce, Apr. 28, 1925, HRL.

Boxer Rebellion and return to China: Emmavail Severinghaus, July 17, 1969, WAS; W. A. Swanberg, *Luce and His Empire,* pp. 20–23; B. A. Garside, *One Increasing Purpose,* pp. 94–98, 100–13; Henry W. Luce to "home friends," ca. Christmas 1904, SF; Henry W. Luce to Mary Linen, Mar. 25, 1903, SF; Elizabeth R. Luce to Mary Linen, June 20, 1904, SF; Henry W. Luce to Mary Linen, Apr. 8, 1905, SF; Henry W. Luce to Emmavail Luce, Jan. 24, 1917, SF; Henry W. Luce to Emmavail Luce, Mar. 11, 1917, SF; Henry R. Luce to Henry W. Luce and Elizabeth R. Luce, Oct. 15, 1911, HRL; Elisabeth Luce Moore, "Henry R. Luce Letters to His Family, 1903–22," HRL; Elisabeth Luce Moore, Apr. 17, 1991, TIA.

Luce's first years in China: Elisabeth Luce Moore, Mar. 4, 1965, TIA; Elisabeth Luce Moore, Oct. 19, 1968, WAS; Elisabeth Luce Moore, "A Spoken History," May 1989, TIA; Elisabeth Luce Moore, Apr. 17, 1991, TIA; Joe Garner Estill, quoted in Lilian Rixey, "Notes on early competition between Hadden and Luce," July 1, 1948, TIA; Elizabeth R. Luce to Mary Linen, Dec. 7, 1902, SF; Henry R. Luce, childhood letters, 1903, TIA; Henry R. Luce, "Sermon by the most likely Rev. Henry Robinson Luce," ca. 1905, HRL; Henry R. Luce, "Sermon-1," ca. 1905, HRL; Emmavail Severinghaus, July 17, 1969, WAS; Elizabeth R. Luce, "Frequent sayings of H.W.L.," "Random Thoughts on Religion of H.W.L.," "notes and thoughts for book on H.W.L.," SF; Henry R. Luce, "Sight and Insight," Apr. 26, 1961, TIA; Henry R. Luce, "Speech Delivered by Henry R. Luce Before a Group of Time Inc. Executives," May 4, 1950, TIA; Ralph G. Martin, *Henry & Clare,* p. 20; W. A. Swanberg, *Luce and His Empire,* p. 24; B. A. Garside, *One Increasing Purpose,* pp. 9, 18, 23, 53, 85.

Furlough year: Henry R. Luce, Jan. 11, 1965, TIA; Henry R. Luce, "Sight and Insight," Apr. 26, 1961, TIA; Elisabeth Luce Moore, Mar. 4, 1965, TIA; Elisabeth Luce Moore, Oct. 19, 1968, TIA; Elisabeth Luce Moore, "A Spoken History," May 1989, TIA; Elisabeth Luce Moore, Apr. 17, 1991, TIA; W. A. Swanberg, *Luce and His Empire*, pp. 25–26; B. A. Garside, *One Increasing Purpose*, p. 122.

The Luces' "Renaissance villa": Elizabeth R. Luce to Mary Wood, May 29, 1911, SF; Elisabeth Luce Moore, Mar. 4, 1965, TIA; Elisabeth Luce Moore, Oct. 19, 1968, WAS; Elisabeth Luce Moore, Apr. 17, 1991, TIA; Emmavail Severinghaus, July 17, 1969, WAS; Ralph G. Martin, *Henry & Clare*, p. 18; B. A. Garside, *One Increasing Purpose*, pp. 134, 314.

Chefoo: Sheila Miller, *Pigtails, Petticoats and the Old School Tie*; Gordon Martin, *Chefoo School 1881–1951*; Elisabeth Luce Moore, Oct. 19, 1968, WAS; Elisabeth Luce Moore, Apr. 17, 1991, TIA; Elizabeth R. Luce to Mary Linen, July 16, 1908, WAS; Henry W. Luce to Mary Linen, July 26, 1908, SF; Elizabeth R. Luce to Mary Wood, Dec. 10, 1909, Mar. 8, 1910, SF; Henry R. Luce to Henry W. Luce and Elizabeth R. Luce, Sept. 7, 1908, Sept. 20, 1908, Nov. 1908, Feb. 21, 1909, Mar. 27, 1909, Apr. 3, 1909, Apr. 23, 1909, Oct. 10, 1909, Oct. 17, 1909, Oct. 18, 1909, Nov. 7, 1909, Nov. 21, 1909, Feb. 20, 1910, Apr. 8, 1910, May 22, 1910, May 29, 1910, Sept. 4, 1910, undated, ca. Feb. 1912, Mar. 10, 1912, July 14, 1912, Feb. 13, 1921, HRL; Henry R. Luce, "Speech Delivered by Henry R. Luce Before a Group of Time Inc. Executives," May 4, 1950, TIA.

Friendship and rivalry with Sydney Cecil-Smith: Henry R. Luce to Henry W. Luce and Elizabeth R. Luce, Sept. 17, 1911, Oct. 22, 1911, Oct. 29, 1911, Nov. 12, 1911, Feb. 1912, undated, ca. Feb. 1912, Feb. 11, 1912, Feb. 18, 1912, Mar. 24, 1912, Mar. 31, 1912, May 18, 1912, July 21, 1912, HRL; Henry R. Luce to Henry W. Luce, Feb. 13, 1913, HRL; Henry R. Luce to "Miss Dolph," Mar. 24, 1912, HRL; Mary Bancroft, Oct. 29, 1970, WAS; William Benton to W. A. Swanberg, undated, ca. 1969, WAS; Ralph Ingersoll, *High Time*, Apr. 15, 1962, RI; Thomas Griffith, *Harry and Teddy*; Noel F. Busch, *Life, Luce and the Pursuit of God Knows What*, pt. 2, p. 6, NAB.

Chinese Revolution: Henry R. Luce to Henry W. Luce and Elizabeth R. Luce, Oct. 5, 1911, Feb. 11, 1912, HRL; Henry R. Luce to Emmavail Luce and Elisabeth Luce, Feb. 11, 1912, HRL; Elizabeth R. Luce to Mary Wood, July 1, 1910, SF; Elizabeth R. Luce to Mary Linen McWithey, July 13, 1910, SF; Elisabeth Luce Moore, July 17, 1991, TIA; B. A. Garside, *One Increasing Purpose*, pp. 131–32.

Luce's travels: Henry R. Luce to Henry W. Luce and Elizabeth R. Luce, Oct. 31, 1912, Nov. 2, 1912, Nov. 3–4, 1912, Nov. 6–9, 1912, Nov. 9, 1912, Nov. 13, 1912, Nov. 17, 1912, Dec. 1, 1912, Dec. 7, 1912, Dec. 9, 1912, Dec. 12, 1912, Dec. 16, 1912, Dec. 22, 1912, Jan. 19, 1913, Mar. 10, 1913, Mar. 22, 1913, Mar. 30, 1913, Apr. 7, 1913, Apr. 14, 1913, Apr. 15, 1913, Aug. 24, 1913, HRL; Henry R. Luce to Henry W. Luce, Aug. 21, 1912, HRL; Henry R. Luce to Elizabeth R. Luce, undated, ca. Sept. 1913, Sept. 10, 1913, HRL; Frau Netz to Mary Linen McWithey, July 8, 1913, SF; Elizabeth R. Luce to Mary Linen McWithey, Aug. 3, 1913, SF; Emmavail Luce to Henry W. Luce, Feb. 1, 1913, SF; Henry W. Luce to "Miss Dolph," Aug. 6, 1913, SF; Elizabeth R. Luce to Mary Wood, June 23, 1913, Aug. 8, 1913, Sept 1, 1913, SF; Emmavail Severinghaus, July 17, 1969, WAS; Henry R. Luce, Jan. 11, 1965, TIA.

2. THE HILL

Hotchkiss campus and customs: Culbreth Sudler to W. A. Swanberg, undated, ca. Sept. 1968, WAS; Clyde L. Davis, "Hail to Hotchkiss," in *The Hotchkiss School, Class Day Exercises,* June 17, 1916, TIA; Briton Hadden to Elizabeth Pool, undated letters, ca. Sept. 1913, BH; Henry R. Luce to Henry W. Luce and Elizabeth R. Luce, Sept. 18, 1913, HRL; Henry R. Luce to Emmavail Luce, Sept. 24, 1913, HRL; Culbreth Sudler to Robert T. Elson, Mar. 5, 1965, TIA; David Houghtaling, Apr. 27, 1948, TIA; *Hotchkiss Record,* June 2, 1914, p. 7; *Hotchkiss Record,* May 11, 1915, p. 4; *Hotchkiss Record,* Jan. 25, 1916, p. 1; *Mischianza,* 1916, pp. 20–42; Briton Hadden Alumni Records, HAR; Henry R. Luce Alumni Records, HAR; Ernest Kolowrat, *Hotchkiss,* pp. 114, 118, 122–23.

Hadden and Luce as new boys: Donald G. Driscoll to Lilian Rixey, May 3, 1948, TIA; Evans Woollen to Lilian Rixey, Apr. 30, 1948, TIA; Egbert Driscoll to Lilian Rixey, May 3, 1948, TIA; Stuart Heminway to Lilian Rixey, May 19, 1948, TIA; Culbreth Sudler to Lilian Rixey, May 18, 1948, TIA; John M. Hincks, Dec. 20, 1968, WAS; Elisabeth Luce Moore, Oct. 19, 1968, WAS; Seymour Knox, June 25, 1956, TIA; Briton Hadden to Elizabeth Pool, undated, ca. Sept. 1913, undated, ca. winter 1914, "Thursday 1:45," undated, ca. Feb. 14, 1915, Sept. 23, 1915, BH; Henry W. Luce to Emmavail Luce and Elisabeth Luce, Sept. 27, 1913, SF; Henry R. Luce to Emmavail Luce, Sept. 24, 1913, HRL; Elizabeth R. Luce to Mary Linen McWithey, Feb. 14, 1914, SF; Henry R. Luce to Henry W. Luce and Elizabeth R. Luce, various letters, Sept. 1913–May 1914, esp. Oct. 3, 1913, HRL; Henry R. Luce to Henry W. Luce, Dec. 4, 1913, Jan. 8, 1914, Jan. 18, 1914, undated, ca. Nov. 1914, Dec. 4, 1914, HRL; Henry R. Luce to Elizabeth R. Luce, Nov. 4, 1913, Nov. 27,

1913, undated, Feb. 1914, HRL; *Hotchkiss Record,* Apr. 4, 1916, pp. 1–2; *Hotchkiss Record,* Mar. 10, 1914, p. 1; Ralph Ingersoll, *High Time,* 1969, p. 22, RI.

Record and Lit: Briton Hadden to Elizabeth Pool, May 17, 1914, undated, ca. spring 1914, BH; Henry R. Luce to Elizabeth R. Luce, Nov. 4, 1913, HRL; Henry R. Luce to Henry W. Luce and Elizabeth R. Luce, undated letters, ca. Apr. 1914, May 1, 1914, May 12, 1914, May 16–17, 1914, HRL; Stuart Heminway, undated notes, pp. 5–7, TIA; *Hotchkiss Record,* Sept. 23, 1913, p. 4; *Hotchkiss Record,* Nov. 18, 1913, p. 4; *Hotchkiss Record,* Dec. 9, 1913, p. 6; *Hotchkiss Record,* Jan. 20, 1914, p. 5; *Hotchkiss Record,* Feb. 10, 1914, p. 3; *Hotchkiss Record,* Apr. 28, 1914, p. 4; *Hotchkiss Record,* May 5, 1914, p. 1; *Hotchkiss Record,* May 26, 1914, p. 5; *Hotchkiss Record,* June 9, 1914, p. 4; *Hotchkiss Record,* Mar. 2, 1915, p. 1; *Hotchkiss Record,* Apr. 27, 1915, p. 4; *Hotchkiss Record,* June 1, 1915, p. 3.

Spring and summer of 1914: David Houghtaling, Apr. 27, 1948, TIA; Henry R. Luce, commencement address at Hotchkiss, June 13, 1964, HRLLOC; Emmavail Severinghaus, July 17, 1969, WAS; Elisabeth Luce Moore, "A Spoken History," May 1989, TIA; Nettie F. McCormick to Henry R. Luce, Aug. 3, 1914, NFM; Henry R. Luce to Elizabeth R. Luce, Nov. 16, 1914, HRL; Stuart Heminway, undated notes, p. 9, TIA; *Hotchkiss Record,* Oct. 28, 1913, p. 4; *Hotchkiss Record,* Mar. 10, 1914, p. 4; *Hotchkiss Record,* Mar. 16, 1915, p. 1; *Hotchkiss Record,* Nov. 19, 1915, p. 2; Jack C. Lane, *Armed Progressive,* pp. 180, 182, 193–96.

Hadden and Luce as juniors: Briton Hadden to Elizabeth Pool, undated, "Monday morning," ca. 1915, Nov. 29, 1915, BH; Henry R. Luce to Henry W. Luce and Elizabeth R. Luce, Oct. 22, 1913, Oct. 30, 1913, Nov. 4, 1913, Nov. 12, 1913, Nov. 27, 1913, HRL; Henry R. Luce, assorted letters, Sept. 1914–June 1915, HRL; Evans Woollen to Lilian Rixey, Apr. 30, 1948, TIA; John M. Hincks, Apr. 30, 1948, TIA; Elizabeth Pool, May 10, 1948, TIA; Jean Whiting Trowbridge, Apr. 30, 1968, TIA; W. Rice Brewster, May 14, 1948, TIA; Henry R. Luce, Jan. 12, 1965, TIA; Culbreth Sudler, Mar. 9, 1965, TIA; Culbreth Sudler to W. A. Swanberg, Aug. 21, 1968, WAS; Culbreth Sudler, Jan. 2, 1969, WAS; *Mischianza,* 1916, p. 32.

Changes to the Lit and the Record: Erdman Harris, "Harry Luce '16 at Hotchkiss," *Hotchkiss Alumni Weekly,* July 1964, pp. 8–9; Henry R. Luce to Elizabeth R. Luce, undated, ca. spring 1915, HRL; Henry R. Luce to Henry W. Luce and Elizabeth R. Luce, Sept. 12, 1915, Sept. 19, 1915, HRL; Henry R. Luce to Nettie F. McCormick, Sept. 19, 1915, NFM; Charles D. Smith to Lilian Rixey, May 20, 1948, TIA; *Hotchkiss Record,* Feb. 2, 1915, p. 4; *Hotchkiss Record,* Mar. 9, 1915, p. 4; *Hotchkiss Record,* Apr. 13, 1915, p. 4; *Hotchkiss Record,* Oct. 2, 1915–May 12, 1916, p. 2; *Hotchkiss Record,* Oct.

12, 1915, p. 2; *Hotchkiss Record,* Oct. 15, 1915, p. 1; *Hotchkiss Record,* Oct. 29, 1915, p. 1; *Hotchkiss Record,* Nov. 12, 1915, p. 2; *Hotchkiss Record,* Jan. 25, 1916, p. 1.

Hadden's war coverage: Henry R. Luce, commencement address at Hotchkiss, June 13, 1964, HRLLOC; Briton Hadden to Elizabeth Pool, undated, ca. fall 1913, BH; John S. Martin, Apr. 4, 1956, TIA; Winsor French, "*Time's* First Years in City Turbulent," *Cleveland Press,* Feb. 16, 1952; *Hotchkiss Record,* Nov. 19, 1915, p. 1; *Hotchkiss Record,* Jan. 28, 1916, p. 1; *Hotchkiss Record,* Mar. 10, 1916, p. 1; Thomas J. C. Martyn to Henry R. Luce, Apr. 2, 1966, TIA.

***Lit-Record* rivalry:** Lilian Rixey, "Notes on early competition between Hadden and Luce at Hotchkiss," July 1, 1948, TIA; *Mischianza,* 1916, pp. 32, 192; *Hotchkiss Record,* Nov. 30, 1915, p. 3; *Hotchkiss Record,* Dec. 3, 1915, p. 2; *Hotchkiss Record,* Jan. 14, 1916, p. 1; *Hotchkiss Literary Monthly,* 1915–1916, esp. Dec. 1915, pp. 83–84; Briton Hadden to Elizabeth Pool, undated, ca. Dec. 1915, BH; John S. Martin, Apr. 4, 1956, TIA.

Ancient Greek: Lilian Rixey, "Notes on early competition between Hadden and Luce at Hotchkiss," July 1, 1948, TIA; Evans Woollen to Lilian Rixey, Apr. 30, 1948, TIA; John M. Hincks, Apr. 20, 1948, TIA; Charles D. Smith to Lilian Rixey, May 20, 1948, TIA; Culbreth Sudler to Lilian Rixey, May 18, 1948, TIA; Culbreth Sudler, Mar. 9, 1965, TIA; Homer, *Iliad,* Briton Hadden books file, TIA; Briton Hadden to E. G. Driscoll, June 20, 1914, BH; *Mischianza,* 1916, pp. 68, 185.

Luce drew closer to Hadden: Culbreth Sudler, Mar. 9, 1965, TIA; Lila Tyng, May 27, 1948, TIA; Henry R. Luce to Henry W. Luce and Elizabeth R. Luce, June 1914, Oct. 10, 1915, Jan. 30, 1916, Feb. 6, 1916, Mar. 5, 1916, Mar. 23, 1916, May 29, 1916, June 25, 1916, HRL; Briton Hadden to Elizabeth Pool, undated, ca. Jan. 1916, BH; *Hotchkiss Record,* Mar. 7, 1916, p. 1; *Hotchkiss Record,* Mar. 31, 1916, p. 1; *Mischianza,* 1916, pp. 25, 32.

Their interest in journalism: *Mischianza,* 1916, pp. 25, 32, 178, 185, 200; "The Literary Game," *Hotchkiss Literary Monthly,* June 1916, p. 269; "1916 Class Oration," *Hotchkiss Literary Monthly,* June 1916, pp. 301–2; *Hotchkiss Record,* Apr. 11, 1916, p. 1; Henry R. Luce to Henry W. Luce and Elizabeth R. Luce, Apr. 8, 1916, May 29, 1916, Aug. 8, 1916, Sept. 3, 1916, HRL; Henry R. Luce to Elisabeth Luce, July 9, 1916, HRL; Henry W. Luce to Henry R. Luce, Oct. 8, 1916, HWL; Henry R. Luce to Nettie F. McCormick, Oct. 2, 1916, NFM.

3. MOST LIKELY TO SUCCEED

Yale and its "democracy": Briton Hadden to Elizabeth Pool, Oct. 13, 1916, BH; Henry R. Luce to Henry W. Luce and Elizabeth R. Luce, Oct. 15, 1916, HRL; Henry R. Luce, Jan. 11, 1965, TIA; Charles D. Smith to Lilian Rixey, May 20, 1948, TIA; Wilmarth Sheldon Lewis, *One Man's Education*, pp. 93–94, 97, 102–3; George Wilson Pierson, *Yale College*, pp. 18, 21, 28, 41–42; Stephen Vincent Benét, *The Beginning of Wisdom*, p. 26; Charles A. Fenton, *Stephen Vincent Benét*, p. 51; Owen Johnson, *Stover at Yale*, pp. 25–29; Dan A. Oren, *Joining the Club*, pp. 21, 23, 30, 68–69, 81, 338; Maynard Mack, *A History of Scroll and Key*; Alexandra Robbins, *Secrets of the Tomb*; Yale Picture Collection, YRG 41, RU 736, Boxes 1, 2, 6, 7, 8, 10, 12, 16, 17, 18, 26, 30, 36, 42, YMA.

Yale Daily News: Elizabeth R. Luce to Mary Wood, Nov. 2, 1916, SF; Henry W. Luce to Henry R. Luce, Mar. 8, 1917, HWL; Henry R. Luce to Henry W. Luce and Elizabeth R. Luce, Dec. 24, 1916, Mar. 20, 1917, "Easter" [Apr. 8], 1917, HRL; Briton Hadden to Elizabeth Pool, undated, ca. late 1916, undated, "Sunday night," ca. Nov. 15, 1916, Mar. 29, 1917, BH; Henry R. Luce to Emmavail Luce, Apr. 16, 1917, HRL; Henry R. Luce to Nettie F. McCormick, Apr. 6, 1917, NFM; E. V. Hale, June 29, 1948, TIA; William Lyon Phelps, quoted in the *Boston Sunday Globe*, June 7, 1925, p. 23; P. I. Prentice, Mar. 2, 1967, TIA; John E. Woolley, June 4, 1948, TIA; John E. Woolley, Mar. 4, 1958, TIA; Wells Root, Mar. 10, 1964, TIA; Henry R. Luce, Jan. 11, 1965, TIA; Samuel W. Meek, May 7, 1962, TIA; Lila Tyng, May 27, 1948, TIA; John M. Hincks to Lilian Rixey, May 17, 1948, TIA; Henry R. Luce, speech at the *Yale Daily News* eightieth-anniversary dinner, Apr. 16, 1958, TIA; Briton Hadden, "The Modern News," *Yale Daily News 50th Anniversary, 1878–1928*, pp. 35–36, 90, YMA; Hans L. Wydler, *The Late Gargantuan Man*, p. 9, TIA; Owen Johnson, *Stover at Yale*, p. 44; Noel F. Busch, *Briton Hadden*, p. 32; W. A. Swanberg, *Luce and His Empire*, p. 37.

Great War: *Yale Daily News*, Dec. 18, 1917, p. 1; John E. Woolley, Feb. 4, 1958, TIA; Walter Isaacson and Evan Thomas, *The Wise Men*, pp. 90–3; "War History," in Morehead Patterson, ed., *History of the Class of Nineteen Hundred and Twenty*, pp. 63–79, YMA; George Wilson Pierson, *Yale College*, pp. 435–76; Henry R. Luce to Henry W. Luce and Elizabeth R. Luce, June 3–4, 1917, HRL; Briton Hadden to Elizabeth Pool, Apr. 29, 1917, BH; Henry R. Luce to Emmavail Luce, July 21, 1927, SF; Elisabeth Luce to Henry W. Luce and Elizabeth R. Luce, Aug. 2, 1917, SF; Emmavail Luce to Henry W. Luce and Elizabeth R. Luce, Aug. 3, 1917, Aug. 26, 1917, SF; Briton Hadden to Henry R. Luce, Aug. 23, 1917, LT; Thayer Hobson to Henry R. Luce, Aug. 21, 1917, LT; Henry R. Luce, Jan. 11, 1965, TIA.

Hadden and Luce as sophomores in 1917: *Yale Daily News,* Sept. 28, 1917, p. 1; Culbreth Sudler to W. A. Swanberg, Oct. 20, 1968, WAS; Henry R. Luce, Jan. 12, 1965, TIA; Henry R. Luce to Henry W. Luce and Elizabeth R. Luce, Oct. 22, 1917, Oct. 28, 1917, Nov. 12–13, 1917, HRL; Briton Hadden to Henry R. Luce, ca. Aug. 1917, LT.

Yale Daily News election: John E. Woolley, June 4, 1948, TIA; Henry R. Luce to Henry W. Luce and Elizabeth R. Luce, Jan. 1918, Jan. 10, 1918, Jan. 20, 1918, HRL; Elizabeth R. Luce to Henry R. Luce, Feb. 20, 1918, HWL; Henry R. Luce, *Yale Daily News* election file, TIA; Elizabeth R. Luce to Henry R. Luce, Feb. 20, 1918, HWL; Emmavail Luce to Elizabeth R. Luce, May 18, 1919, SF; E. V. Hale, June 29, 1948, TIA; Elmore McKee, "Of scoops, subs and inky fingers," in John B. Harris and Jonathan Kaufman, eds., *100: A History of the Yale Daily News,* pp. 9–10; Henry R. Luce, Jan. 11, 1965, TIA.

Hadden's chairmanship: Briton Hadden to Elizabeth Pool, Jan. 13, [1918], July 26, 1918, BH; Henry R. Luce to Nettie F. McCormick, Mar. 30, 1917, NFM; Culbreth Sudler, Oct. 20, 1968, WAS; Henry R. Luce to Elizabeth R. Luce, Mar. 1918, HRL; Henry W. Luce to Henry R. Luce, July 6, 1918, HWL; *Yale Daily News,* Jan. 26, 1918, p. 2; *Yale Daily News,* Mar. 15, 1918, p. 2; *Yale Daily News,* May 21–24, 1918; James F. Neville, fence speech, *Yale Daily News,* June 1, 1918, p. 7; Henry R. Luce, speech at *Time*'s twentieth-anniversary dinner, Mar. 11, 1943, TIA; W. Rice Brewster, May 14, 1958, TIA.

Camp Jackson: Briton Hadden to Crowell Hadden III and Elizabeth Hadden, Aug. 13, 1918, BH; Briton Hadden to Elizabeth Pool, Aug. 18, 1918, Sept. 9, 1918, Oct. 26, 1918, Nov. 12, 1918, BH; Briton Hadden to Maud Hadden, Sept. 11, 1918, BH; Henry R. Luce, speech at *Time*'s twentieth-anniversary dinner, Mar. 11, 1943, TIA; Henry R. Luce to Nettie F. McCormick, undated postcards, ca. Aug. 8, 1918, NFM; Clare Boothe Luce, Feb. 21, 1969, WAS; Culbreth Sudler to W. A. Swanberg, undated, ca. 1969, WAS; Culbreth Sudler, Mar. 9, 1965, TIA; Henry R. Luce, Jan. 11, 1965, TIA.

Running the Yale Daily News as upperclassmen: Briton Hadden to Elizabeth Pool, Apr. 10, 1919, Apr. 17, 1919, BH; *Yale Daily News,* Apr. 25, 1919; *Yale Daily News,* May 28, 1919, p. 2; *Yale Daily News,* June 3–4, 1919; *Yale Daily News,* Jan. 15, 1920; John Berdan, Nov. 1, 1948, TIA; Joseph Kastner, Apr. 19, 1956, TIA; Culbreth Sudler, Mar. 9, 1965, TIA; Winthrop Hoyt to Henry R. Luce, Mar. 21, 1929, TIA; John M. Hincks, Apr. 30, 1948, TIA; John M. Hincks, "Briton Hadden," in C. Stuart Heminway, ed., *Twenty Years with Nineteen-Twenty*, p. 492, YMA; Briton Hadden, "The Modern News," in *Yale Daily News*, ed., *Yale Daily News 50th Anniversary, 1878–1928*, p. 36, YMA; Jennifer Cohen and Jonathan Liebman, "1920–1930," in John B. Harris and Jonathan Kaufman, eds., *100: A History of the Yale Daily News*, pp. 12–18, YMA.

Hadden's stature and personality: John M. Hincks, Apr. 30, 1948, TIA; W. Rice Brewster to Lilian Rixey, Jan. 4, 1949, TIA; Evans Woollen Jr. to Lilian Rixey, Apr. 30, 1948, TIA; Henry R. Luce, Jan. 12, 1965, TIA; John Farrar, undated interview, ca. 1965, TIA; Henry R. Luce to Henry W. Luce, Feb. 19, 1919, HRL; George Frazier, *It's About Time*, p. 23, GF; Emmavail Luce to Henry R. Luce and Elizabeth R. Luce, Mar. 2, 1920, SF.

Tap Day: "Yale Will Revive Tap Day This Year," *New York Times*, May 4, 1919, p. 25; Henry R. Luce to Henry W. Luce, Mar. 1919, May 1919, May 16, 1919, HRL; Culbreth Sudler to W. A. Swanberg, undated, ca. 1969, WAS; Emmavail Luce to Elizabeth R. Luce, May 18, 1919, SF; Briton Hadden to Elizabeth Pool, May 15, 1919, BH; Morehead Patterson, ed., *History of the Class of Nineteen Hundred and Twenty*, p. 38, YMA; Noel F. Busch, *Briton Hadden*, p. 41.

Skull and Bones and growing friendship: David Ingalls, July 28, 1948, TIA; Lewis G. Adams, Dec. 28, 1955, TIA; Elisabeth Luce Moore, Mar. 4, 1965, TIA; John M. Hincks, Apr. 30, 1948, TIA; W. Rice Brewster, May 14, 1948, TIA; Alexandra Robbins, *Secrets of the Tomb*, pp. 109–10, 115–22, 125–49; Hans L. Wydler, *The Late Gargantuan Man*, pp. 21–22, TIA; Jennifer Cohen and Jonathan Liebman, "1920–1930," in John B. Harris and Jonathan Kaufman, eds., *100: A History of the Yale Daily News*, pp. 12–18, YMA; Morehead Patterson, ed., *History of the Class of Nineteen Hundred and Twenty*, pp. 81, 152–53, 201–2, 211–12, 218–19, 220–22, 236–38, 269–70, 275–76, 304–5, 330–32, 335–6, 240–42, 399–400, 418–19, YMA.

Desire to be journalists: Henry R. Luce, address at the second-annual *Life* managing editor's dinner, June 13, 1963, TIA; Henry W. Luce to Henry R. Luce, Apr. 19, 1918, HWL; Henry R. Luce to Henry W. Luce and Elizabeth R. Luce, undated, ca. fall 1919, undated, ca. Mar. 1920, HRL; John M. Hincks, Apr. 30, 1948, TIA; John M. Hincks, "Briton Hadden," in C. Stuart Heminway, ed., *Twenty Years with Nineteen-Twenty*, p. 493, YMA; Niven Busch, "Biographical Notes—Briton Hadden," June 8, 1948, TIA.

4. DESTINY

Political conventions: Briton Hadden to William and Elizabeth Pool, June 29, 1920, July 1920, BH; Briton Hadden to Elizabeth Pool, July 9, 1920, BH; Elizabeth

Pool, May 10, 1948, TIA; Henry R. Luce to Elizabeth R. Luce, undated, ca. June 1920, HRL; Henry R. Luce, Jan. 11, 1965, TIA; Jack C. Lane, *Armed Progressive*, pp. 247–49.

Hadden at the *New York World*: F. Darius Benham, June 3, 1948, TIA; John S. Martin, Apr. 4, 1956, TIA; Briton Hadden, Cub Reporting file, TIA; Herbert Bayard Swope Jr., author's interview, June 24, 2003; Herbert Bayard Swope, quoted in Irma Kuté, untitled memorandum, Feb. 27, 1929, Briton Hadden Death Condolences file, TIA; Henry R. Luce to Herbert Bayard Swope, Mar. 5, 1929, TIA; Niven Busch, "Biographical Notes—Briton Hadden," June 8, 1948, TIA; Dorothy McDowell, June 12, 1961, TIA; Manfred Gottfried, Aug. 16, 1961, TIA; John M. Hincks, Apr. 30, 1948, TIA; John M. Hincks, Dec. 20, 1968, WAS; John S. Martin, *A Grab-Bag for My Grandsons*, "Beginning of *Time*," p. 5, TIA; E. J. Kahn Jr., *The World of Swope;* Alfred Allan Lewis, *Man of the World*, pp. x, 96; Noel F. Busch, *Briton Hadden*, pp. 44–46, 103; Marion Meade, *Dorothy Parker,* pp. 113–14; Bruce Gould and Beatrice Blackmar Gould, *American Story*, pp. 99–100.

Luce at Oxford: Henry R. Luce to Henry W. Luce and Elizabeth R. Luce, June 9, 1920, July 18, 1920, July 30, 1920, undated, ca. Aug. 1920, Aug. 7, 1920, Aug. 10, 1920, Aug. 29, 1920, Sept. 16, 1920, Sept. 29, 1920, Oct. 9, 1920, Oct. 19, 1920, Oct. 28, 1920, Nov. 15, 1920, Nov. 28, 1920, Dec. 11, 1920, Feb. 13, 1921, Mar. 6, 1921, HRL; Henry R. Luce to family, July 14, 1920, ca. July 1920, Sept. 2, 1920, HRL; Henry R. Luce to Emmavail Luce, Sept. 14, 1920, HRL; Henry R. Luce to Nettie F. McCormick, Nov. 5, 1920, Feb. 12, 1921, NFM; Henry R. Luce, Jan. 11, 1965, TIA; Henry R. Luce Photographs file, 1916–22, TIA.

Luce's social life and optimism in 1920–21: Henry R. Luce to family, July 14, 1920, HRL; Henry R. Luce to Henry W. Luce and Elizabeth R. Luce, Aug. 10, 1920, Jan. 30, 1921, Feb. 24, 1921, Mar. 6, 1921, Mar. 24, 1921, Apr. 7, 1921, Apr. 28, 1921, HRL; Henry R. Luce to Henry W. Luce, Nov. 15, 1920, Jan. 22, 1921, HRL; Henry R. Luce to Nettie F. McCormick, Dec. 17, 1920, Mar. 22, 1921, undated, ca. Apr. 1921, Apr. 10, 1921, NFM; "pilgrim": David H. C. Read, eulogy for Henry R. Luce, Mar. 3, 1967, HAR; John M. Hincks, Dec. 20, 1968, WAS; Lila Tyng, July 2, 1957, TIA.

Meeting Lila Hotz: Lila Tyng, journal, Jan. 3, 1921, June 16–25, 1921, LT; Lila Hotz to Lila F. R. Hotz, various letters, 1920–21, esp. Jan. 1, 1921, LT; Henry R. Luce to Henry W. Luce and Elizabeth R. Luce, Dec. 24, 1920, Apr. 7, 1921, HRL; Lila Tyng, July 2, 1957, TIA; Lila Tyng, June 13, 1967, TIA; Lila Tyng, Mar. 30, 1969, WAS; Lila Tyng, May 2, 1969, WAS; Culbreth Sudler to W. A. Swanberg, undated, ca. Aug.

1968, WAS; Elisabeth Luce Moore, June 12, 1991, TIA; C. D. Spence to Lila Hotz, undated, ca. 1917, LT; John S. Martin, Sept. 1965, TIA; P. I. Prentice, Sept. 17, 1968, WAS; Peter Paul Luce, author's interview, May 27, 2003.

Luce's return to the United States: Henry R. Luce, Jan. 11, 1965, TIA; *Time,* Mar. 10, 1967, p. 29; Ralph G. Martin, *Henry & Clare,* p. 64; Elisabeth Luce Moore, May 17, 1960, TIA; Elisabeth Luce Moore, Mar. 4, 1965, TIA; Elisabeth Luce Moore, June 12, 1991, TIA; Lewis G. Adams, Dec. 28, 1955, TIA.

Hadden's trip to South America: Elizabeth Pool, May 10, 1948, TIA; Morris Phinney, *A Trip to Ecuador and Peru,* TIA; Briton Hadden to William Pool, Aug. 27, 1921, BH; Briton Hadden to Elizabeth Pool, Aug. 27, 1921, Sept. 4, 1921, BH; Briton Hadden to Elizabeth Pool and William Pool, Sept. 20, 1921, Sept. 25, 1921, Oct. 1, 1921, Oct. 7, 1921, BH; Briton Hadden to Crowell Hadden III, Aug. 30, 1921, BH; J. C. Dobbie, note to the operators of trains no. 4 and no. 2 of the Guayaquil & Quito Railway Company, Sept. 26, 1921, BH; Edwin Hardy, invitation to a Paper Chase, Sept. 23, 1921, BH; Walter Millis, Sept. 13, 1948, TIA; W. Rice Brewster to Lilian Rixey, May 21, 1948, TIA; Morris Phinney to Robert T. Elson, Apr. 9, 1965, TIA.

Luce in Chicago: Henry R. Luce to Henry W. Luce and Elizabeth R. Luce, Aug. 4, 1921, Aug. 8, 1921, undated, ca. fall 1921, HRL; Henry R. Luce to Elizabeth R. Luce, Aug. 16, 1921, undated letters, ca. Sept. 15, 1921, HRL; William MacAdams, *Ben Hecht;* Doug Fetherling, *The Five Lives of Ben Hecht;* Ben Hecht, *A Thousand and One Afternoons in Chicago;* transcript of *The Ben Hecht Show,* WABC-TV, Sept. 23, 1958, TIA; Bill Furth to Alex Groner, Sept. 30, 1958, TIA; Lila Hotz, journal, Sept. 13–Nov. 27, 1921, LT; Lila Tyng, June 13, 1967, TIA; Elisabeth Luce Moore, June 12, 1991, TIA; Henry R. Luce, Jan. 11, 1965, TIA; Henry R. Luce to Henry Justin Smith, undated, ca. Dec. 1, 1921, TIA; "Student Lost After Hazing," *Chicago Daily Tribune,* Sept. 23, 1921; "Father Looks for Boy Back Home Today," *Chicago Daily Tribune,* Sept. 24, 1921; "View Vanishing of Freshman As Teapot Tempest," *Chicago Daily Tribune,* Sept. 25, 1921; "Leighton Mount Found Dead," *Chicago Daily Tribune,* May 1, 1923; "Mount Boy Buried in Lime," *Chicago Daily Tribune,* May 2, 1923; "Mount 'Burial Witness' Found; Case Reopened," *Chicago Daily Tribune,* June 17, 1923.

Luce's last days in Chicago: Lila Hotz, journal, Nov. 24–26, 1921, LT; Lila Hotz, "A HISTORICAL ROMANCE in Four Acts," undated poem, LT; Lila Tyng, Mar. 30, 1969, WAS; Henry R. Luce to Nettie F. McCormick, Feb. 6, 1922, NFM; Henry R.

Luce to Elizabeth R. Luce, undated, ca. fall 1921, HRL; Henry R. Luce to Henry W. Luce and Elizabeth R. Luce, undated, ca. fall 1921, HRL; Walter Millis, Sept. 13, 1948, TIA; John M. Hincks, Dec. 20, 1968, WAS; Culbreth Sudler to W. A. Swanberg, undated, ca. Aug. 1968, WAS; Culbreth Sudler to W. A. Swanberg, Oct. 27, 1968, WAS; Niven Busch, "Biographical Notes—Briton Hadden," June 8, 1948, TIA; Noel F. Busch, *Briton Hadden*, p. 50.

5. TIME WILL TELL

Baltimore News: Henry R. Luce to Henry W. Luce and Elizabeth R. Luce, undated, ca. fall 1921, HRL; Henry R. Luce, Jan. 11, 1965, TIA; Elizabeth Pool, May 10, 1948, TIA; Henry R. Luce to John M. Hincks, Nov. 12, 1948, TIA; Walter Millis, Sept. 13, 1948, TIA; Lila Tyng, July 2, 1957, TIA; Noel F. Busch, *Briton Hadden*, pp. 50–53; George Britt, *Forty Years—Forty Millions;* John S. Martin, *A Grab-Bag for My Grandsons*, "Beginning of *Time*," p. 2, TIA.

Rise of the media: Paul Starr, *The Creation of the Media*, pp. 124, 131–34, 146, 252–66, 298–304, 319, 328, 331, 335, 386–87; Matthew Schneirov, *The Dream of a New Social Order*, pp. 12, 68–72, 75–76, 96, 98, 208–38, 252–55; Loren Baritz, *The Good Life*, pp. 72, 76–77, 79–83; Edward Bliss Jr., *Now the News*, pp. 6–10; Robert S. Lynd and Helen Merrell Lynd, *Middletown*, p. 46–47, 81–82, 86, 88, 156, 161, 172–73, 230–31; Gerald J. Baldasty, *The Commercialization of News in the Nineteenth Century*, pp. 66–71, 83; Michael Schudson, *The Power of News*, pp. 53–71; Edwin Emery and Michael Emery, *The Press and America*, pp. 223–26, 245–49, 270, 364–66; David Nasaw, *The Chief*, pp. 95–185; James L. Baughman, *Henry R. Luce and the Rise of the American News Media*, pp. 29–31; Jan Cohn, *Creating America*, pp. 5, 10, 28, 32, 47, 66, 102, 135, 144, 155, 165–66; George H. Douglas, *The Smart Magazines*, p. 19; Susan E. Tifft and Alex S. Jones, *The Trust*, pp. 41–46, 64; Peter Canning, *American Dreamers*, p. 24; *The Literary Digest* and *Saturday Evening Post*, Nov.–Dec. 1921, Jan. 1922.

The middle class: James L. Baughman, *Henry R. Luce and the Rise of the American News Media*, p. 34; Robert S. Lynd and Helen Merrell Lynd, *Middletown*, pp. 148, 182, 183, 187, 213, 263, 265, 267, 472–74; Loren Baritz, *The Good Life*, pp. 86, 94, 96; Lyman P. Powell, "Coué," *American Review of Reviews* (July–Dec., 1922), pp. 622–24; Roy E. Larsen to Briton Hadden, Feb. 14, 1928, TIA.

Working out the idea: Henry R. Luce, Jan. 11, 1965, TIA; Walter Millis, Sept. 13, 1948, TIA; "The Story of an Experiment," *Time*, Mar. 8, 1948, p. 56; W. A. Swanberg, *Luce and His Empire*, p. 49; John Berdan, Nov. 1, 1948, TIA; Henry Seidel Canby, June 24, 1948, TIA; *Time* prospectus, 1922, TIA; "Announcing the publication of a brief, readable chronicle of significant events," *Time* subscription circular, TIA; "Boys in School Had an Idea—Now It's a Surprise in Magazine World," *Boston Sunday Globe,* June 7, 1925, p. 23; Henry R. Luce to Henry W. Luce, undated, ca. Jan. 1922, HRL; *International News Service v. Associated Press,* 248 U.S. 215 (1918); Paul Starr, *The Creation of the Media,* p. 185; Briton Hadden, "*Time* Publisher Protests," *Editor & Publisher,* Nov. 12, 1928; Edwin J. Heath to Henry R. Luce, Mar. 4, 1948, *Time* twenty-fifth-anniversary files, TIA; Culbreth Sudler to Lilian Rixey, May 18, 1948, TIA; Culbreth Sudler to Alex Groner, June 28, 1955, TIA; Sheldon Luce, July 17, 1969, WAS; Robert T. Elson, *Time Inc.,* p. 6.

East 17th Street: Culbreth Sudler to Lilian Rixey, May 18, 1948, TIA; Culbreth Sudler to Alex Groner, June 28, 1955, TIA; Culbreth Sudler, Mar. 5, 1965, TIA; Henry R. Luce, Jan. 11, 1965, TIA; John S. Martin, Apr. 4, 1956, TIA; Manfred Gottfried, Aug. 14, 1961, TIA; Lillian Owens, untitled memorandum, Aug. 22, 1973, TIA; W. H. Eaton, June 4, 1948, TIA; W. H. Eaton, Oct. 31, 1961, TIA; Roy E. Larsen, Feb. 1, 1965, TIA; Dickinson W. Richards to James A. Linen III, Nov. 29, 1968, TIA; Samuel W. Meek, May 7, 1962, TIA; Walter Millis, Sept. 13, 1948, TIA; Lewis G. Adams, Dec. 28, 1955, TIA; John F. Carter, Aug. 1966, TIA; John W. Hanes, June 4, 1948, TIA; Lila Hotz, journal, Apr. 1, 1922, LT; "Boys in School Had an Idea—Now It's a Surprise in Magazine World," *Boston Sunday Globe,* June 7, 1925, p. 23; George Frazier, *It's About Time,* p. 13, GF; W. A. Swanberg, *Luce and His Empire,* p. 53; James L. Baughman, *Henry R. Luce and the Rise of the American News Media,* p. 31; Noel F. Busch, *Briton Hadden,* p. 66.

Raising funds: O. D. Keep, "SUCCESS comes mysteriously," *Time* promotion booklet, *Time* Publishing files, 1929, TIA; Henry R. Luce to Henry W. Luce, ca. Jan. 1922, HRL; Henry R. Luce, Jan. 11, 1965, TIA; John S. Martin, Apr. 4, 1956, TIA; E. V. Hale, June 29, 1948, TIA; Lila Tyng, July 2, 1957, TIA; *Time* traveling journal, 1922, TIA; Alexander Lowenthal to Hedley Donovan, Nov. 16, 1968, TIA; Culbreth Sudler, Mar. 9, 1965, TIA; Edward L. Bernays, Jan. 13, 1969, WAS; Elisabeth Luce Moore, Mar. 4, 1965, TIA; Elisabeth Luce Moore, Oct. 19, 1968, TIA; Elisabeth Luce Moore, Apr. 17, 1991, TIA; "12,000,000 Heiress, Miss Harkness, Wed," *New York Times,* June 28, 1922, p. 12; Wells Root, Mar. 10, 1964, TIA; Seymour Knox, June 25, 1956, TIA; William Hale Harkness, Oct. 22, 1948, TIA; David Ingalls, July 28, 1948, TIA; Henry R. Luce to Elizabeth R. Luce and Henry W. Luce, undated, ca. 1924, HRL; John S. Martin, *A Grab-Bag for My Grandsons,* "Beginning of *Time,*" p. 9, TIA; Noel F. Busch, *Briton Hadden: His Life and TIME,* pt. 2, p. 11, NOB; W. A. Swanberg, *Luce and His Empire,* pp. 54–55; Ralph Ingersoll, *High Time,* "Britton [*sic*] Hadden, in Memoriam," vol. 2, ch. 3, May 1962, retyped Jan. 1966, p. 17, 18, 20, 21, RI; Ralph Ingersoll, *High Time,* outline for ch. 2, p. 4, undated, ca. 1962, RI; Noel F. Busch, *Briton Hadden,* pp. 69, 76–80; Robert T. Elson, *Time Inc.,* pp. 13–14; Rosalie Heffelfinger Hall, author's interview, Apr. 16, 2003; Daniel P. Davison, author's interview, Apr. 9, 2003; Henry R. Luce, "Henry Pomeroy Davison Jr.: A Memoir," Aug. 30, 1961, TIA; Henry R. Luce to Henry P. Davison Jr., Sept. 3, 1929, TIA; Time Inc., certificate of incorporation, Nov. 28, 1922, TIA.

6. LONG SHOT

W. H. Eaton, June 4, 1948, TIA; Stanley Resor to Henry R. Luce, Feb. 27, 1929, TIA; John S. Martin, Apr. 4, 1956, TIA; Henry R. Luce, Jan. 11, 1965, TIA; Manfred Gottfried, Aug. 10, 1961, TIA; Roy E. Larsen, Aug. 7, 1956, TIA; Roy E. Larsen, Aug. 28, 1956, TIA; *Time,* specimen issue, Dec. 30, 1922 TIA, Feb. 17, 1923, TIA; Manfred Gottfried, diary excerpts, Jan. 2, 7, 25, Feb. 4, 1923, quoted in Manfred Gottfried, Mar. 7, 1955, TIA; Harry Reasoner and Mary Fickett, "Calendar," CBS, May 7, 1963, TIA.

Jan.–Feb. 1923: John F. Carter, Aug. 1966, TIA; Manfred Gottfried, Aug. 16, 1961, TIA; Roy E. Larsen, Aug. 7, 1956, TIA; Roy E. Larsen, Aug. 28, 1956, TIA; Elizabeth Luce Moore, Apr. 17, 1991, TIA; O. D. Keep, Aug. 27, 1959, TIA; "*Time's* Business Program," undated memorandum, ca. Jan. 1923, TIA; Henry R. Luce to Lila Hotz, Feb. 1923, LT; Williams Printing Company to Henry R. Luce, Dec. 8, 1922, TIA; Sidney Carroll to Roy E. Larsen, Mar. 30, 1948, TIA; John S. Martin, *A Grab-Bag for My Grandsons,* "Beginning of *Time,*" TIA; *Newsweek* staff, *Newsweek, The First 50 Years,* ca. 1983, p. 1; Noel F. Busch, *Briton Hadden,* p. 86; Howell C. Martyn, author's interview, Dec. 11, 2003.

First issue: *Time,* Mar. 3, 1923; Henry R. Luce, quoted in "He Ran the Course," *Time,* Mar. 10, 1967; Eric Hodgins, "The Span of Time," 1944, quoted in Julia Fay to Bob Fisler, Jan. 29, 1965, TIA; Roy E. Larsen, July 13, 1965, TIA; Edward L. Bernays to Henry R. Luce, June 5, 1944, TIA; *Time* press release, Mar. 1923, TIA; "'*Time,*' A New Weekly," *New York Times,* Mar. 2, 1923, p. 15; "New Weekly Out To-Day," *New York Herald,* Mar. 2, 1923, p. 7.

Assembling an audience: Henry R. Luce to Lila Hotz, Mar. 1923, LT; Roy E. Larsen, Aug. 7, 1956, TIA; Bob Brody, "Broad Brush Approach," memorandum on 1923 circulation figures, May 10, 1965, TIA; Patricia Divver, "Notes on Lunch with Roy Larsen," June 28, 1939, TIA; "*Time's* Business Program," undated memorandum, ca. Jan. 1923, TIA; Dorothy McDowell, June 12, 1961, TIA; Elisabeth Luce Moore,

Mar. 4, 1965, TIA; John S. Martin, Apr. 4, 1956, TIA; O. D. Keep, Aug. 27, 1959, TIA; Henry R. Luce, Jan. 12, 1965, TIA; Sidney Carroll to Roy E. Larsen, Mar. 30, 1948, TIA; "For Christmas," *Time* advertisement, ca. 1923, TIA; David Ahern to James A. Linen III, Nov. 12, 1952, TIA; Thomas M. Laney to James A. Linen III, Oct. 31, 1952, TIA; Peter Paul Luce, author's interview, Aug. 18, 2003.

Building the business: Samuel W. Meek, May 7, 1962, TIA; Robert L. Johnson, June 9, 1948, TIA; Robert L. Johnson, Mar. 5, 1956, TIA; John S. Martin, Apr. 4, 1956, TIA; W. H. Eaton, June 4, 1948, TIA; W. H. Eaton, Oct. 31, 1961, TIA; Noble Cathcart, Nov. 26, 1956, TIA; Polly Groves, May 19, 1960, TIA; Mary Fraser, June 16, 1939, TIA; Roy E. Larsen, Aug. 7, 1956, TIA; Roy E. Larsen to Celia Sugarman, Nov. 26, 1962, TIA; Roy E. Larsen, Feb. 1, 1965, TIA; Roy E. Larsen, July 13, 1965, TIA; undated letter to subscribers, ca. 1923, TIA; Christopher Larsen, author's interview, Oct. 4, 2002; "Sloan Wilson," obituary, *Variety*, June 29, 2003; Dorothy McDowell to Hedley Donovan, Nov. 2, 1968, TIA; Henry R. Luce to Lila Hotz, July 2, 1923, LT; Henry R. Luce, Jan. 12, 1965, TIA; Patricia Divver, "Notes on Lunch with Roy Larsen," June 28, 1939, TIA; Noel F. Busch, *Briton Hadden: His Life and TIME*, pt. 2, p. 5, NOB; Briton Hadden, "President's Report," Time Inc. Annual Report, Dec. 31, 1923, TIA; Robert T. Elson, *Time Inc.*, p. 59, 75.

Brewery: Roy E. Larsen, Aug. 7, 1956, TIA; Agnes Cowap, Dec. 1962, TIA; Manfred Gottfried, Aug. 23, 1961, TIA; John S. Martin, Apr. 4, 1956, TIA; Mary Fraser, June 16, 1939, TIA; "Weekly Budget for 30,000 Mail Subs," [Nov. 1, 1923], *Time* Publishing files, 1923, TIA; John F. Carter, Aug. 1966, TIA.

Covering the news: *Time*, July 2, 1923, p. 13; *Time*, July 16, 1923; *Time*, Aug. 20, 1923, pp. 1, 5; *Time*, Oct. 1, 1923, pp. 6, 19; *Time*, Oct. 8, 1923, pp. 1, 19; *Time*, Feb. 4, 1924, p. 1; *Time*, Mar. 22, 1926, p. 19; *Time*, Mar. 31, 1924, p. 20; *Time*, Apr. 21, 1924, pp. 19–20; *Time*, Apr. 28, 1924, esp. pp. 19–20; *Time*, Jan. 26, 1925, p. 22; *Time*, Feb. 23, 1925, p. 1; *Time*, June 22, 1925, p. 1; *Time*, June 29, 1925, p. 1; *Time*, Nov. 15, 1926, pp. 26–27; *Time*, Mar. 4, 1929, p. 10; Harry Sand to James A. Linen III, Nov. 13, 1952, TIA; David Ahern to James A. Linen III, Nov. 12, 1952, TIA; John Shaw Billings, Jan. 16, 1966, TIA; Joseph Kastner, Apr. 19, 1956, TIA.

Hadden's editing style and sensibility: John S. Martin, Apr. 4, 1956, TIA; John S. Martin, "Briton Hadden as Editor and Co-Founder of *Time*," Apr. 27, 1932, TIA; John S. Martin, Dec. 1965, TIA; Manfred Gottfried, Aug. 23, 1961, TIA; Dorothy McDowell, July 30, 1948, TIA; Wells Root, Mar. 10, 1964, TIA; *Time*, Jan. 28, 1924,

p. 4; *Time,* May 19, 1924, p. 5; *Time,* May 26, 1924, p. 7; *Time,* July 28, 1924, p. 4; *Time,* Nov. 3, 1924, p. 6; *Time,* Sept. 28, 1925, p. 2; *Time,* June 7, 1926, pp. 8–9; *Time,* Nov. 29, 1926, p. 11; *Time,* Mar. 17, 1927, p. 4.

Writers: Joseph Kastner, untitled memorandum, ca. June 1939, p. 2, TIA; Manfred Gottfried, Aug. 16, 1961, TIA; Thomas J. C. Martyn to Henry R. Luce, May 2, 1966, TIA; Niven Busch, Mar. 11, 1965, TIA; Noel F. Busch, *Life with Luce,* pp. 19–24, NAB; Jerry Busch, author's interview, May 22, 2003; Terry Busch, author's interview, June 7, 2003.

Researchers: Nancy Ford and Ruth Ogg, Feb. 12, 1958, TIA; Dorothy McDowell, July 30, 1948, TIA; Dorothy McDowell, June 12, 1961, TIA; Elizabeth Armstrong, Oct. 11, 1960, TIA; Manfred Gottfried, Aug. 16, 1961, TIA; Henry R. Luce, Jan. 11, 1965, TIA; Agnes Cowap, Dec. 1962, TIA; Faith Willcox, Mar. 1, 1960, TIA; Alan R. Jackson, July 20, 1960, Aug. 22, 1960, TIA; Florence Horn, ca. June 1939, TIA; Mary Fraser to Robert T. Elson, Sept. 8, 1965, TIA; John S. Martin, Apr. 4, 1956, TIA; John S. Martin, Sept. 29, 1965, TIA; Ben Yagoda, *About Town,* pp. 202–3; Thomas Kunkel, *Genius in Disguise,* pp. 153, 191, 259–63.

Deborah Douglas: Bob Aden, author's interview, Apr. 10, 2003; Susan Aguilar, author's interview, Oct. 30, 2005; Rebecca C. Morey, author's interview, Apr. 10, 2003; Elisabeth Krueger, author's interview, June 1, 2003; John S. Martin, Sept. 29, 1965, TIA; John M. Hincks, Apr. 30, 1948, TIA; Dorothy McDowell, June 12, 1961, TIA; Agnes Cowap, May 15, 1958, TIA; George Frazier, *It's About Time,* p. 114, GF.

Luce's work and social life: John Humphrey Stevenson, May 19, 1960, TIA; Noble Cathcart, Nov. 26, 1956, TIA; Elisabeth Luce Moore, May 17, 1960, TIA; Henry R. Luce, Jan. 12, 1965, TIA; Joseph Kastner, Apr. 19, 1956, TIA; John S. Martin, Apr. 4, 1956, TIA; Wells Root, Mar. 10, 1964, TIA; Dorothy McDowell, June 12, 1961, TIA; Lilian Rixey, "Who Did What When," memorandum, Oct. 1, 1948, TIA; Elizabeth Tobin, "Apotheosis of *Time,*" unidentified news clipping, Publicity files, 1929, TIA.

Luce's wedding and vacation: Manfred Gottfried, Aug. 23, 1961, TIA; Lila Hotz, journal, June 13, 1923, Dec. 22, 1923, LT; Lila Tyng, June 13, 1967, TIA; unidentified society column, Dec. 22, 1923, LT; Elizabeth R. Luce to Emmavail Luce, written in the margin of Henry R. Luce to Elizabeth R. Luce, Dec. 27, 1923, HRL; Henry P. Davison Jr. ["G–g"] to Henry R. Luce ["B–l"], Dec. 12, 1923, LT; *New York Evening Journal,* ca. Dec. 23, 1923, LT; Henry W. Luce to family, ca. Dec. 27, 1923, SF; Lila Luce to Elizabeth R. Luce, Dec. 27, 1923, HRL; Henry R. Luce to Elizabeth R. Luce,

Dec. 27, 1923, HRL; Lila Tyng to Robert T. Elson, undated, ca. 1967, WAS; Lila Tyng to Robert T. Elson, Feb. 10, 1969, TIA; Lila Tyng, June 13, 1967, TIA; Elisabeth Luce Moore, June 12, 1991, TIA; Peter Paul Luce, author's interview, May 29, 2003; Alexandra Robbins, *Secrets of the Tomb,* pp. 154–57; Deborah Tighe, "But—We Have a Theatre," *Countryside,* June 1941, quoted in Bob Aden, *The Way It Was,* p. 6.

The Pop Question Game: "Genesis of M.O.T.," "Radio Broadcasts by *Time,* Chronology," Broadcasting history files, 1928–29, TIA; John S. Martin, Apr. 4, 1956, TIA; Roy E. Larsen, Aug. 7, 1956, TIA; Roy E. Larsen, Aug. 28, 1956, TIA; Roy E. Larsen, Jan. 13, 1965, TIA; Joseph Kastner, Apr. 19, 1956, TIA; *New York Herald,* Mar. 4, 1924, quoted in "Genesis of M.O.T.," Broadcasting history files, 1928–29; Paul Starr, *The Creation of the Media,* p. 338.

The Saturday Review of Literature: Henry Seidel Canby, June 24, 1948, TIA; Henry Seidel Canby to Lilian Rixey, Nov. 8, 1948, TIA; "Re: Founding of *The Saturday Review of Literature* as explained by members of the SRL staff," June 27, 1969, TIA; *The Saturday Review of Literature,* "Reviewing Ten Years: A Personal Record of *The Saturday Review of Literature,*" pp. 4–8, TIA; Roy E. Larsen, Aug. 7, 1956, TIA; Roy E. Larsen, Feb. 1, 1965, TIA; Manfred Gottfried, Aug. 23, 1961, TIA; Henry R. Luce, Jan. 12, 1965, TIA; Amy Loveman, June 23, 1948, TIA; John S. Martin, Apr. 4, 1956, TIA.

Hadden's breakup with Deborah Douglas: Lila Tyng, journal, Feb. 27, 1924, LT; Henry R. Luce, Jan. 12, 1965, TIA; Dorothy McDowell, June 12, 1961, TIA; F. P. Heffelfinger to Henry R. Luce, Mar. 17, 1948, HRL; "Ambrose Tighe, Leading Attorney, Dies at His Home," *Saint Paul Pioneer Press,* Nov. 12, 1928, p. 7; "R. L. Tighe, State Solon, Found Dead," *Minneapolis Journal,* Apr. 30, 1938, p. 1; Elisabeth Krueger, author's interview, June 1, 2003; Rebecca C. Morey, author's interview, Apr. 10, 2003; Bob Aden, author's interview, Apr. 10, 2003, Bob Aden, author's interview, June 7, 2003; Bob Aden, *This Was Us*; Bob Aden, *The Way It Was.*

Hadden's temperament: Manfred Gottfried, Aug. 23, 1961, TIA; Niven Busch, "Biographical Notes—Briton Hadden," June 8, 1948, TIA; Niven Busch, Mar. 11, 1965, TIA; John M. Hincks, Apr. 30, 1948, TIA; Ruth Flint, July 23, 1948, TIA; Joseph Kastner, Apr. 19, 1956, TIA; Henry R. Luce, Jan. 12, 1965, TIA.

Time at the close of 1924: Henry R. Luce, "President's Report," Time Inc. Annual Report, Dec. 31, 1924, TIA; Time Inc. Publisher's Statement for the Audit Bureau of Circulations, Dec. 31, 1924, TIA; Noble Cathcart, Nov. 26, 1956, TIA; Nancy Ford and Ruth Ogg, Feb. 12, 1958, TIA.

7. BALLGAMES

Description of the staff: Niven Busch, "Biographical Notes—Briton Hadden," June 8, 1948, TIA; Niven Busch, Mar. 11, 1965, TIA; Joseph Kastner, ca. June 1939, TIA; Joseph Kastner, Apr. 19, 1956, TIA; Nancy Ford and Ruth Ogg, Feb. 12, 1958, TIA; Dorothy McDowell, July 30, 1948, TIA; Dorothy McDowell, June 12, 1961, TIA; Mary Fraser, June 16, 1939, TIA; Elizabeth Robert, Feb. 2, 1956, TIA; Manfred Gottfried, Aug. 16, 1961, TIA; Manfred Gottfried, Aug. 21, 1961, TIA; Manfred Gottfried, June 20, 1966, TIA; John S. Martin, Dec. 1965, TIA; Howard Black, June 20, 1956, TIA; F. D. Dusossoit, Sept. 16, 1958, TIA; Barry M. Osborn, author's interview, Apr. 6, 2002; *F.Y.I.*, Mar. 6, 1953, p. 1, TIA.

Thursday–Friday: Henry R. Luce to Lila Hotz, undated, ca. 1923, LT; Ruth Ogg, Feb. 12, 1958, TIA; Wells Root, Mar. 10, 1964, TIA; Mimi Martin, Aug. 4, 1948, TIA; Elisabeth Luce Moore, Mar. 4, 1965, TIA; Elisabeth Luce Moore, Apr. 17, 1991, TIA; John S. Martin, Apr. 4, 1956, TIA; John S. Martin, Sept. 29, 1965, TIA; Henry R. Luce, Jan. 12, 1965, TIA; John Kobler, Aug. 5, 1969, WAS; Agnes Cowap, May 15, 1958, TIA; Mary Fraser, June 16, 1939, TIA; Robert T. Elson, *Time Inc.*, p. 157.

Saturday–Monday: Dorothy McDowell, July 30, 1948, TIA; Dorothy McDowell, June 12, 1961, TIA; Nancy Ford and Ruth Ogg, Feb. 12, 1958, TIA; Elizabeth Armstrong, Oct. 11, 1960, TIA; Wells Root, Mar. 10, 1964, TIA; Joseph Kastner, undated, ca. June 1939, TIA; Joseph Kastner, Apr. 19, 1956, TIA; John S. Martin, Apr. 4, 1956, TIA; John S. Martin, Sept. 29, 1965, TIA; John S. Martin, *A Grab-Bag for My Grandsons,* "Beginning of *Time,*" pp. 16, 24, TIA; Noel F. Busch, *Briton Hadden,* pp. 231–32.

Death Avenue: Nancy Ford and Ruth Ogg, Feb. 12, 1958, TIA; Agnes Cowap, May 15, 1958, TIA; Agnes Cowap, Dec. 1962, TIA; Joseph Kastner, ca. June 1939, TIA; Joseph Kastner, Apr. 19, 1956, TIA; Henry R. Luce, Jan. 13, 1965, TIA; Wells Root, Mar. 10, 1964, TIA; Ruth Flint, July 23, 1948, TIA; Manfred Gottfried, Aug. 16, 1961, TIA; John S. Martin, *A Grab-Bag for My Grandsons,* "Beginning of *Time,*" pp. 21–22, TIA.

Party and days off: Wells Root, Mar. 10, 1964, TIA; Dorothy McDowell, June 12, 1961, TIA; Noble Cathcart, Nov. 21, 1956, TIA; O. D. Keep, Aug. 27, 1959, TIA; John S. Martin, Sept. 29, 1965, TIA; Elizabeth Armstrong, Oct. 11, 1960, TIA; Dorothy McDowell to Hedley Donovan, Nov. 2, 1968, TIA; John S. Martin, "Briton Hadden as Editor and Co-Founder of *Time,*" Apr. 27, 1932, p. 6, TIA; John S. Martin, *A Grab-Bag for My Grandsons,* "Beginning of *Time,*" p. 25, TIA.

8. TIMESTYLE

Scopes case: George Frazier, *It's About Time,* p. 30, GF; *Literary Digest,* July 18, 1925, pp. 5, 52; *Literary Digest,* July 25, 1925, pp. 5–7, 18; *Time,* July 20, 1925; *Time,* Apr. 6, 1925; *Time,* May 18, 1925; *Time,* May 25, 1925; *Time,* June 1, 1925; *Time,* June 22, 1925; *Time,* July 27, 1925; *Time,* Aug. 3, 1925; Edward J. Larson, *Summer for the Gods,* pp. 87–91; Mary Lee Settle, *The Scopes Trial,* pp. 37–44.

***The New Yorker* and the *Daily Graphic*:** *Time,* Sept. 22, 1924, p. 22; *Time,* Mar. 2, 1925, p. 18; *Time,* July 12, 1926, p. 22; *Time,* Sept. 27, 1926, p. 22; *Time,* Feb. 7, 1927, p. 31; *Time,* Apr. 30, 1928, p. 24; *Time,* May 7, 1928, p. 25; Niven Busch, Mar. 11, 1965, TIA; Niven Busch, "Biographical Notes—Briton Hadden," June 8, 1948, TIA; Robert L. Johnson, Mar. 5, 1956, TIA.

Hadden's terse style: John S. Martin, "Briton Hadden as Editor and Co-Founder of *Time,*" Apr. 27, 1932, p. 4, TIA; John S. Martin, *A Grab-Bag for My Grandsons,* "Beginning of *Time,*" p. 20, TIA; Niven Busch, "Biographical Notes—Briton Hadden," June 8, 1948, TIA; *Time,* Apr. 6, 1925, p. 15; *Time,* Sept. 7, 1925, p. 14; *Time,* Oct. 5, 1925, p. 32; *Time,* Nov. 16, 1925, p. 18; *Time,* Jan. 25, 1926, p. 14; *Time,* Mar. 8, 1926, pp. 14–15; *Time,* May 31, 1926, p. 19; *Time,* June 14, 1926, p. 12; *Time,* July 26, 1926, p. 20; *Time,* Aug. 2, 1926, p. 14; *Time,* Aug. 9, 1926, p. 12.

***Iliad*'s influence:** Homer, *Iliad,* Briton Hadden books files, TIA; Thayer Hobson to Eric Hodgins, July 26, 1945, Sept. 6, 1945, TIA; Eric Hodgins to Thayer Hobson, Aug. 23, 1945, TIA; Henry R. Luce, Jan. 11, 1965, TIA; John S. Martin, Apr. 4, 1956, TIA; John S. Martin, *A Grab-Bag for My Grandsons,* "Beginning of *Time,*" pp. 13, 18, 20, TIA; *Time,* July 21, 1924, p. 10; *Time,* Sept. 7, 1925; *Time,* Dec. 7, 1925, p. 13; *Time,* Dec. 21, 1925, p. 30; *Time,* Jan. 11, 1926, p. 13; *Time,* May 24, 1926, p. 11; *Time,* May 31, 1926, pp. 2, 17; *Time,* June 14, 1926, p. 15; *Time,* June 28, 1926, p. 11; *Time,* Aug. 2, 1926, p. 5; *Time,* Sept. 13, 1926, p. 7; *Time,* Nov. 8, 1926, p. 17; *Time,* June 25, 1928, p. 18; *Time,* July 30, 1928, p. 2.

Depictions of newsmakers: Culbreth Sudler, May 18, 1948, TIA; John S. Martin, "Briton Hadden as Editor and Co-Founder of *Time,*" Apr. 27, 1932, p. 7, TIA; John S. Martin, *A Grab-Bag for My Grandsons,* "Beginning of *Time,*" p. 19, TIA; Niven Busch, "Biographical Notes—Briton Hadden," June 8, 1948, p. 5, TIA; George Frazier, *It's About Time,* p. 119, GF; Robert Ernst, *Weakness Is a Crime,* pp. 22–23, 33–34, 97–98; *Time,* June 2, 1924, p. 13; *Time,* Aug. 10, 1925, cover; *Time,* Jan. 11, 1926, p. 16; *Time,* Mar. 15, 1926, p. 15; *Time,* July 19, 1926, pp. 10, 20–22; *Time,* Feb. 22, 1926, p. 11; *Time,* Apr. 9, 1927, cover.

Hadden's interest in unusual words: Homer, *Iliad,* p. 205, Briton Hadden books files, TIA; Briton Hadden, *Style Book for Time,* 1927, TIA; *Time,* Sept. 22, 1924, p. 22; *Time,* Aug. 24, 1925, p. 18; *Time,* May 17, 1926, p. 20; *Time,* May 31, 1926, p. 32; *Time,* July 5, 1926, p. 10; *Time,* July 19, 1926, pp. 20–22, 30; *Time,* Aug. 2, 1926, pp. 2, 8; *Time,* Aug. 16, 1926, p. 6; *Time,* Sept. 13, 1926, pp. 7, 34; *Time,* Jan. 3, 1927, cover; *Time,* Oct. 3, 1927, p. 17; *Time,* Dec. 12, 1927, p. 14; *Time,* Aug. 20, 1928, p. 19; *Time,* Oct. 8, 1928, p. 30; *Time,* Dec. 31, 1928, p. 30; Ruth Flint, July 23, 1948, TIA; Nancy Ford, Feb. 12, 1958, TIA; John S. Martin, Apr. 4, 1956, TIA; Culbreth Sudler, Mar. 9, 1965, TIA; Faith Willcox, Mar. 24, 1958, TIA; Elizabeth Pool, May 10, 1948, TIA.

Narrative story structure: *Time,* Sept. 3, 1923, p. 7; *Time,* Sept. 10, 1923, p. 7; *Time,* Dec. 10, 1923, p. 11; *Time,* Feb. 4, 1924, p. 10; *Time,* Mar. 31, 1924, p. 8; *Time,* Aug. 25, 1924, p. 10; *Time,* Jan. 5, 1925, p. 18; *Time,* Jan. 26, 1925, p. 22; *Time,* Feb. 15, 1926, p. 1; *Time,* Feb. 22, 1926, p. 8; *Time,* Mar. 1, 1926, p. 17; *Time,* June 28, 1926, p. 10; *Time,* July 5, 1926, p. 13; *Time,* Aug. 16, 1926, p. 22; Faith Willcox, Mar. 1, 1960, TIA; Manfred Gottfried, undated interview, ca. 1950, JM; David Cort, *The Sin of Henry R. Luce,* p. 33.

Inventions and formulaic style: *Time,* Sept. 10, 1923, cover, p. 24; *Time,* Apr. 7, 1924, p. 7; *Time,* Jan. 12, 1925; *Time,* Feb. 23, 1925, p. 28; *Time,* Sept. 14, 1925, p. 31; *Time,* Dec. 14, 1925, p. 34; *Time,* Dec. 21, 1925, p. 13; *Time,* Jan. 11, 1926, p. 13; *Time,* Jan 25, 1926, pp. 11, 15; *Time,* Jan. 25, 1926, p. 15; *Time,* Feb. 1, 1926, p. 37; *Time,* Feb. 8, 1926, p. 12; *Time,* Feb. 15, 1926, p. 16; *Time,* Mar. 29, 1926, p. 12; *Time,* Apr. 12, 1926, p. 22; *Time,* May 24, 1926, pp. 12–13; *Time,* Aug. 2, 1926, p. 14; *Time,* Sept. 13, 1926, p. 2; *Time,* Sept. 20, 1926, p. 13; *Time,* Oct. 4, 1926, pp. 28–30; *Time,* Nov. 1, 1926, pp. 6, 19; *Time,* Nov. 8, 1926, p. 13; *Time,* Apr. 18, 1927, p. 16; *Time,* Apr. 25, 1927, p. 15; *Time,* June 13, 1927, p. 26; *Time,* Sept. 19, 1927, p. 15; *Time,* Oct. 31, 1927, p. 14.

Praise and blame: Marshall McLuhan quoted in *Fact,* Jan.–Feb. 1964, p. 15, Publicity files, 1964, TIA; James Rowland Angell to Briton Hadden, May 28, 1926, *Time* Edit files, 1926, TIA; *Time,* Dec. 8, 1924, p. 30; *Time,* Feb. 2, 1925, p. 27; *Time,* Mar. 2, 1925, pp. 24–25; *Time,* Apr. 27, 1925, p. 26; *Time,* Aug. 24, 1925, p. 28; *Time,* Mar. 15, 1926, p. 2; *Time,* Aug. 9, 1926, p. 31; *Time,* June 20, 1927, p. 24; *Time,* Jan. 2, 1928, p. 2; John S. Martin, Apr. 4, 1956, TIA.

***Time* expressed Hadden's personality:** Evans Woollen, Apr. 30, 1948, TIA; Stuart Heminway, May 19, 1948, TIA; Newton Hockaday, Feb. 22, 1960, TIA; Katherine

Abrams, June 22, 1948, TIA; John S. Martin, Sept. 29, 1965, TIA; Charles D. Smith to Lilian Rixey, May 20, 1948, TIA; Niven Busch, "Biographical Notes—Briton Hadden," June 8, 1948, p. 5, TIA; Mimi Martin, Feb. 3, 1958, TIA; W. Rice Brewster, May 14, 1948, TIA; Henry Luce III, author's interview, Dec. 27, 2001.

9. BURNING BOTH ENDS

Hadden's relationship with Luce: "Boys in School Had an Idea—Now It's a Surprise in Magazine World," *Boston Sunday Globe,* June 7, 1925, p. 23; Henry R. Luce to Lila Hotz, numerous letters, ca. June 1923; undated, "Thursday P.M.," 1923, LT; Polly Groves, May 19, 1960, TIA; Dorothy McDowell, June 12, 1961, TIA; Dorothy Lindner, Apr. 6, 1964, TIA; Wells Root, Mar. 10, 1964, TIA; Manfred Gottfried, Aug. 16, 1961, TIA; Katherine Abrams, June 22, 1948, TIA; Mimi Martin, Aug. 5, 1948, TIA; Lila Tyng, June 13, 1967, TIA; Lila Tyng, Sept. 8, 1969, WAS; Mary Fraser, June 16, 1939, TIA; Elizabeth Armstrong, Oct. 11, 1960, TIA; Archibald MacLeish, Mar. 17, 1965, TIA; John S. Martin, Apr. 4, 1956, TIA; Niven Busch, "Biographical Notes—Briton Hadden," June 8, 1948, TIA; Noel F. Busch, *Life with Luce,* undated draft, pp. 11–12, NAB; Noel F. Busch, *Life with Luce,* pt. 3, p. 3, NAB; Noel F. Busch, *Life with Luce,* undated draft segment, NAB; Noel F. Busch, *Briton Hadden,* p. 42; Ralph Ingersoll, *High Time,* 1966, p. 38, RI.

Luce's home life: Lila Luce, journal, Feb. 15, 1924, Aug. 20, 1924, Mar. 12–13, 1925, LT; Henry R. Luce to Lila Luce, June 7, 1924, LT; Lila Tyng, June 13, 1967, TIA; Lila Tyng, Mar. 30, 1969, WAS; Lila Tyng, Sept. 8, 1969, WAS; Lila Tyng to W. A. Swanberg, Feb. 3, 1969, WAS; Lila Tyng to Robert T. Elson, Feb. 10, 1969, TIA; Peter Paul Luce, author's interview, May 27, 2003; Robert L. Luce, "At the tomb of Napoleon (dedicated to *his* spiritual successor)," Sept. 28, 1925, LT; John S. Martin, Sept. 1965, TIA; D. Jacques Benoliel to James A. Linen III, Nov. 7, 1952, TIA; Sylvia Jukes Morris, *Rage for Fame,* p. 252.

Hadden's social life and sexuality: Ruth Flint, July 23, 1948, TIA; Manfred Gottfried, Aug. 23, 1961, TIA; Henry R. Luce, Jan. 12, 1965, TIA; Mimi Martin, Mar. 20, 1958, TIA; Niven Busch, "Biographical Notes—Briton Hadden," June 8, 1948, TIA; Niven Busch, Mar. 11, 1965, TIA; Culbreth Sudler, Mar. 9, 1965, TIA; Roy E. Larsen, July 13, 1965, TIA; John S. Martin, Sept. 29, 1965, TIA; John S. Martin, Dec. 1965, TIA; Winslow Duke, author's interview, Feb. 14, 2003; Chan Hardwick, author's interview, Apr. 10, 2004; David Dolben, author's interview, Mar. 3, 2004; Thomas H. Black, author's interview, June 20, 2003; Margot Anne Simonson, author's interview, Sept. 5, 2003.

Hadden's drinking and eating habits: Henry R. Luce, Jan. 12, 1965, TIA; Lila Tyng, May 27, 1948, TIA; Elisabeth Luce Moore, Mar. 4, 1965, TIA; Elisabeth Luce Moore, Apr. 17, 1991, TIA; Niven Busch, "Biographical Notes—Briton Hadden," June 8, 1948, TIA; Niven Busch, Mar. 11, 1965, TIA; Mimi Martin, Mar. 20, 1958, TIA; John F. Carter, Aug. 1966, TIA; Elizabeth Armstrong, Oct. 11, 1960, TIA; Manfred Gottfried, Aug. 23, 1961, TIA; Briton Hadden Adult Photographs file, TIA; George Frazier, *It's About Time*, p. 152, GF; Harvey K. Murdock, author's interview, May 31, 2003; Akiko Busch and Mary Fairchild Busch, author's interview, Nov. 2, 2005; Barry M. Osborn, author's interview, Apr. 6, 2002.

Time's **rapid expansion:** Henry R. Luce to Elizabeth R. Luce, Feb. 21, 1925, undated, ca. Apr. 1925, Oct. 24, 1925, HRL; Harry S. New, "Method to Be Followed in the Handling of Newspapers," U.S. Postal Service Order No. 99, Jan. 30, 1924, TIA; Roy E. Larsen to the postmaster of New York, Feb. 20, 1924, TIA; publishers of *Time* to the postmaster of New York, "Brief," ca. Jan. 1924, TIA; E. M. Morgan and J. J. Kiely to publishers of *Time*, Feb. 28, 1924, TIA; Charles D. Hilles to Henry R. Luce, Mar. 12, 1924, TIA; Time Inc. Annual Report, 1924, Dec. 31, 1924, TIA; Time Inc. Annual Report, 1925, Jan. 2, 1926, TIA; John H. Schnackenberg & Associates, "Time Inc. Financial Statements," Apr. 30, 1925, TIA; Katherine Abrams, June 22, 1948, TIA; E. V. Hale, "Recollections of Briton Hadden," June 29, 1948, TIA.

Last days before Hadden's vacation: Lila Luce, journal, Mar. 13, 1925, LT; Lila Tyng, May 27, 1948, TIA; Manfred Gottfried, Aug. 23, 1961, TIA; Dorothy McDowell, July 30, 1948, TIA; Dorothy McDowell, June 12, 1961, TIA; Dorothy McDowell, Jan. 6, 1964, TIA; Elizabeth Armstrong, Oct. 11, 1960, TIA; Joseph Kastner, quoted in W. A. Swanberg, *Luce and His Empire*, p. 61; Joseph Kastner, Apr. 19, 1956, TIA; David Dolben, author's interview, Mar. 9, 2004; Chan Hardwick, author's interview, Apr. 10, 2004.

Hadden's vacation: Lila Luce, journal, Mar. 28, 1925, LT; Briton Hadden to Elizabeth Pool, Apr. 25, 1925, BH; Roy E. Larsen, Feb. 1, 1965, TIA; Roy E. Larsen to Robert T. Elson, Sept. 12, 1967, TIA; Lewis G. Adams, Dec. 28, 1955, TIA; Lewis G. Adams to Hedley Donovan, Nov. 25, 1968, TIA; David Dolben, author's interview, Mar. 9, 2004; Chan Hardwick, author's interview, Apr. 10, 2004; Christopher Larsen, author's interview, Oct. 4, 2002; Noel F. Busch, *Briton Hadden*, pp. 163–68, TIA.

Luce's plan to move to Cleveland: Henry R. Luce to Henry P. Davison Jr., Apr. 15, 1925, HPD; Henry R. Luce to Elizabeth R. Luce, Oct. 24, 1925, HRL; Time Inc.

board of directors minutes, June 23, 1925, TIA; Time Inc. board of directors minutes, May 27, 1926, TIA; Henry R. Luce, Jan. 12, 1965, TIA; Roy E. Larsen, Aug. 7, 1956, TIA; Roy E. Larsen, Aug. 28, 1956, TIA; Roy E. Larsen, Feb. 1, 1965, TIA; Manfred Gottfried, Aug. 23, 1961, TIA; Manfred Gottfried, Aug. 24, 1961, TIA; Dorothy McDowell, July 30, 1948, TIA; Joseph Kastner, Apr. 19, 1956, TIA; Robert L. Johnson, Mar. 5, 1956, TIA; Noel F. Busch, *Briton Hadden*, p. 169.

Breakup of the staff: Robert L. Johnson, Mar. 5, 1956, TIA; Eileen Murphy, Jan. 8, 1958, TIA; Roy E. Larsen, Aug. 7, 1956, TIA; Roy E. Larsen, Aug. 28, 1956, TIA; Amy Loveman, June 23, 1948, TIA; Henry R. Luce, Jan. 12, 1965, TIA; Henry Seidel Canby, June 24, 1948, TIA; Noble Cathcart, Nov. 26, 1956, TIA; Dorothy McDowell, June 12, 1961, TIA; Joseph Kastner, Apr. 19, 1956, TIA; Manfred Gottfried, Aug. 23, 1961, TIA; John F. Carter, Aug. 1966, TIA; John S. Martin, Apr. 4, 1956, TIA; Katherine Abrams, June 9, 1962, TIA; "Dupie" to Katherine Halle, ca. June 1948, TIA; Howell C. Martyn, author's interview, Dec. 11, 2003; *Newsweek* staff, *Newsweek, The First 50 Years*, p. 1, ca. 1983, Noel F. Busch, *Life with Luce*, pt. 2, pp. 29–30, NAB.

10. HAMMER AND TONGS

Cleveland: William Ganson Rose, *Cleveland*, p. 623; Jan Cigliano, *Showplace of America*, pp. 2–3, 8–9, 11, 28, 32, 185, 309, 320, 322, 324–25, 328, 337; Carol Poh Miller and Robert A. Wheeler, *Cleveland*, p. 79; Ralph Ingersoll, *High Time*, Jan. 1966, p. 30, RI; Lila Luce to Lila F. R. Hotz, undated letters, ca. fall 1926, LT; Mimi Martin, Feb. 3, 1958, TIA; "The Living Descendants of Dr. and Mrs. Henry Winters Luce," Luce family genealogy, Apr. 1, 2002, LT; Henry R. Luce to Elizabeth R. Luce, Oct. 24, 1925, HRL; Henry R. Luce to Lila Luce, undated, ca. fall 1925, LT.

Editorial and financial troubles: Henry R. Luce to Elizabeth R. Luce, Oct. 24, 1925, HRL; William J. Shultz to the editor of *Time*, Feb. 19, 1964, *Time* Publishing files, 1925, TIA; Briton Hadden to William J. Shultz, Aug. 6, 1925, *Time* Publishing files, 1925, TIA; Henry R. Luce to Elizabeth R. Luce, Oct. 24, 1925, HRL; Henry R. Luce to Lila Luce, undated, ca. 1925, LT; Lila Luce to Lila F. R. Hotz, undated, ca. Jan. 27, 1926, LT; Niven Busch, Mar. 11, 1965, TIA; John S. Martin, Apr. 4, 1956, TIA; Mimi Martin, Feb. 3, 1958, TIA; Myron Weiss, Mar. 13, 1956, TIA; Dorothea Spieth, Mar. 30, 1955, TIA; Ruth Flint, July 23, 1948, TIA.

Circulation drive and Postal Service campaign: Henry R. Luce to Lila Luce, undated, ca. Jan. 1926, LT; Henry R. Luce to Elizabeth R. Luce, Oct. 24, 1925, HRL; Henry R. Luce, Jan. 12, 1965, TIA; Patricia Divver, "Notes on Lunch with Roy

Larsen," June 28, 1939, TIA; Roy E. Larsen, Aug. 7, 1956, TIA; Roy E. Larsen, Aug. 28, 1956, TIA; Harry L. Richey, June 26, 1956, TIA; Ruth Flint, July 23, 1948, TIA; Noel F. Busch, *Briton Hadden*, pp. 181–82.

Pop Question tours: "Chamber Eats Luncheon Like 'Main Street,'" *Cleveland Press*, Jan. 27, 1926; "Forum Guests Facing Skull Test By Luce," *Ohio State Journal*, Feb. 3, 1927; "Editor's Brain Teasers Stump City's Captains of Industry," *Ohio State Journal*, Feb. 5, 1927; "Chamber Members Enjoy Quiz," *Brooklyn Daily Eagle*, Mar. 12, 1927, p. 13; Lila Luce to Lila F. R. Hotz, undated, ca. 1925, undated, ca. Jan. 27, 1926, Mar. 18, 1926, undated, ca. spring 1926, LT; John S. Martin, Apr. 4, 1956, TIA; Henry R. Luce, Jan. 12, 1965, TIA.

Luce's public persona: Henry R. Luce to Lila Luce, undated, ca. 1926, LT; Lila Luce to Lila F. R. Hotz, undated, ca. fall 1925, undated letters, ca. 1926, LT; Faith Willcox, Mar. 1, 1960, TIA; Katherine Halle, Nov. 14, 1961, TIA; Henrietta Force, Apr. 15, 1958, TIA.

Hadden's social life: Niven Busch, "Biographical Notes—Briton Hadden," June 8, 1948, TIA; Niven Busch, Mar. 11, 1965, TIA; Mimi Martin, Feb. 3, 1958, TIA; Roy E. Larsen, Aug. 28, 1956, TIA; Laird Goldsborough to Henry R. Luce, undated, ca. 1927, LT; Winsor French, June 26, 1956, TIA; Winsor French, "Early Days with *Time* and Its Briton Hadden," *Cleveland Press*, Feb. 9, 1952; Winsor French, "Colorful Staff Aided Hadden, Luce with *Time*'s Birth Pains," *Cleveland Press*, Feb. 23, 1952; "Dupie" to Katherine Halle, ca. June 1948, TIA; John S. Martin, Apr. 4, 1956, TIA; Ruth Flint, July 23, 1948, TIA; Faith Willcox, Mar. 1, 1960, TIA; E. V. Hale, "Recollections of Briton Hadden," June 29, 1948, TIA; George Frazier, *It's About Time*, p. 145, GF; *Time*, July 26, 1926, p. 29; Sinclair Lewis, *Babbitt*, pp. 9, 10, 32–50, 157–71, 179–89; Noel F. Busch, *Briton Hadden*, p. 105; Winslow Duke, author's interview, Feb. 14, 2003; Christopher Larsen to author, June 6, 2003; Coralee McInerney, author's interview, Sept. 6, 2003.

Mimi Martin: Lila Luce to Lila F. R. Hotz, undated, ca. winter 1926, undated, ca. Mar. 1926, LT; Mimi Martin, Aug. 5, 1948, TIA; Mimi Martin, Feb. 3, 1958, TIA; Richardson Wood, Mar. 14, 19, 25, Apr. 9, 1963, TIA; Barry M. Osborn, author's interview, Sept. 8, 2003.

Winsor French: Winsor French, "An Old Letter Recalls *Time*'s Dawning Hours," *Cleveland Press*, Feb. 2, 1952; Winsor French, "Early Days with *Time* and Its Briton Hadden," *Cleveland Press*, Feb. 9, 1952; Winsor French, "*Time*'s First Years in City Turbulent," *Cleveland Press*, Feb. 16, 1952; Winsor French, June 26, 1956, TIA;

Winsor French to J. O. Eaton, Nov. 14, 1927, WF; Manfred Gottfried, Aug. 24, 1961, TIA; Mimi Martin, Feb. 3, 1958, TIA; Faith Willcox, Mar. 1, 1960, TIA; Mary Fraser to Robert T. Elson, Sept. 8, 1965, TIA; Harold Lateiner, June 14, 1939, TIA.

Laird Goldsborough and the Robinn letters: John S. Martin, Sept. 1965, TIA; John S. Martin, Dec. 1965, TIA; John S. Martin, Apr. 4, 1956, TIA; Laird Goldsborough to Henry R. Luce, undated, ca. 1927, TIA; *Time,* Feb. 28, 1927, p. 4; *Time,* May 9, 1927, p. 4; *Time,* May 31, 1926, p. 2; *Time,* Feb. 7, 1927, p. 4; *Time,* May 2, 1927, p. 4; *Time,* Dec. 12, 1927, pp. 4, 6; *Time,* Dec. 13, 1926, p. 4; Robert T. Elson, *Time Inc.,* pp. 259–61; *Time Insider,* ca. 1989, p. 8, TIA; Henry R. Luce, Dec. 15, 1965, TIA.

Advertising: Robert L. Johnson, Mar. 5, 1956, TIA; O. D. Keep, Sept. 1, 1959, TIA; Henry R. Luce, Jan. 12, 1965, TIA; Mimi Martin, Feb. 3, 1958, TIA; *Time,* Apr. 20, 1925, front inside cover; *Time,* May 4, 1925, front inside cover; *Time,* May 25, 1925, front inside cover; *Time,* Sept. 7, 1925, p. 4; *Time,* Oct. 5, 1925, pp. 4, 25; *Time,* Nov. 30, 1925, pp. 19, 28–29; Henry R. Luce to Lila Luce, undated, ca. Dec. 1925, LT.

Luce's honorary degree: Robert Maynard Hutchins to Henry R. Luce, Mar. 25, 1926, May 14, 1926, LT; Lila Luce to Lila F. R. Hotz, undated, ca. Mar. 1926, LT; John S. Martin, *A Grab-Bag for My Grandsons,* "Beginning of *Time,*" p. 4, TIA; Thomas J. C. Martyn to Roy E. Larsen, May 18, 1971, TIA; Mimi Martin, Feb. 3, 1958, TIA; Niven Busch, "Biographical Notes—Briton Hadden," June 8, 1948, p. 6, TIA; Niven Busch, Mar. 11, 1965, TIA; W. A. Swanberg, *Luce and His Empire,* p. 66.

11. HOT STUFF
Hadden's dissatisfaction with Cleveland: Stuart Heminway, May 19, 1948, TIA; Daniel Longwell, June 30, 1939, TIA; Briton Hadden, "*Time* likes Cleveland," *Clevelander,* June 1926, Publicity files, 1926, TIA; Mimi Martin, Feb. 3, 1958, TIA; Mimi Martin, Mar. 20, 1958, TIA; Lila Tyng, June 13, 1967, TIA; Lila Tyng, Mar. 30, 1969, WAS; Katherine Abrams, June 22, 1948, TIA.

Regional feuds and rising popularity: *Time,* Sept. 6, 1926, p. 2; *Time,* Feb. 28, 1927, p. 2; *Time,* Mar. 14, 1927, pp. 2, 4; *Time,* Nov. 5, 1928, p. 4; Patricia Divver, "Notes on Lunch with Roy Larsen," June 28, 1939, TIA; Roy E. Larsen, Aug. 7, 1956, TIA; Roy E. Larsen to Briton Hadden, undated memorandum, Publicity files, 1926, TIA; Roy E. Larsen to Briton Hadden and Henry R. Luce, Oct. 4, 1927, TIA; *School and Society,* June 5, 1926, Publicity files, 1926, TIA; William Nichols to Briton Hadden, June 23, 1926, TIA; *Evening Gazette* of Cedar Rapids, Iowa, Aug. 5, 1926, Publicity files, 1926, TIA; *Auburn Citizen,* Aug. 13, 1926, Publicity files, 1926, TIA; *Word* *and Way,* undated press clipping, Publicity files, 1927, TIA; E. A. Solomon to *Time,* Jan. 15, 1927, Publicity files, 1927, TIA; Faith Willcox, Mar. 24, 1958, TIA; Henry R. Luce, Jan. 12, 1965, TIA; Time Inc. Annual Report, 1926, Jan. 1, 1927, TIA.

Advertising and circulation gains: Time Inc. Annual Report, 1926, Jan. 1, 1927, TIA; Time Inc. Annual Report, 1927, Jan. 1, 1928, TIA; Time Inc. Annual Report, 1928, Feb. 28, 1929, TIA; Roy E. Larsen to Briton Hadden, May 18, 1927, *Time* Publishing files, Jan.–Aug. 1927, TIA; Robert L. Johnson, June 9, 1948, TIA; Roy E. Larsen, 1927 circulation and promotion report, p. 30, Publishing files, 1927, TIA; Roy E. Larsen, Aug. 7, 1956, TIA; *Time,* Jan. 3, 1927.

Hadden as business manager: Henry R. Luce, Jan. 12, 1965, TIA; Katherine Abrams, June 9, 1962, TIA; Patricia Divver, "Notes on Lunch with Roy Larsen," June 28, 1939, TIA; *This Class-Ridden Democracy,* advertising promotion booklet, ca. 1927, TIA; Howard Black, Sept. 27, 1956, TIA; Paul Synnott, June 4, 1953, TIA; Time Inc. Annual Report, 1927, Jan. 1, 1928, TIA; Thomas H. Black, author's interview, June 20, 2003.

Tide: *Tide,* Apr. 1927, pp. 1–2; *Tide,* May 1927, p. 4; *Time,* Jan. 2, 1928, p. 29; *Tide,* June 1928, p. 9; *Tide,* Nov. 1928, p. 1; John S. Martin, Apr. 4, 1956, TIA; Elizabeth Robert to Roy E. Larsen, Apr. 11, 1927, TIA; Isabella Van Meter, Feb. 7, Apr. 24, 1956, TIA; "*Time* Editor Now Clerk," *Post-Standard,* Jan. 15, 1956; William L. White to Robert T. Elson, May 6, 1969, TIA; William L. White to Robert T. Elson, May 16, 1969, TIA; Nathan Miller, *New World Coming,* p. 152.

Luce as editor: Lila Tyng, June 13, 1967, TIA; Henry R. Luce, Jan. 12, 1965, TIA; John S. Martin, Sept. 29, 1965, TIA; Elizabeth Armstrong, Oct. 11, 1960, TIA; Myron Weiss, Mar. 13, 1956, TIA; Faith Willcox, Mar. 24, 1958, TIA; Manfred Gottfried, diary excerpts, July 1, 1927, Sept. 30, 1927, quoted in Manfred Gottfried, Mar. 7, 1955, TIA; *Time,* Mar. 22, 1926, p. 20; *Time,* Apr. 5, 1926; *Time,* Apr. 26, 1926, p. 15; *Time,* Oct. 18, 1926, p. 27; *Time,* May 30, 1927; *Time,* June 6, 1927.

Foreign News under Goldsborough: Henry R. Luce, Jan. 12, 1965, TIA; Laird Goldsborough to Henry R. Luce, Dec. 24, 1937, Dec. 1942, Dec. 29, 1948, Jan. 1950, TIA; Alan R. Jackson, July 20, Aug. 22, 1960, TIA; Elisabeth Luce Moore, Apr. 17, 1991, TIA; Ralph Ingersoll to Laird Goldsborough, Nov. 11, 1938, TIA; Mary Fraser to Robert T. Elson, Oct. 18, 1965, TIA; John S. Martin, Sept. 1965, TIA; *Time,* Sept. 21, 1925, p. 16; Henry R. Luce to *Time* writers and editors, Dec. 8, 1938, TIA; Time Inc. board of directors minutes, Apr. 22, 1941, Nov. 19, 1942, TIA; "Writer Killed in 9-Floor Plunge from Rockefeller Plaza Office," *New York Herald Tribune,* Feb. 15,

1950; *New York Times,* Feb. 15, 1950, p. 1; Robert T. Elson, *Time Inc.,* pp. 104, 258, 261–64, 322–23, 369–70; W. A. Swanberg, *Luce and His Empire,* pp. 75–78.

Luce received public notice: *Cincinnati Times-Star,* Jan. 1927, Publicity files, 1927, TIA; Lila Luce to Lila F. R. Hotz, undated, ca. Good Friday, 1926, LT; undated, ca. Jan. 27, 1926, LT; Henry R. Luce to Lila Luce, ca. Jan. 1926, undated, ca. 1927, LT; Mary Bancroft, Oct. 28, 1970, WAS; *A Tour Through Time Colony,* advertising promotion booklet, 1928, TIA; Henry R. Luce, Jan. 12, 1965, TIA.

Luce's vacation and the move to New York: Henry R. Luce, Jan. 12, 1965, TIA; Archibald MacLeish, July 26, 1968, WAS; Lila Tyng, Mar. 30, 1969, WAS; Briton Hadden, "A Proposal to Move from Cleveland to New York as Much of Time as Possible," July 15, 1927, HPD; Time Inc. board of directors minutes, June 18, 1927, July 1927, Sept. 16, 1927, TIA; Roy E. Larsen, Aug. 7, 1956, TIA; Roy E. Larsen, Aug. 28, 1956, TIA; W. A. Swanberg, *Luce and His Empire,* p. 67.

R. R. Donnelley & Sons: Henry R. Luce to Thomas E. Donnelley, Aug. 31, 1927, Sept. 17, 1927, TIA; R. R. Donnelley & Sons to Henry R. Luce, Sept. 16, 1927, TIA; "Concerning Production Requirements for *Time* in 1928," undated Time Inc. memorandum, ca. Sept. 14, 1927, TIA; Henry R. Luce, Jan. 12, 1965, TIA; *Bookman,* Oct. 1927, Publicity files, 1927, TIA.

Triumphant return: Time Inc. Annual Report, 1925, Jan. 2, 1926, TIA; Time Inc. Annual Report, 1926, Jan. 1, 1927, TIA; Time Inc. Annual Report, 1927, Jan. 1, 1928, TIA; *Do You Own a HORSE? Time* subscriber survey, Oct. 1928, TIA; Roy E. Larsen, Aug. 7, 1956, TIA; Roy E. Larsen, Aug. 28, 1956, TIA; Winsor French, June 26, 1956, TIA.

12. MAN OF THE YEAR

Time's popularity: "The Start's the Thing," *Time* advertisement, Agency Promotion files, 1928, TIA; Harold Lateiner, June 14, 1939, TIA; Henrietta Force, Apr. 15, 1958, TIA; Manfred Gottfried, diary entry, Sept. 30, 1927, quoted in Manfred Gottfried, Mar. 7, 1955, TIA; New York offices file, 1937 and before, TIA; *Time,* Oct. 31, 1927, p. 4; *Time,* Nov. 14, 1927, p. 6; *Time,* Dec. 26, 1927, p. 20; *New York Herald Tribune,* June 6, 1927, *Time* Publicity files, 1927, TIA; Henry R. Luce to Lila Luce, undated letter, ca. 1928, LT; O. D. Keep, Aug. 27, 1959, TIA.

Office atmosphere: Harold Lateiner, Dec. 6, 1960, TIA; Wells Root, Mar. 10, 1964, TIA; John O'Hara, Sept. 16, 1964, TIA; Dorothea Spieth, Mar. 30, 1955, TIA; Wilder Hobson, quoted in A. J. Liebling, "*Time* Magazine Notes," undated, ca.

1949, AJL; Winsor French to Katherine Halle, quoted in Katherine Halle to Noel F. Busch, June 20, 1948, TIA; Briton Hadden, "Memo to all Writers, all Researchers and Typists," Aug. 18, 1927, TIA; "Noel F. Busch," corporate biography, June 10, 1947, TIA; Noel F. Busch, *Life with Luce*, p. 17, NAB; Beatrix Miller, author's interview, July 11, 2003; *Esquire*, Dec. 1944, Noel Busch Pictures and Biography file, TIA; *Time*, May 9, 1927, p. 3; *Time*, Sept. 12, 1927, p. 2; *Time*, Jan. 9, 1928, p. 4; Geoffrey Wolff, *The Art of Burning Bridges*, pp. 89–91, 94–95.

New departments and features: *Time*, Mar. 17, 1924, p. 16; *Time*, Mar. 24, 1924, p. 10; *Time*, Aug. 1, 1927, p. 14; *Time*, Aug. 15, 1927, pp. 20–23; *Time*, Sept. 12, 1927, p. 22; *Time*, Nov. 14, 1927, p. 24; *Time*, Nov. 21, 1927, pp. 14, 16, 32; *Time*, Nov. 28, 1927, p. 2; *Time*, Dec. 12, 1927, pp. 6, 11–15; *Time*, Mar. 17, 1967, p. 52; Andrew Heiskell, "How They Invented *People*," *Columbia Journalism Review*, Nov.–Dec., 1998.

Conflicts over Hadden's cracks: Roy E. Larsen to Briton Hadden, Sept. 1, 1927, Nov. 14, 1927, Dec. 3, 1927, Dec. 23, 1927, TIA; Briton Hadden to Roy E. Larsen, written by hand on Roy E. Larsen to Briton Hadden, Sept. 21, 1927, Oct. 6, 1927, TIA; Henry R. Luce to Lila Luce, undated letters, ca. 1927, TIA; Noel F. Busch, *Life with Luce*, p. 8, NAB; Roy E. Larsen, Aug. 7, 1956, TIA; *Time*, May 2, 1927, p. 4; *Time*, June 20, 1927, p. 24; *Time*, Aug. 15, 1927, p. 2; *Time*, Aug. 22, 1927, p. 2; *Time*, Sept. 5, 1927, p. 2; *Time*, Sept. 19, 1927, p. 34; *Time*, Sept. 26, 1927, p. 28; *Time*, Oct. 3, 1927, p. 4; *Time*, Oct. 10, 1927, p. 4.

Circulation and advertising growth: Time Inc. Annual Report, 1927, Jan. 1, 1928, TIA; Time Inc. Annual Report, 1928, Feb. 28, 1929, TIA; Time Inc. Annual Report, 1929, Mar. 13, 1930, TIA; Time Inc. budget for 1928, p. 3, TIA; Robert T. Elson, *Time Inc.*, p. 117.

Man of the Year: Mary Fraser to Robert T. Elson, Oct. 18, 1965, TIA; *Time*, May 30, 1927, p. 26; *Time*, June 6, 1927, p. 12; *Time*, June 20, 1927, p. 25; *Time*, June 27, 1927, p. 24; *Time*, Oct. 31, 1927, pp. 4, 19; *Time*, Jan. 2, 1928, pp. 5, 10, 14–15, 20, 30; "The First Man of the Year," *Time* Man of the Year file, TIA; A. Scott Berg, *Lindbergh*, pp. 3–9, 158; Frederick S. Voss, *Man of the Year*, pp. 2–3, 6–7.

13. GENIUSES

New production system: *Chicago Daily News*, Jan. 13, 1928, Publicity files, 1928, TIA; *Printers' Ink*, Jan. 19, 1928, *Chicago Commerce*, Jan. 28, 1928, Publicity files, 1928, TIA; Robert Draper, May 1948, TIA; Alice Weigel, May 21, 1958, TIA; Henry R. Luce, Jan. 12, 1965, TIA; *Time*, Sept. 17, 1928, p. 3.

Luce's changes to *Time*: Noel F. Busch, *Life with Luce,* two undated drafts, NAB; *Time,* June 14, 1926, p. 10; *Time,* Dec. 26, 1927, p. 21; *Time,* Jan. 2, 1928; *Time,* Jan. 9, 1928, pp. 3–4; *Time,* Jan. 16, 1928; *Time,* Jan. 23, 1928, p. 21; *Time,* Jan. 30, 1928, pp. 4–5, 18, 20; *Time,* Feb. 6, 1928, p. 16; *Time,* Apr. 2, 1928, pp. 2, 34, 36; *Time,* Nov. 26, 1928, p. 20; *Time,* Dec. 3, 1928, p. 3; *Time,* Dec. 10, 1928, p. 18; Robert T. Elson, speech before a *Life* advertising convention, June 4, 1967, TIA; Henry R. Luce to Briton Hadden, Robert L. Johnson, and Roy E. Larsen, July 20, 1928, TIA; Roy E. Larsen to John S. Martin, June 1, 1928, TIA; Alan Jackson, July 20, 1960, Aug. 22, 1960, TIA; Elizabeth Armstrong, Oct. 11, 1960, TIA; John S. Martin, Apr. 4, 1956, TIA; John S. Martin, Sept. 29, 1965, TIA; Ralph Ingersoll, Mar. 28, 1956, TIA; Niven Busch to Robert T. Elson, Apr. 6, 1965, TIA; "What I Am Reading—and Why," *The World's Work,* undated clipping, Publicity files, 1928, TIA; Archibald MacLeish, Mar. 17, 1965, TIA.

Smith and Hoover: Manfred Gottfried, Aug. 23, 1961, TIA; Manfred Gottfried, undated interview, ca. 1950, JM; Henry R. Luce, Jan. 12, 1965, TIA; Lila Tyng, June 13, 1967, TIA; Lila Tyng, Sept. 8, 1969, WAS; Emmavail Severinghaus, July 17, 1969, WAS; Henry R. Luce, handwritten notes on 1928 candidates, ca. 1928, LT; Henry R. Luce, $100 certificate from the Alfred E. Smith campaign, Oct. 29, 1928, LT; G. W. Johnstone, manager of NBC's press relations department, undated press release, Publicity files, 1928, TIA; John S. Martin to Roy E. Larsen, July 6, 1928, TIA; W. W. Commons to Roy E. Larsen, Jan. 11, 1929, TIA; *Rochester Times-Union,* Mar. 17, 1928, Publicity files, 1928, TIA; *Rochester Times-Union,* Mar. 22, 1928, Publicity files, 1928, TIA; *Democrat & Chronicle,* Mar. 29, 1928, Publicity files, 1928, TIA; *New York Evening Post,* Sept. 19, 1928, Publicity files, 1928, TIA; *Time,* Mar. 26, 1928, pp. 7–9; *Time,* Apr. 30, 1928, pp. 9–11; *Time,* June 25, 1928, p. 11; *Time,* July 2, 1928, p. 2; *Time,* July 9, 1928, pp. 9–11; *Time,* Oct. 29, 1928, p. 2; *Time,* Nov. 5, 1928, cover, pp. 7–9, 13; *Time,* Nov. 12, 1928, pp. 23–25; Robert A. Slayton, *Empire Statesman,* pp. ix–xv, 310–17.

***Time*'s growth and popularity:** Time Inc. Annual Report, 1928, Feb. 28, 1929, TIA; Henry R. Luce to Lila Luce, ca. 1928, July 6, 1928, TIA; "Preface to the 1929 Budget," undated, ca. late 1928, TIA; *Time,* Sept. 3, 1928; *Time,* Sept. 24, 1928; *Time,* Oct. 1, 1928; *Time,* Oct. 15, 1928; *Time,* Oct. 29, 1928; *Time,* Nov. 12, 1928; *Time,* Nov. 19, 1928; *Time,* Dec. 10, 1928; *Saturday Evening Post,* undated clipping, p. 81, Publicity files, 1928, TIA; *Cincinnati Enquirer,* Feb. 3, 1928, Publicity files, 1928, TIA; *Colorado Lookout,* June 9, 1928, p. 1; *Town Talk,* July 18, 1928, cover; Mimi Martin, Feb. 3, 1958, TIA; John O'Hara, quoted in A. J. Liebling, undated notes, ca. 1949, AJL; Lewis G. Adams, Dec. 28, 1955, TIA.

14. OLIVER TWISTING

Hadden's drinking: Sheldon Luce, July 17, 1969, WAS; Lila Tyng, Mar. 30, 1969, WAS; Celia Sugarman, Jan. 23, 1969, WAS; P. I. Prentice, Sept. 17, 1968, WAS; Henry Thorne, Nov. 30, 1948, TIA; Mimi Martin, Feb. 3, 1958, TIA; Briton Hadden, "He is not drunk," cartoon panel, Briton Hadden Cartoons file, TIA; Roy E. Larsen to Thomas J. C. Martyn, Sept. 25, 1967, TIA; W. Rice Brewster, May 14, 1948, TIA; Henry R. Luce, Jan. 12, 1965, TIA; Lewis G. Adams, Dec. 28, 1955, TIA; Noel F. Busch, *Life with Luce,* pt. 3, p. 3, NAB; Niven Busch, "Biographical Notes—Briton Hadden," June 8, 1948, pp. 7–8, TIA; Winsor French, June 26, 1956, TIA; Christopher Larsen, author's interview, Oct. 4, 2002.

Hadden's restlessness: Niven Busch, "Biographical Notes—Briton Hadden," June 8, 1948, pp. 8–9, TIA; John M. Hincks, Apr. 30, 1948, TIA; Celia Sugarman to Alex Groner, May 3, 1955, TIA; Elisabeth Luce Moore, Mar. 4, 1965, TIA; Robert L. Johnson, Mar. 5, 1956, TIA; Thornton Wilder to James A. Linen III, May 11, 1949, TIA; Thomas H. Black, author's interview, June 20, 2003; Winslow Duke, author's interview, Feb. 14, 2003.

Tide: John S. Martin, Apr. 4, 1956, TIA; Elizabeth Robert, Feb. 13, 1956, TIA; *Tide,* Jan. 1928–Jan. 1929, esp. Apr. 1928, pp. 13–14; *Tide,* Feb. 1928, pp. 4–5; Mimi Martin, Feb. 3, 1958, TIA; Robert L. Johnson, Mar. 5, 1956, TIA; Roy E. Larsen, Aug. 28, 1956, TIA; Roy E. Larsen, Oct. 29, 1956, TIA; Howard Black, June 20, 1956, TIA; O. D. Keep, Aug. 27, 1959, TIA; George Sadler, Feb. 28, 1956, TIA.

Hadden's ideas for expansion: *Do You Own A HORSE? Time* subscriber survey, Oct. 1928, TIA; Briton Hadden, notebook, "Expansion," BH; Roy E. Larsen, Aug. 28, 1956, TIA; Celia Sugarman to Alex Groner, May 3, 1955, TIA; Henry R. Luce, Jan. 12, 1965, TIA; E. Robin Little, Jan. 16, 1953, TIA; John S. Martin, Apr. 4, 1956, TIA; John S. Martin, Sept. 1965, TIA; Robert L. Johnson, Mar. 5, 1956, TIA; Noel F. Busch, *Life with Luce,* pt. 12, p. 30, TIA; Noel F. Busch, *Life with Luce,* untitled and undated manuscript draft segment, ca. 1970s, NAB; E. Robin Little to Briton Hadden, undated note on *Tone,* proposed fashion magazine, Publishing files, 1927, TIA; Katherine Halle, Nov. 14, 1961, TIA; Lila Tyng to W. A. Swanberg, Jan. 14, 1972, WAS.

Newscasting and *Newsacting:* Celia Sugarman to Alex Groner, May 3, 1955, TIA; Roy E. Larsen, Aug. 7, 1956, TIA; Roy E. Larsen, Aug. 28, 1956, TIA; *Tide,* Oct. 1928; *Time,* Oct. 8, 1928, p. 33; Time Inc. Annual Report, 1928, Feb. 28, 1929, TIA; "Bitten by Ducks," *Editor & Publisher,* Nov. 3, 1928, Publicity files, 1928, TIA; "*Time* Publisher Protests," *Editor & Publisher,* Nov. 17, 1928, Publicity files, 1928, TIA; Marlen Pew, "Shop Talk at Thirty," *Editor & Publisher,* ca. Nov. 1928, p. 52, Publicity files, 1928, TIA; "Genesis of M.O.T.," Broadcasting History files, 1928–29, TIA.

***Fortune*:** Henry R. Luce, untitled notes on Hotel Astoria stationery, ca. 1928, TIA; Henry R. Luce to Henry P. Davison Jr., "Announcing Fortune," Oct. 21, 1929, HPD; Henry R. Luce, speech before the Ad Men's Club of Rochester, New York, Jan. 1929, TIA; Henry R. Luce, "The American Tycoon," Mar. 22, 1929, TIA; Daniel Longwell, Aug. 18, 1957, TIA; Lila Tyng, June 13, 1967, TIA; O. D. Keep, Sept. 1, 1959, TIA; Henry R. Luce, Jan. 12, 1965, TIA; Roy E. Larsen, Aug. 28, 1956, TIA; Roy E. Larsen, July 13, 1965, TIA; John S. Martin, Apr. 4, 1956, TIA; Charles L. Stillman, June 14, 1956, TIA; Briton Hadden, notebook, "Expansion," BH; Henry R. Luce, "Special Report to the Board of Directors," Feb. 8, 1929, TIA; Florence Horn, *"Fortune,"* undated reminiscences, ca. June 1939, TIA; Florence Horn, Oct. 4, 1961, TIA; Mary Fraser to Patricia Divver, June 16, 1939, TIA.

Hadden's absences and ill health: E. Robin Little, Jan. 16, 1953, TIA; Niven Busch, "Biographical Notes—Briton Hadden," June 8, 1948, pp. 2–3, TIA; Noel F. Busch, *Life with Luce,* p. 24, NAB.

Move to the Bartholomew: Mary Fraser, June 16, 1939, TIA; E. Robin Little, Jan. 16, 1953, TIA; W. Rice Brewster to Lilian Rixey, May 21, 1948, TIA; Mimi Martin, Aug. 5, 1948, TIA; John E. Woolley, June 4, 1948, TIA; Celia Sugarman to Alex Groner, May 3, 1955, TIA; Isabella Van Meter, Feb. 7, Apr. 24, 1956, TIA; Isabella Van Meter to Eric Hodgins, June 14, [1939], TIA; Henry R. Luce, Jan. 12, 1965, TIA; George Frazier, *It's About Time,* p. 106, GF; *New York Evening Graphic,* Oct. 22, 1928, Publicity files, 1928, TIA.

15. THE FINAL FIGHT

Hadden's illness: Katherine Abrams, June 22, 1948, TIA; Henry R. Luce, Jan. 12, 1965, TIA; Mimi Martin, Aug. 5, 1948, TIA; Mimi Martin, Feb. 3, 1958, TIA; F. Darius Benham, June 3, 1948, TIA; Oswald Jones, Aug. 9, 1948, TIA; George Frazier, prospectus for a book about *Time,* p. vii, GF.

Hadden in the hospital: Lucy Wolinski, undated interview, ca. 1950, JM; Henry R. Luce to Daniel R. Winter, Jan. 19, 1929, Briton Hadden Illness and Death file, TIA; Time Inc. board of directors minutes, Jan. 21, 1929, TIA; Katherine Halle, Nov. 14, 1961, TIA; Harold Lateiner, June 6, 1939, TIA; Elizabeth Robert, Feb. 13, 1956, TIA; Coralee McInerney, author's interview, Sept. 6, 2003.

Luce's visits: Henry R. Luce, Jan. 12, 1965, TIA; John S. Martin, Apr. 4, 1956, TIA; Lucy Wolinski, undated interview, ca. 1950, JM; Mimi Martin, Feb. 3, 1958, TIA; James Munves, author's interview, Jan. 13, 2005; Ralph Ingersoll, *High Time,* "Britton [*sic*] Hadden, in Memoriam," vol. 2, ch. 3, May 1962, p. 36, RI.

Hadden's stock and will: Henry R. Luce, Jan. 12, 1965, HRL; Lucy Wolinksi, undated interview, ca. 1950, JM; Briton Hadden, Last Will and Testament, Jan. 28, 1929, SCNY; John Barkham, June 20, 1969, WAS; Ralph Ingersoll, *High Time,* "Britton [*sic*] Hadden, in Memoriam," vol. 2, ch. 3, May 1962, p. 36, RI.

Hadden's treatment and transfusions: Oswald Jones, Aug. 9, 1948, TIA; Hugh H. Young, J. H. Hill, and W. W. Scott, "The Treatment of Infections and Infectious Diseases with Mercurochrome-220 Soluble," *Archives of Surgery,* May 1925, pp. 829–55; James S. Simmons, "The Intravenous Use of Acriviolet and of Mercurochrome in Bacterial Infections," *Journal of Infectious Diseases,* vol. 39, 1926, pp. 273–85; John S. Martin, "Bulletin on Mr. Hadden," Jan. 30, 1929, Briton Hadden Illness and Death file, TIA; Howard Black, June 20, 1956, TIA; Howard Black, Mar. 2, 1967, TIA; Thomas M. Cleland, Sept. 2, 1960, TIA; Henry R. Luce, Jan. 12, 1965, TIA.

Hadden's last days: Harold Lateiner, June 14, 1939, TIA; [John S. Martin], *A Thorough-Going Round of Schnitzel-Banck,* Feb. 18, 1929, Briton Hadden Cartoons file, TIA; Henry R. Luce, "A Bulletin on Mr. Hadden," Feb. 5, 1929, Briton Hadden Illness and Death file, TIA; Henry R. Luce to Henry P. Davison Jr., Feb. 7, 1929, HPD; Henry R. Luce, "Special Report to the Board of Directors," Feb. 8, 1929, HPD; Lila Luce to Henry R. Luce, undated, ca. Feb. 1929, LT; Lucy Wolinksi, undated interview, ca. 1950, JM; Oswald Jones, Aug. 9, 1948, TIA; Manfred Gottfried, diary excerpt, Feb. 26, 1929, quoted in Manfred Gottfried, Mar. 7, 1955, TIA; Roy E. Larsen to Nicholas L. Wallace, Feb. 27, 1929, Briton Hadden Illness and Death file, TIA.

Hadden's death: Manfred Gottfried diary excerpt, Feb. 27, 1929, quoted in Manfred Gottfried, Mar. 7, 1955, TIA; Briton Hadden Death Condolences file, TIA; Dorothea Spieth, Mar. 30, 1955, TIA; Irma Kuté, notes on a telegram from William Lyon Phelps to Henry R. Luce, ca. Feb. 28, 1929, TIA; "A Death Too Early," *New York Times,* Feb. 28, 1929; George M. Murray to Robert L. Johnson, Feb. 28, 1929, TIA; Henry Emerson Tuttle to Henry R. Luce, Feb. 28, 1929, TIA; *Time,* Mar. 11, 1929, p. 64; *Chicago Journal of Commerce,* Mar. 14, 1929, Briton Hadden obituaries file, TIA.

Hadden's funeral service: Henry R. Luce to Seymour H. Knox, Mar. 1, 1929, TIA; unidentified press clipping, Mar. 1, 1929, Briton Hadden Miscellaneous file, TIA;

John O'Hara, quoted in A. J. Liebling, "*Time* Magazine Notes," undated, ca. 1949, AJL; Mimi Martin, Feb. 3, 1958, TIA; Green-Wood Cemetery, Section 163, Lot 15791, Brooklyn, New York.

Reaction to Hadden's death: C. D. Trowbridge to Henry R. Luce, Feb. 27, 1929, TIA; E. V. Hale to Henry R. Luce, Feb. 28, 1929, TIA; Henry R. Luce to F. P. Heffelfinger, Mar. 2, 1929, TIA; Henry R. Luce to T. E. Donnelley, Mar. 2, 1929, TIA; Henry R. Luce to Annie B. Jennings, Mar. 4, 1929, TIA; Henry R. Luce to Langhorne Gibson, Mar. 5, 1929, TIA; Robert W. Griggs to Henry R. Luce, Mar. 11, 1929, TIA; F. P. Heffelfinger to John M. Hincks, Mar. 18, 1929, TIA; John W. Hincks, author's interview, Nov. 22, 2005; also see: Briton Hadden Death Condolences file, TIA.

Speculation about Hadden's death: W. Rice Brewster, May 14, 1948, TIA; Henry R. Luce, Jan. 12, 1965, TIA; Robert Blum, Apr. 15, 1965, TIA; Mimi Martin, Feb. 3, 1958, TIA; Oswald Jones, Aug. 9, 1948, TIA; Dr. Scott Podolsky, author's interview, Oct. 25, 2005; Dr. Selim Suner, author's interview, Oct. 28, 2005; Dr. Richard S. Hotchkiss, author's interview, Oct. 25, 2005; Bernarr Macfadden, "Body Loving," *New York Evening Graphic,* Sept. 26, 1929, Publicity files, 1929, TIA.

16. BURIAL

Luce's claim that he and Hadden traded jobs "year by year": Henry R. Luce to the managing editor of the *Yale Daily News,* Feb. 27, 1929, TIA; *Time,* Feb. 28, 1938, p. 38; "Henry R. Luce—Editor-in-Chief," Dec. 15, 1947, TIA; "Henry R. Luce, Editor-in-Chief of all Time Inc. Publications," Feb. 1953, TIA; Time Inc. Annual Report, 1949, TIA; Henry R. Luce, personal biography, in C. Stuart Heminway, ed., *Twenty Years with Nineteen-Twenty*; Henry Luce III, July 9, 1969, WAS.

***Time*'s coverage of Hadden's death:** *Time,* Mar. 11, 1929, pp. 9, 63–64; Henry R. Luce, Jan. 11, 1965, TIA; *Shenandoah* coverage: *Time,* Sept. 14, 1925, cover, pp. 31–32; Elizabeth Pool to Roy E. Larsen, May 10, 1932, TIA.

Sale of Hadden's stock: Henry R. Luce to Henry P. Davison Jr., Apr. 23, 1929, TIA; Honorable John P. O'Brien, "Decree Admitting Will to Probate," Briton Hadden estate files, Mar. 12, 1929, SCNY; Henry R. Luce to Elizabeth R. Luce, Apr. 1929, HRL; Time Inc. board of directors minutes, May 17, 1929, May 27, 1929, TIA; Henry R. Luce to Henry W. Luce and Elizabeth R. Luce, undated letter, ca. Sept. 1929, HRL; Henry R. Luce, Jan. 12, 1965, TIA; Lila Tyng, June 13, 1967, TIA; Manfred Gottfried, Aug. 29, 1961, TIA; Thomas J. C. Martyn to Henry R. Luce, Mar. 15, 1966, TIA; Thomas J. C. Martyn, Sept. 11, 1967, TIA; Charles L. Stillman, July 26, 1965, TIA; Robert T. Elson to James A. Linen III, Apr. 19, 1966, TIA; "Time

Inc. Stock, Hadden Estate and Disposition of the Hadden Stock at the time of his death, based on analysis of the Stock Books by Stephen Finnerty, Comptroller's Dept.," Nov. 15, 1967, TIA; Briton Hadden Estate file, TIA.

Aftermath of the sale: Charles L. Stillman, July 26, 1965, TIA; A. J. Liebling, "*Time* Magazine Notes, Briton Hadden's Estate," undated, ca. 1949, AJL; "Accounting of Dermod Ives and Irving Trust Company as Executors of the Estate of Elizabeth Busch Pool," Apr. 5, 1968, SCNY; Dermod Ives and Irving Trust Company, "Affidavit of Services," June 9, 1968, SCNY; Dermod Ives and Irving Trust Company, "Affidavit of Services," Sept. 27, 1968, SCNY; "Luce Foundation gets Time Stock," *New York Times,* Mar. 11, 1967; Robert T. Elson, *Time Inc.,* p. 123.

Employees who purchased Hadden's shares: Henry R. Luce to Henry P. Davison Jr., Sept. 23, 1929, HPD; A. J. Liebling, "*Time* Magazine Notes, Briton Hadden's Estate," undated, ca. 1949, AJL; Briton Hadden Estate file, TIA; Robert T. Elson to James A. Linen III, Apr. 19, 1966, TIA; Robert T. Elson, *Time Inc.,* pp. 123–25.

Fortune, March of Time, Life: Garland Smith, "The Young Man Behind *Time,*" *Brooklyn Daily Eagle,* Oct. 6, 1929, Publicity files, 1929, TIA; George Frazier, *It's About Time,* p. 106, GF; Ralph Ingersoll, *High Time,* "How Come PM? Second Typescript," undated, pp. 15–17, RI; Roy E. Larsen, July 3, 1956, TIA; Roy E. Larsen, Aug. 28, 1956, TIA; Roy E. Larsen, July 22, 1957, TIA; "We Nominate for the Hall of Fame," *Vanity Fair,* Aug. 1930; W. A. Swanberg, *Luce and His Empire,* p. 84; Sylvia Jukes Morris, *Rage for Fame,* pp. 241–42; Peter Paul Luce, author's interview, May 27, 2003; Robert T. Elson, *Time Inc.,* pp. 133–298.

Luce's personality: Mary Fraser, June 15, 1945, TIA; Wilder Hobson, quoted in A. J. Liebling, "*Time* Magazine Notes," undated, ca. 1949, AJL; Howard Black, June 20, 1956, TIA; Ralph Ingersoll, *High Time,* "Britton [*sic*] Hadden, in Memoriam," May 1962, p. 38, RI; Alfred Kazin, *New York Jew,* pp. 54–56.

Briton Hadden Memorial: "A Building for the *Yale Daily News* in Memory of Briton Hadden, '20," Apr. 1930, TIA; Alex Groner to Allen Grover, "Financing of Briton Hadden Memorial," July 20, 1955, TIA; Thomas W. Farnam to Henry R. Luce, June 30, 1931, TIA; "Briton Hadden's Career Lauded by John S. Martin," *Yale Daily News,* Apr. 28, 1932, p. 1; John S. Martin, "Briton Hadden as Editor and Co-Founder of *Time,*" Apr. 27, 1932, TIA; Roy E. Larsen to Robert Draper, May 31, 1932, TIA; Henry R. Luce, Jan. 11, 1965, TIA; Lewis G. Adams, Dec. 28, 1955, TIA; *Time,* May 9, 1932, pp. 28, 30; Elizabeth Pool to Roy E. Larsen, May 5, 1932, TIA.

Rumors that Hadden was *Time*'s genius: *Washington Post,* Feb. 27, 1938, p.B8; Clare Boothe Luce, Feb. 21, 1969, WAS.

Luce would not bring up Hadden: Hugh Sidey, author's interview, Mar. 23, 2004; Otto Fuerbringer, author's interview, June 7, 2003; Gloria Mariano, author's interview, July 20, 2003; Peter Paul Luce, author's interview, May 27, 2003; Henry Luce III, author's interview, Dec. 27, 2001; Culbreth Sudler, Mar. 9, 1965, TIA; Henry R. Luce to Stuart Heminway, Jan. 22, 1940, HRLLOC; C. Stuart Heminway, ed., *Twenty Years with Nineteen-Twenty,* YMA.

Luce's speeches: Henry R. Luce, "Can Business Be Patriotic?" Apr. 3, 1939, TIA; Henry R. Luce, untitled speech, Nov. 10, 1937, TIA; Henry R. Luce, "Putting Our House in Order," Apr. 22, 1963, TIA; Henry R. Luce, untitled speech, Apr. 20, 1939, TIA; Henry R. Luce, untitled speech, Mar. 12, 1941, TIA; Henry R. Luce, "China: To the Mountains," June 6, 1941, TIA; Henry R. Luce, untitled speech, Sept. 29, 1949, TIA; Henry R. Luce, untitled speech, Mar. 11, 1943, TIA; Henry R. Luce, untitled speech, May 27, 1939, TIA; Henry R. Luce, untitled speech, May 15, 1961, TIA; Henry R. Luce, untitled speech, Mar. 4, 1963, TIA.

Luce reminisced in his speeches: Henry R. Luce, rough notes on an untitled speech, Nov. 17, 1932, TIA; Henry R. Luce, untitled speech, Apr. 21, 1938, TIA; Henry R. Luce, untitled speech, Apr. 20, 1939, TIA; Henry R. Luce, untitled speech, Mar. 12, 1941, TIA; Henry R. Luce, untitled speech, Oct. 10, 1941, TIA; Henry R. Luce, speech at *Time*'s twentieth-anniversary dinner, Mar. 11, 1943, TIA; Henry R. Luce, "The World's Need for the Church," Dec. 10, 1944, TIA; Henry R. Luce, "The Christianity of the Missionary," Sept. 10, 1946, TIA; Henry R. Luce, speech before the Montclair Yale Club, Dec. 4, 1947, TIA; Henry R. Luce, "Christian Responsibility," Nov. 16, 1948, TIA; Henry R. Luce, untitled speech, May 4, 1950, TIA; Henry R. Luce, untitled speech, Oct. 8, 1952, TIA; Henry R. Luce, speech at a *Time* editorial dinner, Nov. 14, 1952, TIA; Henry R. Luce, untitled speech at the *Yale Daily News* eightieth–anniversary party, Apr. 16, 1958, TIA; Henry R. Luce, speech at the University of Miami Fifth Annual Photojournalism Conference, Apr. 26, 1961, TIA; Henry R. Luce, speech before the Second Annual *Life* Managing Editor's Dinner, June 13, 1963, TIA; Henry R. Luce, commencement address at Hotchkiss, June 13, 1964, TIA; Henry R. Luce, speech before a *Sports Illustrated* sales convention, May 16, 1965, TIA.

Speeches mentioning Hadden: Henry R. Luce, speech at *Time*'s twentieth-anniversary dinner, Mar. 11, 1943, TIA; Henry R. Luce, speech before a group of Time Inc. executives at the Union Club, Nov. 14, 1952; Henry R. Luce, "Management in an Editorial Enterprise, Lecture II: Purpose and Profit," May 1, 1963, TIA; Henry R. Luce, "Magazines and the Great Society," Sept. 21, 1965, TIA.

1942 *Yale Daily News* **banquet:** Henry R. Luce, address at *Yale Daily News* dinner, Feb. 16, 1942, TIA; *Yale Daily News*, Feb. 17, 1942, p. 3; Stirling Tomkins Jr., author's interview, Jan. 11, 2006.

Luce's talk on the *March of Time*: Show transcript, *March of Time*, July 9, 1942, TIA; Henry R. Luce, untitled drafts of a talk to be delivered on the *March of Time*, July 8–9, 1942, TIA.

Time's **twentieth-anniversary dinner:** Henry R. Luce, speech at *Time*'s twentieth-anniversary dinner, Mar. 11, 1943, TIA.

Hadden's fading legacy: London *Observer*, May 19, 1963, Publicity files, 1963, TIA; *Time*, Mar. 8, 1948, pp. 55–66; Henry R. Luce to Max Ways, Feb. 15, 1948, TIA; *Business Week*, Mar. 6, 1948, twenty-fifth anniversary files, TIA; David Ahern to James A. Linen III, Nov. 12, 1952, TIA; David Dolben, author's interview, Mar. 9, 2004; Bob Aden, author's interview, Apr. 10, 2003; John M. Hincks, Apr. 30, 1948, TIA; Elizabeth Pool to P. I. Prentice, Mar. 14, 1940, TIA.

Proposal for a book about Hadden: Stuart Heminway to Henry R. Luce, Feb. 24, 1948, TIA; Stuart Heminway, notes for a book about Briton Hadden, undated, TIA; Henry R. Luce to Stuart Heminway, Mar. 3, 1948, TIA; John G. Rohrbach to Henry R. Luce, Nov. 19, 1947, HRLLOC; Henry R. Luce to John G. Rohrbach, Nov. 24, 1947, HRLLOC; Corinne Thrasher to John G. Rohrbach, Feb. 3, 1948, Feb. 16, 1948, HRLLOC; John G. Rohrbach to Corinne Thrasher, Feb. 10, 1948, HRLLOC; Corinne Thrasher to Henry R. Luce, undated memorandum, ca. Feb. 10, 1948, HRLLOC; Dorothea Philp to John G. Rohrbach, Mar. 3, 1948, HRLLOC; John G. Rohrbach, author's interview, Jan. 12, 2006.

Noel F. Busch's career: Wilder Hobson, quoted in A. J. Liebling, "*Time* Magazine Notes," undated, ca. 1949, AJL; "Milestones," *F.Y.I.*, Oct. 1, 1983, TIA; "Which one is the *Life* editor?" *Life* advertisement, Feb. 1944; Noel F. Busch, *Life with Luce*, pt. 7, pp. 18a, 19, 21, 23, 28, NAB; Noel F. Busch, untitled manuscript on Clare Boothe Luce, NAB; Orville Prescott, "Books of the Times," *New York Times*, Mar. 5, 1948; Pearl Kroll, Apr. 26, 1963, May 10, 1963, TIA; Roy E. Larsen to Henry R. Luce, "Re: Noel Busch," Jan. 17, 1946, TIA; John Shaw Billings to Henry R. Luce, "Busch," confidential memorandum, Feb. 4, 1948, TIA; Henry R. Luce to John Shaw Billings, "In re Busch," Feb. 11, 1948, TIA.

Noel F. Busch's biography of Hadden: Allen Grover to Henry R. Luce, May 20, 1952, TIA; Henry Luce III, author's interview, Dec. 27, 2001; Noel Fairchild Busch papers, NOB; Noel Fairchild Busch manuscripts and notes, NAB; Robert T. Elson to Henry R. Luce, Dec. 18, 1964, TIA; Noel F. Busch, Jan. 22, 1969, WAS; Noel F. Busch, *Briton Hadden,* pp. 29–40, 43, 53, 99, 102, 168–69, 189–90, 195–98, 227–28; John M. Hincks to Henry R. Luce, Nov. 17, 1948, TIA; Calvin Fixx, "Re: Noel Busch," Mar. 3, 1949, TIA; Noel F. Busch to Henry R. Luce, Oct. 12, 1948, TIA; Rosalind Constable to Mary Fraser, "Subject: Briton Hadden," Nov. 12, 1948, TIA; Calvin Fixx to Noel F. Busch, Nov. 23, 1948, TIA; Maurice T. Moore to Roy E. Larsen, Jan. 24, 1949, TIA; Calvin Fixx to Roy E. Larsen, Mar. 4, 1949, TIA.

Responses of readers: [Lilian Rixey], memorandum on a conversation with Elizabeth Pool, Mar. 2, 1949, TIA; John G. Rohrbach, author's interview, Jan. 12, 2006; Jerry Busch, author's interview, May 22, 2003; Terry Busch, author's interview, June 7, 2003.

The book's publication and its aftermath: Roger W. Straus Jr. to Noel F. Busch, Dec. 16, 1948, TIA; Roy E. Larsen to Henry R. Luce, July 18, 1949, TIA; Henry R. Luce to Niven Busch, July 19, 1949, TIA; Calvin Fixx to Roy E. Larsen, Mar. 4, 1949, TIA; George Frazier, *It's About Time,* p. 27, GF; James T. Babb to Noel F. Busch, Nov. 11, 1948, TIA; Lilian Rixey to James T. Babb, Nov. 19, 1948, TIA.

A. J. Liebling: John Sousa III to Bob Joose, Sept. 28, 1949, TIA; James Munves to Judith Lowry, Jan. 21, 1988, AJL; James Munves, author's interview, Jan. 13, 2005; Walter Winchell, *New York Daily Mirror,* Mar. 20, 1959; A. J. Liebling to Bill Welling, Nov. 27, 1949, AJL; Larry Hoover to Bernard Barnes, May 4, 1951, TIA.

George Frazier: George Frazier to Roy E. Larsen, undated letter, ca. 1950, TIA; John Sousa III to James A. Linen III, confidential memorandum, Mar. 14, 1950, TIA; James Munves, author's interview, Jan. 13, 2005; George Frazier to W. A. Swanberg, May 16, 1970, WAS; "George Frazier, Writer, 63, Dies," *New York Times,* June 15, 1974; Charles Fountain, *Another Man's Poison,* pp. 1–6, 13–34, 101, 131–36, 184, 238, 328.

James Munves: John Sousa III to Bernard Barnes, Oct. 3, 1949, TIA; James Munves, author's interview, Jan. 13, 2005; John Denson to Otto Fuerbringer, Mar. 13, 1950, TIA; John Sousa III to James A. Linen III, Mar. 14, 1950, TIA; James A. Linen III to A. E. Winger, Mar. 17, 1950, TIA; John Sousa III to Bernard Barnes and senior Time Inc. officials, Dec. 6, 1950, TIA; George Frazier to W. A. Swanberg, May

16, 1970, GF, quoted in Charles Fountain, *Another Man's Poison,* p. 136; Bernard Barnes to Larry Hoover, May 4, 1951, TIA.

1951–60: Henry R. Luce, "Journalism and Responsibility," Feb. 20, 1953, TIA; Henry R. Luce, untitled speech at the *Yale Daily News* eightieth-anniversary party, Apr. 16, 1958, TIA; Henry R. Luce, Time-Life Building cornerstone ceremony address, June 23, 1959, TIA; Henry R. Luce, cornerstone ceremony photographs, TIA; Henry R. Luce, handwritten edits of CBC *Closeup* interview transcript, Robert Crone Pictures, Sept. 20, 1960, TIA; Lawrence E. Laybourne to Bill Furth, edited transcript for CBC *Closeup,* Oct. 18, 1960, TIA.

Elson's corporate history: "Elson, Robert T.," Time Inc. career profile, TIA; Hedley Donovan to Time Inc. staff, Nov. 2, 1964, TIA; Frank Kelly, M.A.I., appraisal of Forty-Three Biltmore Estates, Feb. 28, 1967, CBL; Letitia Baldrige, author's interview, Dec. 2, 2005; Henry R. Luce, Jan. 12, 1965, TIA; *New York Times,* Jan. 7, 1969, p. 39.

***Time*'s masthead:** Thomas J. C. Martyn to Henry R. Luce, Apr. 2, 1966, TIA; Otto Fuerbringer, author's interview, Nov. 28, 2005; *Time,* Mar. 17, 1967, p. 19.

Luce missed Hadden: Letitia Baldrige, author's interview, Dec. 2, 2005.

EPILOGUE: THE PARTY OF ALL TIME

The crowd: James E. Pitt to Bernhard Auer, Lawrence E. Laybourne, and Bernard Barnes, May 14, 1963, TIA; "*Time*'s 40th Anniversary," *F.Y.I.,* May 10, 1963, pp. 1–2, 7, TIA; "Covering Four Decades," fortieth-anniversary guest list, May 6, 1963, TIA; fortieth-anniversary Miscellaneous file, TIA; fortieth-anniversary Publicity file, TIA; Louis C. Stengel, May 7, 1963, fortieth-anniversary Correspondence file, TIA; Geoffrey T. Hellman, *The New Yorker,* May 18, 1963, pp. 32–33; James E. Pitt, "How a News Magazine Made Headlines with Its Anniversary Celebration," *Public Relations Journal,* July 1964; "Miller, Thimmesch, Clark, Gruin to Parker," Time Inc. report, May 7, 1963, CBL.

The dinner: James E. Pitt to Bernhard Auer, Lawrence E. Laybourne, Bernard Barnes, May 14, 1963, TIA; James E. Pitt, "How a News Magazine Made Headlines with Its Anniversary Celebration, *Public Relations Journal,* July 1964; "*Time*'s 40th Anniversary Party," *Time,* May 17, 1963, pp. 64, 66; Henry R. Luce photographs, fortieth-anniversary, TIA; "Time 40th Anniversary Party, No. 549, 1963," Beta tape, TIA; Loye Miller, "Mood and Narrative (Special Section)," Time Inc. report, May 7, 1963, CBL; Alfred Kazin, *New York Jew,* p. 55.

The scope of Time Inc.: Time Inc. Annual Reports, 1945–63; Richard Decker, *The New Yorker,* ca. 1962, quoted in Robert T. Elson, *Time Inc.,* "Leaves from a Company Album," picture insert between pp. 246–47; Hubert Kay to Henry R. Luce, Mar. 5, 1963, TIA; Henry R. Luce to Hubert Kay, Mar. 8, 1963, TIA; Henry R. Luce to John F. Kennedy, Feb. 21, 1963, TIA.

Intoning the names: "*Time* 40th Anniversary Party, No. 549, 1963," Beta tape, TIA; "Cover Dinner Speeches," Time Inc. transcript, May 6, 1963, pp. 3, 4, 10–11, 53–54, TIA; Peter Paul Luce, author's interview, Mar. 25, 2004; Loye Miller, "Mood and Narrative (Special Section)," Time Inc. report, May 7, 1963, CBL; Henry R. Luce, "Management in an Editorial Enterprise, Lecture II: Purpose and Profit," May 1, 1963, TIA.

Party lasted late: Hugh Sidey, author's interview, Mar. 23, 2004; Gloria Mariano, author's interview, Nov. 28, 2005; W. A. Swanberg, *Luce and His Empire,* p. 434; Hedda Hopper to Roy E. Larsen, May 29, 1963; oversize photographs, *Time*'s fortieth-anniversary, CBL; Henry R. Luce photographs, fortieth-anniversary, TIA.

Luce's last years: "A Profile of Henry R. Luce," WNBC television transcript, May 8, 1966, TIA; Henry R. Luce to Thomas Griffith, Feb. 10, 1967, TIA; Henry R. Luce "Invitation to a Ride," draft preface for *Time Capsule,* ca. Feb. 10, 1967, TIA; Henry R. Luce, introduction to Time Inc., *Time Capsule 1923.*

Daniel Winter: Daniel R. Winter to Henry R. Luce, May 20, 1963, HRL; Jan. 19, 1964, HRL; "Henry R. Luce to Daniel R. Winter, Feb. 5, 1964, HRL.

BIBLIOGRAPHY

Time Inc. magazines
Tide
Time
Fortune
Letters
Life
Sports Illustrated

Time Inc. radio programs
March of Time

Time Inc. books
Time Capsule 1923
Time Capsule 1924
Time Capsule 1925
Time Capsule 1926
Time Capsule 1927
Time Capsule 1928
Time Capsule 1929

Internal Time Inc. publications
F.Y.I. (company news sheet)

Magazines
Brooklyn Life
Editor & Publisher
Reader's Digest
The Literary Digest
The New Yorker
The Saturday Evening Post
The Saturday Review of Literature
Vanity Fair

School publications
Mischianza (Hotchkiss yearbook)
The Hotchkiss Literary Monthly
The Hotchkiss Record
Yale Daily News
Yale Literary Monthly

Books

Aden, Bob. *The Way It Was: A Highly Personal Account of the Old Log Theater's Early Years*. Excelsior, Minn.: Old Log Theater, 1989.

Allen, Frederick Lewis. *Only Yesterday: An Informal History of the 1920's*. New York: Harper & Row, 1931. Reprint, New York: Perennial Classics, 2000.

Augspurger, Michael. *An Economy of Abundant Beauty: Fortune Magazine and Depression America.* Ithaca, N.Y.: Cornell University Press, 2004.

Baldasty, Gerald J. *The Commercialization of News in the Nineteenth Century.* Madison, Wis.: University of Wisconsin Press, 1992.

Baritz, Loren. *The Good Life: The Meaning of Success for the American Middle Class.* New York: Knopf, 1989.

Barrett, James Wyman, ed. *The End of "The World."* New York: Harper & Row, 1931; reprint, Freeport, N.Y.: Books for Libraries Press, 1970.

Baughman, James L. *Henry R. Luce and the Rise of the American News Media.* With an Afterword by the author. Twayne's twentieth-century American biography series, no. 5. Boston: Twayne, 1987; reprint, Baltimore: Johns Hopkins University Press, 2001.

Beatty, Jerome, Jr., ed. *The Saturday Review Gallery.* With an introduction by John T. Winterich. New York: Simon and Schuster, 1959.

Behr, Edward. *Prohibition: Thirteen Years that Changed America.* New York: Arcade Publishing, 1996.

Benét, Stephen Vincent. *The Beginning of Wisdom.* New York: Holt, 1921.

Berg, A. Scott. *Max Perkins: Editor of Genius.* New York: Dutton, 1978; reprint, New York: Riverhead, 1997.

———. *Goldwyn: A Biography.* New York: Knopf, 1989; New York: Riverhead, 1998.

———. *Lindbergh.* New York: Putnam's, 1998; New York: Berkeley, 1999.

Bernays, Edward. *Propaganda.* New York: Liveright, 1928.

———. *Biography of an Idea.* New York: Simon and Schuster, 1965.

Bessie, Simon Michael. *Jazz Journalism: The Story of the Tabloid Newspapers.* New York: Dutton, 1938.

Blakey, George T. *Historians on the Homefront: American Propagandists for the Great War.* Lexington, Ky.: University Press of Kentucky, 1970.

Bliss, Edward, Jr. *Now the News: The Story of Broadcast Journalism.* New York: Columbia University Press, 1991.

Bradshaw, Jon. *Dreams That Money Can Buy: The Tragic Life of Libby Holman.* New York: Morrow, 1985.

Brian, Denis. *Pulitzer: A Life.* New York: Wiley, 2001.

Britt, George. *Forty Years—Forty Millions: The Career of Frank A. Munsey.* New York: Farrar & Rinehart, 1935.

Brooklyn Savings Bank. *Old Brooklyn Heights.* New York: privately published, 1927.

Brown, Charles H. *The Correspondents' War: Journalists in the Spanish-American War.* New York: Scribner's, 1967.

Busch, Noel F. *Briton Hadden: A Biography of the Co-founder of Time*. New York: Farrar, Straus, 1949.

Callander, James H. *Yesterdays on Brooklyn Heights*. New York: Dorland Press, 1927.

Canning, Peter. *American Dreamers: The Wallaces and Reader's Digest. An Insider's Story*. New York: Simon & Schuster, 1996.

Chauncey, George. *Gay New York: Gender, Urban Culture, and the Making of the Gay Male World, 1890–1940*. New York: Basic Books, 1994.

Childs, Marquis, and James Reston. *Walter Lippmann and His Times*. New York: Harcourt, Brace & World, 1959; reprint, Freeport, N.Y.: Books for Libraries Press, 1968.

Cigliano, Jan. *Showplace of America: Cleveland's Euclid Avenue, 1850–1910*. Kent, Ohio: Kent State University Press, 1991.

Clifford, John Garry. *The Citizen Soldiers: The Plattsburg Training Camp Movement, 1913–1920*. Lexington, Ky.: University Press of Kentucky, 1972.

Clurman, Richard M. *To the End of Time: The Seduction and Conquest of a Media Empire*. New York: Simon & Schuster, 1992.

Cohn, Jan. *Creating America: George Horace Lorimer and the Saturday Evening Post*. Pittsburgh: University of Pittsburgh Press, 1989.

Cooper, John Milton, Jr. *Pivotal Decades: The United States, 1900–1920*. New York: Norton, 1990.

Cort, David. *The Sin of Henry R. Luce: An Anatomy of Journalism*. Secaucus, N.J.: Lyle Stuart, 1974.

Davis, Kenneth S. *FDR: The Beckoning of Destiny, 1882–1928*. New York: Putnam's, 1972.

Dell, Floyd. *Intellectual Vagabondage*. New York: Doran, 1926.

Dewey, John. *The Public and Its Problems*. New York: Holt, 1927; reprint, Athens, Ohio: Swallow Press/Ohio University Press, 1954.

Donovan, Hedley. *Right Places, Right Times: Forty Years in Journalism Not Counting My Paper Route*. New York: Holt, 1989.

Douglas, Ann. *Terrible Honesty: Mongrel Manhattan in the 1920s*. New York: Farrar, Straus and Giroux, 1995.

Douglas, George H. *The Smart Magazines: 50 Years of Literary Revelry and High Jinks at Vanity Fair, the New Yorker, Life, Esquire and the Smart Set*. Hamden, Conn.: Archon Books, 1991.

Dumenil, Lynn. *The Modern Temper: American Culture and Society in the 1920s*. New York: Hill & Wang, 1995.

Elson, Robert T. *Time Inc.: The Intimate History of a Publishing Enterprise, 1923–1941*. Edited by Duncan Norton-Taylor. New York: Atheneum, 1968.

——. *The World of Time Inc.: The Intimate History of a Publishing Enterprise, Volume Two: 1941–1960*. Edited by Duncan Norton-Taylor. New York: Atheneum, 1973.

Emery, Edwin, and Michael Emery. *The Press and America: An Interpretative History of the Mass Media,* 4th ed. Englewood Cliffs, N.J.: Prentice-Hall, 1978.

Ernst, Robert. *Weakness Is a Crime: The Life of Bernarr Macfadden.* Syracuse, N.Y.: Syracuse University Press, 1991.

Everdell, William R., and Malcolm MacKay. *Rowboats to Rapid Transit: A History of Brooklyn Heights.* New York: Brooklyn Heights Association, 1973.

Fass, Paula S. *The Damned and the Beautiful: American Youth in the 1920s.* New York: Oxford University Press, 1977.

Fenton, Charles A. *Stephen Vincent Benét: The Life and Times of an American Man of Letters, 1898–1943.* New Haven: Yale University Press, 1958.

Fetherling, Doug. *The Five Lives of Ben Hecht.* Toronto: Leter and Orpen, 1977.

Feuer, A. B. *The U.S. Navy in World War I: Combat at Sea and in the Air.* Westport, Conn.: Praeger, 1999.

Finnegan, John Patrick. *Against the Specter of a Dragon: The Campaign for American Military Preparedness, 1914–1917.* Contributions in Military History, no. 7. Westport, Conn.: Greenwood Press, 1974.

Fountain, Charles. *Another Man's Poison: The Life and Writing of Columnist George Frazier.* Introduction by Matthew J. Bruccoli. Chester, Conn.: Globe Pequot Press, 1984.

Gallagher, Brian. *Anything Goes: The Jazz Age Adventures of Neysa McMein and Her Extravagant Circle of Friends.* New York: Times Books, 1987.

Garside, B. A. *One Increasing Purpose: The Life of Henry Winters Luce.* With an introduction by Henry P. Van Dusen. New York: Revell, 1948.

Gilbert, Martin. *The First World War: A Complete History.* New York: Holt, 1994.

Goldberg, David J. *Discontented America: The United States in the 1920s. The American Moment.* Stanley I. Kutler. ed. With a foreword by Stanley I. Kutler. Baltimore: Johns Hopkins University Press, 1999.

Gould, Bruce, and Beatrice Blackmar Gould. *American Story.* New York: Harper & Row, 1968.

Griffith, Thomas. *Harry and Teddy: The Turbulent Friendship of Press Lord Henry R. Luce and His Favorite Reporter, Theodore H. White.* New York: Random House, 1995.

Gruber, Carol S. *Mars and Minerva: World War I and the Uses of the Higher Learning in America.* Baton Rouge: Louisiana State University Press, 1975.

Grunwald, Henry. *One Man's America: A Journalist's Search for the Heart of His Country.* New York: Doubleday, 1997.

Hadley, Morris. *Arthur Twining Hadley*. New Haven: Yale University Press, 1948.

Halberstam, David. *The Powers That Be*. New York: Knopf, 1975; reprint, Urbana, Ill.: University of Illinois Press, 2000.

Hamblin, Dora Jane. *That Was the LIFE*. New York: Norton, 1977.

Harris, John B., and Jonathan Kaufman, eds. *100: A History of the Yale Daily News*. New Haven: OCD Foundation, 1978.

Hecht, Ben. *A Thousand and One Afternoons in Chicago*. Reprint, Chicago: University of Chicago Press, 1992.

Heidenry, John. *Theirs Was the Kingdom: Lila and DeWitt Wallace and the Story of the Reader's Digest*. New York: Norton, 1993.

Heiskell, Andrew, with Ralph Graves. *Outsider, Insider: An Unlikely Success Story*. Foreword by Vartan Gregorian. New York: Marian-Darien Press, 1998.

Heminway, C. Stuart, ed. *Twenty Years with Nineteen-Twenty: Vicennial Record of the Class of 1920 Yale College*. Pasadena, Calif.: San Pasqual Press, 1940.

Herzstein, Robert E. *Henry R. Luce: A Political Portrait of the Man Who Created the American Century*. New York: Scribner, 1994.

Hicks, Frederick C. *William Howard Taft, Yale Professor of Law & New Haven Citizen: An Academic Interlude in the Life of the Twenty-Seventh President of the United States and the Tenth Chief Justice of the Supreme Court*. New Haven: Yale University Press, 1945.

Hobson, Laura Z. *Laura Z: The Early Years and Years of Fulfillment*. With an introduction by Norman H. Cousins and an afterword by Christopher Z. Hobson. New York: Fine, 1986.

Hodgson, Godfrey. *The Colonel: The Life and Wars of Henry Stimson, 1867–1950*. New York: Knopf, 1990.

Homer, *The Iliad*, books 1–9. Pocket Literal Translations of the Classics. Translated by Theodore Alois Buckley. With an introduction by Edward Brooks Jr. Philadelphia: McKay, 1896.

———. *The Iliad*. Translated by Robert Fitzgerald. New York: Anchor Books, 1974; reprint, New York: Anchor Books, 1989.

Hoopes, Roy. *Ralph Ingersoll: A Biography*. Foreword by Max Lerner. New York: Atheneum, 1985.

Ingersoll, Ralph. *The Great Ones: The Love Story of Two Very Important People*. New York: Harcourt, Brace, 1948.

Isaacson, Walter, and Evan Thomas. *The Wise Men: Six Friends and the World They Made*. New York: Simon & Schuster, 1986.

Johnson, Owen. *Stover at Yale*. Introduction by Judith Ann Schiff. New York: Stokes, 1912; reprint, New Haven: The Yale Bookstore, 1997.

Kahn, E. J., Jr. *The World of Swope*. New York: Simon and Schuster, 1965.

Kahn, Roger. *A Flame of Pure Fire: Jack Dempsey and the Roaring '20s.* New York: Harcourt Brace, 1999.

Karabel, Jerome. *The Chosen: The Hidden History of Admission and Exclusion at Harvard, Yale, and Princeton.* New York: Houghton Mifflin, 2005.

Kastendieck, Miles Merwin. *The Story of Poly.* With a foreword by Hiram Austin Tuttle. Wilmington, Del.: Matthews, 1940.

Kaytor, Marilyn. *"21": The Life and Times of New York's Favorite Club.* New York: "21" Club, 1975.

Kazin, Alfred. *New York Jew.* New York: Knopf, 1978.

Kelley, Brooks Mather. *Yale: A History.* The Yale Scene, University Series, no. 3. New Haven: Yale University Press, 1974.

Kennedy, David M. *Over Here: The First World War and American Society.* New York: Oxford University Press, 1980.

Kobler, John. *Luce: His Time, Life, and Fortune.* New York: Doubleday, 1968.

Kolowrat, Ernest. *Hotchkiss: A Chronicle of an American School.* New York: New Amsterdam, 1992.

Kronenberger, Louis. *No Whippings, No Gold Watches: The Saga of a Writer and His Jobs.* Boston: Little, Brown, 1970.

Kunkel, Thomas. *Genius in Disguise: Harold Ross of the New Yorker.* New York: Random House, 1995.

Lancaster, Clay. *Old Brooklyn Heights: New York's First Suburb. Including Detailed Analyses of 619 Century-old Houses.* 2d ed. With photographs by Edmund V. Gillon Jr. Rutland, Vt.: Tuttle, 1961; reprint, Mineola, N.Y.: Dover, 1979.

Lane, Jack C. *Armed Progressive: General Leonard Wood.* San Rafael, Calif.: Presidio Press, 1978.

Larson, Edward J. *Summer for the Gods: The Scopes Trial and America's Continuing Debate over Science and Religion.* Cambridge: Harvard University Press, 1997.

Leuchtenberg, William E. *The Perils of Prosperity, 1914–32.* Chicago History of American Civilization, ed. Daniel J. Boorstin. Chicago: University of Chicago Press, 1958.

Levin, Gerald M. *Values for the Digital Age: The Legacy of Henry Luce.* Washington, D.C.: Aspen Institute, 2000.

Lewis, Alfred Allan. *Man of the World. Herbert Bayard Swope: A Charmed Life of Pulitzer Prizes, Poker and Politics.* Indianapolis: Bobbs-Merrill, 1978.

Lewis, Sinclair. *Babbitt.* New York: Harcourt, Brace, 1922.

Lewis, Wilmarth Sheldon. *One Man's Education.* New York: Knopf, 1967.

Lippmann, Walter. *Liberty and the News.* New York: Harcourt, Brace & Howe, 1920.

————. *Public Opinion*. New York: Harcourt, Brace, 1922.

Luce, Henry Robinson. *The Ideas of Henry Luce*. Edited with an introduction by John K. Jessup. New York: Atheneum, 1969.

Lynd, Robert S., and Helen Merrell Lynd. *Middletown: A Study in American Culture*. Foreword by Clark Wissler. New York: Harcourt, Brace, 1929; reprint, New York: Harcourt Brace Jovanovich, 1957.

MacAdams, William. *Ben Hecht: The Man Behind the Legend*. New York: Scribner's, 1990.

MacCambridge, Michael. *The Franchise: A History of Sports Illustrated Magazine*. New York: Hyperion, 1997.

Mack, Maynard. *A History of Scroll and Key: 1842–1942*. New Haven: Scroll and Key, 1978.

Martin, Gordon. *Chefoo School 1881–1951*. Braunton, U.K.: Merlin Books, 1990.

Martin, Ralph G. *Henry & Clare: An Intimate Portrait of the Luces*. New York: Putnam's, 1991.

Matthews, T. S. *Name and Address*. London: Anthony Blond, 1961.

McBrien, William. *Cole Porter: A Biography*. New York: Knopf, 1998.

Meade, Marion. *Dorothy Parker: What Fresh Hell Is This?* New York: Villard Books, 1988; reprint, New York: Penguin Books, 1989.

Merlis, Brian, and Lee A. Rosenzweig. *Brooklyn Heights & Downtown, Volume 1: 1860–1922*. New York: Israelowitz Publishing with Brooklyn Editions, 2001.

Miller, Carol Poh, and Robert A. Wheeler. *Cleveland: A Concise History, 1796–1996*. 2d ed. Bloomington: Indiana University Press, 1997.

Miller, Nathan. *New World Coming: The 1920s and the Making of Modern America*. New York: Scribner, 2003.

Miller, Sheila. *Pigtails, Petticoats and the Old School Tie*. Sevenoaks, U.K.: OMF Books, 1981.

Milton, Joyce. *The Yellow Kids: Foreign Correspondents in the Heyday of Yellow Journalism*. New York: Harper & Row, 1989.

Morris, Lloyd. *Incredible New York: High Life and Low Life from 1850 to 1950*. New York: Random House, 1951; reprint, Syracuse, N.Y.: Syracuse University Press, 1996.

Morris, Sylvia Jukes. *Rage for Fame: The Ascent of Clare Boothe Luce*. New York: Random House, 1997.

Mott, Frank Luther. *A History of American Magazines, 1885–1905*. Cambridge: Harvard University Press, 1957.

Munk, Nina. *Fools Rush In: Steve Case, Jerry Levin, and the Unmaking of AOL Time Warner*. New York: HarperCollins, 2004.

Nasaw, David. *The Chief: The Life of William Randolph Hearst.* New York: Houghton, Mifflin, 2000.

Neils, Patricia. *China Images in the Life and Times of Henry Luce.* Savage, Md.: Rowman & Littlefield, 1990.

Nettleton, George Henry, ed. *Yale in the World War.* Vol. 1. New Haven: Yale University Press, 1925

O'Keefe, Kevin J. *A Thousand Deadlines: The New York City Press and American Neutrality, 1914–17.* The Hague: Nijhoff, 1972.

Oren, Dan A. *Joining the Club: A History of Jews and Yale.* New Haven: Yale University Press, 1985.

Parrish, Michael E. *Anxious Decades: America in Prosperity and Depression, 1920–1941.* John Morton Blum, ed. Norton Twentieth Century America Series. New York: Norton, 1992.

Patterson, Morehead, ed. *History of the Class of Nineteen Hundred and Twenty.* New Haven: Tuttle, Morehouse and Taylor, 1920.

Pearman, Phil, ed. *Dear Editor: Letters to Time Magazine, 1923–1984.* Dee Why West, Australia: privately printed, 1985.

Phelps, William Lyon. *Autobiography with Letters.* New York: Oxford University Press, 1939.

Pierson, George Wilson. *Yale College: An Educational History, 1871–1921.* New Haven: Yale University Press, 1952.

Prendergast, Curtis, with Geoffrey Colvin. *The World of Time Inc.: The Intimate History of a Changing Enterprise, Volume Three: 1960–1980.* Edited by Robert Lubar. New York: Atheneum, 1986.

Robbins, Alexandra. *Secrets of the Tomb: Skull and Bones, the Ivy League, and the Hidden Paths of Power.* New York: Little, Brown, 2002.

Rose, William Ganson. *Cleveland: The Making of a City.* Cleveland: World, 1950.

Ryan, A. P. *Lord Northcliffe.* New York: Macmillan, 1953.

Samuels, Peggy, and Harold Samuels. *Remembering the Maine.* Washington, D.C.: Smithsonian Institution Press, 1995.

Sanger, William. *Brooklyn Heights.* New York: American Printing, 1929.

Santayana, George. *The Middle Span.* New York: Scribner's, 1945.

Saturday Review of Literature and Farrar & Rinehart. *Stephen Vincent Benét.* New York: Saturday Review of Literature and Farrar & Rinehart, 1943.

Schlesinger, Arthur M., Jr. *The Crisis of the Old Order: The Age of Roosevelt, vol. 1, 1919–1933.* New York: Houghton Mifflin, 1957; reprint, New York: Mariner Books, 2003.

Schneirov, Matthew. *The Dream of a New Social Order: Popular Magazines in America, 1893–1914*. New York: Columbia University Press, 1994.

Schudson, Michael. *The Good Citizen: A History of American Civic Life*. New York: Free Press, 1998.

———. *The Power of News*. Cambridge: Harvard University Press, 1995.

Seebohm, Caroline. *The Man Who Was Vogue: The Life and Times of Condé Nast*. New York: Viking Press, 1982.

Seldes, George. *One Thousand Americans*. New York: Boni & Gaer, 1947.

Settle, Mary Lee. *The Scopes Trial: The State of Tennessee v. John Thomas Scopes*. New York: Franklin Watts, 1972.

Slayton, Robert A. *Empire Statesman: The Rise and Redemption of Al Smith*. New York: Free Press, 2001.

Sokolov, Raymond. *Wayward Reporter: The Life of A. J. Liebling*. New York: Harper & Row, 1980.

Spellman, Howard Hilton, ed. *Another Quarter Century for 1920. 1940–1965*. New Haven: privately printed, 1965.

Starfield, Martin J. *Starfield's Brooklyn: Historical Sketches of Brooklyn Heights*. New York: Brooklyn Heights Periodicals, 1984.

Starr, Paul. *The Creation of the Media: Political Origins of Modern Communications*. New York: Basic Books, 2004.

Steel, Ronald. *Walter Lippmann and the American Century*. Boston: Little, Brown, 1980.

Stevenson, Elizabeth. *Babbitts and Bohemians: The American 1920s*. New York: Macmillan, 1967.

Sullivan, Mark. *Our Times*. Vols. 1–6. New York: Scribner's, 1926.

Swanberg, W. A. *Luce and His Empire*. New York: Scribner's, 1972.

Talese, Gay. *The Kingdom and the Power*. New York: World, 1969.

Teachout, Terry. *The Skeptic: A Life of H. L. Mencken*. New York: HarperCollins, 2002.

Thomas, John. *Dry Martini: A Gentleman Turns to Love*. Lost American Fiction, ed. Matthew J. Bruccoli. Afterword by Morrill Cody. New York: Doran, 1926; reprint, Carbondale, Ill.: Southern Illinois University Press, 1974.

Thompson, Edward K. *A Love Affair with Life & Smithsonian*. Columbia, Mo.: University of Missouri Press, 1995.

Thurber, James. *The Years with Ross*. With a foreword by Adam Gopnik. New York: Little, Brown, 1957; reprint, New York: Perennial Classics, 2001.

Tifft, Susan E., and Alex S. Jones. *The Trust: The Private and Powerful Family Behind The New York Times*. New York: Little, Brown, 1999.

Tuesday Evening Club. *The Second Book of the Tuesday Evening Club*. Princeton, N.J.: privately printed, 1923.

Tye, Larry. *The Father of Spin: Edward L. Bernays and the Birth of Public Relations*. New York: Crown, 1998.

Voss, Frederick S. *Man of the Year: A TIME Honored Tradition*. Washington, D.C.: Smithsonian Institution Press, 1987.

Wainwright, Loudon. *The Great American Magazine: An Inside History of Life*. New York: Knopf, 1986.

Walker, Stanley. *The Night Club Era*. With an introduction by Alva Johnston. New York: Stokes, 1933; reprint, Baltimore: Johns Hopkins University Press, 1999.

———. *City Editor*. With a foreword by Alexander Woollcott. New York: Stokes, 1934; reprint, Baltimore: Johns Hopkins University Press, 1999.

Welch, Lewis Sheldon, and Walter Camp. *Yale: Her Campus, Class-Rooms, and Athletics*. With an introduction by Samuel J. Elder. Boston: Page, 1899.

White, Norval, and Elliot Willensky. *AIA Guide to New York City*, 4th ed. New York: Crown, 2000.

Wilson, Sloan. *The Man in the Gray Flannel Suit*. New York: Simon and Schuster, 1955.

Winks, Robin W. *Cloak & Gown: Scholars in the Secret War, 1939–1961*. 2d ed. New Haven: Yale University Press, 1996.

Wolff, Geoffrey. *The Art of Burning Bridges: A Life of John O'Hara*. New York: Knopf, 2003.

Yagoda, Ben. *About Town: The New Yorker and the World It Made*. New York: Scribner, 2000.

Yale Daily News, eds. *Yale Daily News 50th Anniversary, 1878–1928*. New Haven: Yale Daily News, 1928.

Zieger, Robert H. *America's Great War: World War I and the American Experience*. Lanham, Md.: Rowman & Littlefield, 2000.

Unpublished manuscripts

Aden, Bob. *This Was Us: A Memoir*. Typed and bound manuscript, undated.

Busch, Noel Fairchild. *Briton Hadden: His Life and TIME*. Typed manuscript draft, ca. 1948.

———. *Life, Luce and the Pursuit of God Knows What: A Game of Music Chairs to the Jive Music of Time Inc.* Typed manuscript, multiple drafts, undated, ca. 1976.

———. *Life with Luce: A Long March to the Music of Time Inc.* Typed manuscript, multiple drafts, undated, ca. 1970–85.

Frazier, George. *It's About Time.* Typed manuscript, multiple drafts, ca. 1950.

Hotz, Lila. *A Line a Day.* Handwritten journal, 1921–25.

Ingersoll, Ralph, *High Time.* Typed manuscript, multiple drafts, 1962–69.

Martin, John S. *A Grab-Bag for My Grandsons.* Typed manuscript, undated.

Newsweek staff. *Newsweek, The First 50 Years.* Manuscript draft, ca. 1983.

Phinney, Morris. *A Trip to Ecuador and Peru.* Typed manuscript, undated.

Wydler, Hans L. *The Late Gargantuan Man: Briton Hadden, the Other Founder of Time.* Yale senior essay, Apr. 18, 1988.

Magazine and journal articles

Heiskell, Andrew. "How They Invented *People*," *Columbia Journalism Review*, Nov.–Dec. 1998.

Larsen, Jonathan Z. "Forty Years on A Roller Coaster." *Columbia Journalism Review*, Nov.–Dec., 2001.

Powell, Lyman P. "Coué," *American Review of Reviews*, July–Dec. 1922, pp. 622–24.

Simmons, James S. "The Intravenous Use of Acriviolet and of Mercurochrome in Bacterial Infections," *Journal of Infectious Diseases*, vol. 39 (1926): pp. 273–85.

Stoker, Kevin, and Brad L. Rawlins. "The Light of Publicity in the Progressive Era, from Searchlight to Flashlight," *Journalism History*, vol. 30, no. 4 (Winter 2005): 177–88.

Young, Hugh H., and J. H. Hill, and W. W. Scott. "The Treatment of Infections and Infectious Diseases with Mercurochrome-220 Soluble," *Archives of Surgery* (May 1925): 829–55.

INDEX